VISUAL QUICKSTART GUIDE

PINNACLE STUDIO 8

FOR WINDOWS

Jan Ozer

Visual QuickStart Guide

Pinnacle Studio 8 for Windows

Jan Ozer

Peachpit Press
1249 Eighth Street
Berkeley, CA 94710
510/524-2178
800/283-9444
510/524-2221 (fax)
Find us on the World Wide Web at: http://www.peachpit.com
To report errors, please send a note to errata@peachpit.com.
Peachpit Press is a division of Pearson Education.

Editor: Suki Gear
Copy Editor: Jacqueline K. Aaron
Tech Editor: Stephen Nathans
Production Coordinator: Judy Zimola
Composition: David Van Ness
Cover Design: The Visual Group
Cover Production: Nathalie Valette
Indexer: Karin Arrigoni

ISBN 0-321-18653-2

9 8 7 6 5 4 3 2 1

Printed and bound in the United States of America

For the three girlies in my life:
Barb, Whatley, and Rose.

Acknowledgements

I'd like to thank the Peachpit team: Clifford Colby, Kelly Ryer, and Rebecca Ross for making it easy to join, Jacqueline Aaron, for her exacting and precise editing, Stephen Nathans, for his extraordinarily insightful tech read, David Van Ness for going the extra mile to implement my last-minute changes, Judy Zimola, for her patience and management, and most of all, Suki Gear, for pushing and pulling, demanding and giving, dotting all the Is and crossing the Ts, and generally making the project straightforward, fun, and best of all, done. Let's do another.

Special thanks to the Pinnacle folks for their responsiveness during this project.

TABLE OF CONTENTS

INTRODUCTION

When I started working with digital video in 1991, the sheer ability to play video on a computer was a technical marvel. If you showed it to the average consumer, however, the typical response was, "Gee, why doesn't it look as good as my TV?" Tough to explain when the computer cost $3,000 and the TV cost $300.

Thus began my search for "apology-free video"—video I could show my wife, children, and friends without apologizing for poor sound or image quality.

As interest in digital video grew, friends and family asked with increasing frequency for a video editor they could both afford and quickly learn to use. Wary of the unspoken technical-support obligation that comes with recommending just any software program, I began my search for a product I could recommend without getting an unlisted phone number.

As you've probably guessed, I found that product in Pinnacle Systems' Studio 8.

Studio 8 delivers apology-free video courtesy of its MPEG-2 encoding engine, which is the same format used on DVDs coming from Hollywood. Hey, if it's good enough for *The Matrix* and *When Harry Met Sally*, it's good enough for me.

After working on software-review teams that awarded Studio several *PC Magazine* Editor's Choice awards, I knew that even newcomers to video editing could quickly master Studio's interface. With Studio 8, the first program ever to merge traditional video editing with DVD authoring, Pinnacle extended this ease of use to DVD production, now made practical by inexpensive DVD-Recordable burners and low-cost media.

Studio offers an unprecedented range of movie creation options. Want to quickly convert your 60-minute digital videotape to DVD and send it to the in-laws? It's a simple two-step process—no muss, no fuss. Want to invest hours to produce a polished, Hollywood-style video? Studio can do that too, with distribution options ranging from the Internet to DVD and all points in between.

It's a program that can easily be mastered by beginners and also satisfy intermediate or even advanced users with its breadth of features.

Using This Book

If you bought Studio 8 through a retail channel, you already have a manual that explains how to use the various components of the Studio interface. This book complements the manual in two ways.

First, like all *Visual QuickStart Guides*, this one is task oriented, describing and showing you how to perform most common video production tasks. The descriptions are precise and exhaustive, identifying with screen shots and text the best ways to get the job done.

In addition, having worked with digital video for many years, I know that video editing can be an incredible time sink, probably the main reason most folks simply don't edit their camcorder tapes. Thus many sections and tips focus on how to avoid problems and work as efficiently as possible. Sidebars address technical topics to help you make decisions.

Making Movies with Studio

Within its uniquely unified video-editing/DVD-authoring interface, Studio 8 gives you an unparalleled range of production activities. Depending on your equipment, you can capture footage from a digital or analog camcorder, edit the footage, integrate video from other sources, and output the results for streaming on the Internet, playing back on your desktop or delivering via DVD or CD.

What I appreciate as a busy parent is the range of editing styles that Studio promotes. Invest a little time, get great results. Invest more time, get even better results. To illustrate this, I took my two little girls to Zoo Atlanta this past holiday season and shot about 40 minutes of tape you'll see throughout the book. Their former nanny accompanied us, shooting still images with a Kodak digital still-image camera.

What you can do

Using the raw input I got from that tape, I put together a list of potential projects along with estimated editing and authoring time (net of capturing and rendering plus DVD-R burning time) for each project.

Create a quick and dirty DVD to send to the grandparents. Use Studio's scene detection feature (Chapter 3) to break the captured footage into scenes, then combine scenes in the Album (Chapter 6) by animal visited. Drag the clips to the Timeline (Chapter 7) and then drag a menu (Chapter 12). Studio will automatically create all necessary links with DVD menus. Each menu will display a thumbnail image from the video clip and a generic title ("Chapter 1," "Chapter 2," and so on). Start burning the DVD. *Estimated editing time: 10 minutes.*

Customize the above presentation. Change generic menu titles like "Chapter 1," "Chapter 2," and "Chapter 3" to Lions, Tigers, and Bears (oh, my!) (see Chapter 12). Change a thumbnail image from initial frame in sequence to best image of subject animal (Chapter 12). Insert transitions between scenes so grandparents can play back the video smoothly from start to finish (Chapter 8). Insert a background music track (Chapter 11). Start burning DVD. *Estimated editing time: 30 minutes.*

Add a slide show. Enter Storyboard view, drag all still images down in desired order (Chapter 7). Add a ripple transition so the images dissolve smoothly from one to another (Chapter 8). Insert a background music track for the slide show (Chapter 11). Start burning DVD. *Estimated editing time: 20 minutes.*

Output to tape for dubbing to VHS. Delete the DVD menu, and you're ready to go. *Estimated editing time: 1 minute.*

Output to RealVideo or Windows Media file to post to a Web site. No extra time required. Just select the different output option. *Editing time: 0 minutes.*

I've found that these quick and dirty productions are the best options when life is busy. When you have time to tinker or want to create a visual masterpiece, the list of customizable options is almost unlimited. For example, you can do the following:

- Trim the source videos to delete unwanted sections (Chapter 7).
- Add titles and still image overlays to your clips (Chapter 10).
- Add a narration track describing the events of the day (Chapter 11).
- Add special effects (sepia, black and white), or speed up or slow down playback (Chapter 9).
- Customize your DVD menus with background video, audio, or motion buttons (Chapter 12).

Editing and production

After you've shot your source videos, the process of editing and production involves the following four steps:

- **Gathering assets.** This is where you capture your video, import still images, or grab them from your camcorder or captured video, and import any background audio files. These activities in covered in Chapters 3, 4, and 5.
- **Trimming and organizing.** In most instances, you won't want to include every minute that you shot in the final production. Accordingly, you trim unwanted sections, then place your video clips and still images in the desired order. Chapter 7 describes how to get this done.
- **Garnishing.** Here's where the true editing comes in. During this stage, you add transitions between clips, title tracks, still image overlays, and any special effects. You can also input a narration track, add music ripped from a CD, or create your own custom background track using SmartSound (a utility included with Studio). Chapters 8 through 11 cover these activities.
- **Rendering.** This is where you produce your final output. Though "encoding into a streaming format" may sound complicated, Studio includes easy-to-follow templates that simplify the task, making this stage the most mechanical of all. Chapter 14 describes how to output your videos as digital files for posting to a Web site, sending via email, or copying to CD-ROM.

If you're outputting to DVD there's another stage, of course, typically called *authoring*. This is when you create your menus, link videos and still image assets, and preview to ensure that your project flows as desired. Then you burn your disc. DVD production is covered in Chapter 12.

You can also write your production back to your camcorder, where you can dub copies for VHS or other analog players. I describe how to do this in Chapter 13.

Finally, Pinnacle provides a free service for posting your video files online, appropriately called StudioOnline. I discuss how you can best utilize this service in Chapter 15.

System Requirements

Most products ship with two sets of requirements, minimum and recommended. Here are Studio 8's minimum requirements.

Minimum system requirements

- 500 MHz or faster Intel Pentium or AMD Athlon processor
- 128 MB of random access memory, or RAM (256 MB recommended)
- Microsoft Windows 98 Second Edition, Windows Millennium Edition, Windows 2000, or Windows XP operating system
- Microsoft DirectX-compatible sound and graphics card
- Mouse
- CD-ROM drive
- 300 MB of hard disk space to install software (Disc Two, Content, requires another 600 MB)
- 4.5 GB of hard disk space for every 20 minutes of video captured at best quality
- Hard disk capable of sustained throughput of at least 4 MB per second. All SCSI and most ultra direct memory access (UDMA) drives are fast enough; dedicated hard drive recommended. (Studio will automatically test your hard drive for sufficient speed for real-time video capture when you first enter Capture mode.)
- CD-Recordable or CD-Rewritable drive for creating VideoCDs or Super VideoCDs that will play on most living room DVD players
- DVD-Recordable, DVD-Rewritable, or DVD+RW drive for creating DVDs

Disk requirements

A faster processor and more RAM are certainly better when it comes to video production, but the most significant area of potential trouble relates to disk requirements. Here's a quick example that illustrates how to estimate how much disk space you'll need for your projects.

Assume that you've shot 60 minutes of video that you want to edit down to a 30-minute production. You plan on including both a narration and background audio track, and will burn the result to DVD.

Table I.1, which presents a worst-case estimate of required disk space, assumes that you'll be applying edits to every single frame in the production footage. If you edit more sparingly, you'll need less space.

Back in 1994, the required 22 GB would have cost close to $30,000, and your electrical bill would jump significantly. Today, you can buy an 80 GB drive for well under $300, a great investment if you plan on pursuing multiple editing projects.

Table I.1

Calculating Disk Requirements

Item	Duration	MB/Minute	Total
Capture footage	60 minutes	216	12.96 GB
Production footage	30 minutes	216	6.48 GB
Narration track	30 minutes	10.5	315 MB
Background audio	30 minutes	10.5	315 MB
DVD files	30 minutes	60	1.8 GB
Total disk space required			21.87 GB

PART I

GETTING STARTED

1

The Interface

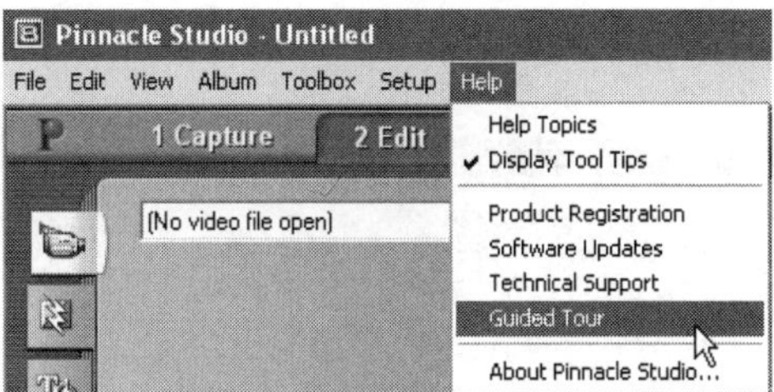

Figure 1.1 Taking Pinnacle Studio's guided tour will familiarize you with the various program components.

Figure 1.2 Use the controls at the bottom of the screen to control your tour experience.

Though generally straightforward, Pinnacle Systems' Studio 8 interface has a few nooks and crannies that aren't obvious at first glance. Fortunately, Studio includes a fairly comprehensive guided tour to get you familiar with the landscape fast. This chapter starts by showing you how to take the tour, then quickly introduces you to Studio's primary modes: Capture, Edit, and Make Movie. Finally, the chapter shows you how to undo or redo your work, discusses online help including keyboard shortcuts, and explains how and when to name and save your project file.

The Guided Tour

Studio 8 includes a guided tour that's a great first step toward getting familiar with the program's interface.

To take the guided tour:

- Choose Help > Guided Tour (**Figure 1.1**).

  The Pinnacle Studio Guided Tour starts (**Figure 1.2**). Use the controls at the bottom of the tour window to control the experience.

Edit Mode

When you first enter Studio, you're in Edit mode (**Figure 1.3**), where you'll spend the overwhelming bulk of your time. Capture mode and Make Movie mode, accessible via tabs in the upper-left corner, enable their namesake activities.

Edit mode is composed of three windows: the Album, the Player, and the Movie Window. While in Edit mode you have access to Undo, Redo, and Help buttons on the upper-right side.

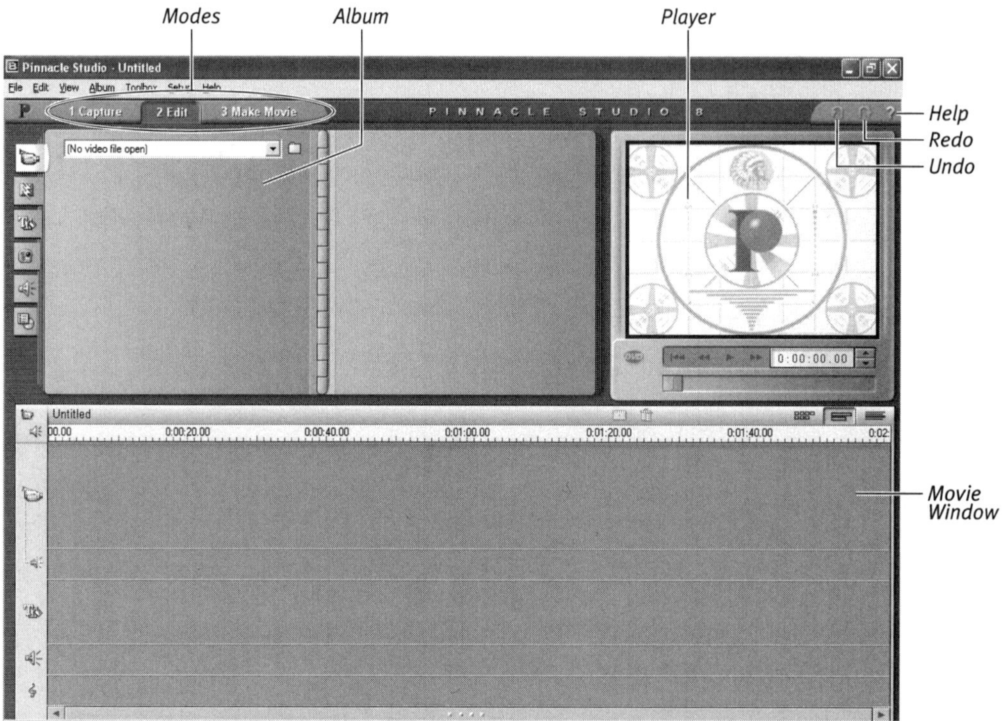

Figure 1.3 When you first run Studio you're in Edit mode, where you'll spend most of your time.

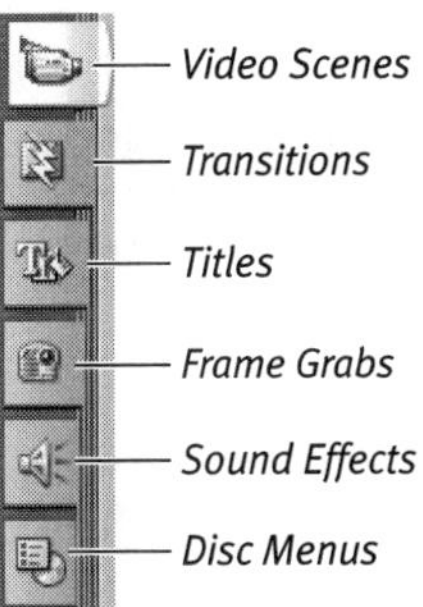

Figure 1.4 These tabs on the left side of the Album let you navigate between the various content types.

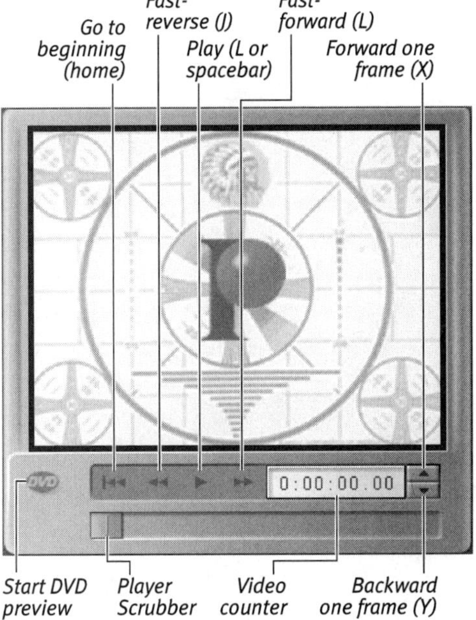

Figure 1.5 The Player has the usual VCR-like playback controls, plus a Scrubber that lets you manually move through the video files. The DVD button transforms the Player into a DVD remote (see Chapter 12).

Figure 1.6 Here's how you switch between the Timeline, Storyboard, and Text views of the Movie Window. Note the omnipresent razorblade, for splitting your videos, and the trash can, for deleting them.

The Album

The Album comprises six windows, selectable using the icons located on the left-hand panel (**Figure 1.4**). Three of these windows are for collecting video, audio, and still image files for including in a project (for details on how to do this, see Chapter 6).

The other three windows contain libraries of effects supplied by Pinnacle, including transitions, titles, and disc menus. For a discussion on how to apply and customize these, see Chapters 8, 10, and 12, respectively.

The Player

The Player is where you preview content and effects contained in the various albums and preview your editing progress in the Movie Window (**Figure 1.5**). Click the little DVD symbol on the lower left, and you convert the Player into a DVD playback remote for previewing your DVD titles.

Note that you can't detach or enlarge the Player; like all interface components, it's fixed for simplicity. Since the Player is integral to virtually all editing operations, its use is discussed in most of the chapters in this book.

The Movie Window

The Movie Window has three views—Timeline (as shown in **Figure 1.6**), Storyboard, and Text (called Edit List view in the Studio menu)—that you toggle through using controls at the upper-right corner of the Movie Window (Figure 1.6). See Chapter 7 to learn how and when to use these modes. Two icons, the razorblade for splitting clips and the trash can for deleting clips, are available in all three modes.

The Video Toolbox. In the upper-left corner of the Movie Window are two small icons, a camcorder and a speaker (**Figure 1.7**). Click the camcorder icon and the Video Toolbox opens (**Figure 1.8**), revealing six editing functions.

Figure 1.7 The camcorder icon opens and closes the Video Toolbox, while the speaker icon opens and closes the Audio Toolbox.

Figure 1.8 shows the Clip Properties tool, which you use to trim your videos to the desired length. For more on this tool, see Chapter 7.

Other functions in the Video Toolbox include the following:

- *Titles and still images.* Here you edit the name and duration of images and access title-editing screens (see Chapter 10).
- *Set menu links.* Here you link menus to content and customize the DVD menus (see Chapter 12).
- *Grab video frames.* Use this tool to grab still frame images from your camcorder or disk-based video files (see Chapter 5).
- *Adjust color/visual effects.* Here you access Studio's color correction facilities and other special effects (see Chapter 9).
- *Vary playback speed.* This control lets you create fast- and slow-motion effects (see Chapter 9).

You can click through the various options at will, and click the camcorder icon again to close the Video Toolbox.

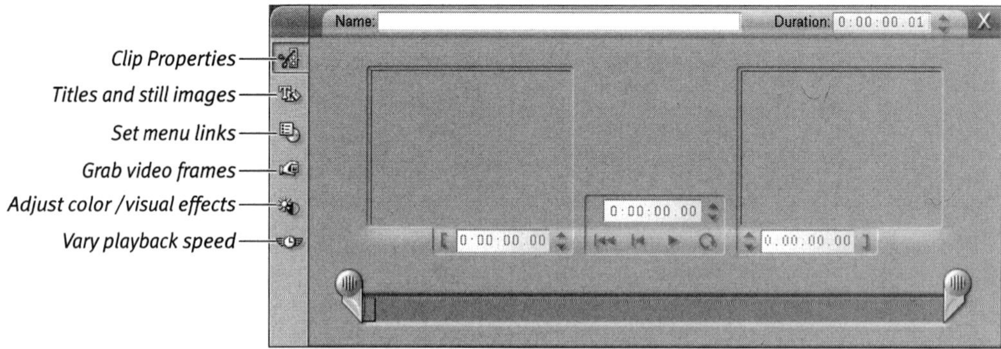

Figure 1.8 The various editing tools of the Video Toolbox.

The Audio Toolbox. Click the speaker icon (in the upper-left corner of the Movie Window) and you open the Audio Toolbox, which contains its own set of unique tools (**Figure 1.9**). In the Audio Clip Properties window, which is open here, you trim audio files to the desired length.

Other functions in the Audio Toolbox include the following (see Chapter 11 for more information):

- *Volume and fades.* For adjusting the volumes of the three audio tracks.
- *Voice-overs.* Where you record your voice-over track.
- *CD audio.* For ripping CD-Audio tracks to include in your projects.
- *SmartSound.* This feature lets you create custom background music of any length.

✔ Tip

- Double-clicking any of the icons in the Video or Audio Toolbox will return you to the main Movie Window.

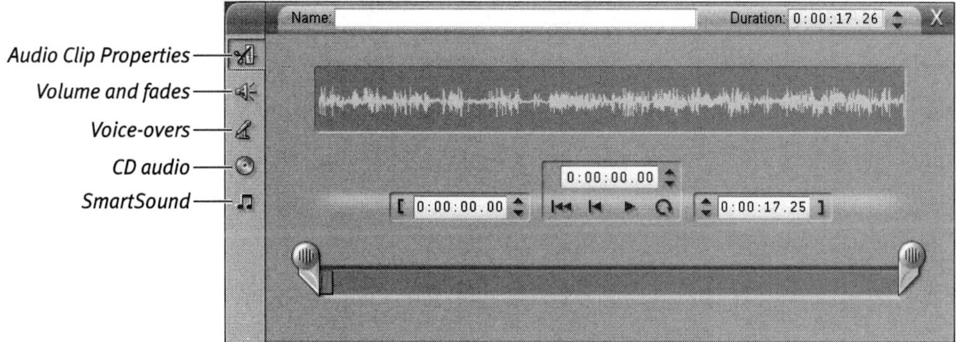

Figure 1.9 The various editing tools of the Audio Toolbox.

Capture Mode

You enter Capture mode by selecting the Capture tab in the upper-left corner of the Studio interface (Figure 1.3). Here you transfer video from camcorder or another source to your computer. Studio has two interfaces for capturing, one for digital video (DV) and MicroMV devices and one for analog camcorders and decks.

As discussed in the last section, Pinnacle designed Studio so that you grab still images from your videos in Edit mode, using the Frame Grab tool in the Video Toolbox. Still-image capture is covered in Chapter 5.

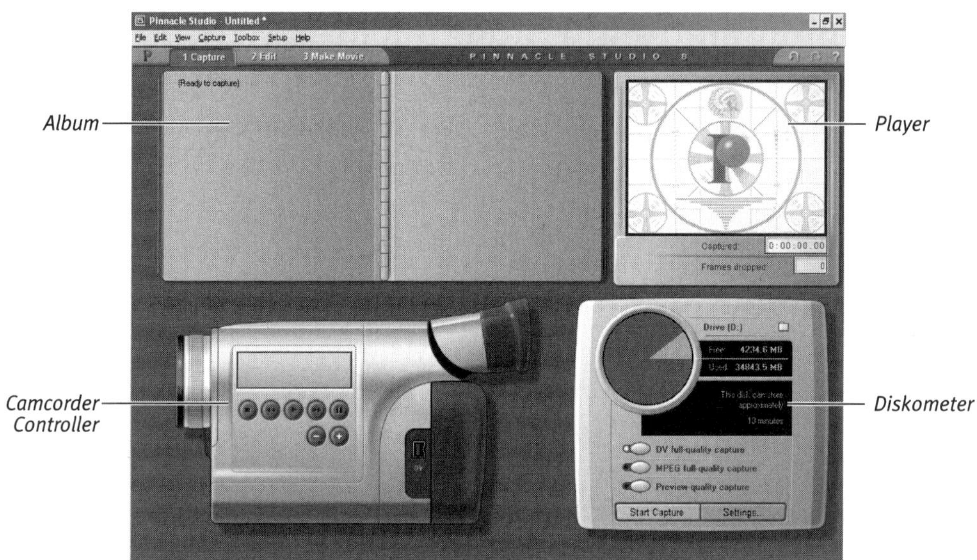

Figure 1.10 Meet the Capture screen, configured to capture DV video. Note the four major components: the Album, the Player, the Camcorder Controller, and the Diskometer.

Capturing from DV source devices

Figure 1.10 shows the four basic windows of Capture mode: the Album, the Player, the Camcorder Controller, and the Diskometer.

The Album. Holds the captured video files, which are added dynamically during capture when Studio detects additional scenes in your source video. After capture, you can change the comments associated with each scene (see Chapters 3 and 4) and thus search for scenes while in Edit mode. However, you can't play back your videos in Capture mode; you must switch to Edit mode.

The Player. Previews the captured video, providing information on capture duration and the number of frames dropped during capture, if any. As you can see, there are no playback controls, so you have to switch to Edit mode to play your captured videos.

The Camcorder Controller. Lets you control your DV or MicroMV camcorder. Briefly, one of the key advantages of these digital formats is the ability to control your camcorder over the same FireWire connection that transfers video from camcorder to computer (see the sidebar "FireWire to the Rescue" in Chapter 3). This makes capture from these sources much easier than analog capture.

The Diskometer. Contains the controls for starting and stopping capture, lets you select your capture drive, and lets you know how much disk space remains on your capture drive (in megabytes as well as time remaining for the selected capture format). There are also several capture options you can select on its face; to choose all other relevant options, you click the Settings button.

Capturing from analog sources

Figure 1.11 shows Studio's interface for capturing analog video. As you can see, the Album and Player remain unchanged, but there are two additional panels, for adjusting the brightness and color of the captured video and for adjusting incoming audio volume. These are unnecessary with DV or MicroMV source video as you're simply transferring the digital video from camera to computer.

Capturing from an analog source, however, usually involves some fine-tuning, especially for audio, and Studio provides a strong tool set for doing so. Also, when capturing analog video, you have to select the format for storing your video and, often, quality options associated with that format—the reason for the additional controls on the Diskometer.

If all this sounds scary, don't sweat. Capturing analog video is more meticulous than mysterious, and it's all spelled out in Chapter 4.

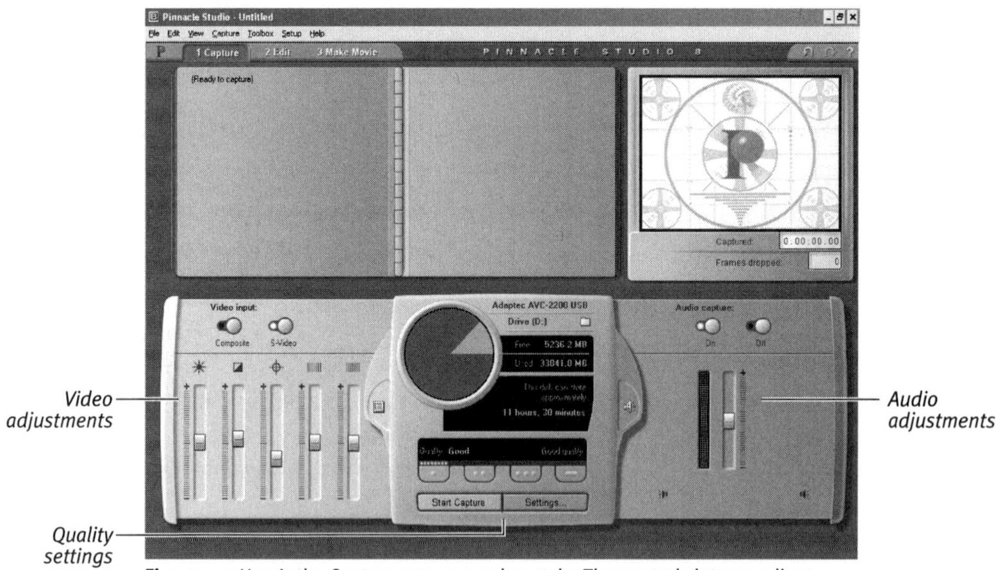

Figure 1.11 Here's the Capture screen, analog style. The controls let you adjust the incoming audio and video.

Figure 1.12 The Make Movie screen is your last stop in the production process. Say hello to baby Whatley! Note the panels on the upper left that let you select output type.

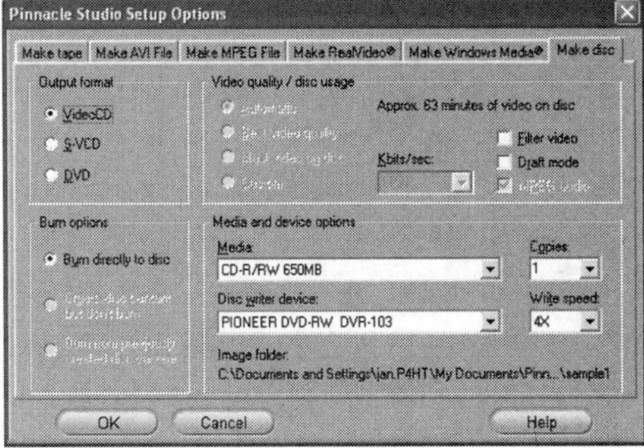

Figure 1.13 Click Settings and choose an output type, in this case from the Make disc tab.

Make Movie Mode

Enter Make Movie mode (**Figure 1.12**) by selecting the Make Movie tab in the upper-left corner of the Studio interface (Figure 1.3). This takes you to the controls for outputting your work.

Note that Studio customizes the Make Movie interface based on output type. In the example here, I'm about to produce a DVD of my first daughter's birth. As you can see, Studio shows a Diskometer-like view of the amount of space available on the DVD, and clicking the Settings button launches a screen with options specific to your output medium of choice. Select Make disc, and you'll see choices for output to VideoCD, S-VCD (Super VideoCD), and DVD (see **Figure 1.13**).

As shown on the vertical panel on the top left of Figure 1.12, you can also output to tape (see Chapter 13), produce AVI, MPEG, or streaming media files (see Chapter 14), and you can share your file by uploading it to Pinnacle's StudioOnline Web site (see Chapter 15).

Undo and Redo

Experimentation is a major part of the video creation process, which means trying and discarding lots of options. Studio makes this painless with an exhaustive Undo and/or Redo feature that saves all edit decisions made since the project was loaded for the current editing session. You can even save your file and then undo previous edit decisions (a rare option in my experience) and, of course, redo them all if you change your mind again.

To undo an edit:

- To undo the immediately preceding edit that you've made, select one of the following:
  - Click the Undo icon at the upper-right corner of the Studio interface (**Figure 1.14**).
  - Select Edit > Undo (**Figure 1.15**).
  - Press Ctrl+Z on your keyboard to activate the Undo keyboard shortcut.

  Studio will undo the last edit—in this case, a trim end.

  Note that Studio stores edits sequentially, so to undo the third previous edit, you must first undo the two more recent edits.

To redo an edit:

- To redo an edit, select one of the following:
  - Click the Redo icon at the upper-right corner of the Studio interface (**Figure 1.16**).
  - Select Edit > Redo (**Figure 1.17**).
  - Press Ctrl+Y on your keyboard to activate the Redo keyboard shortcut.

  Studio will redo the last edit—in this case, a trim end.

  As with edits, Studio stores Undo commands sequentially, so you have to apply Redo commands sequentially to reverse previously applied Undo commands.

Figure 1.14 Video requires lots of experimentation, so Studio gives you an Undo icon...

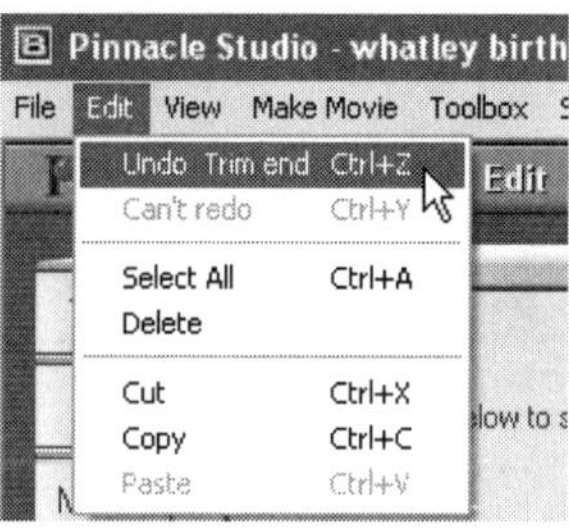

Figure 1.15 ...menu control (pull-down), and a keyboard shortcut (Ctrl+Z).

Figure 1.16 Changed your mind again? Simply turn to the Redo icon...

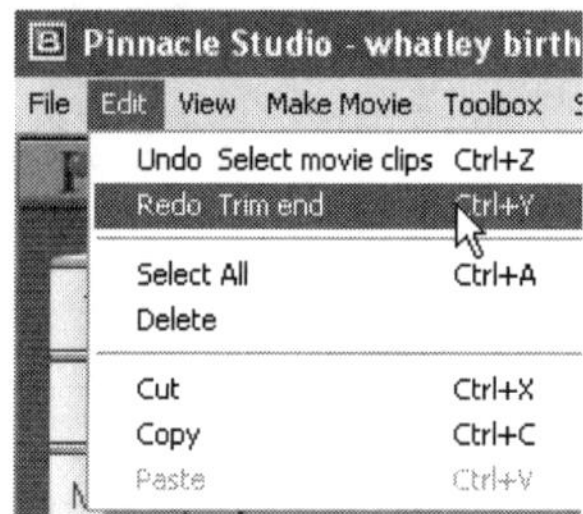

Figure 1.17 ...menu control, or keyboard shortcut (Ctrl+Y).

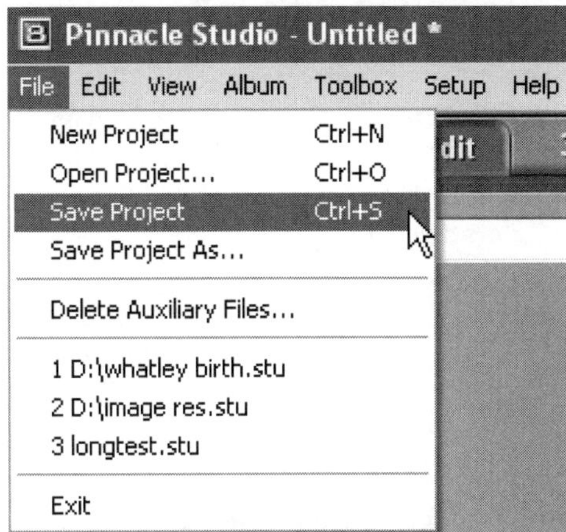

Figure 1.18 Nothing is more irritating than losing the fruits of your editing. Saving your file early is a great way to prevent this from occurring.

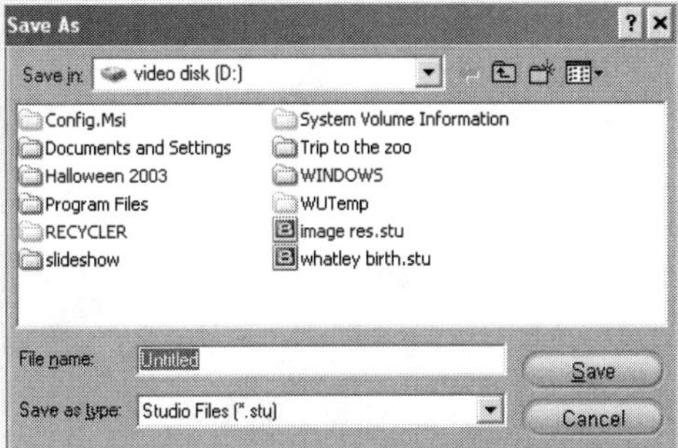

Figure 1.19 Here's the familiar dialog for choosing what to name your file and where to save it. I usually save the file in the same directory where I capture my files.

Saving Your Projects

Like most design products, Studio lets you save a project any time, preserving your careful editing so you can return later and continue working. Unlike many other programs, however, Studio doesn't have a true "bin" that saves assets captured and/or imported into the project.

Rather, the Album merely displays the assets available in the currently selected directory. If all you've done is capture files, there is no reason to save the project file, and Studio won't prompt you to do so when you exit the program. So long as you don't change the directories for your captured files (see "Loading Video Files" in Chapter 6), the files will appear in the Album next time you load Studio.

Once you drag an asset into the Movie Window and start editing, however, the project has officially begun. If you try to close the program or start a new project, Studio ensures that you don't lose your work. Or, you can be proactive and save the file yourself. Both options are covered below.

I typically create a separate folder for each project, using an obvious name like "Trip to the Zoo" so I know exactly what's in the folder. Then I save all relevant video, still image, and auxiliary files in that folder, as well as the project file. This makes everything easier to find and clean up later on.

To save a project for the first time:

1. Do one of the following (**Figure 1.18**):
   - ▲ Choose File > Save Project.
   - ▲ Choose File > Save Project As.
   - ▲ Press Ctrl+S.

   The Save As dialog opens (**Figure 1.19**).
2. Find the desired folder and type the desired name, then click Save.

   Studio saves the project as an .stu file.

To save a project after naming it:

- Choose File > Save Project, or press Ctrl+S.

To save a project to a new name and/or location:

1. Choose File > Save Project As.
   The Save As dialog opens.
2. Find the desired folder, type the desired name, and click Save.
   Studio saves the project file.

To respond to Studio's automatic save functions:

1. Attempt to exit Studio by doing one of the following:
   - Choose File > Exit (**Figure 1.20**).
   - Click the X icon at the upper-right corner of the screen (**Figure 1.21**).

   The dialog shown in **Figure 1.22** appears.
2. Do one of the following:
   - Click No.

   Studio exits.
   - Click Cancel.

   You return to Studio.
   - Click Yes.

   The Save As dialog opens.
3. Find the desired folder and type the desired name.
4. Click Save.
   Studio saves the project file.

✔ Tip

- Studio can automatically save your file at selectable periods, a good insurance policy against system crashes. The default Autosave interval is 90 seconds. For details on how to enable and configure this option, see "Setting Default Durations" in Chapter 2.

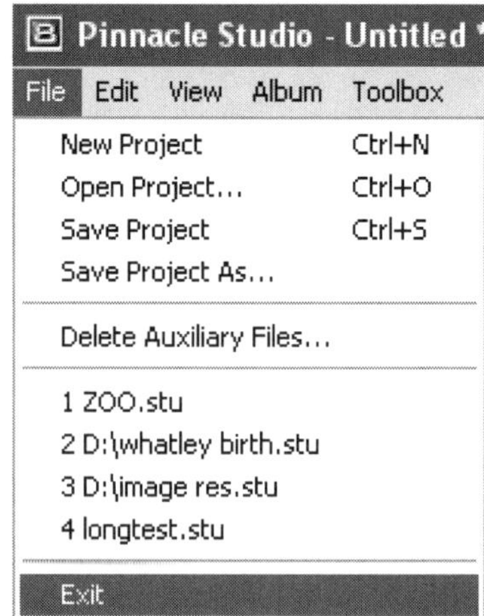

Figure 1.20 Try to exit the program by using the menu command.

Figure 1.21 Or exit via the icon.

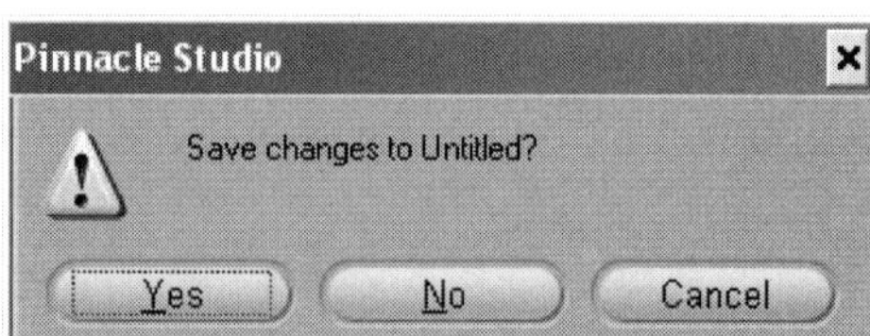

Figure 1.22 Either way Studio prompts you to save your project file. Studio can also automatically save your file at periodic intervals.

Saving Your Projects

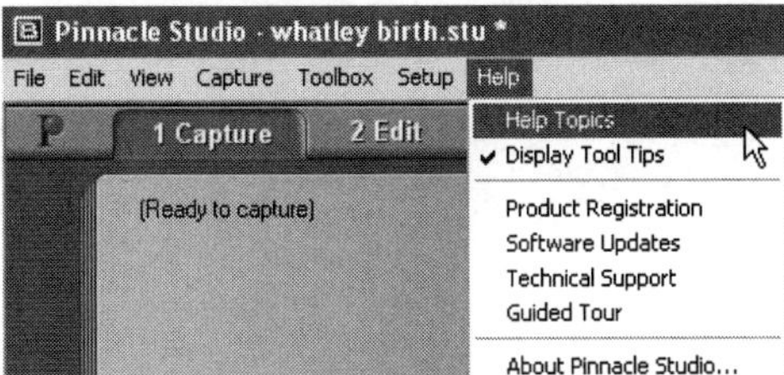

Figure 1.23 Here's how you open Studio's online Help screen.

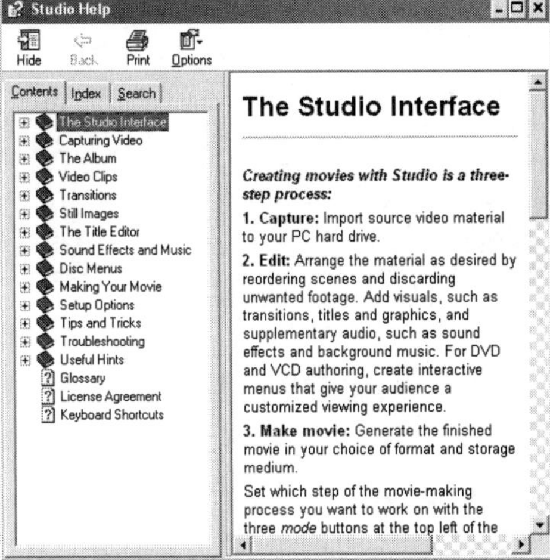

Figure 1.24 What you get is essentially an online version of the manual.

Online Help Facilities

Studio includes extensive online help, essentially a digital version of the product manual. Studio also has "tool tips," those little flags that explain an icon's function when you hover over it with your cursor for a moment or two. If you find these irritating, Studio lets you disable them.

In addition, Studio provides keyboard shortcuts for many common activities. In this book I present the keyboard shortcuts that I find most useful, and a list of all keyboard shortcuts can be found in Appendix A. Studio also offers an online list of shortcuts, with access described below.

To open Studio's Help screen:

- Do one of the following:
  - Press the F1 key.
  - Click the question mark icon in the upper-right corner of the screen (see Figure 1.14).
  - Choose Help > Help Topics (**Figure 1.23**). Studio's Help screen appears (**Figure 1.24**).

To disable Studio's tool tips:

- Choose Help > Display Tool Tips (**Figure 1.25**).

  When you select Display Tool Tips, the check mark beside the Display Tool Tips menu item is removed (**Figure 1.26**). You can reenable tool tips by selecting Display Tool Tips in the Help menu again.

To view Studio's keyboard shortcuts:

- With Studio Help open, select Keyboard Shortcuts at the bottom of the menu.

  A list of keyboard shortcuts appears in the display window (**Figure 1.27**).

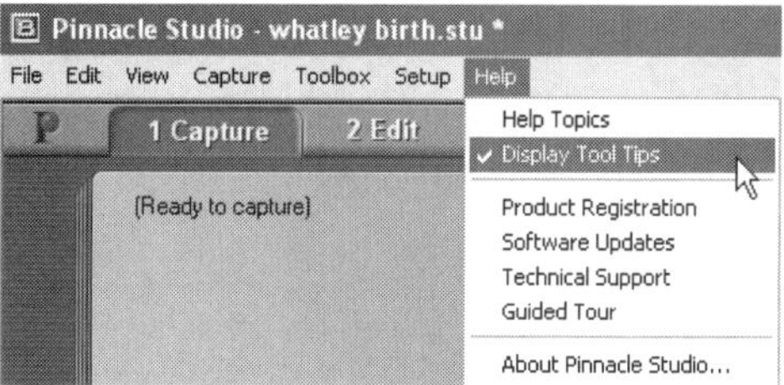

Figure 1.25 If you find tool tips irritating, you can disable them.

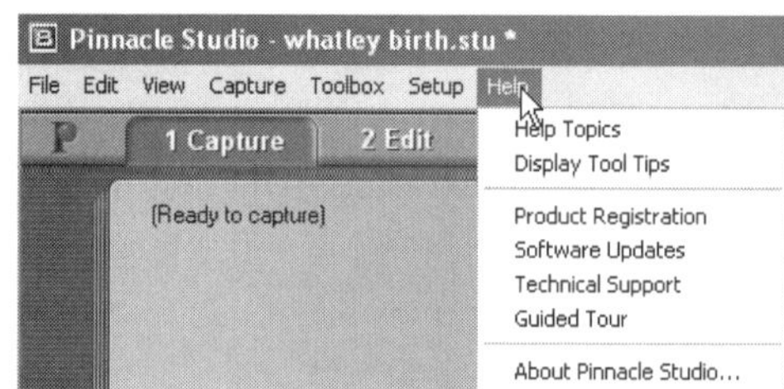

Figure 1.26 Tool tips are disabled when the check mark is gone from the side of the menu item.

Figure 1.27 If you're a fan of keyboard shortcuts, Pinnacle makes them easy to learn by making them available online.

2

Getting Started

Pinnacle Studio 8 is a very accessible program, so it's easy (and tempting) to just jump in and get started. Still, there are a few options for each project that you should set beforehand. For example, you'll need to choose the location of your captured video and auxiliary files, and you should perform a disk performance test to see if your system is up to the rigors of video editing.

Most of these options are "set 'em and forget 'em"; Studio will maintain them from project to project until you manually change them.

Just a quick note: Studio displays housekeeping options like file locations in the same dialogs that display configuration options relevant to particular activities like capture or transition rendering. This chapter focuses mainly on those housekeeping options (other options, like using hardware to view transitions, are covered later in the book).

Selecting Your Capture Drive

Most video old-timers use two or more disk drives in their systems—one for the operating system and applications, and one for captured video and project files. This goes back to the days of underpowered computers and cranky disk drives that were barely up to the task of capturing video. To capture effectively, you needed a separate, high-powered SCSI drive that cost thousands of dollars, required frequent defragmenting, and had to be dedicated to video capture.

Things have changed since then. Most computers purchased since 2000 are more than capable of video capture and editing. Still, with 80 GB drives costing well under $300, most video producers should consider purchasing a separate drive, especially for long projects or DVD production.

Even if you're working on one drive, you may want to create a separate folder for captured video and auxiliary files so they're easier to find during production and easier to delete when your project is done. Here's how.

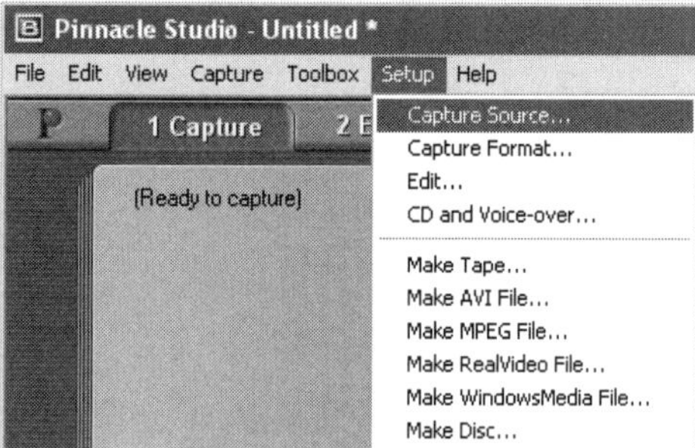

Figure 2.1 Choose Setup > Capture Source to access disk selection and test settings.

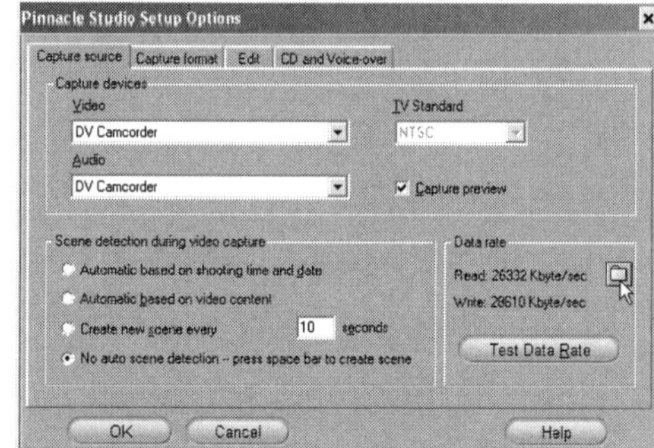

Figure 2.2 Click the yellow folder icon to select your capture drive and folder.

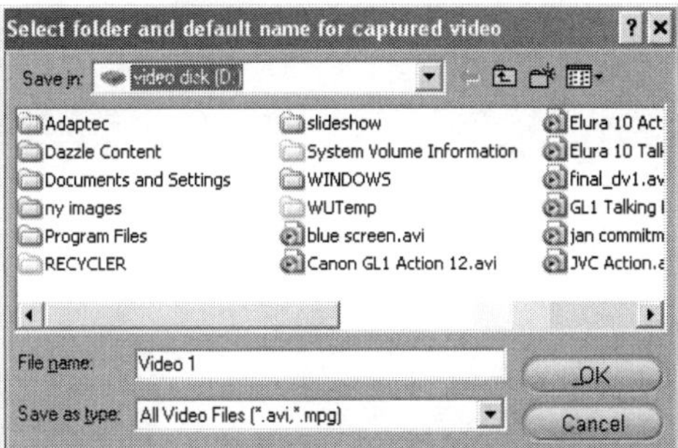

Figure 2.3 Click the Save in box to change capture drives.

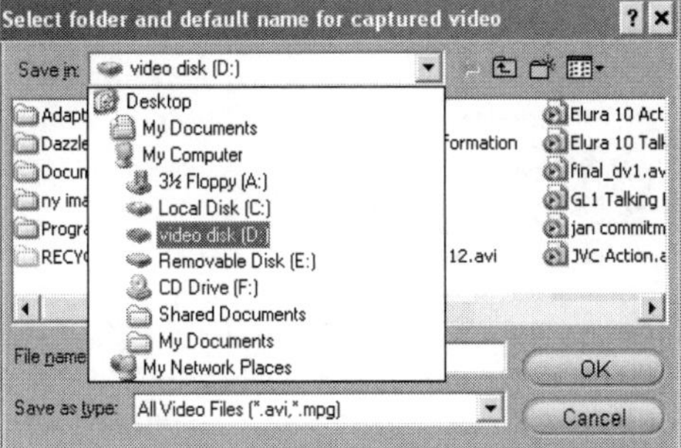

Figure 2.4 Select the target drive for your captured video.

To select your capture drive:

1. From the Studio menu, choose Setup > Capture Source (**Figure 2.1**).

   The Pinnacle Studio Setup Options dialog appears set to the Capture source tab.

2. In the Data rate box (in the lower-right corner of the Setup Options dialog), click the little yellow folder icon (**Figure 2.2**).

   The "Select folder and default name for captured video" dialog appears.

3. To change drives, click the Save in list box at the top of the screen (**Figure 2.3**).

   The list of available drives drops down.

4. Click to select the target drive (**Figure 2.4**).

✔ Tips

- Even if you're running a fast network at home, don't select a network drive as your capture disk. Performance is best with a local drive.
- If you have multiple drives, sometimes it's helpful to label your capture drive "video disk."

To create a new folder and name your clips:

1. At the top of the "Select folder and default name for captured video" dialog, click the yellow folder icon to the right of the selected disk drive.

   When you hold the mouse over the icon, the tool tip "Create New Folder" appears (**Figure 2.5**).

2. Studio creates a new folder, which you can name at will (**Figure 2.6**).

3. If desired, type the name of the captured file in the File name box.

   If you capture sequential files, Studio simply updates the file from Video 1 to Video 2, and so on.

✔ Tips

- Don't stress about what to name your files at this point, as you'll revisit this during the capture process.
- It helps to make your folder names descriptive; otherwise you'll have trouble figuring out what's in them six months later.

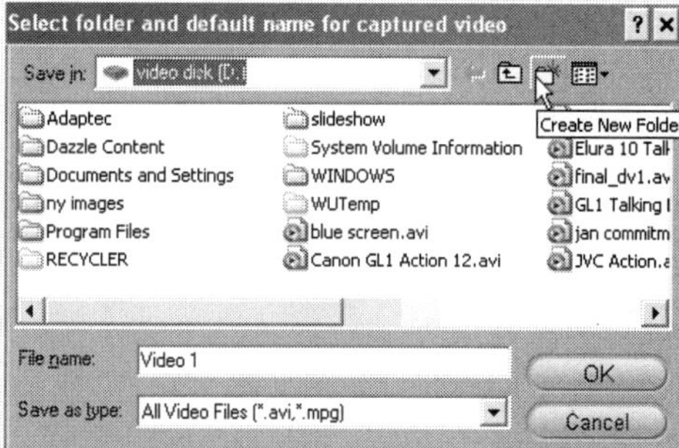

Figure 2.5 Click the Create New Folder icon to create a new folder.

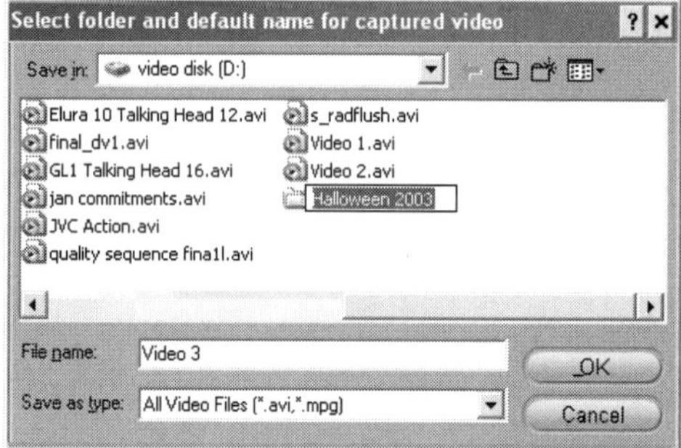

Figure 2.6 It helps to give your folders descriptive names so you can remember what's in them.

Defragmenting Your Capture Drive

Although most current (say, 2000 or more recent) computers have enough power to handle digital video capture and editing, Studio includes a performance test so you can be sure. Run this test as soon as you install Studio to identify any problems that may prevent smooth operation.

If you're using a disk that contains lots of data for your capture and edit drive, you should defragment the drive before performing this test. This is because during normal disk operation, Windows copies and deletes files all over the drive, sometimes splitting up longer files when writing them to disk. *Defragmenting* the drive reunites all file components, and packs the files efficiently together on the drive, opening up large contiguous spaces for the performance test and video editing projects.

The Windows Disk Defragmenter has a tool that lets you analyze the drive to see if it needs defragmenting. We'll skip that test and defragment anyway, just to be sure that your disk is in the optimal condition to take the performance test.

To defragment your capture drive:

1. From the Windows Start screen, choose Start > Accessories > System Tools > Disk Defragmenter (**Figure 2.7**).

   The Disk Defragmenter application window appears.

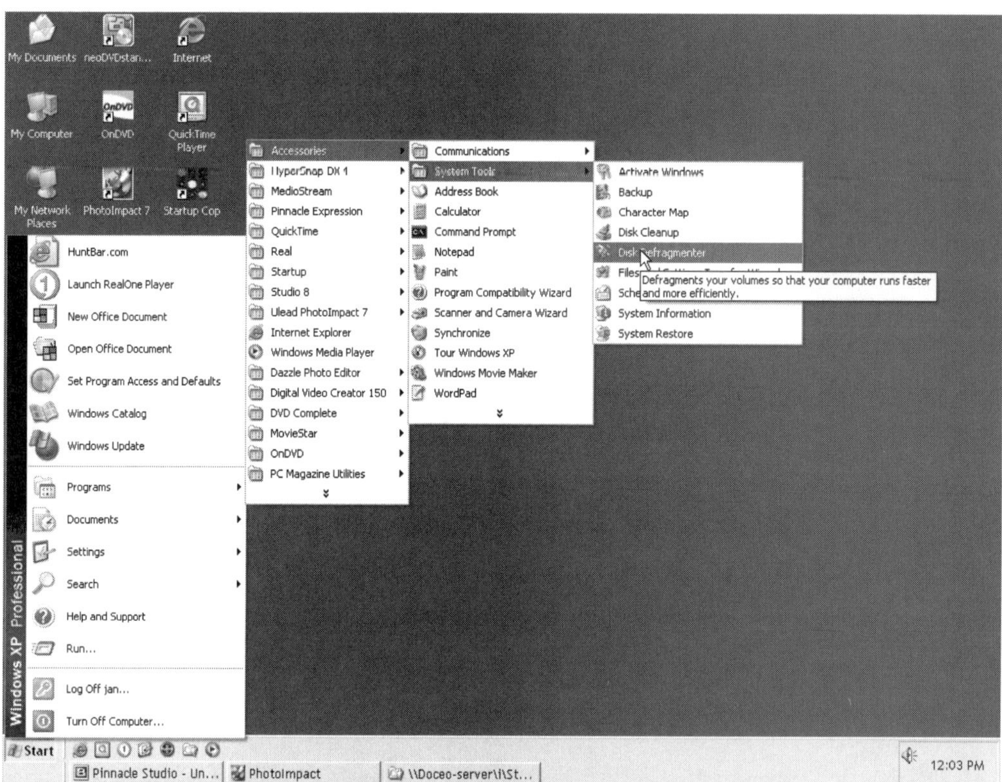

Figure 2.7 The long and winding road to the Disk Defragmenter utility, a hard drive's best friend.

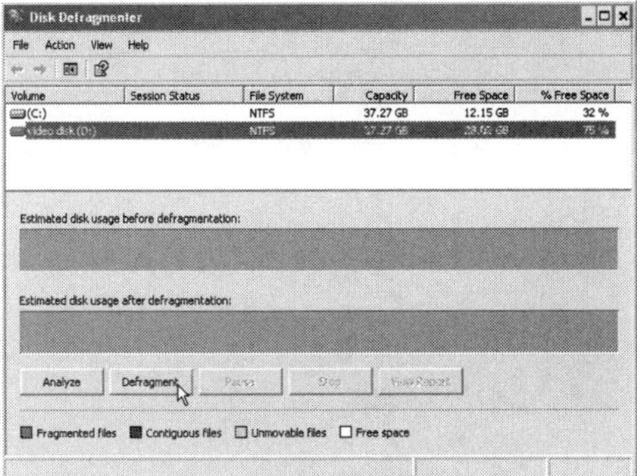

Figure 2.8 Select your target drive and click the Defragment button to get started.

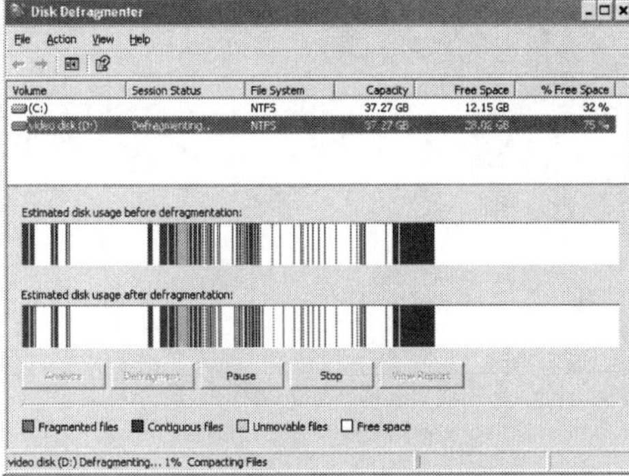

Figure 2.9 The Disk Defragmenter first analyzes your file, and then starts to consolidate files, compacting them to the inner tracks of the drive.

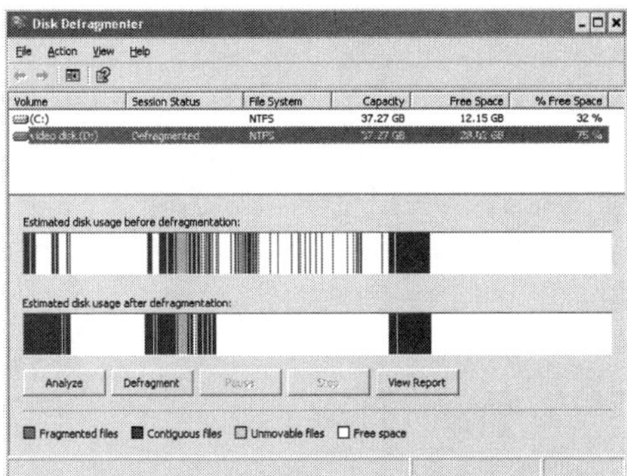

Figure 2.10 The freshly defragmented disk has wide open spaces, perfect for efficient video capture.

2. Choose the video disk by clicking it in the application window, then click the Defragment button (**Figure 2.8**).

   While you're waiting, go get a cup of coffee. You're pretty much done, but if you care to watch, here's what you should be seeing:

   The program analyzes disk usage before defragmenting. Although you can't see it in the black-and-white screen shots, most of the small lines surrounded by white spaces are fragmented files that will be consolidated during the defragmentation process (**Figure 2.9**).

   In the defragmented disk, which is ready for testing, all files are consolidated and efficiently packed, leaving plenty of contiguous disk space (**Figure 2.10**).

✔ Tips

- Depending on the size of the drive and how much data is on the disk, defragmenting can take anywhere from 30 seconds to several hours. Keep this in mind before starting this operation.
- Turn off all background programs and don't use the computer when you're defragmenting the drive. If any program writes data to disk while the system is defragmenting, it often stops and restarts the Disk Defragmenter, extending the completion time significantly.
- Large files slow the disk defragmentation process. If you have large video files or other files on the capture drive that you don't need, delete them and any other extraneous files before defragmenting.

Testing Your Capture Drive

Now that your drive is freshly defragmented, let's see how it performs in the Pinnacle drive test.

For perspective, keep in mind that DV streams from the camera at about 3.6 MB of video data per second. To successfully capture DV, a disk must be able to write, or store, at least 3.6 MB of data per second. To successfully transfer DV back to the camera, the disk must be able to read at least 3.6 MB of data per second.

As you'll see, the video disk on my two-year-old 1.5 GHz Dell Pentium 4 computer can read 18 MB of data per second and write about 25 MB of data per second, well above the DV requirements. In all likelihood your computer will also pass this test with flying colors, but it's better to test early to identify any problems than to experience balky operation during capture and editing.

To test your capture drive:

1. From the Studio menu, choose Setup > Capture Source (**Figure 2.11**).

   The Pinnacle Studio Setup Options dialog appears set to the Capture source tab.

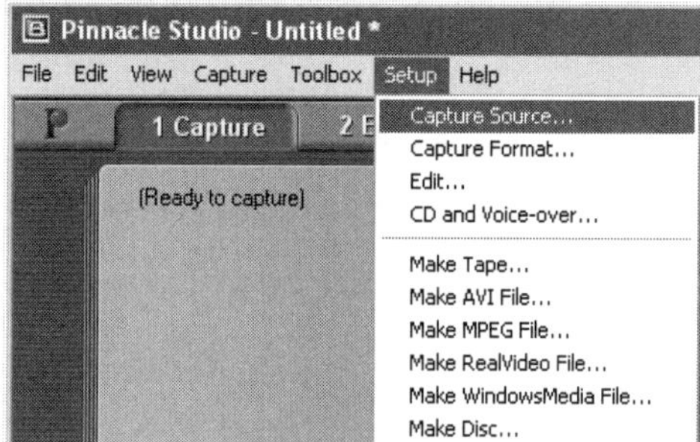

Figure 2.11 Choose Setup > Capture Source to access Studio's disk test utility.

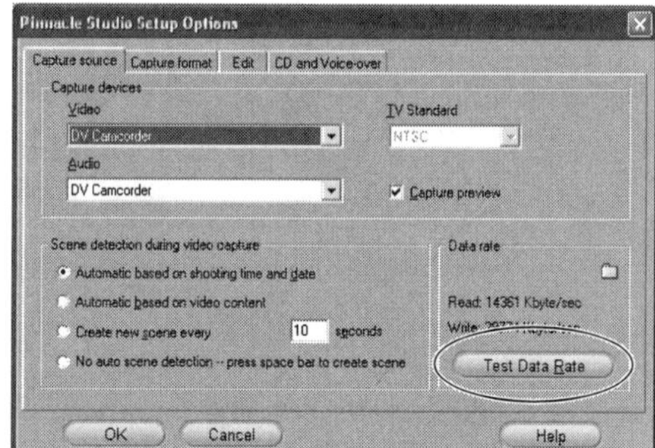

Figure 2.12 Click the Test Data Rate button in the lower-right corner to check disk performance.

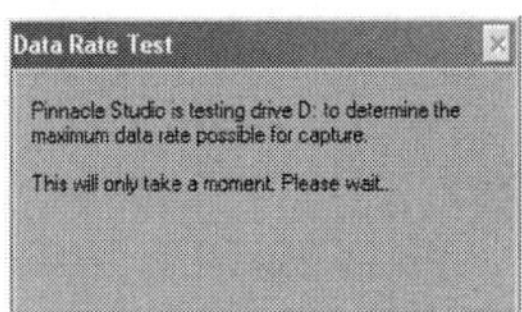

Figure 2.13 You should see this dialog for 10 to 15 seconds.

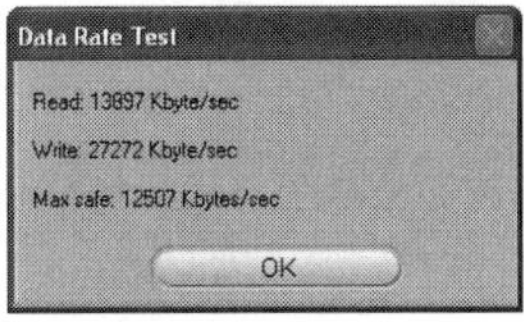

Figure 2.14 Voilà! I passed the test and am almost ready to get started.

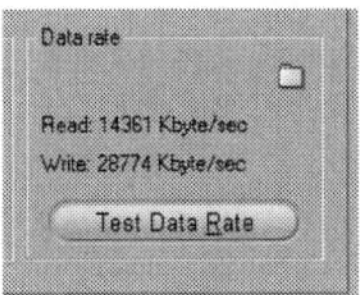

Figure 2.15 Studio notes the results in the Capture source dialog's Data rate box.

2. Click the Test Data Rate button in the lower-right corner of the Capture source screen (**Figure 2.12**).

   Studio starts the tests, and the Data Rate Test dialog appears (**Figure 2.13**). The test should take no longer than about 10 seconds, and then a Data Rate Test results screen appears (**Figure 2.14**). I passed!

   Studio stores these results in the Capture source screen (**Figure 2.15**). You can retest anytime. For example, if you start experiencing dropped frames during capture or you can't write video back to the camera, retest and make sure that performance is up to par.

Optimizing System Disk Performance

Assuming the Disk Defragmenter doesn't indicate that your hardware is faulty, two conditions could be the cause of poor disk performance. First, if you're running Windows 98, direct memory access (DMA) may not be enabled for your capture disk. Enable DMA in the System Properties control by selecting the properties window for your disk drive. DMA is automatically enabled in all operating systems after Windows 98, so this shouldn't be a problem in Windows 2000, Windows Millennium Edition, or Windows XP.

Another possible cause of poor disk performance is having programs that are loaded into background memory. You'll know this is the culprit if your Windows taskbar on the bottom right has more icons than a NASCAR racer. You can attack this problem in two ways. First, click on each icon, thus loading each corresponding program. In the properties or similar window, you should find a control for disabling the background process. For example, to disable QuickTime, choose Edit > Preferences and make sure that "QuickTime System Tray Icon" is not selected. While you wouldn't want to disable your virus checker, you probably don't need RealPlayer, QuickTime Player, the Microsoft Office taskbar, and other items running all the time.

The other alternative is to use a program called a startup manager, which lets you control which programs load in the background and when. *PC Magazine* offers a free utility called Startup Cop that provides basic functionality (www.pcmag.com). The program I've used most extensively is Shensoft Power Launcher Plus, but it doesn't appear to have been updated since 2000 (www.shensoft.com). Most recently, *PC Magazine* recommended Startup Manager by Kissco (www.startupmgr.com). If none of these suits you, search under *startup manager* for other options in your favorite search engine.

Setting Default Durations

When you insert transitions, titles, still images, and audio fades into your video projects, Studio assigns default durations to these assets. You can modify these defaults for each asset or effect during editing, but here's where you set the default values.

To set default durations:

1. From the Studio menu, choose Setup > Edit (**Figure 2.16**).

   The Pinnacle Studio Setup Options dialog appears (**Figure 2.17**).

2. To change the default duration for transitions, titles, still images, and/or volume fades, do one of the following:
   - Click on the number you want to change and enter a new number (**Figure 2.18**).
   - Use the arrow controls next to each duration and adjust the numbers manually (**Figure 2.19**).

To enable Autosave and set duration:

1. To enable Autosave, click the checkbox labeled "Save project automatically every" (Figure 2.17).

2. To modify the default duration of 180 seconds, select the number to activate it, then enter another value (**Figure 2.20**).

   The Autosave function saves your project periodically, so if your computer crashes or you lose power, most of your work is preserved. The only downside is a momentary loss of responsiveness as the system freezes slightly during the save process. Unless you're in the middle of an edit, you probably won't notice a thing, leaving little reason to disable this helpful process. The default duration is probably acceptable for most users.

Figure 2.16 Choose Setup > Edit to access basic editing default settings.

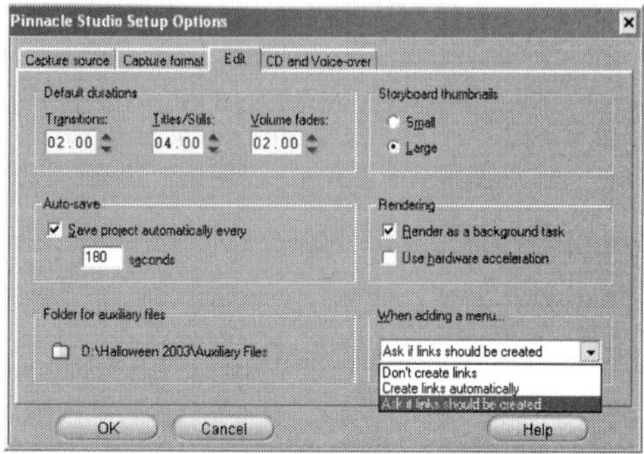

Figure 2.17 Default durations for transitions, titles, still images, and audio volume fades are in the upper-left corner of the screen.

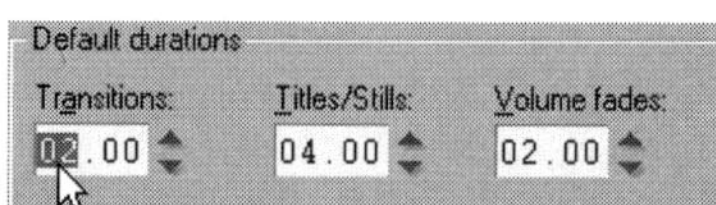

Figure 2.18 To change duration, you can touch the number and enter another, or...

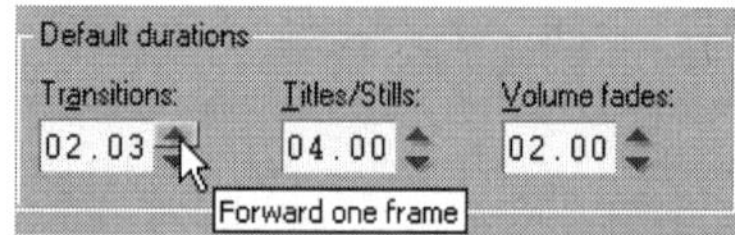

Figure 2.19 ...you can also change duration using the arrow controls next to each value.

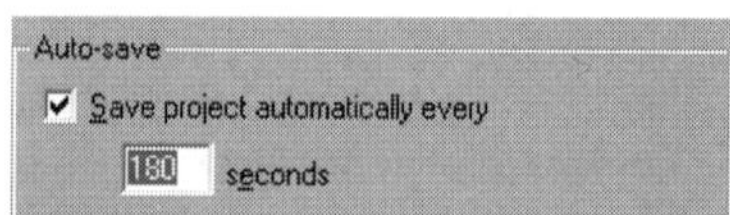

Figure 2.20 Modify the default Autosave value by touching the number and typing in another.

Setting Auxiliary File Location

I don't know about you, but it drives me crazy when I don't know the location of all the files associated with a project. These can include background audio files, narration tracks, DVD image files, and the other file detritus associated with project development.

Fortunately, Studio makes it simple to keep track of these auxiliary files by letting you set their location. This makes it easy to find them for reuse, or to delete them en masse once your project is complete.

Generally, I like to place my auxiliary files in the same drive and folder as my captured files so they're easy to find. The only reason to select another location is if you're running out of space on your capture drive and need to use another location for extra space. When you're writing a DVD, you may need close to 5 GB of extra storage for the DVD image file; most other auxiliary files are much, much smaller.

There are several other presets in the Edit dialog, but leave these at their default settings for now; they're covered in detail later in the book.

To set auxiliary file location:

1. From the Studio menu, choose Setup > Edit (Figure 2.16).

   The Pinnacle Studio Setup Options dialog appears (**Figure 2.21**).

   In the lower-left corner you'll see a yellow folder icon under the label "Folder for auxiliary files."

2. Click the yellow folder to open the Browse for Folder dialog (**Figure 2.22**).

3. Click the desired drive and folder for your auxiliary files.

   Studio creates a separate directory structure off the selected drive and folder (**Figure 2.23**) and doesn't mix the files with your captured files.

✔ Tip

- According to the technical-support discussion forums on Pinnacle's Web site, some users have experienced problems when changing the auxiliary file location in midproject. At the very least, you'll end up copying all auxiliary files from the old to the new location, which could be time-consuming. At worst—and this appears to be rare—you'll corrupt your project file and have to start over. So make sure you have enough space before selecting the auxiliary file location.

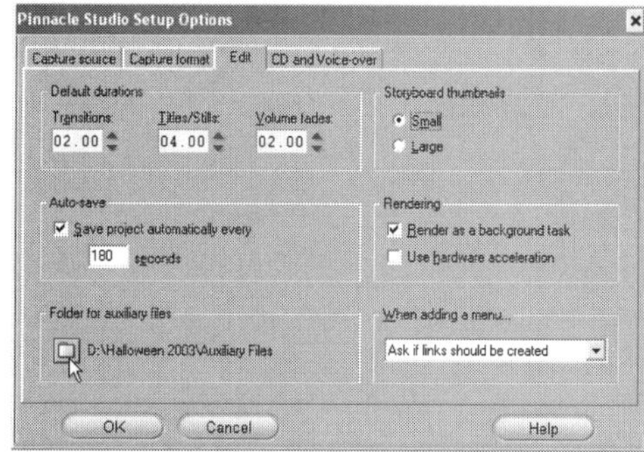

Figure 2.21 Click the yellow folder at the bottom-left corner to change the auxiliary file location.

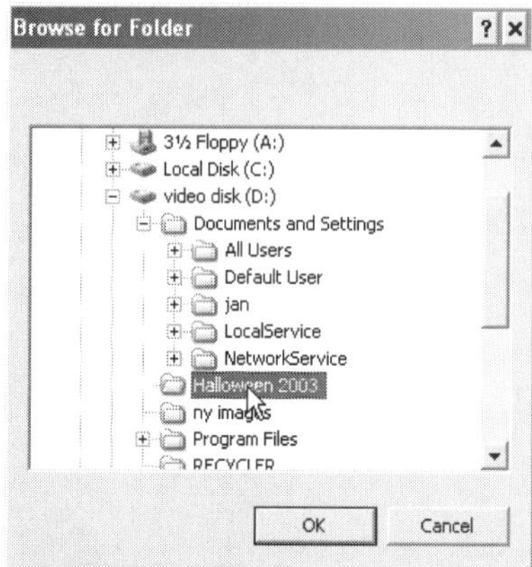

Figure 2.22 Scroll down to choose the drive and folder for the auxiliary files.

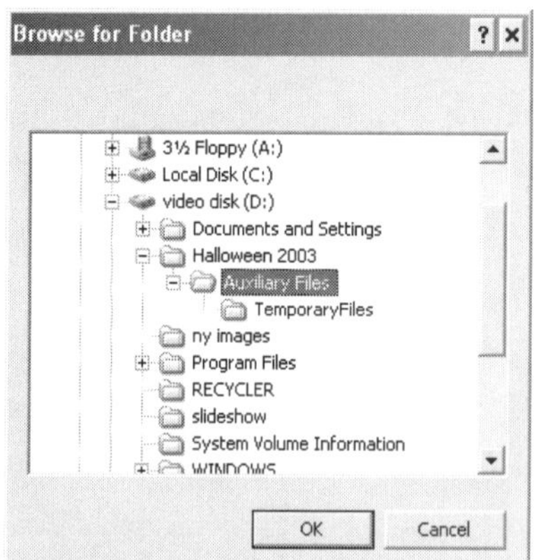

Figure 2.23 Studio creates an entirely new folder for the auxiliary files and doesn't intermingle them with your captured video clips.

PART II

GATHERING YOUR ASSETS

3

Capturing DV

I've been a big fan of the digital video format since I first got my hands on a DV camcorder back in 1996. In addition to capture simplicity, DV video quality is generally superior to that of most analog camcorders. And since DV camcorders record the time and date of each shot, Pinnacle Studio 8 can divide captured video into scenes, making it easier to find the clips you want to include in your project.

The term *video capture* was coined in the olden days, when transferring video from camcorder to computer required a "capture card." The card converted the analog signal to digital, and then compressed the video so it would fit on disk. Today, all that magic occurs on the DV camcorder, which stores the video on tape as a digital file rather than analog. This makes video capture from a DV camcorder more like a file transfer; some even refer to the process as a file import. Call it what you will, getting DV video from your camcorder to your computer is a snap. No video resolution to set or audio volume to adjust; just press start and stop.

The same cable that carries the DV video to your computer lets you control the camera, so you can start, stop, rewind, and fast-forward your DV camera within Studio—a useful capability unavailable with most analog camcorders. All these factors make DV capture fast, painless, and highly functional.

The DV Capture Interface

Let's have a quick look at the tools you'll use to control and monitor DV capture. Note that the interface is different when you're capturing from a DV camcorder than it is when capturing from an analog camcorder. (See Chapter 4 for the scoop on analog capture.)

You access the main capture window by clicking the Capture tab in the upper-left corner of the Studio interface (**Figure 3.1**). In Capture mode, Studio has four main components: the Album, where Studio displays the captured clips; the Player, which displays video during capture; the Camcorder Controller; and the Diskometer.

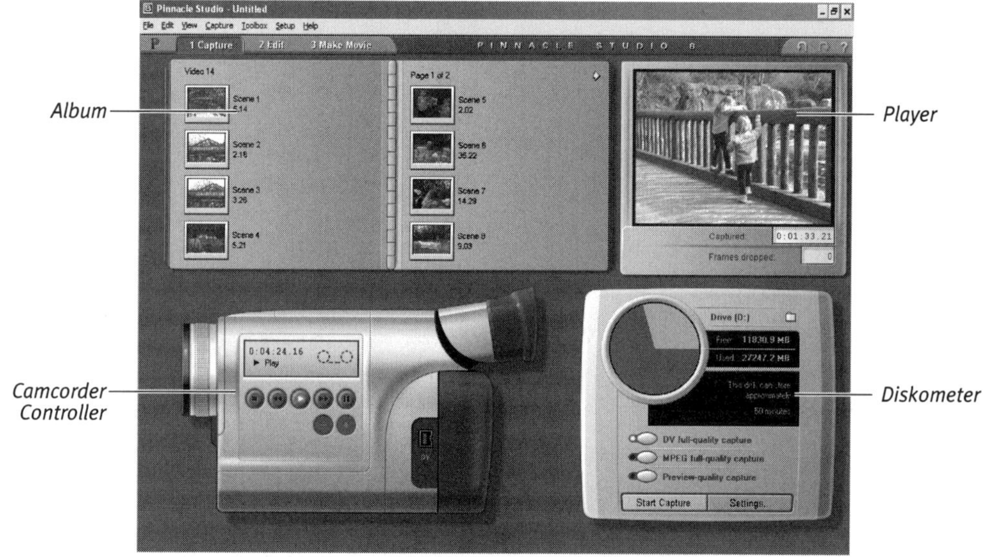

Figure 3.1 Studio's DV capture interface has four main windows: the Album, the Player, the Camcorder Controller, and the Diskometer.

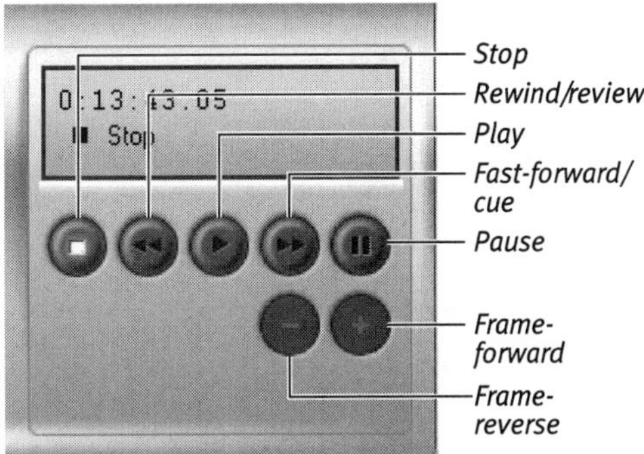

Figure 3.2 The Camcorder Controller lets you control the playback of your DV camcorder.

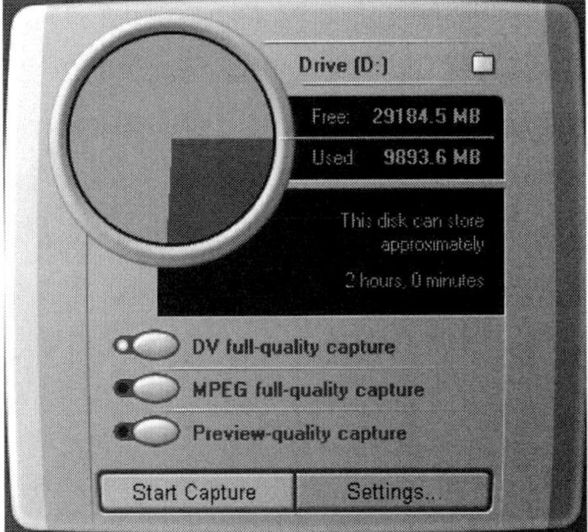

Figure 3.3 The Diskometer lets you know how much video you can store to your capture drive, lets you choose among the three capture options, and contains the Start Capture button.

The Album. The Album contains your captured clips, though you can't play them back while in Capture mode. Note that only one captured file appears in the Album at a time. If you enable scene detection (see the sidebar "Making the Scene with Scene Detection"), each scene from that file appears in the Album, thus accounting for the multiple icons in the Album in Figure 3.1. At the upper-right page of the Album is a little white arrow, which lets you know that there are more scenes stored on subsequent pages.

Studio stores captured files either during capture or, in the case of MPEG files, immediately after capture (Studio has to convert them before storage). Either way, no user intervention is needed to store the files. Once you start to capture another file, your previously captured files disappear from the Album, but don't worry; they are safely stored and accessible in Edit mode.

The Player. Note the lack of playback controls in the Player window. The Player's role during capture is to preview the incoming video and provide information about dropped frames. To play the captured files, you have to switch into Edit mode.

The Camcorder Controller. The controls in the Camcorder Controller mimic those on your camcorder (see **Figure 3.2**). Use these to navigate around the tape to find the scenes you want to include in your project.

The Diskometer. The Diskometer serves multiple purposes. First, the wheel and associated text describe how much additional video you can store on the capture drive at the selected format and capture quality. For example, in **Figure 3.3**, about 29 GB of space is left on the capture drive, which means the drive has enough available space to hold two hours (at 13 GB per hour) of video recorded in DV format.

In the middle of the Diskometer are controls for toggling between DV, MPEG, and preview-quality capture, options discussed later in this chapter (see "Choosing Your Capture Format"). You also control capture from the Diskometer, clicking Start Capture to start. After you start a capture, this button toggles into Stop Capture, which you click to stop the capture (**Figure 3.4**).

Click the Settings button in the lower-right corner to open the Setup Options dialog set to the Capture format tab (**Figure 3.5**). This is where you choose your capture parameters if you capture in a format other than DV.

At the far left of the top panel is the Capture source tab (**Figure 3.6**), where you select your capture device and scene detection options. This is also where you chose and tested the capture drive (see Chapter 2).

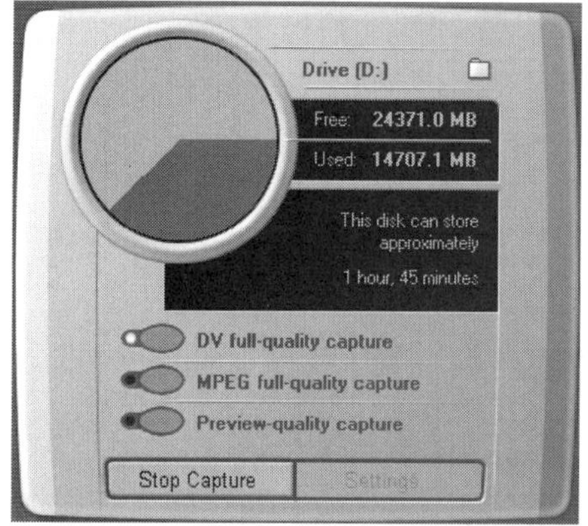

Figure 3.4 The Start Capture button changes to Stop Capture during the capture. You can also press the Esc key on your keyboard to end the capture.

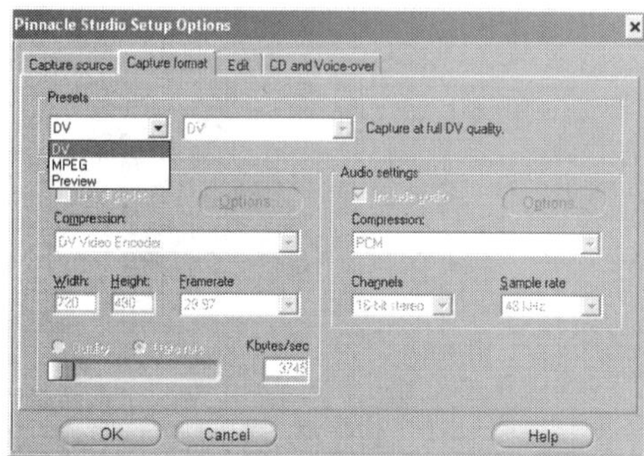

Figure 3.5 The Capture format tab. Since DV is a standard format, there are no options, but you'll have to select options here when capturing in MPEG or Preview format.

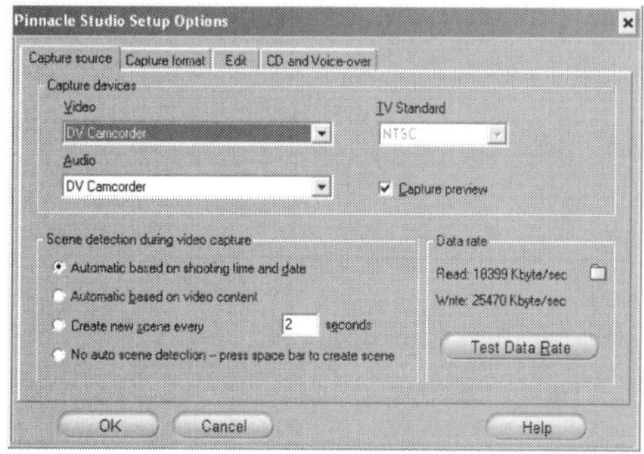

Figure 3.6 Here's the Capture source screen again. The last chapter explained how to select and test the capture drive here; this chapter explores the scene detection options and how to choose among various capture devices.

Making the Scene with Scene Detection

Sifting through and finding the scenes to include in your final project can be extraordinarily time-consuming. Fortunately, Studio automates much of this with its comprehensive scene-detection feature.

Studio offers three scene-detection modes (see Figure 3.6), accessed via the Capture source tab in the Setup Options dialog (click Settings in the Diskometer or choose Setup > Capture Source). The mode I've found most useful is "Automatic based on shooting time and date," an option that analyzes time codes embedded on the DV tape to identify new scenes.

Here's how it works: Personally, I chronicle family events with my DV camcorder continuously, usually taking two or three months to complete a 60-minute tape of holidays, school events, and other camera-worthy moments. When it's time to produce a video, Studio can scan the tape, examine the time codes, and break the captured video into multiple scenes that appear in the Album. Without scene detection, I'd have to view the video and perform that work manually, which is time-consuming and tedious. Although the scenes are all part of a single video file, during editing they look and act like discrete files, so I can easily pull one or more scenes into the Timeline for editing. For many productions, the time saving is enormous.

"Automatic based on video content" analyzes the video frame by frame, identifying a scene change when the amount of interframe change is significant. This mode is useful for DV cameras when the source video contains one long scene with no breaks. This can occur when dubbing a tape from analog to DV or when using a single camera to film one long event.

You can break a scene into regular intervals of 1 second or more (choose "Create new scene every *x* seconds") or eschew automated scene detection and manually create scenes by pressing the spacebar (choose "No auto scene detection").

Connecting for DV Capture

Before setting up for DV capture, quickly review the sections "Selecting Your Capture Drive," "Defragmenting Your Capture Drive," and "Testing Your Capture Drive" in Chapter 2.

I'm assuming that you have a FireWire connector or card installed in your computer. If you don't, start there, and make sure it's up and running. Don't spend too much on the connector; for your purposes, virtually all cards will serve equally well, from the $19 variety on up, and they all plug into an available PCI card slot inside your PC. Choosing one with at least two ports will allow you to connect both your camcorder and a FireWire hard drive, as needed, for additional storage space for your captured video.

FireWire to the Rescue

FireWire technology was invented by Apple Computer and then standardized by the Institute of Electrical and Electronic Engineers as IEEE 1394. Sony's name for FireWire is i Link, and companies refer to the connectors as FireWire, DV, or IEEE 1394. Whatever the name, they should all work together seamlessly.

Some newer DV cameras, like the Canon GL2, have Universal Serial Bus (USB) ports to transfer still images from camera to computer, but it doesn't work for DV video. To capture DV, ignore this connector (and the traditional analog connectors) and find the FireWire plug.

While most computers use a six-pin port, some computers (like my Dell Precision laptop) use a four-pin connector identical to that in most cameras. Identify which connector you have before buying a cable, which come in three varieties: four-pin to six-pin, four-pin to four-pin, and six-pin to six-pin.

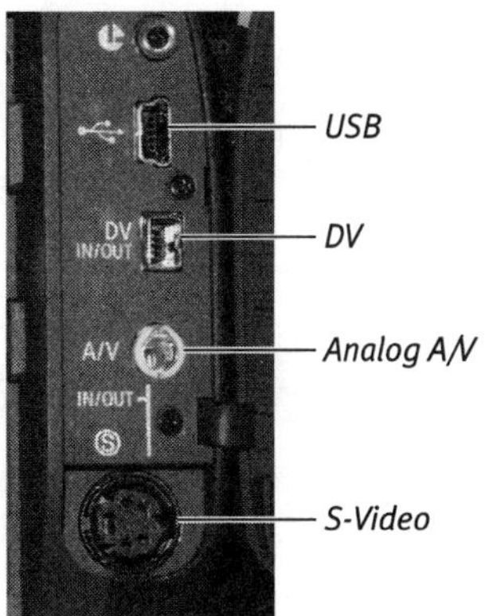

Figure 3.7 The DV port on my loaner Canon GL2 camera. Note the single analog A/V connector for composite video and both audio channels.

Figure 3.8 A four-pin (on the left) to six-pin DV cable. DV cables also come with dual four-pin and dual six-pin connectors.

Figure 3.9 The typical six-pin DV connector is found on most—but not all—computers.

To connect camera and computer for DV capture:

1. Plug in your DV camcorder to AC power.

   Battery power should work, but it doesn't work with all cameras.
2. Make sure that the camcorder is in VCR, VTR, or Play mode.
3. Connect your FireWire cable to the camera's DV connector (**Figure 3.7**).

   Virtually all cameras use a tiny four-pin connector like that shown on the left-hand side of **Figure 3.8**.
4. Connect the FireWire cable to your computer (**Figure 3.9**) using the larger six-pin connector shown on the right in Figure 3.8.

   You're now ready to run Studio and enter Capture mode.

✔ Tip

- Speaking of buying a cable, basic FireWire cables are priced between $12 and $50, depending on brand and store. If you're buying, check out www.cables.com, which offers a complete line of FireWire cables at very reasonable prices.

Entering DV Capture Mode

As the name suggests, Capture mode is where Studio manages all video capture activities. Entering Capture mode isn't as simple as it sounds; as soon as you select the Capture tab, Studio checks to ensure that your DV capture device is running properly and that your camera is connected, turned on, and in the proper mode.

If everything is configured and connected properly, you won't notice any of this; you'll just be ready to capture. If there are problems, this section will help you tackle them.

To enter DV Capture mode:

1. Run Studio, and in the upper-left corner, select the Capture tab (Figure 3.1).

   You are in Capture mode. If this is the first time you've entered Capture mode, Studio runs a quick diagnostic on your system disk to determine its capacity to capture video (**Figure 3.10**).

   If Studio reports that your drive is too slow to capture video, check your options in Chapter 2.

   When the check is completed, Studio attempts to load the DV capture driver and find the DV camera.

   If Studio finds the driver and the camera, the LCD panel in the Camcorder Controller will show the time code position of the tape in the DV camera and indicate that playback is stopped (**Figure 3.11**). You are clean, green, and ready for takeoff. Proceed to Step 2.

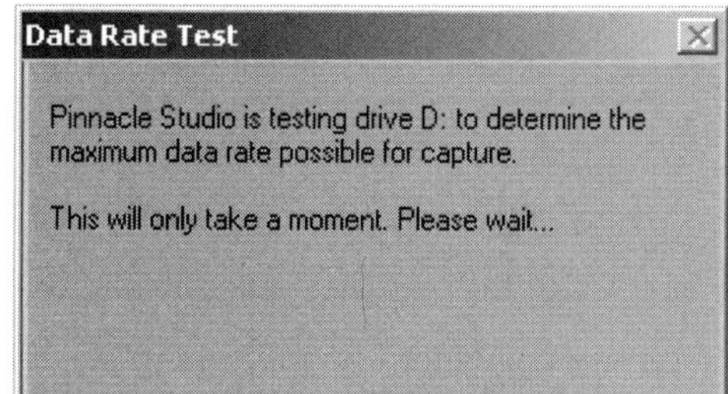

Figure 3.10 Studio runs a quick test on your system disk the first time you enter Capture mode. To read about selecting and testing your capture disk, see Chapter 2.

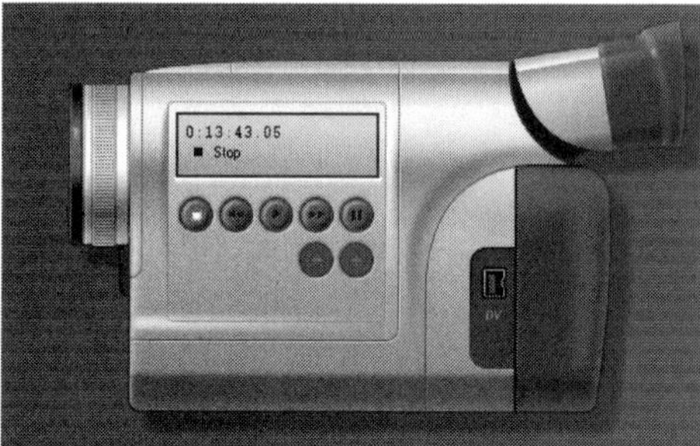

Figure 3.11 Your best clue that Studio sees your DV capture board and DV camera is the time code in the Movie Window.

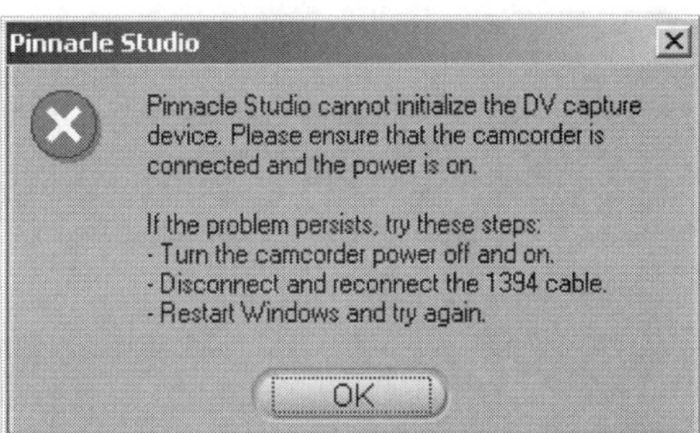

Figure 3.12 Ruh-roh, Scoobie Doo. Something's gone wrong. This is what you get when Studio isn't finding the driver or camera.

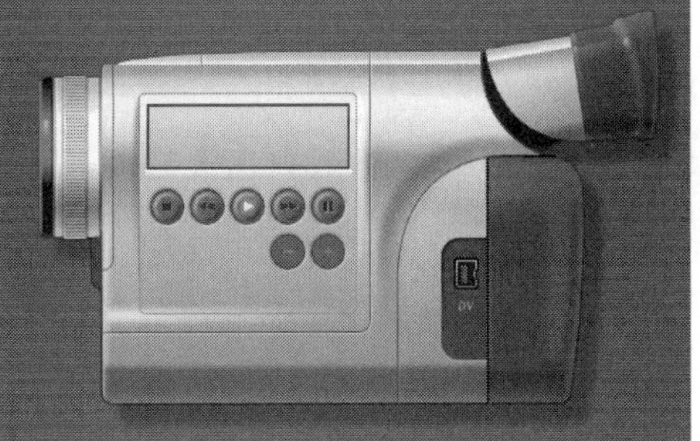

Figure 3.13 The "dead camera" means you're in Capture mode, but Studio can't "see" your DV camcorder.

Figure 3.14 When you see video in the Player, your setup is working and you're ready to capture.

If Studio doesn't find either the driver or the camera, an error message appears (**Figure 3.12**). If you click OK, you enter Capture mode, but the camera LCD is completely blank and you aren't able to capture (**Figure 3.13**). Take the steps recommended in the error message:

- ▲ Turn the DV camera off and on.
- ▲ Disconnect and reconnect the 1394 cable.
- ▲ Restart Windows and try again.

After each step, see if you can enter into Capture mode without error. If so, move to Step 2; if not, check Appendix B for troubleshooting information.

2. Click the Play control button, the middle button on the top row (Figure 3.11).

   Video should appear in the Player window, signifying that you're ready to capture (**Figure 3.14**). Pause the video and turn to the next section for instructions on capturing.

   If you can't see video in the Player window, check Appendix B for troubleshooting information.

✔ Tip

- Studio doesn't pass audio through the system during DV capture, so don't sweat it if you don't hear audio during capture. Besides, unlike capturing from an analog device, it's virtually impossible to transfer the DV video without the audio: It's stored in the same file in the camera.

Capturing DV Video

There are several capture options and other settings you could mess with, but let's throw caution to the wind and capture some video using Studio's default settings. I cover key capture options later in the chapter.

Start by going through the steps in the two immediately preceding sections. Once you enter Capture mode, the Camcorder Controller should appear, with live time code information. If it doesn't, run through the steps in the previous two sections again.

To capture DV video:

1. Select the Capture tab to enter Capture mode.
2. Use the Camcorder Controller to move the DV tape in the camera to the desired starting point.
3. Click the Start Capture button in the Diskometer (**Figure 3.15**).

   The Capture Video dialog opens (**Figure 3.16**), and the Start Capture button changes to Stop Capture (**Figure 3.17**).
4. For this test, change the duration in the Capture Video dialog to 1 minute and 00 seconds.

   If the duration shown in your program is *less than* 1 minute, either your capture disk is almost full or you're pointing toward the wrong disk. See "Selecting Your Capture Drive" in Chapter 2.

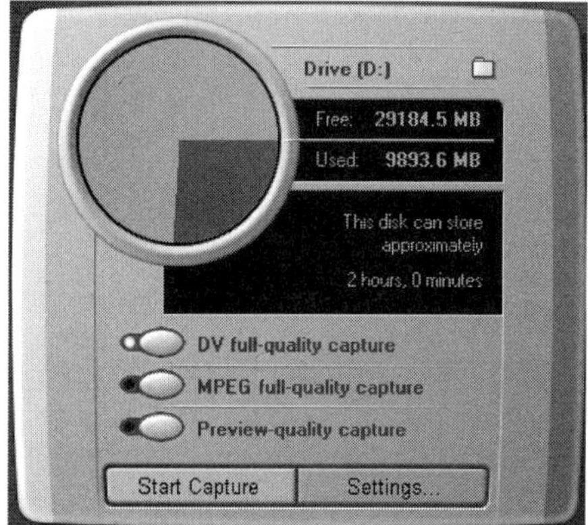

Figure 3.15 Click the Start Capture button on the Diskometer.

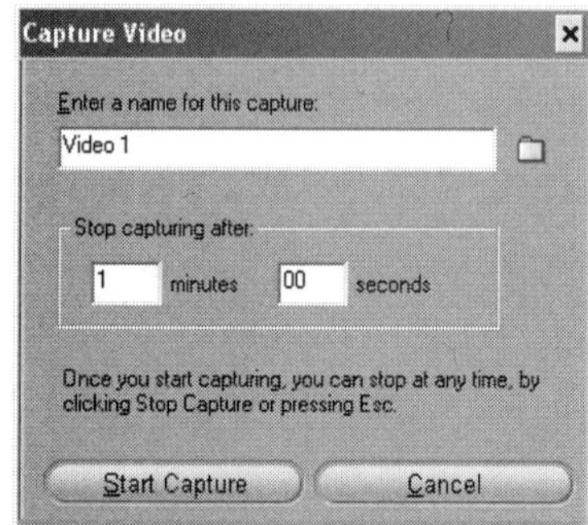

Figure 3.16 You can name your file before capture, and elect to capture for a specified interval. This is useful when you want to capture a 60-minute tape while you're away from the computer.

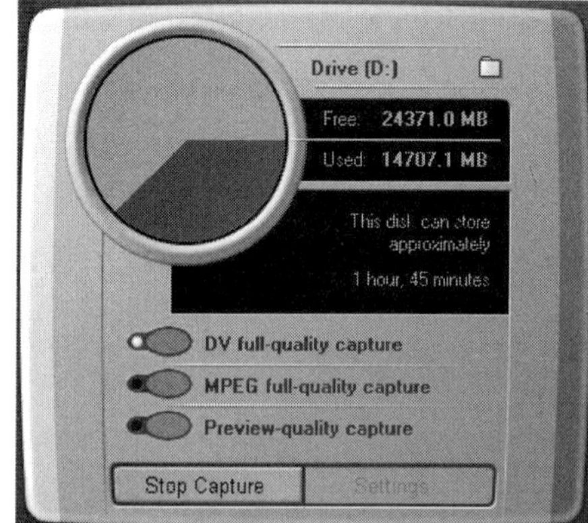

Figure 3.17 Click Stop Capture in the Diskometer, or simply press the Esc key on your keyboard.

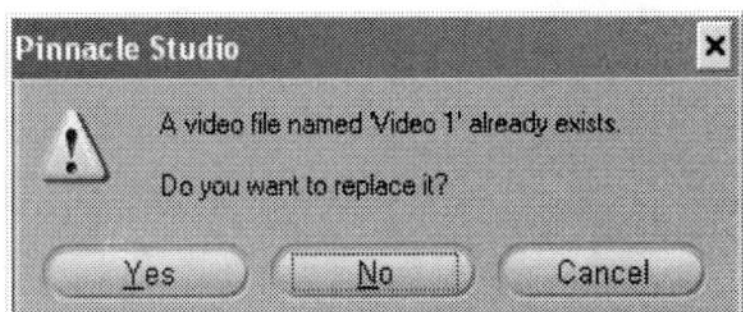

Figure 3.18 Studio won't automatically overwrite previously captured files, a nice feature.

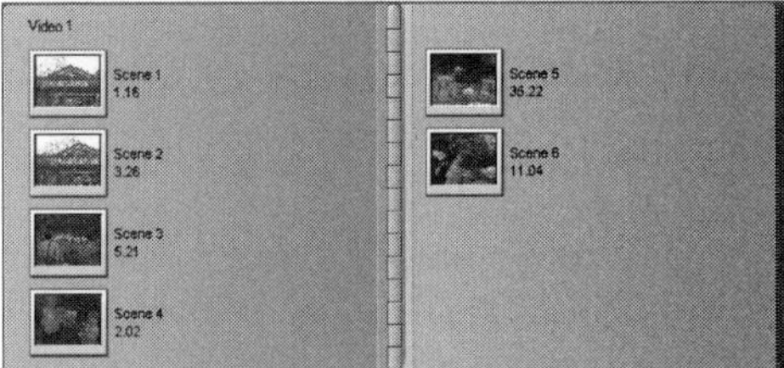

Figure 3.19 Your captured file appears in the Album, with a separate icon for each scene identified by Studio during capture.

5. Click Start Capture in the Capture Video dialog to start capturing.
6. If an error message appears (**Figure 3.18**), you've already captured some video using the same filename. Do one of the following:
   - ▲ Click Yes to overwrite the file and start the capture.
   - ▲ Click No to return to the Capture Video dialog and rename the file. Then click Start Capture to start capturing.

   Your DV camera starts playing and capture begins.
7. Studio should capture one minute of video. To stop capture before then, do one of the following:
   - ▲ Click Stop Capture in the Diskometer.
   - ▲ Press the Esc key on your keyboard.

   After the capture stops, a file labeled Video 1 (or whatever name you may have chosen) appears in the Album (**Figure 3.19**). You'll see multiple files if any scene changes occurred in the source video during the one-minute capture. (See the sidebar "Making the Scene with Scene Detection" for scene detection options.)

(continued on next page)

✔ Tips

- You can't view your captured video in Edit mode. To play back your captured file, see the section "Viewing Your Captured Video," later.
- Note the "Frames dropped" counter under the Player in Figure 3.14. Dropped frames are frames that the computer couldn't capture, usually because the disk wasn't fast enough to keep up with the incoming video. This counter updates in real time during capture. If you drop more than one or two frames, stop capturing and check Appendix B to diagnose and fix your problem.
- The first several hundred times I used Studio, I would start the video rolling, click the Start Capture button, and get frustrated when Studio asked me for a filename before starting capture, since the video I wanted to capture would be speeding by while I named the file. Then the nickel dropped in my brain that I should simply move the video to the desired spot and let Studio do the rest. See Step 1 above for the correct procedure.
- Studio's default scene-detection mode when capturing DV video automatically detects scenes based on time code. If desired, change this option in the Capture source tab, accessible from the Studio menu by choosing Setup > Capture Source.

Windows File Size Limitations

A consistent thorn in the side of video developers has been file size limitations inherent to Windows. Depending on a bunch of arcane rules, like which version of Windows you're running (Studio runs on Windows 98 SE, Windows Me, Windows 2000, and Windows XP) and how you formatted your drives, the maximum file size your system can store might be 2 GB (about 9 minutes of video) or 4 GB (about 19 minutes of video). It's basically 3.6 MB/second, or 216 MB/minute. In these instances you'll have to divide your capture into 2 GB or 4 GB chunks to capture an entire 60-minute DV tape.

Fortunately, Windows XP and Windows 2000 have no file size limitations so long as you format your drives using the Windows NT file system. That's why most video developers have moved to these versions.

If you're running Windows 98 or Me, however, you're probably on a fairly old computer with lots of out-of-date drivers and other code bits and fragments. Upgrading to Windows XP and reformatting your capture drive will give you unlimited capture size and a cleaner starting point for your programs.

Whichever Windows you're running, Studio should automatically list the maximum duration you can capture in the Capture Video dialog (Figure 3.16).

Choosing Your Capture Format

The previous exercise explained how to capture in DV format, which is appropriate for the vast majority of users and projects. However, when capturing DV video from a DV camcorder, Studio gives you two other options: preview-quality capture and MPEG full-quality capture.

Preview-quality capture. You select this option in the Diskometer or in the Capture format tab of the Setup Options dialog. Preview-quality capture relates to Studio's SmartCapture feature, which stores the DV footage in a reduced-quality format that saves disk space but retains the original DV time code information. You edit using the preview-quality video, then Studio captures the footage at full DV quality before rendering.

SmartCapture was wonderful when it was introduced, because disk drives were so pricey and work space critical. Today, however, an 80 GB drive costs under $150. And although SmartCapture works well, it adds both time and complexity to the production process. For this reason, I won't discuss SmartCapture further; see Studio's manual or Help files for assistance.

MPEG full-quality capture. Capturing in MPEG format is a slightly different story with a similar ending. Capturing in MPEG saves you file space and production time if you're producing a DVD, VideoCD (VCD), or Super VideoCD (SVCD) project with MPEG video.

However, the algorithm that Studio uses to encode MPEG during capture is optimized for speed, not quality, so Studio can store the video to disk in as near to real time as possible. In contrast, when Studio outputs into MPEG format during final project rendering, say for DVD production, the algorithm is optimized for quality, not speed.

Note also that when you insert effects like transitions, titles, or color correction into captured MPEG video, Studio implements the effects and then re-renders the affected portions of the video into MPEG format. So if your edits affect substantial portions of the video, your production time savings will be minimal. In addition, the edited sections are encoded into MPEG twice, once during capture and once during rendering, the digital equivalent of photocopying a photocopy.

So, unless you're producing a disk-based project and your edits will be minimal—and production time is absolutely critical—you should capture in DV and then render into MPEG format after editing. This approach will maximize production quality, though production time may be extended.

This leaves DV video as the best capture format for virtually all projects.

To choose your capture format:

- On the Diskometer, click the button for the desired capture format (Figure 3.15).

  The light to the left of the button lights up.

  If you choose DV full-quality capture, you're all set; there are no other options to select.

  If you choose MPEG full-quality capture, you need to set several options before capture. (See the next section in this chapter.)

  If you choose Preview-quality capture, check Pinnacle's Studio 8 manual for additional help.

Time Code: What You Need to Know

As you shoot, your DV camcorder stamps each frame with a sequential time code that looks like this:

01:02:03:04

Here's what it stands for:

Hours:minutes:seconds:frames

Time code gives your DV camcorder and programs like Studio the ability to locate and access any particular frame on the DV tape.

Note that DV tapes don't come with time code embedded; these codes are stored on the tape by the camera as you shoot. Ideally, time code is consecutive from start to finish, so each frame is unique. If there is a break in time code, the camera starts counting again at 00:00:00:01, which means duplicate time codes and potential confusion.

This can occur, for example, when you watch video that you've recorded and play past the end point of the recorded video. If you start recording anew from that subsequent point, the camera restarts the time code from the beginning.

Studio handles time code breaks fairly well, but other programs don't—especially higher-end programs that use continuous time code for features like batch capture. For this reason, it's good practice to maintain a continuous time code on each recorded tape. You can accomplish this in one of two ways:

- Put each tape in your DV camcorder with the lens cap on and record from start to finish. Then rewind and start your normal shooting, which will overwrite the previously recorded frames but maintain the time code structure.
- Whenever you film with your DV camcorder, be sure you don't start beyond the last previously written time code segment. This will be apparent if you see nothing but lines in the time code field.

Don't confuse time code with the time and date stamp the DV format uses to produce scene changes. These are stored on a different part of the tape. On many camcorders, including most Sony DV camcorders, you can see this information by pressing the data code control.

Capturing DV Video to MPEG Format

The most obvious time to capture directly into MPEG format is when you're creating projects using MPEG-formatted video, such as in DVDs, VCDs, and SVCDs. Studio simplifies these captures with presets that deliver the properly formatted video for each project.

First remember that during MPEG capture, Studio defaults to an encoding algorithm optimized for encoding speed rather than quality (see the previous section). This means that quality will be optimized if you capture with DV and encode into MPEG format during final rendering.

Also note that all versions of Studio before 8.6 reencode all MPEG footage during final rendering, even if there are no edits that require it. Version 8.6 introduced smart rendering for MPEG, so that only the segments of video affected during editing are reencoded before production. This makes the upgrade to version 8.6 essential to all producers who capture MPEG video.

Finally, remember that if your edits affect significant portions of the video in the project, you will have to rerender these anyway before producing your disc. If this is the case, capturing in DV format will produce better overall quality with minimal increase in production time.

Knowing all these caveats, if you still want to capture in MPEG format, here's how.

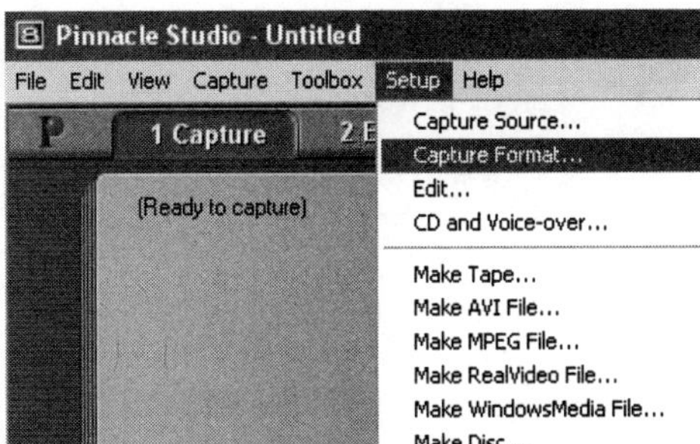

Figure 3.20 Access the Capture format tab to change your capture format to MPEG.

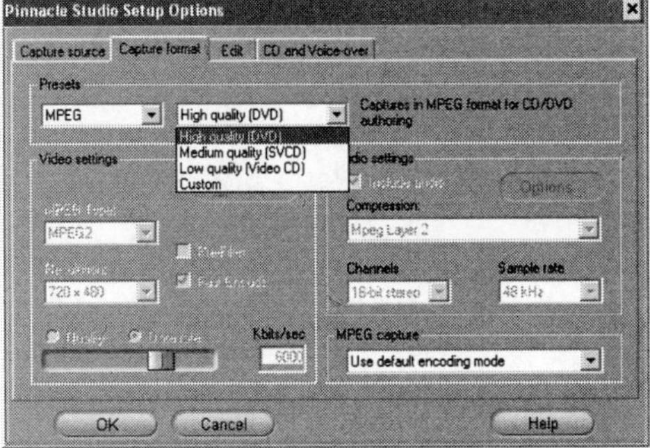

Figure 3.21 Choose the preset format for your project.

To capture DV video into MPEG format:

1. Open the Setup Options dialog to the Capture format tab in one of two ways:
   - ▲ From the Studio menu, choose Setup > Capture Format (**Figure 3.20**).
   - ▲ In Capture mode, click the Settings button in the Diskometer.
2. Click the text in the first list box in the Presets section and select MPEG (**Figure 3.21**).

   This also changes your selection in the Diskometer, so you don't have to change it there separately.
3. In the second list box in the Presets section, choose one of the following options:
   - ▲ If encoding for a DVD project, choose High quality.
   - ▲ If encoding for an SVCD project, choose Medium quality.
   - ▲ If encoding for a VCD project, choose Low quality.
   - ▲ If you wish to customize your encoding settings, choose Custom (but be sure to read the following tips first).
4. Click OK to close the Setup Options dialog.
5. If not in Capture mode, select the Capture tab.
6. Use the Camcorder Controller to move the DV tape in the camera to the desired starting point.

(continued on next page)

7. Click the Start Capture button in the Diskometer.

   The Capture Video dialog opens, and the Start Capture button changes to Stop Capture.

8. If desired, change the duration of the video capture and/or change the name of the captured file.

9. Click the Start Capture button in the Capture Video dialog to start capturing.

10. If the error message appears (Figure 3.18), do one of the following:
    - ▲ Click Yes to overwrite the file and start the capture.
    - ▲ Click No to return to the Capture Video dialog and rename the file. Then click Start Capture.

    Your DV camera starts playing and capture begins.

11. Allow capture to proceed through the specified duration or, to stop capture before then, do one of the following:
    - ▲ Click Stop Capture in the Diskometer.
    - ▲ Press the Esc key on your keyboard.

    Unless you have an extraordinarily fast computer, it may take Studio a while to compress the DV footage into MPEG format, and you'll see a message like the one shown in **Figure 3.22**.

    After encoding stops, a file labeled Video 1 (or whatever name you may have chosen) appears in the Album. You'll see multiple files if any scene changes occurred in the source video during the capture.

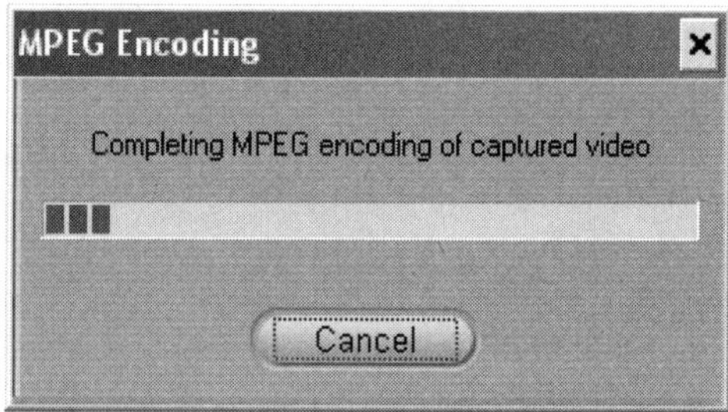

Figure 3.22 On all but the fastest computers, Studio requires a few moments to finish encoding after you stop the tape.

MicroMV Capture

Camcorders using Sony's new MicroMV format have a compelling vision—DV quality at about half the data rate, enabling smaller cassettes and less storage space on the computer.

Technically, MicroMV captures in MPEG-2 format, the same high-quality format used in DVD production, and connects to the computer via the FireWire port. According to the Studio manual, the capture interface for MicroMV is identical to DV, but many features are disabled, like the ability to capture to DV format.

Unfortunately, we did not have access to a MicroMV camera while producing this book and have performed no tests on this format. Judging from comments on the Pinnacle support forums, it appears that there have been some settling-in issues relating to this format, so before starting your work, be sure you have the latest Studio release.

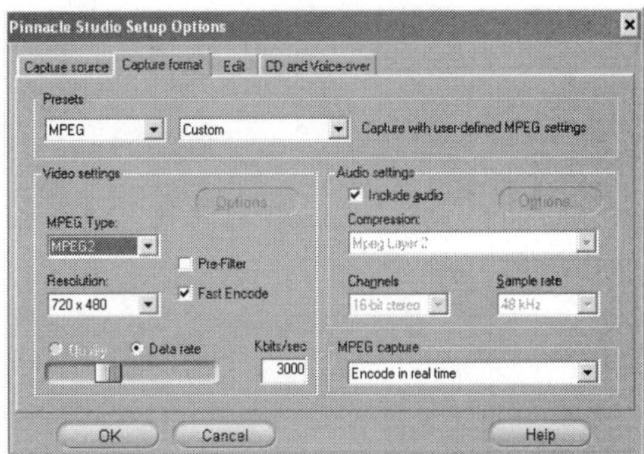

Figure 3.23 Studio lets you customize MPEG capture settings, but most users should stick with the presets whenever possible.

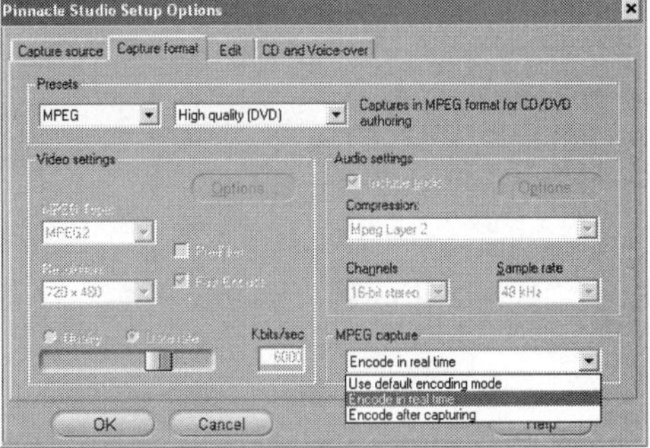

Figure 3.24 Messing with the MPEG capture settings in the lower-right corner almost always causes severe dropped frames.

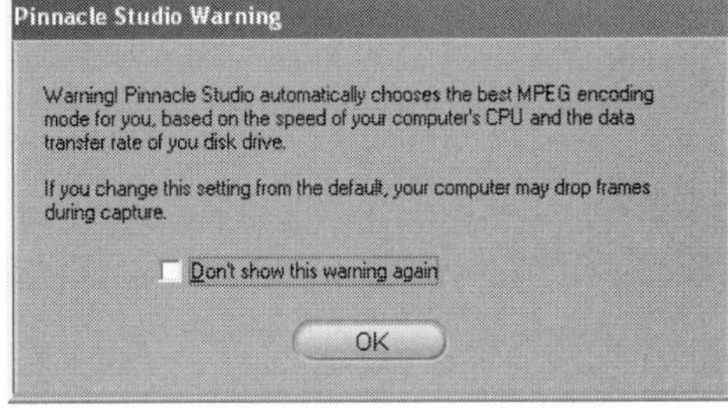

Figure 3.25 Studio will be the first to tell you.

✔ Tips

- Custom (in Step 3) should be used only by advanced users, since it presents additional encoding controls unfamiliar to most users (**Figure 3.23**).

  Don't modify the MPEG capture parameters in the lower-right corner of the screen (**Figure 3.24**). This could lead to dropped frames during capture (**Figure 3.25**).
- Furthermore, if you're capturing video to include on DVD, VCD, or SVCD, stick to the presets and avoid the custom settings. These optical formats define video parameters very tightly, and custom settings could render your video files unusable in these projects.
- If you're using the same captured video in different types of projects, like DVD and VCD, use the lowest-common-denominator format. That is, DVDs can incorporate video encoded for VCD and SVCD, but VCDs can't integrate video encoded for SVCD or DVD.
- If you're capturing video in MPEG format simply to distribute it on CD-ROM or via the Internet, note that virtually every computer on the planet can now play back MPEG-1 files, since MPEG-1 decoders have been standard on Windows and Macintosh computers for years. However, MPEG-2 decoder capabilities are much less prevalent and generally not available for free. Thus MPEG-1 is a much better format for general sharing.

Adding Scene Comments

Immediately after capture, you can annotate your captured scenes in the Album while in Capture mode.

If you intend to do so, note that Studio updates the Album each time you capture, so if you start another capture before changing the name, your files disappear. Don't worry, you can easily find them in the Album in Edit mode and make your changes there (see the section "Working with Scene Comments" in Chapter 6).

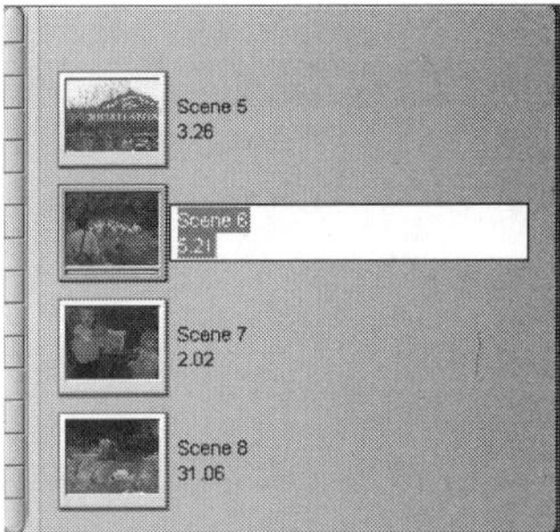

Figure 3.26 To add or change scene comments, touch the text twice slowly...

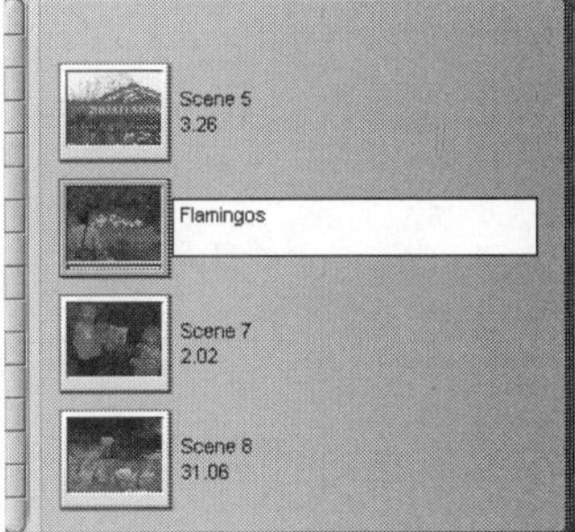

Figure 3.27 ...then type in your description.

To add scene comments to your captured video:

1. In the Album, slowly double-click the text immediately to the right of the video icon to make it editable (**Figure 3.26**).
2. Type the desired comments (**Figure 3.27**).
3. To save the comments do one of the following:
   - ▲ Press Enter.
   - ▲ Click anywhere else on the Studio interface.

✔ Tips

- You're not actually changing the filename; you're merely editing text that can be seen only inside Studio.
- If you plan to combine your scenes in the Edit tab of the Album, note that Studio blows away all screen comments when you combine scenes. You might want to look at the "Combining Scenes" section in Chapter 6 before you invest a bunch of time naming your captured scenes.

Viewing Your Captured Video

If you're like me, the first thing you want to do after capture is watch the video. To do this, switch over to Edit mode and use the Player there.

To view your captured video:

1. Select the Edit tab in the upper-left corner of the Studio interface.
   Studio enters Edit mode.
2. In the Album window, double-click the video you'd like to play (**Figure 3.28**).
   The video starts playing in the Player.
3. Use the controls beneath the Player to stop, rewind, fast-forward, go to the beginning of the video, and move through your video frame by frame.

✔ Tip

- If you captured using scene detection and the Album contains multiple scenes, the Player automatically plays from one scene to the next without breaks.

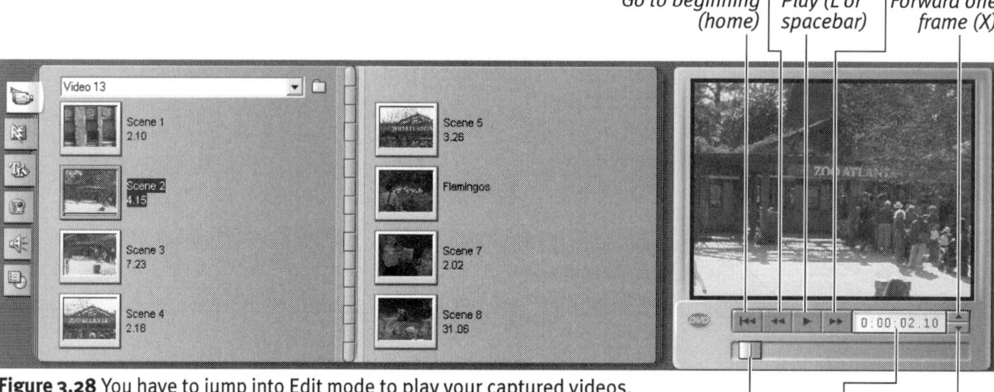

Figure 3.28 You have to jump into Edit mode to play your captured videos.

4

Capturing Analog Video

While DV capture is a simple file transfer with few settings to worry about, analog capture involves a plethora of controls, including resolution, quality, brightness, volume, and much, much more. To paraphrase Zorba the Greek, the sheer number of options can easily turn analog capture into "the whole catastrophe."

Fortunately, Studio simplifies the process with some well-designed presets and an excellent interface for making all the choices and adjustments necessary to capture analog video at top quality. With some care and frequent checking of your captured files, you should be in great shape.

Note that while Studio's DV capture interface is relatively standard among different cameras and FireWire devices, analog capture devices and their software interfaces can be as unique as snowflakes. Although Pinnacle attempts to present a standard approach in Studio, it's impossible to document all the differences between the various devices. The best way to go is use this chapter as a guide and consult the manual or help files that came with your analog capture card for fine-tuning.

The Analog Capture Interface

As you would expect, Studio's analog capture interface (**Figure 4.1**) contains various controls for adjusting your analog capture. Its three main components perform the following roles:

The Album. Your captured clips go directly into the Album, though you can't play them back while in Capture mode. Only one captured file appears in the Album at a time. If you enable scene detection, however (see the sidebar "Scene Detection with Analog Video"), each scene from that file appears in the Album, thus accounting for the multiple icons (**Figure 4.2**). The little white arrow in the Album's upper-right corner lets you know that there are more scenes stored on subsequent pages.

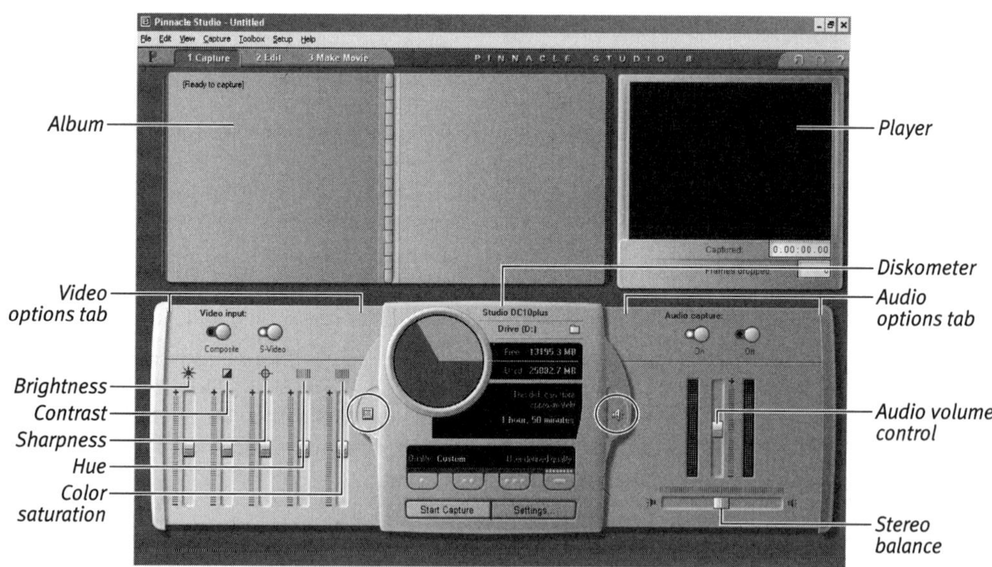

Figure 4.1 In the analog capture interface, the Diskometer has sprouted wings, enabling you to fine-tune the incoming video and control audio volume.

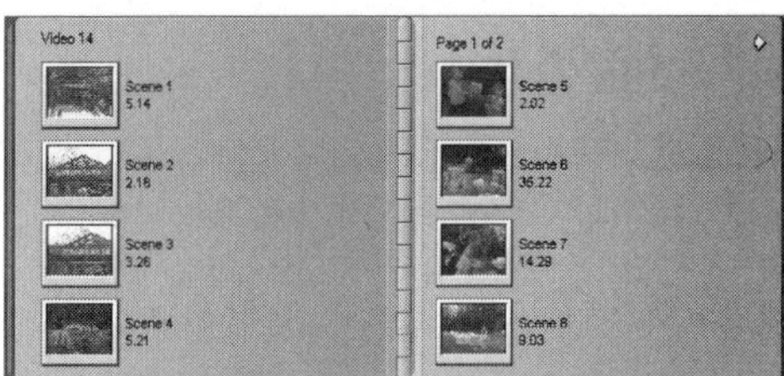

Figure 4.2 The Album, with scene detection enabled.

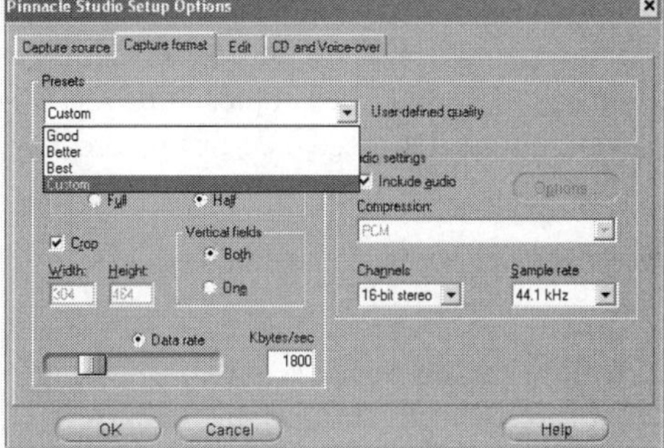

Figure 4.3 Here's where you set your analog capture options.

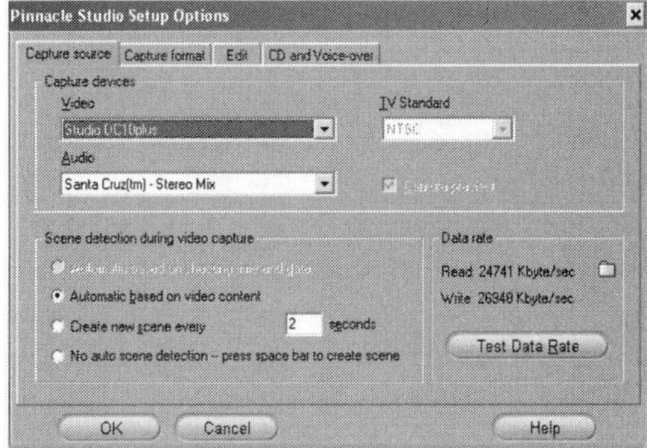

Figure 4.4 Here's where you select your analog video and audio capture devices as well as your option for scene detection.

Studio stores captured files either during capture or immediately after capture, as in the case of MPEG files, which must be converted before storage. Either way, no user intervention is needed to store the files. Once you start to capture another file, your previously captured files disappear from the Album, but don't worry; they are safely stored and accessible in Edit mode.

The Player. Note the lack of playback controls in the Player window. The Player's sole role during capture is to preview the incoming video and provide information about dropped frames; you have to switch into Edit mode to actually play the captured files.

The Diskometer. If you study the analog capture interface in Figure 4.1, you'll see that the Camcorder Controller is missing in action. That's because the lack of a FireWire or similar connection prevents Studio from controlling the camcorder.

The Diskometer looks vaguely similar to the DV capture version, at least on top, where it displays the space remaining on the capture drive. However, the DV, MPEG, and preview capture options are replaced with Good, Better, Best, and Custom settings.

In addition, the Diskometer has sprouted wings, on the left controls for selecting and customizing analog video input and on the right for enabling audio capture and setting volume. You toggle these controls in and out using the circled icons on the sides of the Diskometer (video on the left and audio on the right). You'll learn how to operate these controls later in this chapter.

Click the Settings button in the lower-right of the screen to open the Setup Options dialog set to the Capture format tab (**Figure 4.3**), where you select your analog capture parameters. The next tab to the left is Capture source (**Figure 4.4**), where you choose your capture device and scene detection options.

Scene Detection with Analog Video

With analog footage, sifting through and finding the scenes to include in your project can be extraordinarily time-consuming. When you're using DV footage, however, Studio simply analyzes the data codes on the tape, and identifies scene changes by noting when you stop and start the camera. This makes it a lot easier to choose scenes to include in your final project.

Since analog consumer camcorders don't store this time code, you don't have this option (that's why "Automatic based on shooting time and place" is grayed out in Figure 4.4). Fortunately, Studio provides three analog options that should prove very useful:

- If you choose the first available option, "Automatic based on video content," Studio identifies scene changes based on significant changes between frames. For example, if one second you're filming the birthday cake and the next your child's delighted face, Studio breaks the two Kodak moments into separate scenes.
- If you choose the second option, "Create new scene every *x* seconds," you can break the scene into regular intervals of one second or more.
- Finally, when all else fails, you can watch the video and manually create scenes by pressing the spacebar at the appropriate moments during capture. (Choose the option "No auto scene detection.") Though this is obviously the most time-consuming method, you get reacquainted with all the best moments of your video—helpful when you're editing several months (or years) after filming.

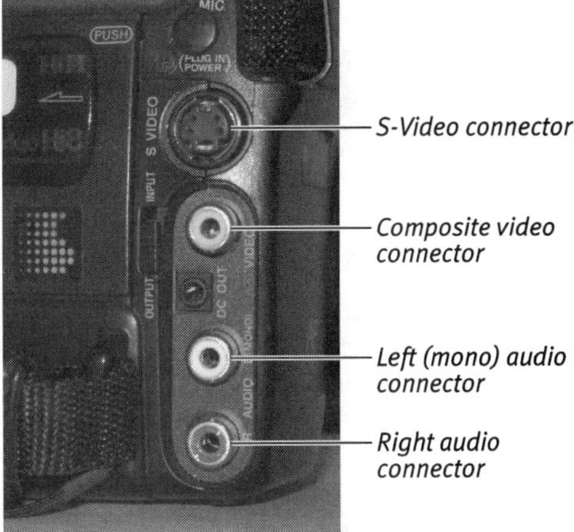

Figure 4.5 The business end of my venerable Sony Hi-8 recorder has separate outputs for S-Video and composite analog video as well as stereo audio.

Figure 4.6 An S-Video cable. Use S-Video whenever it's available, because you'll definitely get higher quality than with composite video.

Connecting for Analog Capture

Although not quite as simple as setting up for DV capture, connecting for analog capture is pretty easy if you can follow color codes and fit square pegs into square holes (metaphorically speaking).

Before taking the steps below, make sure your analog capture card is installed and running. In addition, quickly review the sections "Selecting Your Capture Drive," "Defragmenting Your Capture Drive," and "Testing Your Capture Drive" in Chapter 2.

To connect camera and computer for analog capture:

1. Plug in your analog camcorder to AC power.

   Battery power should work, but it doesn't always with some cameras.

2. Make sure the camcorder is in VCR, VTR, or Play mode.

3. Connect your video cables to the camera (**Figure 4.5**).

   If both your camera and analog capture device have S-Video connectors and you have the necessary cable (**Figure 4.6**), use the S-Video connector.

(continued on next page)

4. If S-Video is not available, use the composite video connectors by doing one of the following:
   - If your analog camera or deck has a separate composite video port (see Figure 4.5), use a cable like the one shown in **Figure 4.7**. In most instances, composite video connectors are yellow, and most three-headed cables are coded yellow (composite video), red (right audio), and white (left audio and mono audio). Follow the color coding at both ends and you'll speed installation.
   - If your camera has a specialty A/V port (see Figure 3.7 in Chapter 3), you should have received a specialty cable that looks like that shown in **Figure 4.8**. Plug the single end into your camera.
5. Connect your audio cables to the camera by doing one of the following:
   - If your camera has separate audio connectors (see Figure 4.5), connect a cable like that shown in Figure 4.7, being careful to match the colors of the connectors and output ports when applicable.
   - If your camera has a specialty A/V port, you should have a specialty cable that looks like the one in Figure 4.8. Plug the single end into your camera.

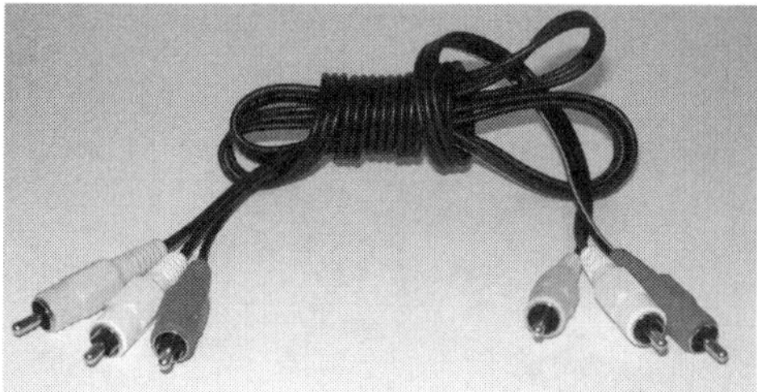

Figure 4.7 The typical three-headed analog cable with separate RCA connectors, for composite video and left and right audio. Fortunately, most are color-coded to help you make proper connections.

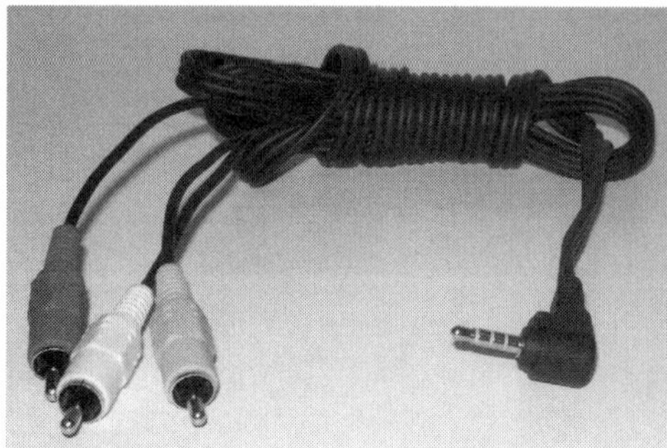

Figure 4.8 If your camcorder has a specialty AV plug like that of the Canon GL2 shown in Figure 3.7 (Chapter 3), you'll need a specialty cable. Note the three rings on the single connector, one for each of the three outputs.

Figure 4.9 The Pinnacle DC10 Plus analog capture card. Note the dual sets of connectors, one for video input and one for video output.

Figure 4.10 A representation of the bracket on my sound card. Use the line-in connector, not the mic-in (microphone), for your analog input.

Figure 4.11 A Y-connector converts the two RCA-type analog connectors to one stereo connector compatible with your sound card.

6. Connect your video cable to the capture card in your computer.

   Most capture cards have input ports and output ports. For example, the Pinnacle DC10 Plus card shown in **Figure 4.9** uses the top two ports for video input, and the bottom two for video output. This provides the connection back to your analog source to write your finished project back to tape. If you see two sets of connectors, check the product's documentation or on the bracket to make sure you're connecting to the analog inputs.

7. Connect your audio cables to the computer by doing one of the following:
   - ▲ If your analog capture card has separate audio inputs, use the audio input on your capture card.
   - ▲ If your analog capture card doesn't have separate audio inputs (like the DC10 Plus), use your sound card's line-in connector (**Figure 4.10**).

   Most computers look for stereo audio inputs (Figure 4.10) rather than separate RCA connectors (Figures 4.7 and 4.8). To convert RCA inputs into stereo audio inputs, you'll need a Y-connector like the one shown in **Figure 4.11**, or a similar adapter. You can pick these up at Radio Shack or on the Web at www.cables.com.

   You're now ready to run Studio, set the proper software options, and start capturing.

Choosing Your Analog Capture Parameters

Now that the hardware side is squared away, it's time to start working on the software side, first selecting your capture source and then setting and adjusting your capture parameters.

To select your capture source:

1. Run Studio, and enter Capture mode by selecting the Capture tab in the upper-left corner of the screen (Figure 4.1).
2. From the top menu, choose Setup > Capture Source (**Figure 4.12**).

   The Pinnacle Studio Setup Options dialog appears.
3. In the Video capture device drop-down box, select your analog video capture device (**Figure 4.13**).
4. In the Audio capture device drop-down box, select your analog audio capture device (**Figure 4.14**).
5. Check the desired scene detection option.

   Remember that the option "Automatic based on shooting time and date" is unavailable because analog tapes don't store this information.
6. Click OK to return to Capture mode.

   If your analog capture card has audio input, it should be one of the listed options. Since in this example the system's sound card is used, line-in is selected on the Turtle Beach Santa Cruz sound card.

   At this point, you should be in analog capture mode, and your screen should look identical to Figure 4.1.

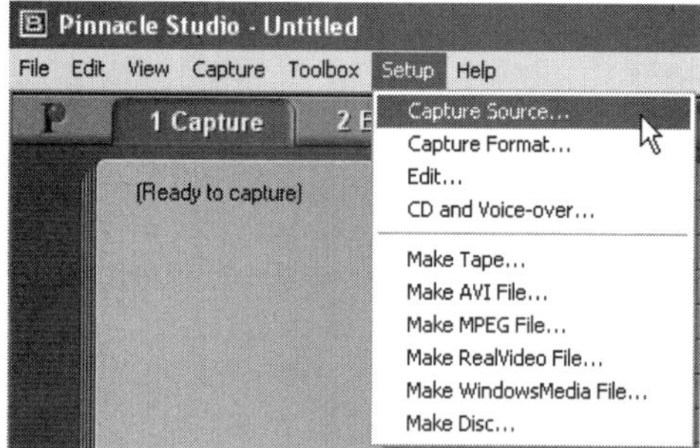

Figure 4.12 Getting to the Capture Source screen.

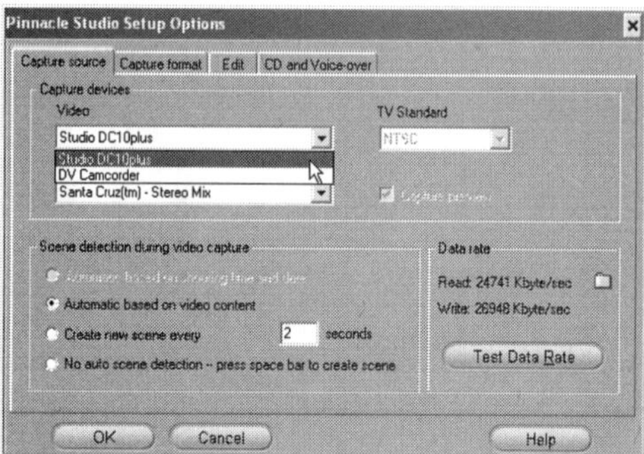

Figure 4.13 Choosing your analog video capture device.

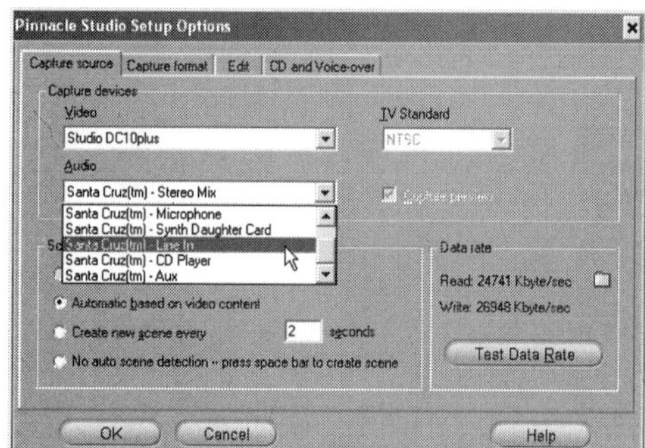

Figure 4.14 Selecting your analog audio capture device. Remember to use line-in!

✔ Tips

- If the video and audio capture controls are not open, open them using the icons on the sides of the Diskometer (Figure 4.1).
- If you see the Camcorder Controller, you're in DV capture mode. Go back and reselect your capture source (Step 3 above).
- If your analog capture source is showing in the list box, it's properly loaded and running under Windows. If it's not showing up, it's not properly installed and you've got some work to do before you can start capturing. Go back to "Connecting for Analog Capture" and try it again.

To configure your capture parameters:

1. Open the Studio Setup Options dialog set to the Capture format tab by performing one of the following steps:
   - ▲ Click the Settings button in the Diskometer.
   - ▲ From the Studio menu, choose Setup > Capture Format (**Figure 4.15**).

   The Capture format tab appears (**Figure 4.16**).
2. Choose the appropriate preset—Good, Better, or Best—for your project (see the sidebar "Navigating Your Analog Capture Format Options").
3. Click OK to return to the capture interface.

To capture audio and configure video input:

1. On the top of the video options tab (Figure 4.1), select the icon that corresponds to your physical cable connection (in this case, S-Video).
2. On top of the audio options tab, choose the On button to enable audio capture.

   Do this to make sure everything is up and running; you can disable audio later if you want.
3. The moment of truth has arrived. Press Play on your camcorder.

   You should see video in the Player and hear audio over your speakers. If you do, try not to jump up and down if people are around. You've crossed a significant hurdle. Now you're ready for analog capture.

   If you don't get video and audio right away, take heart. I've installed hundreds of capture cards and rarely get it right the first time. Run through the steps in this and the previous section one more time. If you still have no signal, check your capture card installation first, then the troubleshooting tips in Appendix B.

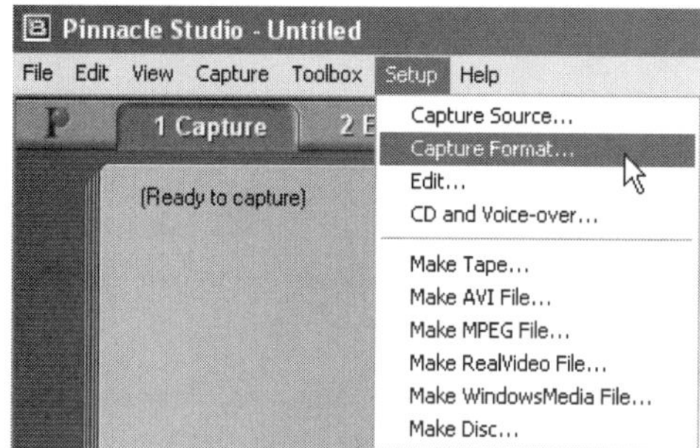

Figure 4.15 Getting to the Capture Format screen.

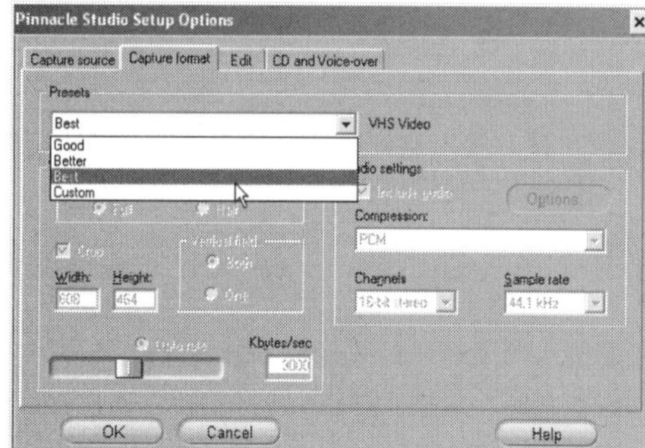

Figure 4.16 Best is always better than Good, right? Check the sidebar "Navigating Your Analog Capture Format Options."

Navigating Your Analog Capture Format Options

Good, Better, Best. Best is always best, right? Well, no. Sometimes Good is superior, and often Good is better than Better. Confused? Here's the skinny.

The most crucial option to consider during analog capture is the video resolution, or the width and height of the captured video in pixels. For example, when you capture at a resolution of 320 x 240 pixels, you produce a captured file that's 320 pixels wide and 240 pixels high.

When determining the best resolution to use during capture, the most important factor is your intended output resolution. For example, suppose you intend to create a DVD using MPEG-2. This high-quality format generally outputs at a resolution of 720 x 480. In contrast, MPEG-1 files, typically used for posting to the Web or sharing on CD-ROM, generally have a resolution of 320 x 240. If you're creating a RealVideo file to post for streaming at modem speeds, the resolution may be as low as 176 x 132.

The general rule for selecting capture resolution is always to capture at the exact output resolution whenever possible. If not, capture at the next available *higher* resolution.

Although all capture devices use different Good, Better, and Best presets, take a look at those in the Pinnacle DC10 Plus capture card as an example.

- Good: 320 x 240 resolution. Use this for AVI, MPEG-1, and all streaming output.
- Better: 304 x 464 resolution. Use this for Super VideoCD projects, which use the so-called half-height MPEG-2 and VideoCD.
- Best: 608 x 464 resolution. Use this for MPEG-2 and DVD projects. Here I might be tempted to customize parameters to see if I could produce a larger-resolution file (like 720 x 480), but novice users should stick to the presets.

So, if you're producing MPEG-1 files at a resolution of 320 x 240, you actually produce slightly better-quality files by capturing at the Good setting, since Studio doesn't have to resize the file during encoding, a process that always causes some degradation. You also save time and disk space, which is why in this case Good is better than Better and Best.

Tuning the Incoming Video Signal

Because DV video is digitized by the camera, video capture is a simple file transfer from camera to computer. In contrast, analog capture involves an analog-to-digital conversion, which is something like a negotiation between two parties speaking a common language with slightly different accents.

This is how it works. The analog camera outputs an analog signal that it perceives as representing reality, adjusting the brightness, color, and contrast accordingly. Then, using factory preset values, the analog capture card looks for and captures a signal that it perceives as representing reality. Seldom do the two realities match.

This is a long way of saying that if you're going to capture analog video, most of the time you will have to mess with the analog input controls to get the video looking right. If you compare the image in **Figure 4.17**, which used the default settings, with the image in **Figure 4.18**, which used optimized settings, the differences can be dramatic.

As you can see from Figure 4.1, the adjustments are for brightness, contrast, sharpness, hue, and color saturation, but these technical terms provide little value (see the sidebar "Adjustments Defined" in Chapter 9). The only way to become skilled at this process is to play with the controls during each capture and fine-tune as you go along.

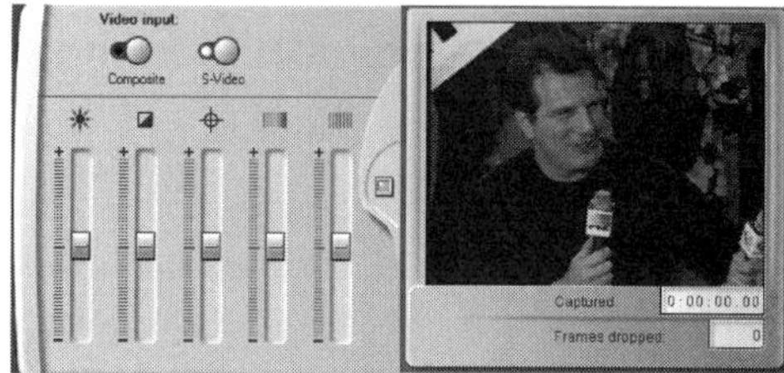

Figure 4.17 My mom insisted that I have at least one picture of me in this book. With brightness and contrast at their default settings, here I am speaking at a trade show. Pretty dark, eh?

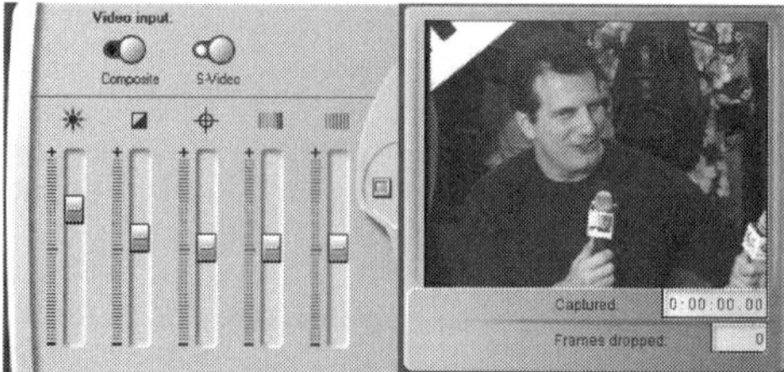

Figure 4.18 Here's the new me, with enhanced brightness and contrast. These controls make a huge difference in the ultimate quality of your video projects.

To adjust incoming video:

1. On your camcorder, press Play to start the video playing. Try to find frames containing objects with known color and brightness values, like faces or clothing.
2. Using the video options tab, adjust the various sliders up and down until the picture looks good (Figure 4.1).
3. Note the adjusted values used during capture so you can re-create your results if necessary.

   This would be easier if Studio offered numerical presets, but it doesn't. Instead, note the relationship to the midline. For example, the adjustments in Figure 4.18 would have a brightness value of plus 10 and a contrast value of plus 3.

✔ Tips

- Studio lets you modify these same values during editing. However, adjusting color and brightness values during editing can degrade quality and takes time, so it's better done while tweaking parameters before capturing your video files.
- If you have radically different scenes on tape, you should adjust for each scene.
- Encoding often darkens video slightly. To make sure your video will be bright enough after encoding, encode a short segment into the final format as early as possible. If you'll be viewing the video on a range of output devices, say laptops or projectors, you might test playback on these as well.

Adjusting the Incoming Audio Volume

Pop quiz: You've just captured some analog video and you play it back to check the volume. Unfortunately, it's way too low. So, here's the question: Is the audio too low because

a) Your speaker system is too low.
b) Your Windows volume control is too low.
c) You didn't boost audio volumes sufficiently during capture.
d) All of the above.

Hmmm. Tough one. The answer is, unless you checked your speakers and playback volume before capture, you don't really know. So don't roll your eyes as you walk through the following steps; it's all about the process.

To adjust incoming audio volume:

1. Make sure your system sound speakers are set at an appropriate playback volume. Disable any treble, bass, or similar boosts, since your ultimate viewer may not have the same tools.

2. Open your computer's volume control by doing either of the following:
   - ▲ Click the speaker icon in the Windows taskbar (**Figure 4.19**).
   - ▲ From the Windows Start menu, choose Programs > Accessories > Entertainment > Volume Control (**Figure 4.20**).

   The Master volume control dialog opens (**Figure 4.21**).

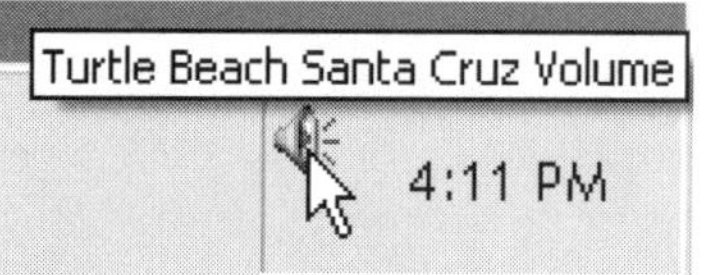

Figure 4.19 Click the speaker icon to load the Master volume control.

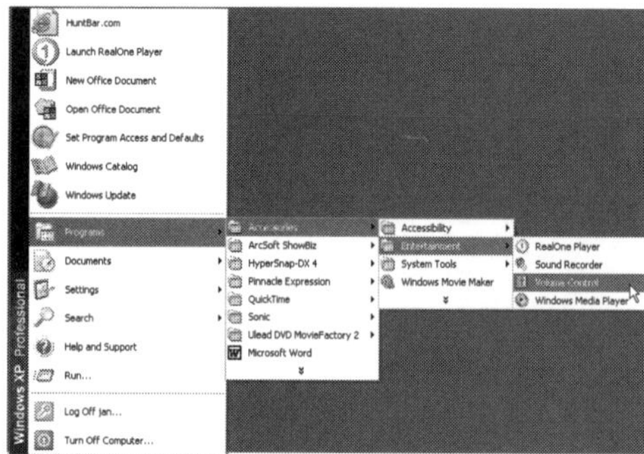

Figure 4.20 Or take the long way.

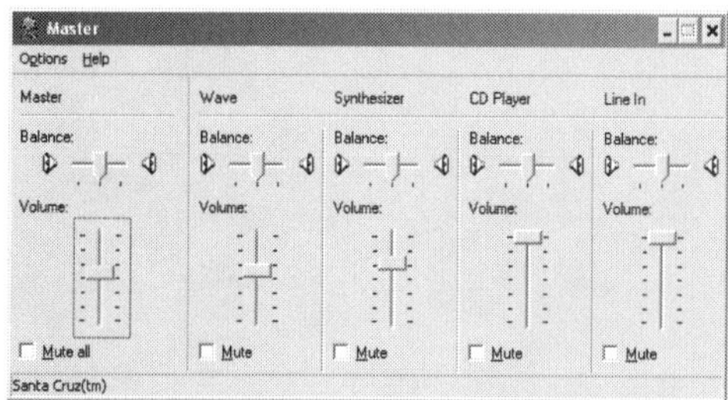

Figure 4.21 However you get here, make sure the Master volume control is around the middle during capture.

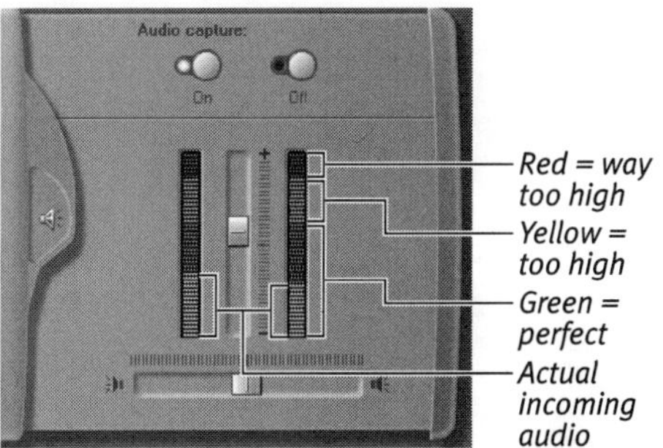

Figure 4.22 Adjust incoming audio volume until it's in the middle to upper regions of the green zone.

3. Make sure that the Master volume control, to the far left in the Master dialog, is near midvolume.
4. Close the Master volume control and return to Studio.
5. Press Play on your camcorder.
6. Use the audio volume control (in the audio options tab, Figure 4.1) to adjust the volume during capture so that the lights occasionally reach into the yellow bar but never into the red (**Figure 4.22**). Be sure to test both high and low volume regions of the clip.
7. After capture, periodically play back your captured files to check audio volume levels.

Capturing Analog Video

The big moment is finally here. It's time to capture some analog video.

To capture analog video:

1. Using your camcorder controls, position your tape about 30 seconds before the initial frame you want to capture.
2. Click the Start Capture button in the Diskometer (**Figure 4.23**).

   The Capture Video dialog opens (**Figure 4.24**), and the Start Capture button changes to Stop Capture (**Figure 4.25**).
3. Change the duration to 1 minute and 00 seconds.

   If the duration shown in your program is *less than* 1 minute, either your capture disk is almost full or you're pointing toward the wrong disk. (See the section "Selecting Your Capture Drive" in Chapter 2.)
4. Press Play on your camcorder to start the video rolling.
5. Watch the video in the Player and click Start approximately 10 to 15 seconds before you actually want capture to start.

   Some capture devices take a few seconds to start capturing; starting early ensures that you capture the desired frames, and provides additional frames for fade-in and fade-out, or for interscene transitions during editing.

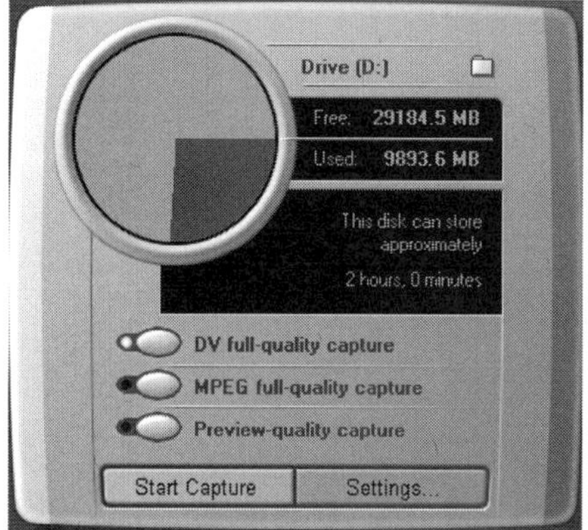

Figure 4.23 Click the Start Capture button in the Diskometer to start capture.

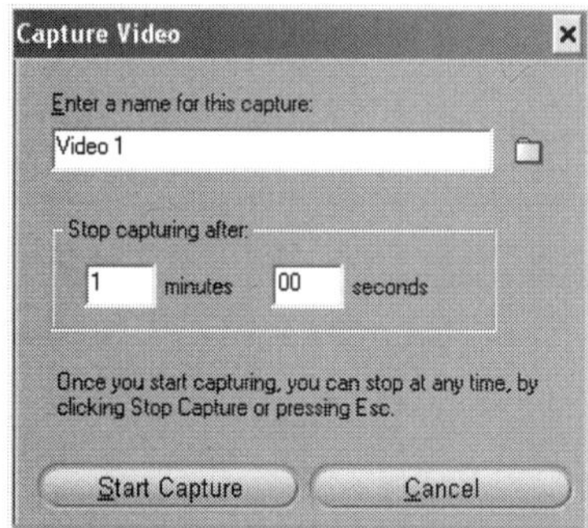

Figure 4.24 You can name your file before capture, and elect to capture for a specified interval. This is useful when you want to capture a 60-minute tape while you're away from the computer.

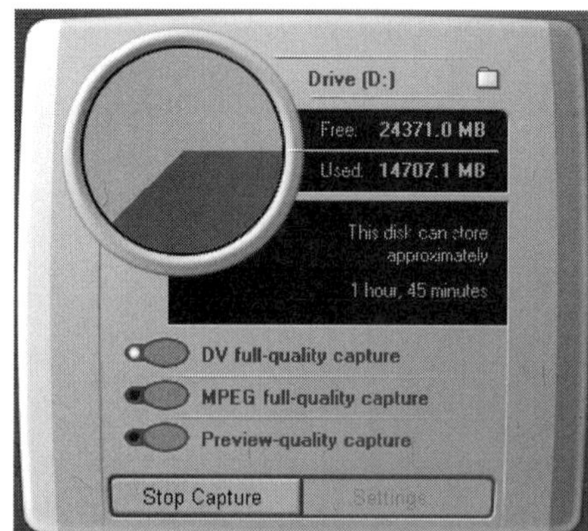

Figure 4.25 Click the Stop Capture button in the Diskometer to stop capture, or simply press the Esc key on your keyboard.

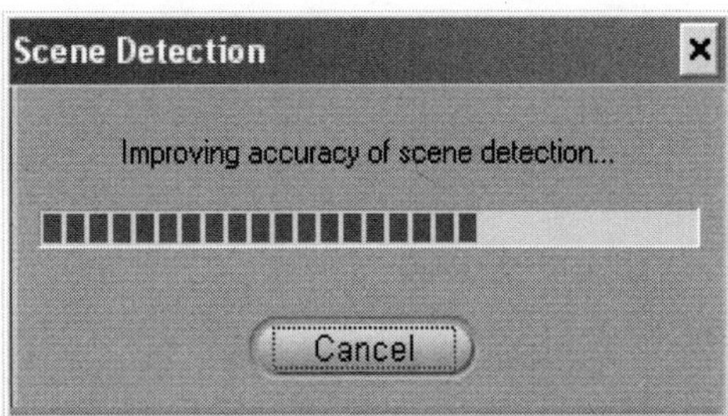

Figure 4.26 After analog capture, Studio takes a moment to check the accuracy of the scene detection settings.

6. Studio will capture 1 minute of video. To stop capture before then, do one of the following:
   - ▲ Click the Stop Capture button in the Diskometer.
   - ▲ Press the Esc key on your keyboard.

   Assuming you enabled scene detection by video content, Studio takes a moment after capture stops to rescan the file for scene changes (**Figure 4.26**). Then your captured scenes appear in the Album (**Figure 4.27**).

✔ Tip

- Note the Frames dropped counter under the Player in Figure 4.27. Dropped frames are frames that the computer couldn't capture, usually because the disk wasn't fast enough to keep up with the incoming video. This counter updates in real time during capture; if you drop more than one or two frames during capture, stop capturing and check Appendix B to diagnose and fix your problem.

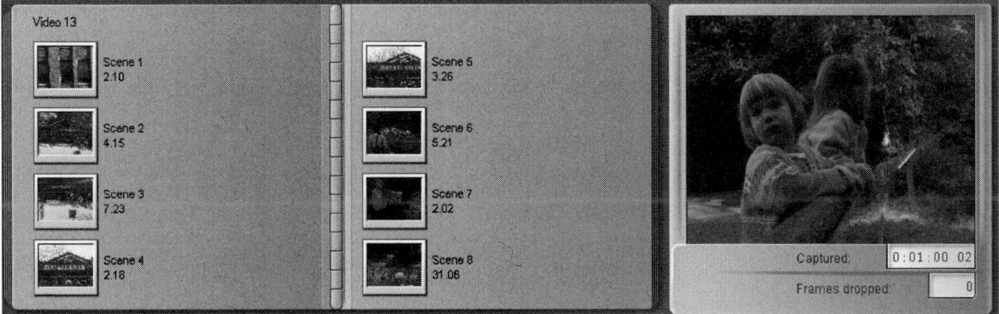

Figure 4.27 Then your scenes appear in the Album in all their glory.

Adding Scene Comments

If you want to rename or annotate your captured scenes to make them easier to find and use in your final production, go to the Album in Capture mode.

If you intend to annotate your scenes, remember that Studio updates the Album each time you capture, so if you start another capture before changing the name, your files disappear. Don't worry, you can easily find them in the Album in Edit mode and make your changes and/or annotations there (see the section "Working with Scene Comments" in Chapter 6).

To add scene comments to your captured video:

1. In the Album, slowly double-click the text immediately to the right of the video icon to make it editable (**Figure 4.28**).
2. Type the desired comments (**Figure 4.29**).
3. To save the comments do one of the following:
   - ▲ Press the Enter key on your keyboard.
   - ▲ Click anywhere else on the Studio interface.

✔ Tips

- You're not actually changing the file name; you're merely editing text that can be seen only inside Studio.
- If you plan to combine your scenes in the Edit tab of the Album, note that Studio blows away all screen comments when you combine scenes. You might want to look at the "Combining Scenes" section in Chapter 6 before you invest a bunch of time naming your captured scenes.

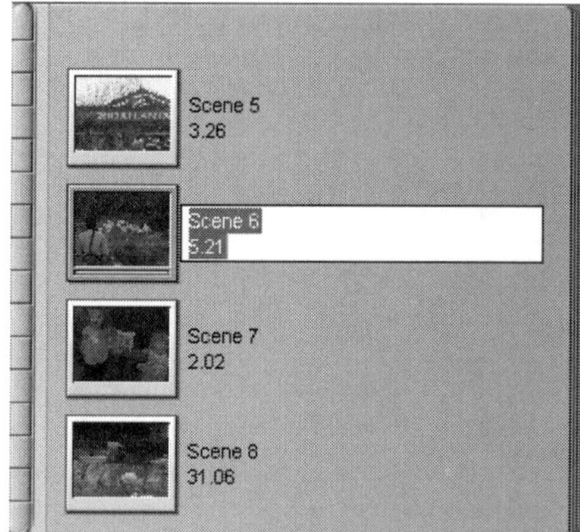

Figure 4.28 To add or change scene comments, touch the text twice slowly...

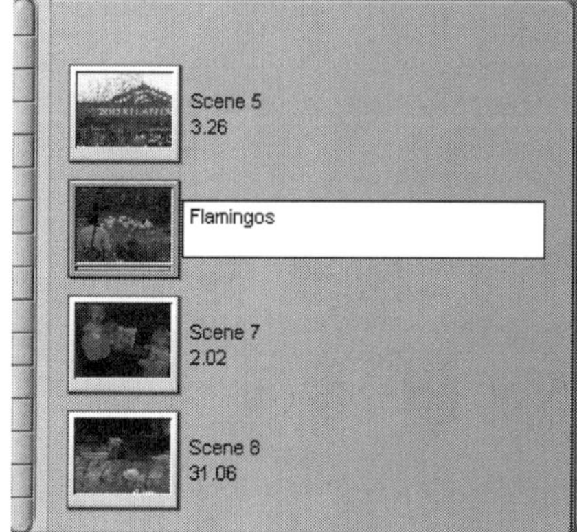

Figure 4.29 ...then type in your description.

Viewing Your Captured Video

If you're like me, the first thing you want to do after capture is watch the video. To do this, toggle over to Edit mode and use the Player.

To view your captured video:

1. Select the Edit tab in the upper-left corner of the Studio interface (Figure 4.1).
   Studio opens Edit mode.
2. In the Album window, double-click the video you'd like to play (**Figure 4.30**).
   The video starts playing in the Player.
3. Controls beneath the Player let you stop, rewind, fast-forward, go to the beginning of the video, and move through each frame of your video.

✔ Tip

- If you capture using scene detection and the Album contains multiple scenes, the Player automatically plays from one scene to the next without breaks.

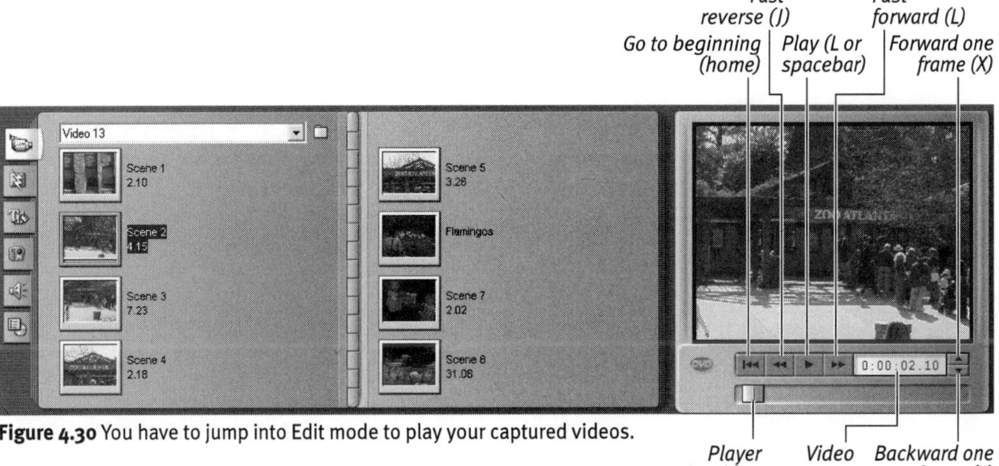

Figure 4.30 You have to jump into Edit mode to play your captured videos.

5 Working with Still Images

I absolutely adore capturing still images from my digital videotapes, especially when shooting videos of the young 'uns. Why? Because although my Kodak DC4800 takes much higher quality, 3.2-megapixel images, it can shoot only about once every six seconds. When you've got DV tape rolling, this gives you about 180 chances to get the shot you really want, compared to one shot with the Kodak.

On the other hand, some days I just don't want to mess with my camcorder, and I grab the Kodak instead. With my 1 GB flash memory card, I can take pictures all day long and usually find many nuggets worth keeping. Of course, these are huge images that often need cropping, cutting, or dropping in resolution to work optimally in Studio.

This chapter covers two topics: grabbing images from your camcorder or movie files, and prepping images from your still camera. As you'll see in Chapter 7, you can combine these images on the Timeline, with background music and/or narration, to produce the perfect slide show.

Capturing Still Images

To capture images from your camcorder, you've got to have everything connected, tested, and turned on (see Chapter 3 and Chapter 4). Operation is similar for digital video (DV) and analog camcorders, so this section covers both. Studio can also grab still images from movie files on disk, whether previously captured within Studio or sourced from another location.

When it comes to capturing still images, DV cameras have one killer feature: the ability to pause on a single frame for multiple seconds without distortion. This makes frame capture from your DV camera frame-accurate. In contrast, most analog camcorders can't pause for more than a moment or two without some image distortion, making it difficult to capture the precise frame you're seeking. For this reason, when you have images you'd like to grab on DV tape, go ahead and grab them from the camera.

On the other hand, if you have images on analog tape that you'd like to capture, it's easier, faster, and more accurate to capture the video to disk first, then grab the frame from the captured file.

To capture still images from your camcorder:

1. Select the Edit tab in the upper-left corner of the Studio interface.

   Studio opens Edit mode.

2. In the top-left corner of the Movie Window, click the camcorder icon to open the Video Toolbox (**Figure 5.1**).

   The Video Toolbox opens (**Figure 5.2**), most likely to the Clip Properties tool.

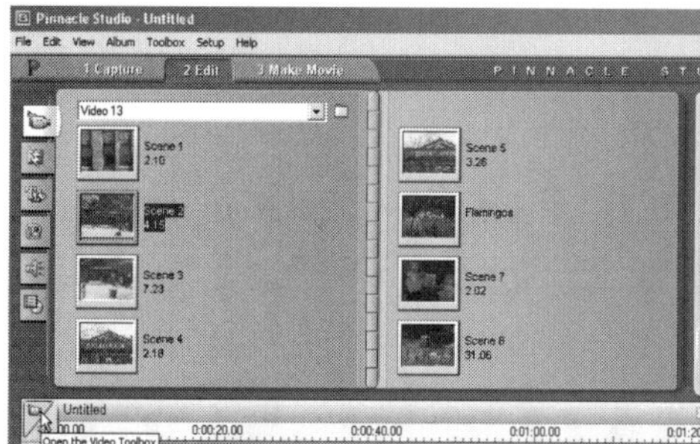

Figure 5.1 Click the camcorder icon to open the Video Toolbox.

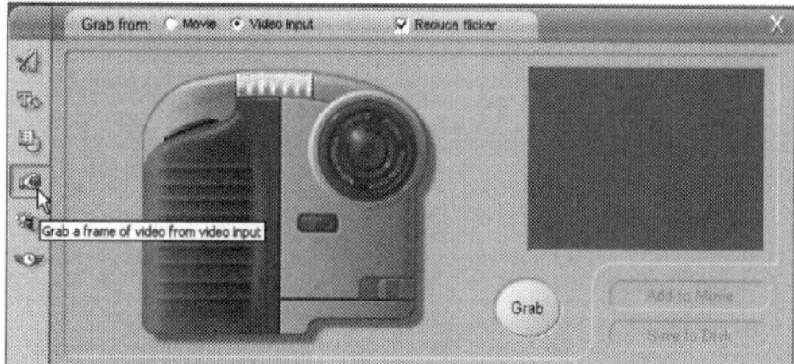

Figure 5.2 The Video Toolbox contains the Frame Grab tool. Note that when you're using an analog camcorder, there are no camcorder controls.

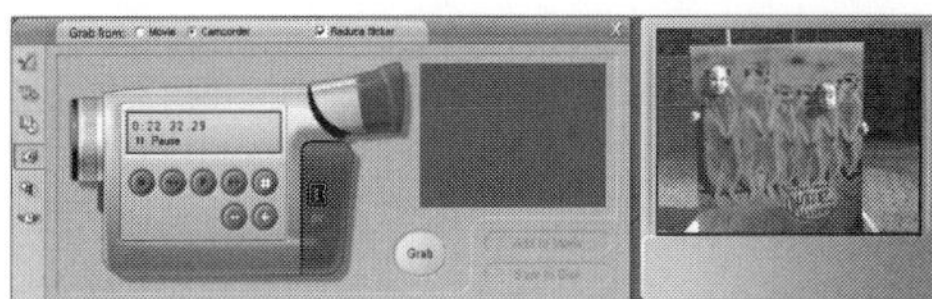

Figure 5.3 When you're using a DV camcorder, Studio provides software controls for getting to the desired frame.

Figure 5.4 Click the Grab button, and Studio grabs the image.

Figure 5.5 Click the Add to Movie button, and Studio places it in the Video track.

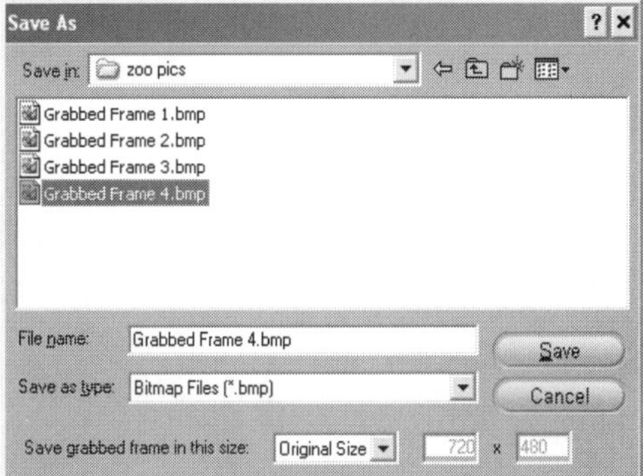

Figure 5.6 Or, save the frame to disk.

3. Click the frame grab icon from the toolbox to open the Frame Grab tool (Figure 5.2).
4. Click the Video input radio button to capture from your camcorder.
5. Use the Camcorder Controller controls to start your DV camcorder, or press Play on your analog camcorder to start the video rolling. Watch the video in the Player window and then do one of the following:
   - ▲ If you have a DV camcorder, you can pause (not stop) at the exact frame you want to capture (**Figure 5.3**).
   - ▲ If you have an analog camcorder, try pausing at the desired capture frame using camcorder controls. If the frame is clear and undistorted, you can move to Step 6. However, many analog devices can't pause on a frame without distortion, so you'll have to capture in real time, which is obviously less accurate.
6. Click the Grab button to capture the frame showing in the Player.

   The frame appears in the Frame grab window (**Figure 5.4**).
7. Do one or both of the following:
   - ▲ Click the Add to Movie button to add the frame to a movie.

     Studio adds the movie to the Video track at the first blank location (**Figure 5.5**).
   - ▲ Click the Save to Disk button to save the still image.

     Studio opens the standard Save As dialog set to store the frames to your default capture drive (**Figure 5.6**).

(continued on next page)

8. In the "Save as type" drop-down box, choose Bitmap Files.
9. In the "Save grabbed frame in this size" drop-down box, choose Original Size.
10. Name the file and click Save (Alt+S).
11. In the top-left corner of the Movie Window, click the camcorder icon to close the Video Toolbox (Figure 5.2).

✔ Tips

- If you're capturing still images from an analog camcorder, and the camera won't pause without distorting the image, you're better off capturing the video to disk and then grabbing your still image from the captured file, as detailed next.
- Note that most camcorders don't include frame advance controls on the camcorder body, but do on the camcorder remote, usually with other nice controls like slow motion.

Figure 5.7 To capture a frame from a video on disk, load the video into the Movie Window.

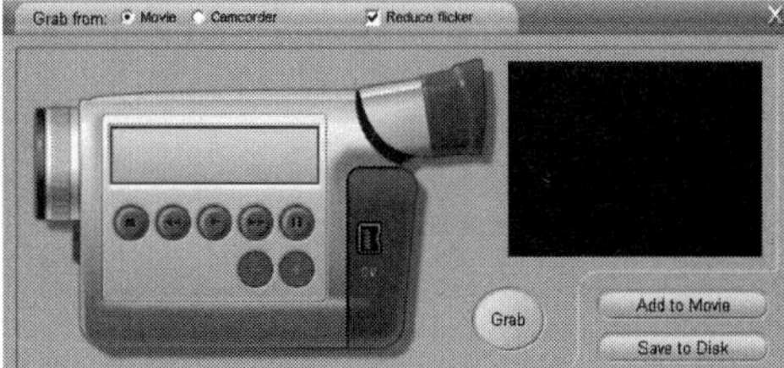

Figure 5.8 Select the Movie button to capture frames from the selected movie.

Figure 5.9 Use the Timeline Scrubber or the Player controls to move to the desired frame, or the jog controls to move one frame at a time.

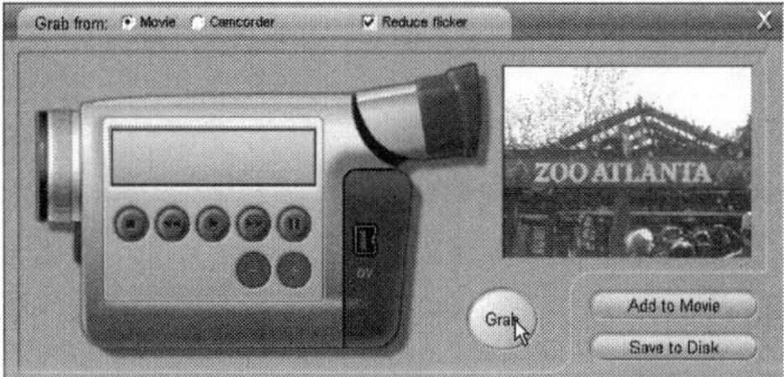

Figure 5.10 Once again, click Grab and you've got your frame.

To capture still images from a file on disk:

1. Select the Edit tab in the upper-left corner of the Studio interface.

   Studio opens Edit mode.

2. Click and drag the video containing the target frames from the Album to the Movie Window (**Figure 5.7**).

   If you're in the Timeline view, drag the video to the Video track. In the other two views, it doesn't matter where you drag the file, so long as it's in the Movie Window.

3. In the top-left corner of the Movie Window, click the camcorder icon to open the Video Toolbox (Figure 5.2).

   The Video Toolbox opens, most likely to the Clip Properties tool.

4. Click the frame grab icon on the left to open the Frame Grab tool.

5. Select the Movie button to grab frames from the Movie Window (**Figure 5.8**).

6. Use the Player controls or the Timeline Scrubber (**Figure 5.9**) to move to the target frame.

   You can use the jog controls to the right of the Player counter (up and down arrows) to move one frame at a time. If the Player controls aren't active, you haven't selected the Movie button in Step 5, above.

7. Click the Grab button to capture the frame showing in the Player.

   The frame appears in the Frame grab window (**Figure 5.10**).

(continued on next page)

8. Do one or both of the following:
   - ▲ Click the Add to Movie button to add the frame to the movie.

     Studio adds the movie to the Video track at the first blank location.
   - ▲ Click the Save to Disk button to save the still image.

     Studio opens the standard Save As dialog, which is set to store the frames to your default capture drive.
9. In the "Save as type" drop-down box, choose Bitmap Files (Figure 5.6).
10. In the "Save grabbed frame in this size" drop-down box, choose Original Size.
11. Name the file and click Save (or Alt+S).
12. In the top-left corner of the Movie Window, click the camcorder icon to close the Video Toolbox.

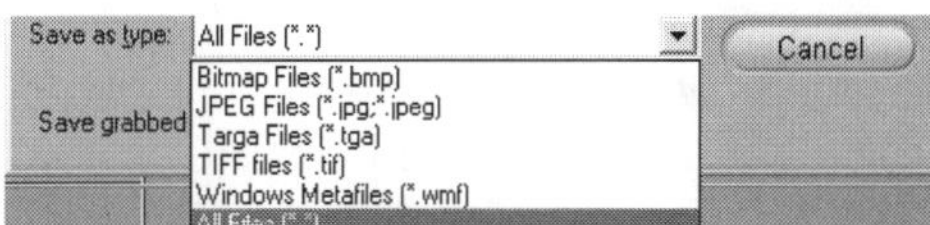

Figure 5.11 Among Studio's many format choices, use bitmap (BMP) unless you have a strong need to use another.

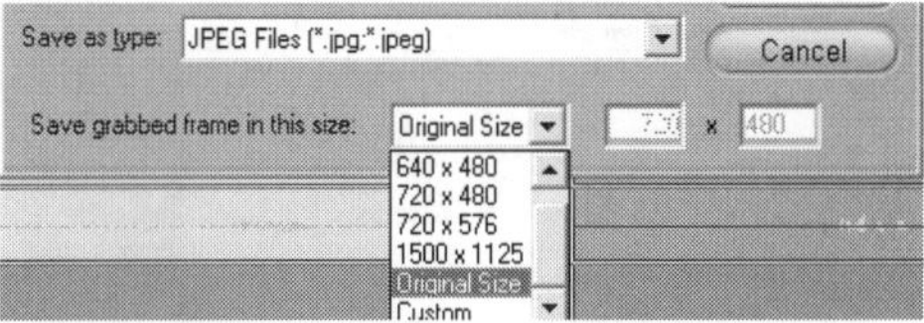

Figure 5.12 You can scale your image up or down at will, but Studio does it anyway, if necessary, once the image is loaded on the Timeline. Save in the original size to avoid potential distortion.

✔ Tips

- Studio lets you save a still image in a number of formats (**Figure 5.11**). Generally, if you plan on using the image in your video production, choose bitmap (BMP), Targa, TIFF, or Windows Metafile format, which are all uncompressed. I like BMP because it's the format most widely recognized by other programs, giving me more flexibility if I decide to use the image again. If you're capturing an image to send via email, you might want to go with JPEG, since it produces a smaller, compressed file (though Studio doesn't have the optimization tools offered by most still image editors).
- Studio also lets you save your still images at a number of different resolutions (**Figure 5.12**). Generally, if you plan on using the image in your video production, your best choice is Original Size, which stores the image at its actual capture resolution.
- I tested flicker reduction (see Figure 5.8) using a number of settings, and the result was that flicker reduction helped slightly when capturing from a DV camcorder or a DV file, but hurt image quality significantly when capturing via analog connections. However, this testing falls far short of a scientific study, and your results may vary. When you're grabbing still frames for your productions, try it with flicker reduction on and off, especially if the first option you try produces poor results.

Editing Still Images

OK. The question on the table is this. Your digital camera takes shots at a princely resolution of, say, 2160 x 1440 pixels. The maximum DVD video resolution is 720 x 480. How do you get from here to there?

Well, let's take a high-level look at how Studio works with still images, then tackle two common problems facing still-image photographers who want to exhibit their work on DVD or tape.

How Studio works with images

Studio takes an admirably laissez-faire attitude toward images, basically displaying them as you place them in the movie. It does not try to fill the screen with your image, stretching it horizontally or vertically, or trim your image to fit; it simply adjusts your image larger or smaller to fit the screen without changing the aspect ratio. If this means that your image doesn't completely fill the 720 x 480-pixel DVD frame, so be it. At least there's no distortion.

Studio also provides excellent visual cues about what your image will look like when it's finally produced. To provide an example, **Figure 5.13** shows the images that will be discussed in the two sample problems.

Rosie 1 is the original 2160 x 1440-pixel image, shot by turning the camera to the side to capture Rosie's full 36-inch height. Rosie 2 is the same image, rotated 90 degrees to the left so she's standing straight up.

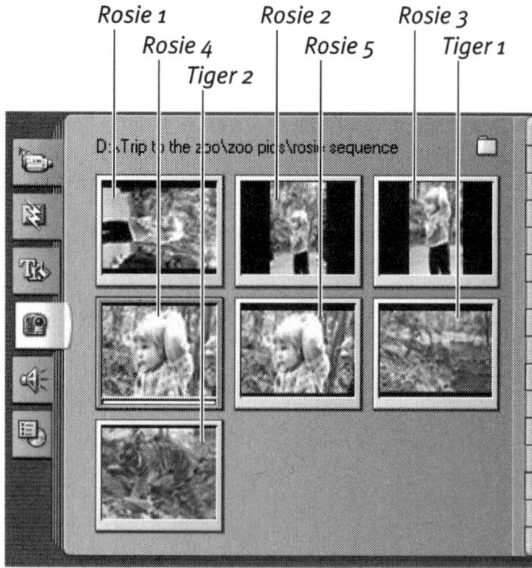

Figure 5.13 The black bars beside Rosie 2 and Rosie 3 are Studio's way of telling you that the image resolution isn't optimal.

Figure 5.14 Here's the big view of Rosie 2. Surely you can show more of this beautiful girl!

Figure 5.15 Rosie 3. The top has been cropped off the image, making Rosie slightly bigger.

Figure 5.16 Rosie 4. Full-screen Rosie, providing a much closer look and filling the screen.

If you click on Rosie 2 to preview her in the Player, you see large areas of black to her left and right, which is precisely the way it would appear in the final DVD or video (**Figure 5.14**). This is Studio's way of telling you that the image doesn't match the final resolution of your project, and Studio is not going to squish or otherwise distort the video to make it appear full screen. Note that these same black areas show up in the Still Images tab of the Album, providing the same message.

Optimizing Rosie

The Rosie picture presents two opportunities. To go with the original impulse of the photographer and display her height, you can crop away as much extraneous material as you'd like from the top, as shown in Rosie 3 (**Figure 5.15**). She's a bit more prominent in the screen, but you still have those black areas on the sides. The other alternative is the full-screen fetching face shot. Here the image has been cropped so that Rosie fills the entire screen, making all involved thankful that she takes after her mother, not her father (**Figure 5.16**).

The obvious question is what image resolution must you use to totally fill the Player window and eliminate those black bars. Since picture resolutions vary immensely between different cameras, the answer isn't a particular resolution, but a specific aspect ratio, which must be 4:3.

What this means is that for every 4 horizontal pixels, you must grab 3 vertical pixels. To grab the image of Rosie, the capture resolution was 1120 pixels across and 840 pixels high. If you divide 1120 by 4, you get 280. Multiply 280 by 3 and you get 840.

It's a pain, but keep a calculator open on your desktop when you're grabbing still images. Once you find the optimal horizontal resolution for your images, divide by four, multiply by three, and you've calculated the ideal height. Or, find an image editor like Ulead Systems' excellent PhotoImpact 8, which does the math for you (**Figure 5.17**). The little lock icon in the top tool panel constrains the crop tool to the selected shape, Digital Camera (4:3).

Figure 5.17 The secret's in the tool. Ulead's PhotoImpact lets you constrain an image to a 4:3 aspect ratio, making it easy to grab the optimal image.

The other obvious question is why you don't capture at an aspect ratio or 4:2.66, which is the aspect ratio for 720 x 480 pixels, the ultimate resolution at which you'll be displaying the video. The complete answer is long, confusing, and involves arcane differences between how computers and televisions display video data.

The quick, empirical answer is this. If you capture at the 4:2.66 aspect ratio, and input the result, Studio tells you via black bars at the top and bottom of the screen that you're not totally filling the screen (**Figure 5.18**). These bars aren't present when the 4:3 aspect ratio is used, so 4:3 must be the optimal setting (see Figure 5.16).

Figure 5.18 Your brain says 720 x 480 resolution, but those black bars above and below the image say no, no, no.

Figure 5.19 The tiger favored us with a close walk-by that day, but I forgot to zoom.

Figure 5.20 The benefit of working with megapixel images is that I can zoom in without distortion. Once again the screen is filled by cropping the photo to create an aspect ratio of 4:3.

Seeing the eyes of the tiger

Now it should be easy to tackle the problem in the second example, the picture of the tiger taken from a distance. You took a great shot of the tiger, but wished you'd had a better telephoto lens, since the noble animal is a mere speck in the Player (**Figure 5.19**).

To enlarge the tiger in the screen, crop your image to an aspect ratio of 4:3, or 720 x 540 pixels. This dramatically increases the size, and now you can actually see the eyes of the tiger (**Figure 5.20**).

✔ Tip

- Always cut out the relevant portion in the shape of the desired aspect ratio. Never change the aspect ratio of an image or resize an image to make it fit a specific area.

Collecting Assets in the Album

The Album is an integral component of Studio's interface: a place for loading video, still image, and audio files—the basic assets your project comprises—into separate tab-selected folders before integrating them into your projects. The Album also contains transitions, titles, and menus—effects discussed in subsequent chapters.

The Album isn't a true bin or library, like those found in many programs, that saves the imported assets in a project file. Rather, the Album simply displays the files in the currently selected directory.

Compared with the richness of features that lie beyond—the flexible Storyboard, the bountiful transitions—the Album may not be the most impressive thing about Studio, but it's unquestionably one of the most valuable. You could easily spend the bulk of your time finding the assets to put into your project; working efficiently in the Album cuts this time considerably.

Opening the Album to Video Scenes

Few things in life are easier than getting to the Video Scenes component of the Album. So let's get right to it.

To open the Album to Video Scenes:

- Do one of the following:
  - If you're not running Studio, load the program.

    Once Studio loads, you're in Edit mode and the Album opens to the Video Scenes tab. Click on a scene to highlight it (**Figure 6.1**).
  - If you're running Studio and you're in Capture or Make Movie mode, select the Edit tab in the three-tab menu at the upper left (**Figure 6.2**).

    Once you're in Edit mode, the Album opens to the video scenes you've accessed or captured most recently.
  - If you're in Edit mode and working in any other Album tab, click the camcorder icon at the top of the column of icons along the left side of the Album window (**Figure 6.3**).

The Album switches to Video Scenes.

Figure 6.1 Here's Studio in Edit mode, with the Album containing the Zoo Atlanta files that were captured earlier.

Figure 6.2 If you're in Capture or Make Movie mode and want to switch to Edit, select Edit in the three-tab menu.

Figure 6.3 If you're in any other Album tab in Edit mode, click the camcorder icon to get to the Video Scenes tab.

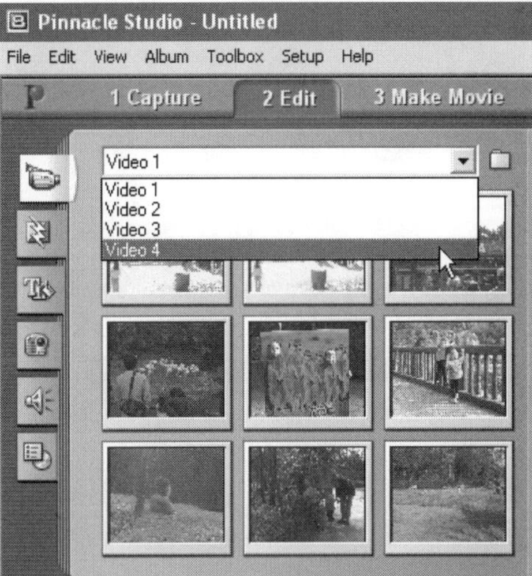

Figure 6.4 The drop-down box in the Album lists all files stored in that capture directory, making it easy for you to switch between captured files. Select the video you want to appear.

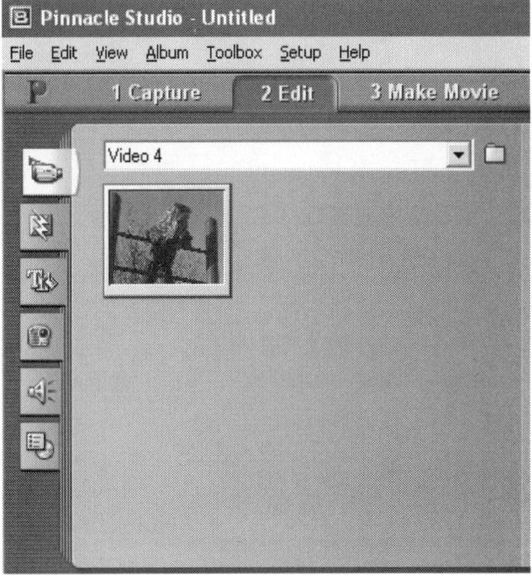

Figure 6.5 And presto, there it is.

Loading Video Files

Before you can split, combine, or annotate your video files, you have to load them into the Album. Here's how.

To load captured files into the Album:

- If you just finished capturing video files, select the Edit tab to enter Edit mode.

  The most recently captured video file appears in the Album.

To load other captured files into the Album:

1. Click the drop-down box in the Album (**Figure 6.4**).

   The drop-down box lists all other files in that folder.

2. Select the file you wish to load.

   The selected file appears in the Video Scenes tab (**Figure 6.5**). Note that Studio performs scene detection on the new clip using whatever option is currently selected in the Capture source tab (see Figure 3.6 in Chapter 3).

To import other videos into the Album:

1. Click the small directory icon to the right of the Album list box (**Figure 6.6**).

   A standard Open file dialog appears (**Figure 6.7**).

2. Navigate to the folder containing the file you want to load (**Figure 6.8**).

3. Select the file you wish to load and click Open (**Figure 6.9**).

   Studio performs scene detection on the new clip using whatever option is currently selected in the Capture source tab (see Chapter 3).

   If Studio can't display all the scenes from that video on one page, it creates multiple pages. Move through the pages by clicking the arrows on the upper-right and upper-left corners of the Album's pages.

✔ Tips

- Studio imports only AVI, MPEG-1, and MPEG-2 video files. Studio cannot import files in RealVideo, Windows Media, or QuickTime, or files saved in animated formats like Autodesk's FLC format.
- The Album can display only one video at a time. Although the Album can display multiple scenes from one video, there is no way to import, combine, or otherwise display scenes from more than one video at a time.
- You can't delete scenes or change their order in the Album. However, Studio provides a great tool for choosing and rearranging the order of your videos: the Storyboard view in the Movie Window, which will be discussed in the next chapter.

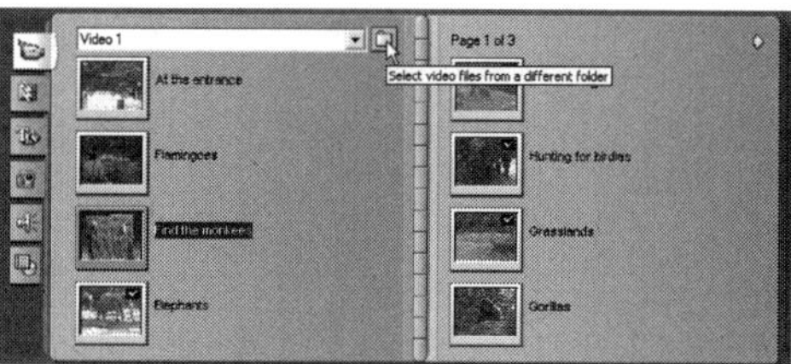

Figure 6.6 To select files in other folders, click the little directory icon to the right of the drop-down box.

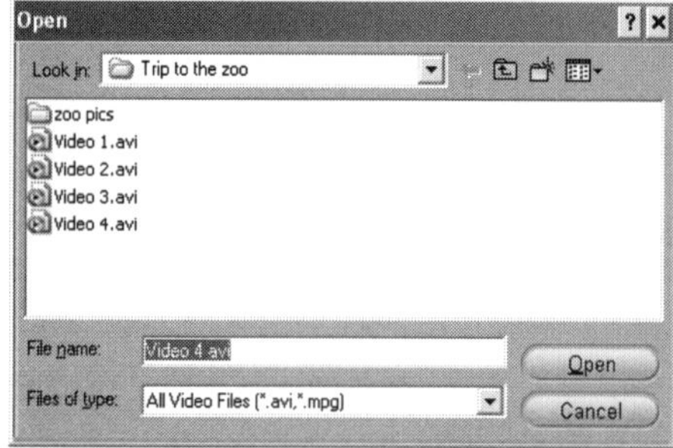

Figure 6.7 The standard file-selection dialog opens.

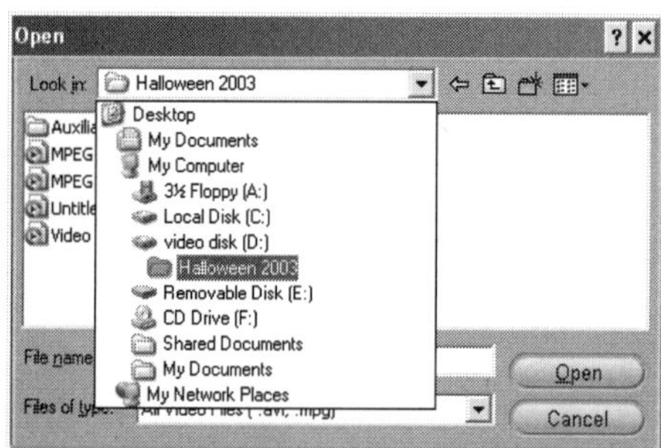

Figure 6.8 Navigate to the folder containing the new files.

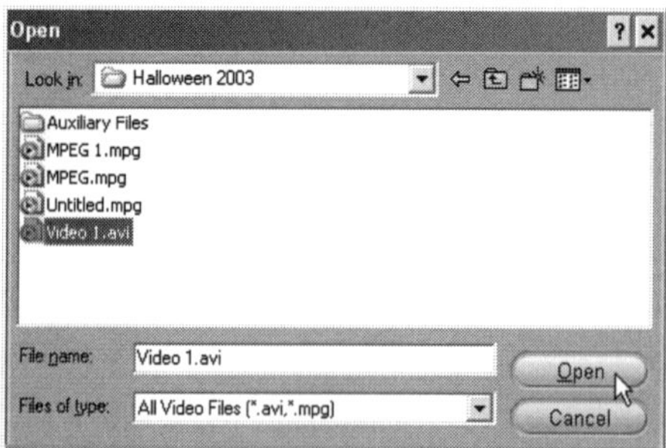

Figure 6.9 Select the file you want to load, and click Open.

Figure 6.10 To play any video file in the Album, double-click it, or click it once and press Play in the Player.

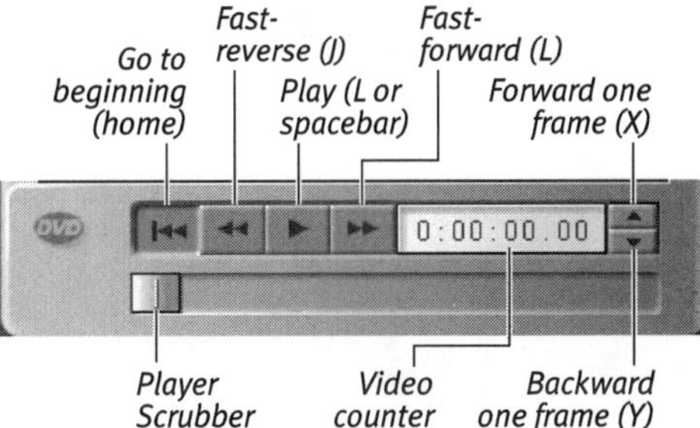

Figure 6.11 To manually move through the scenes, use the familiar VCR playback controls or the Player Scrubber.

Playing Videos

It's tough to select the right scenes for your project without playing the video. For this reason, the Album works closely with the Player to let you view and move through your video scenes.

To play your videos:

1. Double-click on the scene you wish to play.

   The video immediately starts to play in the Player.

Or

1. Touch the scene you wish to play.

   The outline on the video turns from white to blue. If you're in Details view (see "Working with the Album's Views and Tools," later), the scene comments immediately to the right of the video are also highlighted. In addition, the initial frame of the scene appears in the Player (**Figure 6.10**).

2. Under the Player, press Play to start video playback and use the other controls to navigate through the video (**Figure 6.11**).

   Playback shifts automatically from scene to scene when multiple scenes are present.

   While the progress bar represents the playback position within each scene, the Player Scrubber represents the position within the entire video.

✔ Tip

- Keyboard shortcuts are really helpful for playing back video in the Player from both the Album and the Movie Window. Here are the relevant commands:

Spacebar	Play and stop
J	Fast-reverse (hit multiple times for faster speed)
L	Play
L	Fast-forward (hit multiple times for faster speed)

Combining Scenes

Scene detection is a great feature, but often you'll want to combine multiple scenes before moving the composite clip to the Timeline, or perhaps consolidate scenes to reduce clutter in the Album. After all, it's always easier to keep track of one asset than five.

Studio's combine feature has one, very significant limitation: You can only combine contiguous scenes captured from a single video. This means you can undo Studio's scene detection feature, but you can't reorganize your videos to a great degree. No problem, Studio has a great Storyboard feature that's perfect for extensive reorganizing.

The Zoo Atlanta video started out with 101 individual scenes, far too many to navigate easily in a DVD menu. However, combining scenes shot around a particular animal or exhibit reduced this to a much more manageable 24 scenes, making it much simpler to quickly produce a navigable DVD.

To combine scenes:

1. To select the scenes to combine, do one of the following:
   - ▲ While holding down the Shift key, use the pointer to select the desired contiguous scenes (**Figure 6.12**).
   - ▲ Click and drag to select all scenes under the marquee, starting with the pointer over a gray area (not a scene).
   - ▲ While holding down the Shift key, touch a scene with the pointer and use the arrow keys to select the desired scenes.
   - ▲ Choose Edit > Select All to select all scenes on all pages of the Album and reverse scene detection.
   - ▲ Choose Ctrl+A to select all scenes on all pages of the Album.

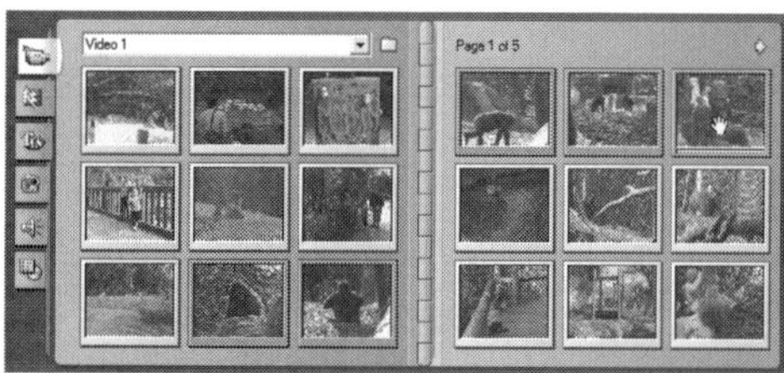

Figure 6.12 To combine multiple scenes into one, you can press the Shift key while touching the desired contiguous scenes with the pointer. In this example, the top three gorilla shots on the second page of the Album are being combined.

Figure 6.13 Studio combines all the gorilla-related scenes.

2. Once the scenes are selected, do one of the following:
   - ▲ From the Studio menu, choose Album > Combine Scenes.
   - ▲ Place the pointer over one of the videos you wish to combine, then right-click and choose Combine Scenes.

   Studio combines all selected scenes (**Figure 6.13**). Had you selected any non-contiguous scenes, Studio would have ignored those selections and combined only the contiguous scenes.

   In addition, had you left any contiguous scenes unselected, Studio would have combined all selected contiguous scenes around the unselected scenes in separate groups, excluding the unselected scene. For example, if you select Scenes 1, 2, 4 and 5, Studio creates two groups, each containing the two contiguous scenes, but leaves Scene 3 as is.

(continued on next page)

✔ Tips

- If you customize scene comments for a scene (see the section "Working with Scene Comments" later in this chapter) and later combine it with another scene, Studio deletes the customized comments and uses the default naming convention, scene number, and duration. Similarly, though you can later subdivide clips and reestablish the original scenes, Studio won't recall your custom comments. If you plan on customizing scene comments, do so after combining or splitting your clips (see the next section, "Splitting Scenes").
- After combining, Studio automatically renumbers all scenes subsequent to the combined scenes. For example, if you combine Scenes 1 through 5, the consolidated scene becomes Scene 1, and the old Scene 6 becomes Scene 2. Keep this in mind if you've been cataloging your videos based on automatic names.
- No matter what method you use to select scenes, Studio ignores the order of selection, combining only the selected contiguous scenes in their original order.
- Don't group scenes if you plan to trim frames from scenes (Chapter 7) or add transitions between them (Chapter 8), as Studio will simply make you resplit them to access the individual scenes.

Splitting Scenes

In addition to combining your scenes, Studio gives you three options for dividing them up in the Album: splitting, subdividing, and scene detection. Splitting is the manual process of dividing one scene into two or multiple scenes, convenient when automatic scene detection doesn't yield useful results.

Subdividing is cutting your clips into regular intervals, useful when working with long continuous videos with no natural breaks. Finally, automatic scene detection breaks the video into intervals based on scene changes in the content or discontinuities in the shooting time and date of the video.

These three options are available during capture, and can be accessed in the Album for scenes captured with scene detection disabled, captured clips with scenes that were manually combined, or videos that were imported. Note that making scene changes based on discontinuities in the shooting date and time requires DV source video, since MPEG and non-DV-source AVI files don't contain the necessary time codes.

To split scenes manually:

1. Select the video to split.
2. Use the Player controls to move to the desired initial frame of the second scene (**Figure 6.14**).

(continued on next page)

Figure 6.14 To create a new scene for Mr. Ostrich, move the Player controls to the desired initial frame of the second scene.

3. Do one of the following:
   - ▲ From the Studio menu, choose Album > Split Scene.
   - ▲ Place the pointer over the video you wish to adjust, then right-click and choose Split Scene.

   Studio splits the scene into two scenes, with the selected frame as the initial frame of the second scene (**Figure 6.15**).

Figure 6.15 Mr. Ostrich gets his own scene, immediately to the right of the scene from which it was split.

To subdivide your scenes into intervals:

1. Select the video to subdivide.
2. Do one of the following:
   - ▲ From the Studio menu, choose Album > Subdivide Scenes.
   - ▲ Right-click and choose Subdivide Scenes.

   The Subdivide Selected Scenes dialog appears.
3. Type the desired interval in the dialog, with the minimum interval being 1 second (**Figure 6.16**).
4. Click OK

   Studio splits the video into scenes of the specified interval, with any remaining time placed in a separate scene. The new scenes are added to the Album (**Figure 6.17**).

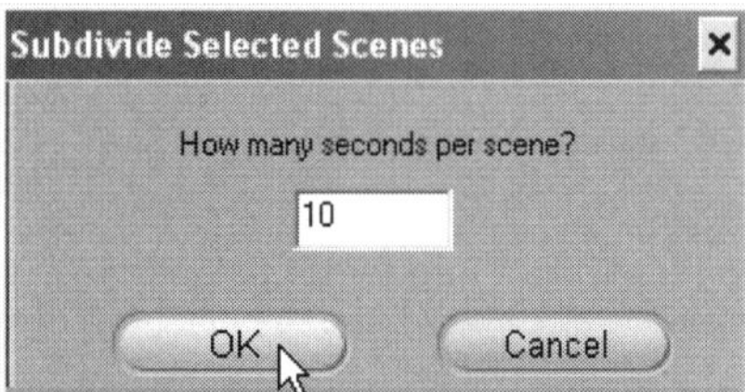

Figure 6.16 Select the desired interval (the minimum is 1 second) and click OK.

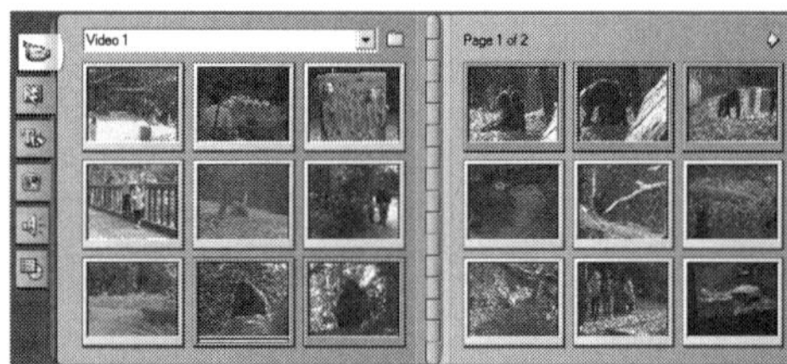

Figure 6.17 See the new gorilla scenes added to the Album.

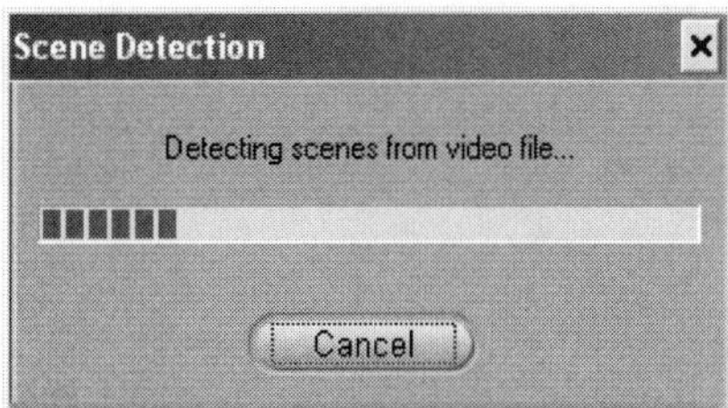

Figure 6.18 When the progress bar appears, Studio is analyzing the clip using the selected scene detection method.

Figure 6.19 At the top of the Album are subdivided clips of flamingos.

To detect scenes in your clips:

1. Select the video to be adjusted.
2. Do one of the following:
   - ▲ In the Studio menu, choose Album > Detect Scenes by Video Content *or* Detect Scenes by Shooting Time and Date.
   - ▲ Right-click and choose Detect Scenes by Video Content *or* Detect Scenes by Shooting Time and Date.

   Studio implements the selected scene detection option. First you see a dialog with a bar tracking Studio's progress (**Figure 6.18**), then the new scenes appear in the Album (**Figure 6.19**).

✔ Tips

- Studio has much more precise tools for *trimming*, or the process of cutting unwanted frames from the beginning and end of each video. Accordingly, use splitting for rough cuts and for making the scenes in the Album easier to manage, and use the tools in the Movie Window for fine-tuning.
- If you customize comments for a scene, and later split, subdivide, or detect scenes for that scene, Studio deletes the customized scene comments and uses the default naming convention, scene number, and duration. If you plan on customizing scene comments, do this after splitting or combining your scenes.
- Splitting also updates the order of all Album scenes, so if you split Scene 1 into two scenes, the former Scene 2 becomes Scene 3. Keep this in mind if you've been cataloging your videos based upon automatic names.

Working with the Album's Views and Tools

The first time you load Studio, the Album is in Icon view, where each scene is represented by an icon—essentially a thumbnail of the initial frame in the scene. However, the Album lets you customize this view to make your videos more accessible. Here's how.

Figure 6.20 To switch to Details view, hold the pointer over any gray area in the Album, right-click, and choose Details View.

To change Icon view to Details view:

- Do one of the following:
  - Hold the pointer over any gray area in the Album, then right-click and choose Details View (**Figure 6.20**).
  - Hold the pointer over any thumbnail in the Album, then right-click and choose Details View.
  - From the Studio menu, choose Album > Details View.

  The Album switches to Details view (**Figure 6.21**).

  The scene comments to the right of each video list the scene number and duration. As you'll see in the next section, you can customize these comments so you can more easily find relevant scenes during production.

Figure 6.21 The Album in Details view.

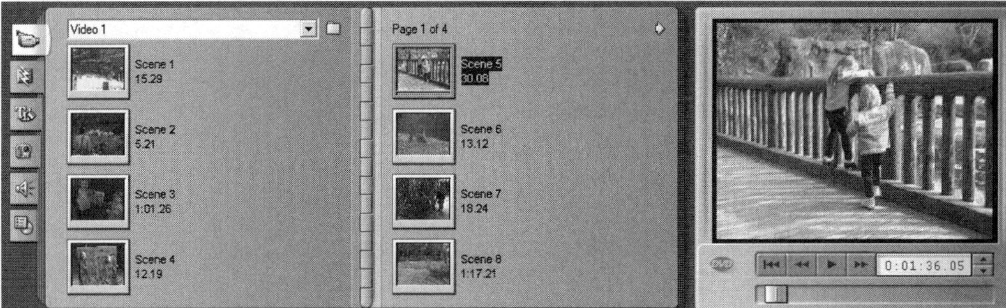

Figure 6.22 Here's the original thumbnail of this scene.

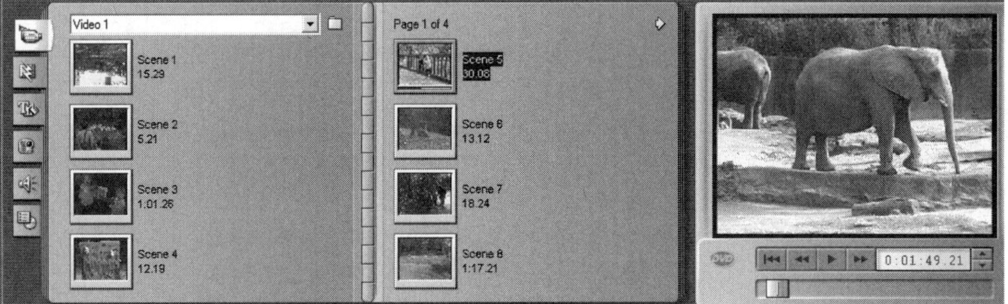

Figure 6.23 Here's a frame that really shows the elephants.

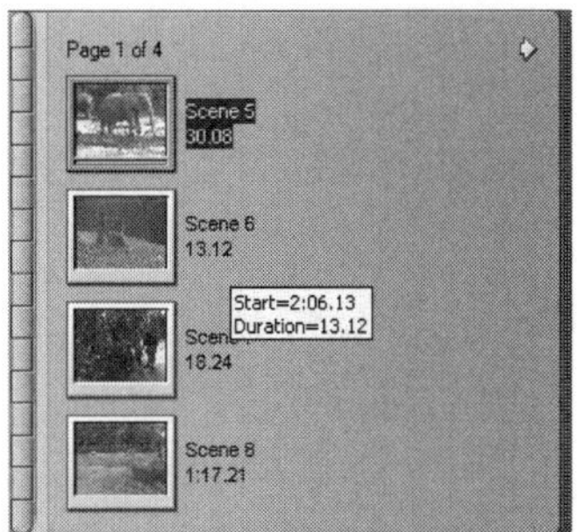

Figure 6.24 Now you can easily tell that this scene relates to elephants.

To change the video thumbnail:

1. Click the video you wish to adjust.

   Studio highlights the scene in the Album and displays the initial frame in the Player (**Figure 6.22**).

2. Use the Player controls to move to the frame you want to be the new thumbnail image (**Figure 6.23**).

3. Do one of the following:

   ▲ From the Studio menu, choose Album > Set Thumbnail.

   ▲ Place the pointer over the video you wish to adjust, then right-click and choose Set Thumbnail.

   Studio changes the thumbnail image to the new frame (**Figure 6.24**).

To locate a clip from the Album in a production:

1. Click on any video with a small green check mark in the upper-right corner (**Figure 6.25**).

   The check mark identifies the videos that are included in the production.

2. Do one of the following:
   - ▲ From the Studio menu, choose Album > Find Scene in Project.
   - ▲ Place the pointer over the video you wish to find, then right-click and choose Find Scene in Project.

   Studio highlights the selected scene in the Movie Window (**Figure 6.26**).

✔ Tip

- If you hold the pointer over any scene for a moment, Studio displays the start time and duration of the scene (**Figure 6.27**). Keep in mind that this and other helpful information found by hovering over a scene or other icon only works with tool tips on—be sure Display Tool Tips is checked in the Help pull-down menu.

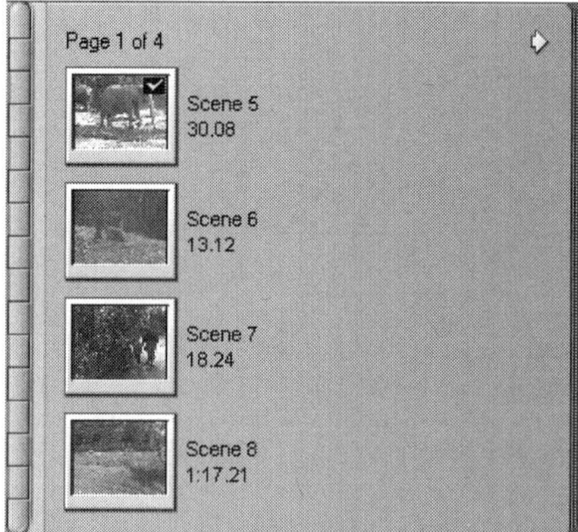

Figure 6.25 The green check mark tells you that you've used the scene somewhere in the production. To find it, select the scene.

Figure 6.26 Studio highlights the video in the Movie Window.

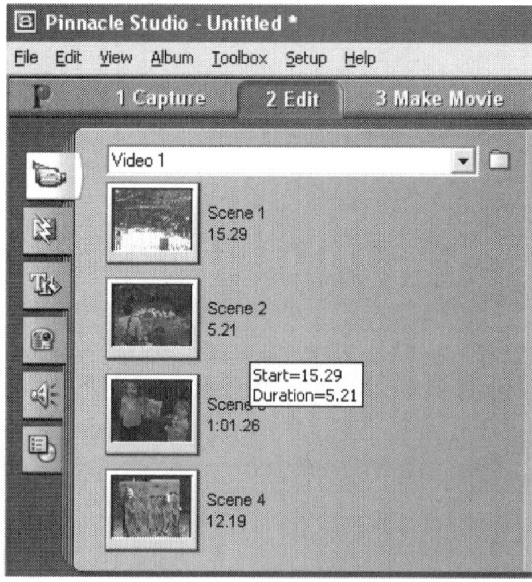

Figure 6.27 The pop-up box that appears when you hold the pointer over a scene's thumbnail identifies the scene's starting time and duration in the video.

Figure 6.28 Changing scene comments helps you find videos fast. Start by clicking the scene.

Figure 6.29 Then type in the desired text.

Working with Scene Comments

In smaller productions, it's easy to keep track of videos and scenes, but when you're tracking multiple videos over many months, scenes can be harder to find. This is where the ability to add descriptive comments to scenes and later search for these scenes can be immensely helpful.

To change scene comments:

1. In Details View mode, select the video you wish to adjust by clicking it, and click again on the comments box.

   The outline around the video turns blue, and the scene comments are highlighted (**Figure 6.28**).

2. Click on the comments box, which turns white, signifying it's ready for editing.

3. Type in the desired scene comments (**Figure 6.29**).

4. To save the scene comments, press Enter or click anywhere else in the Studio interface.

   Studio saves the scene comments.

To select scenes based on keywords:

1. From the Studio menu, choose Album > Select Scenes by Name.

   The Select Scenes by Name dialog appears (**Figure 6.30**).

2. Enter the keyword(s) you wish to search for.

3. Do one of the following:
   - ▲ Click And to find all scenes containing *all* the words typed in the Keywords box.
   - ▲ Click Or to find all scenes containing *any* of the words typed.
   - ▲ Click Not and And to find any scenes that don't contain *all* of the words typed.
   - ▲ Click Not and Or to find any scenes that don't contain *any* of the words typed.

   The Album highlights the scenes conforming to the selected rules (**Figure 6.31**). You'll have to page through the Album to locate the highlighted clips; Studio doesn't move them to a new location.

✔ Tips

- Studio's search function only searches scenes in the video currently loaded in the Album, not other videos saved to disk. This somewhat limits its functionality except with extremely large capture files.
- Unlike Windows Explorer, the Album doesn't prevent you from using duplicate names. Your files won't self-destruct; you'll just end up with different scenes with identical names.

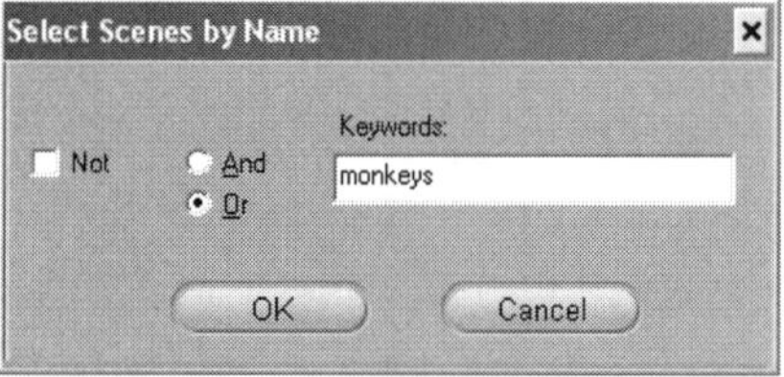

Figure 6.30 Type the word(s) you want to search for, and the conditions.

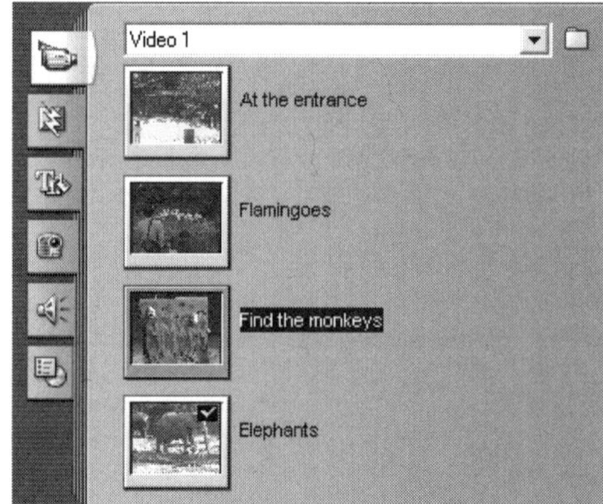

Figure 6.31 Studio highlights the conforming clips.

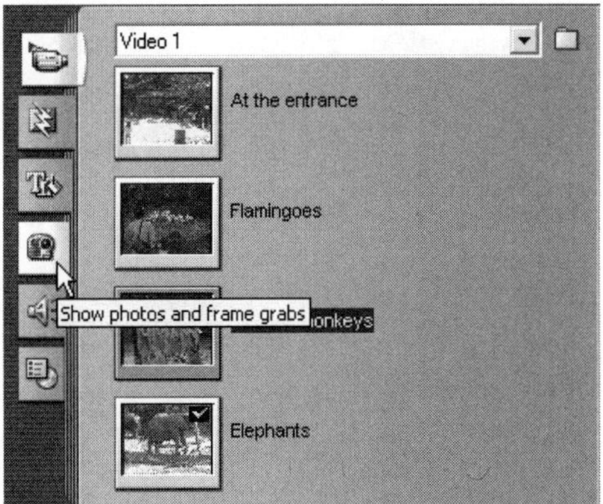

Figure 6.32 Have a look at the still images taken at the zoo.

Working in the Still Images Tab

The Still Images tab is where you load still images from all sources for deployment in your projects. The Album's functions in this area are extremely limited; you can't combine, arrange, or annotate the images in the Album. Don't worry; there'll be plenty of time and functionality for that in the Movie Window.

To open the Album to the Still Images tab:

1. Go to Edit mode.

   When you first open Studio, Edit mode is the default.

   If you're running Studio and are in Capture or Make Movie mode, select the Edit tab.

2. Click the camera icon, the fourth icon from the top along the left side of the Album window (**Figure 6.32**).

The Album switches to the Still Images tab and displays any images in the currently selected folder (**Figure 6.33**).

Figure 6.33 Here they are in the Album.

To display filenames:

- Hover the pointer over any image.

  The pointer immediately changes to a hand and (with tool tips on) then displays the image's filename (**Figure 6.34**).

Figure 6.34 Hover the pointer over an image, and Studio tells you its name.

To load files from a different location:

1. Click the small directory icon to the right of the Album's list box (**Figure 6.35**).

   A standard Open file dialog appears (**Figure 6.36**). Navigate to the folder containing the files to be imported.

2. Select any file in the folder, then click the Open button (**Figure 6.37**).

   Studio loads all files in the folder (**Figure 6.38**).

Figure 6.35 To load files from a different directory, click the folder icon.

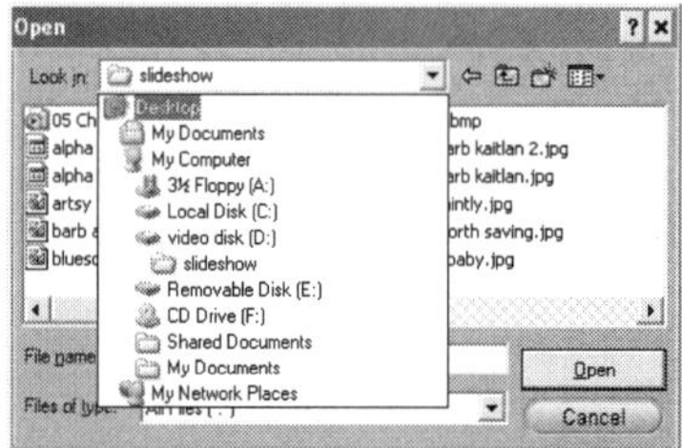

Figure 6.36 Navigate to the desired location.

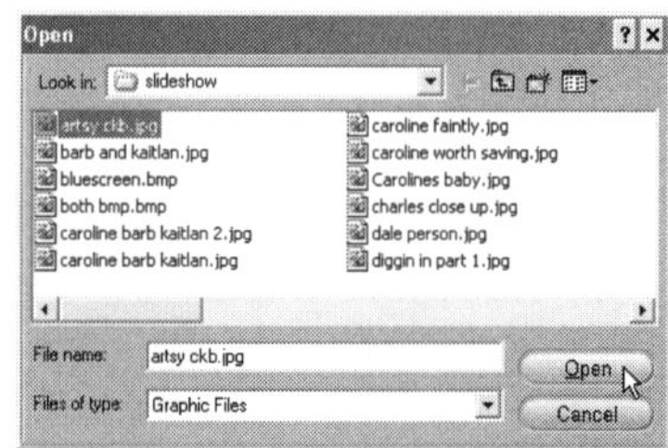

Figure 6.37 Select any file and click Open.

✔ Tips

- If you select a subdirectory with many high-resolution images, it may take several minutes for Studio to create the thumbnails to display in the Album, during which time your hard drive will be chugging like crazy and your computer will feel extremely sluggish. If your still image folders contain lots of images, consider moving the images you wish to incorporate into your production to a separate folder for input into Studio.
- Studio can import files in the following formats: bitmap (BMP), JPEG (JPG, JPEG), Targa (TGA), TIFF (TIFF), Windows Metafiles (WMF), and files created by Title Deko, Studio's titling utility. This pretty much covers the majors, but if you want to use a GIF image or Photoshop document (PSD), you have to convert to one of the supported formats in another program first.

Figure 6.38 Studio loads all the directory's images into the Album.

Figure 6.39 Click the speaker icon to select the Sound Effects tab, where you load audio files into the project.

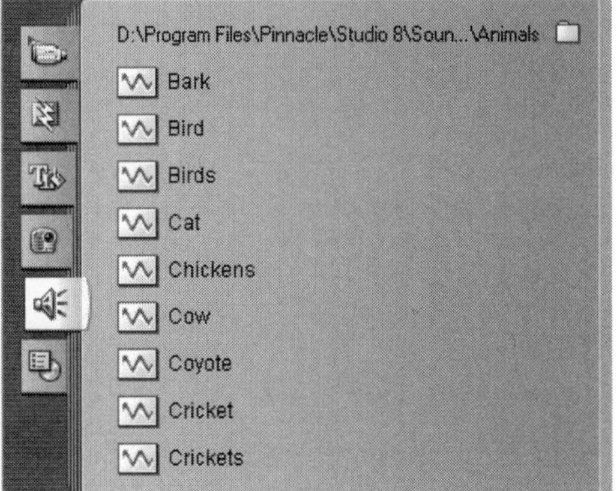

Figure 6.40 The Album defaults to folders containing sound effects that Pinnacle includes with Studio 8.

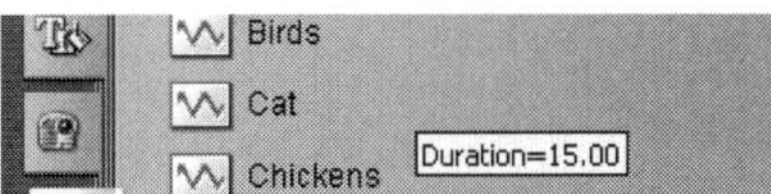

Figure 6.41 As with still images, the Album features for audio files are light, but (with tool tips on) you can ascertain file duration by hovering the pointer over the icon.

Working in the Sound Effects Tab

The Sound Effects tab is where you load audio files for deployment in your projects. As with the Still Images tab, the Album's functions in this area are extremely limited; you can't combine, arrange, or annotate the audio files in the Album, or adjust volume. All this and more are possible in the Movie Window; the Album is here simply to collect and deploy.

To open the Album to the Sound Effects tab:

1. Go to Edit mode.

   When you first open Studio, Edit mode is the default.

   If you're running Studio and are in Capture or Make Movie mode, select the Edit tab.

2. Click the speaker icon, the fifth icon from the top along the left side of the Album window (**Figure 6.39**).

   The Album switches to the Sound Effects tab and displays all supported files in the current folder (**Figure 6.40**).

To display file duration:

◆ Hover the pointer over any audio file.

  The pointer immediately changes to a hand, then displays the file duration in a moment (**Figure 6.41**).

To play any audio file:

◆ Touch any file in the Sound Effects tab with the pointer.

  The file immediately plays through to the end. Use the controls in the Player to replay, rewind, or move through the scene.

To load files from a different location:

1. Click the small directory icon to the right of the Album list box (**Figure 6.42**).

   A standard Open file dialog appears. Navigate to the folder containing the files to be imported.

2. Select any file in the folder and click Open (**Figure 6.43**).

   Studio loads all compatible files in the folder into the Album (**Figure 6.44**).

✔ Tip

- Studio can import WAV files, MP3 files, and audio from AVI files. Notable missing formats include QuickTime, RealAudio, and Windows Media files. The lack of the latter two is a pain given that many folks who collect digital audio files use these formats extensively for their collections.

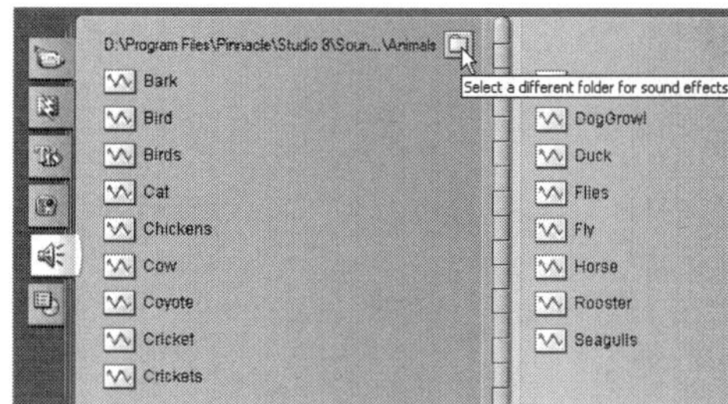

Figure 6.42 You know the drill by now. To open new audio files, click the folder icon.

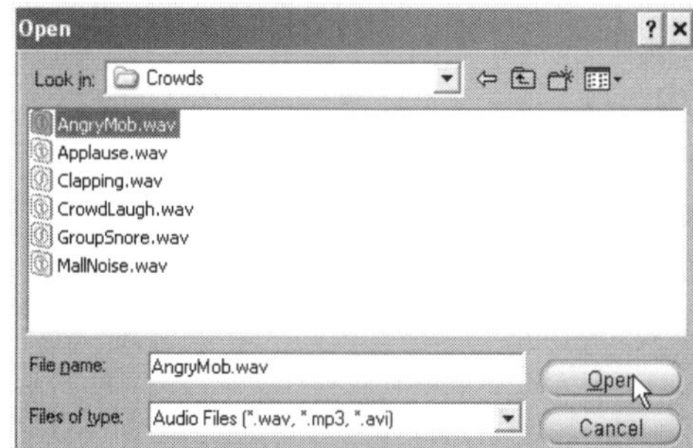

Figure 6.43 Choose any file and click Open.

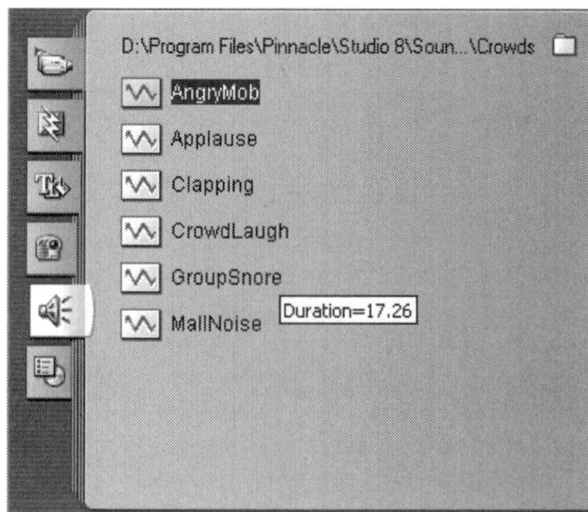

Figure 6.44 Studio displays all compatible audio files in the Album.

PART III

EDITING

7 Producing Videos in the Movie Window

After capturing your video, still image, and audio assets, you've created a huge collection of files—usually far more than you'll want to include in your final production. Now it's time to cut out the fat and assemble the basic pieces of your project, work you'll perform in Studio's Movie Window.

The Movie Window showcases the most flexible part of Studio's interface, providing three views of your assembled assets: Storyboard, Timeline, and Text view (called Edit List view in the Studio menu). This chapter discusses the strengths of each view and teaches you how to customize and efficiently work within them. Considering how much time you'll be spending in the Movie Window—particularly the Timeline—spending a short time on the basics now will save you hours in the future.

Looking at Movie Window Views

The Movie Window offers three views: Storyboard (**Figure 7.1**), Timeline (**Figure 7.2**), and Text (**Figure 7.3**).

Figure 7.1 The Storyboard view, the best view for initially loading and sequencing your assets.

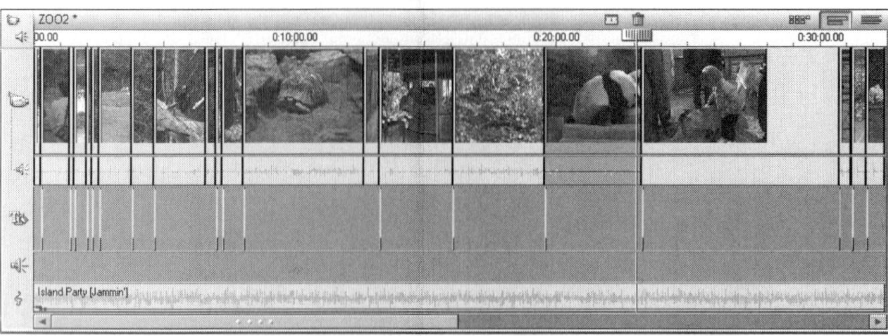

Figure 7.2 The Timeline view, the best view for pulling together all project components.

ZOO2 *

	Name	Trimmed start	Movie duration	Movie start
	Video transition: 'Dissolve'		0:00:02.00	0:16:03.27
	Audio transition: 'Dissolve'		0:00:02.00	0:16:03.27
17	Video clip: 'Majestic tigers'	0:16:32.27	0:03:31.09	0:16:03.27
	Audio clip: 'Majestic tigers'	0:16:32.27	0:03:31.09	0:16:03.27
	Title overlay: 'Tigers'		0:00:04.00	0:16:04.17
	Video transition: 'Dissolve'		0:00:02.00	0:19:33.06
	Audio transition: 'Dissolve'		0:00:02.00	0:19:33.06
18	Video clip: 'Giant pandas'	0:20:04.06	0:03:44.17	0:19:33.06
	Audio clip: 'Giant pandas'	0:20:04.06	0:03:44.17	0:19:33.06
	Title overlay: 'Giant Pandas'		0:00:04.00	0:19:35.06
	Video transition: 'Dissolve'		0:00:02.00	0:23:15.23
	Audio transition: 'Dissolve'		0:00:02.00	0:23:15.23
19	Video clip: 'In the petting zoo'	0:23:48.23	0:07:30.05	0:23:15.23
	Audio clip: 'In the petting zoo'	0:23:48.23	0:07:30.05	0:23:15.23
	Title overlay: 'Petting Zoo'		0:00:04.00	0:23:17.10
	Video transition: 'Dissolve'		0:00:02.00	0:30:43.28

Figure 7.3 The Text view (also called Edit List), best for folks who develop Web pages in Notepad and others who prefer working in text over using visual tools.

Figure 7.4 Switch between views using the Studio menu or the icons atop the Movie Window.

Briefly, the Storyboard view uses a thumbnail image to represent each asset in a project. This is a great view for sequencing your assets and inserting transitions between them, but little else, since you can't access tracks for titles, narration, or background music.

The Timeline view is a graphical representation of an entire project, with each length on the Timeline representing track duration. In Figure 7.2, you can see that the longest tracks are from the Zoo Atlanta's Reptile Hall (see the turtle), giant panda exhibit, and petting zoo. However, many of the smaller tracks are unrecognizable, so it's best to sequence your videos in the Storyboard view, then switch to Timeline view for serious editing.

The Text view is appropriate for those who enjoy working with text descriptors rather than visual assets. I'm not that way and have seldom found use for this view.

To switch between Movie Window views:

- Do one of the following:
  - At the upper-right corner of the Movie Window, click the appropriate button for the desired view (Figure 7.1).
  - In the Studio menu, choose View and the desired view (**Figure 7.4**).

Working in the Storyboard

In traditional video productions, a storyboard is a large chart or series of charts with images representing the various scenes of the project. It's a great tool for conceptualizing the content and flow of your movie, and even better in digital form, since you can easily rearrange your assets.

If you're at all unsure of the order of your scenes, Studio's Storyboard view is a very convenient tool for shuffling them around until you're set. You can even quickly add transitions and preview your project, getting a quick view of the rough cut. When it's time to trim your videos, however, and perform other more sophisticated editing effects, you'll need to use the superior tools available only in the Timeline view.

Note that in default mode, Studio maintains audio/video synchronization in all Movie Window views by automatically tying the Audio track with the Video track through all edits. Accordingly, if you move, delete, split, or combine scenes in the Video track, the audio automatically follows. (Later in this chapter you'll learn how to adjust this default, so you can delete the Original Audio track or perform advanced editing operations that let you edit the Audio and Video tracks separately.)

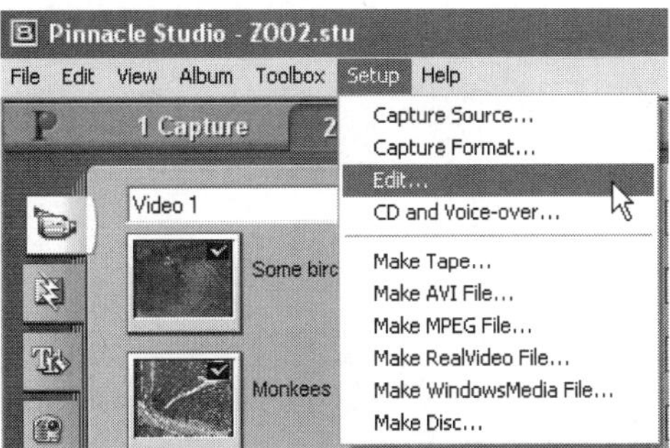

Figure 7.5 Getting to the Pinnacle Studio Setup Options screen.

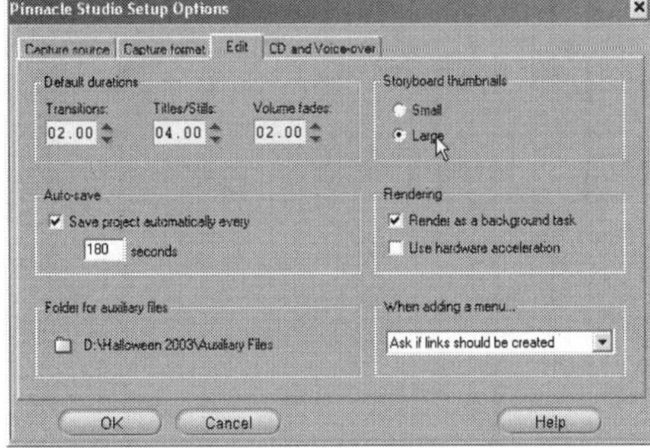

Figure 7.6 With the Edit tab selected, switch from small (the default setting) to large Storyboard thumbnails.

To customize the Storyboard view:

1. From the Studio menu, choose Setup > Edit (**Figure 7.5**).

   The Pinnacle Studio Setup Options screen appears open to the Edit tab (**Figure 7.6**).

2. Check Large to increase the size of the images in the Storyboard.

   Studio increases the size of the individual images and decreases the number of images shown from 27 to 10 (**Figure 7.7**). Use the scroll bar on the right to scroll down and see the additional thumbnails, or use the Page Up or Page Down keys to move through the pages of the Storyboard.

Figure 7.7 Use the large thumbnail view to see more detail in your thumbnails. Note the scroll bar on the right, which you'll use to access the rest of your assets.

To drag videos to the Storyboard:

1. In the Video Scenes tab, select one or more contiguous or noncontiguous scenes with the pointer, while holding down the left mouse button.

   The outlines turn from white to blue, and a small hand appears over the scene or scenes (**Figure 7.8**).

2. Drag the scene or scenes to the Storyboard toward the box in the upper-left corner.

   A green box appears around the box, and a small plus sign appears below the pointer (**Figure 7.9**).

3. Release the mouse button.

   Studio inserts the scenes in the highlighted Storyboard box (**Figure 7.10**).

Figure 7.8 Getting videos into the Movie Window is as simple as selecting and dragging.

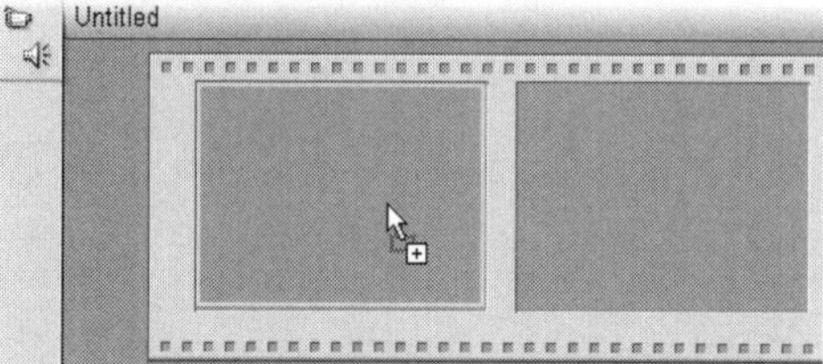

Figure 7.9 The green window and plus sign are your clues that it's safe to drop the asset in the selected box.

Figure 7.10 Voilà. There are your clips.

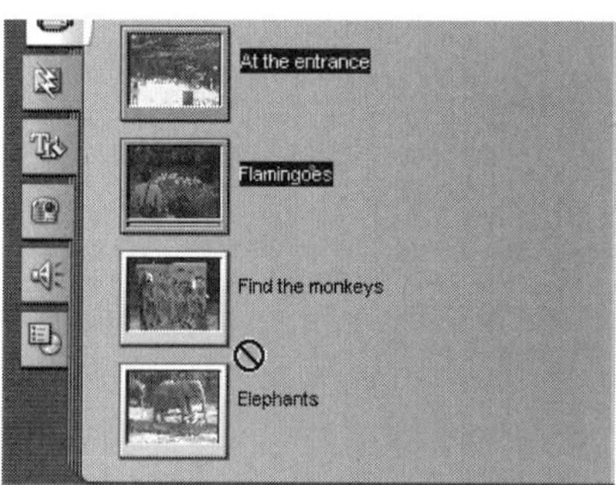

Figure 7.11 Other placement cues include the universal "prohibited" sign, indicating that you can't arrange your clips in the Video Scenes tab.

✔ Tips

- Studio provides visual cues regarding where you can drop all assets. As shown in **Figure 7.11**, if you attempt to drop a scene in a prohibited zone, such as another location in the Video Scenes tab, Studio shows the universal "prohibited" sign.
- Studio drops video and still image assets in the first available space at the beginning of a project. Although you can reorder at will once the assets are in the Storyboard, Studio doesn't let you create gaps in your projects in any Movie Window view.
- To create a black scene at the start of your video, create a full-screen blank title and drag it to the Video track (see Chapter 10).
- You can also use cut and paste commands to move videos and still images to and around the Movie Window, but dragging and dropping is much more intuitive.

Figure 7.12 The green line and a small plus sign tell you that you can drop the assets in that location.

Figure 7.13 The assets, successfully inserted and shifted. Don't those monkeys look natural?

To drag videos between one or more scenes:

1. In the Video Scenes tab, select one scene or more with the pointer, holding down the left mouse button.

   The outlines turn from white to blue, and a small hand appears over the scene.

2. Drag the scene down to the desired location.

   A green line appears between the video scenes, and a small plus sign appears below the pointer (**Figure 7.12**).

3. Release the mouse button.

   Studio inserts the scene between the existing scenes (**Figure 7.13**).

✔ Tip

- Studio inserts the new clip between the selected clips, pushing back all clips after the newly inserted clips. No clips are deleted or otherwise truncated.

To arrange assets in Storyboard view:

1. In the Storyboard, select one or more scenes with the pointer, holding down the left mouse button.

   Studio highlights the clip in blue, and a small hand appears over the scene (**Figure 7.14**).

2. Drag the scene or scenes to the desired location.

   A green line appears each time you cross over an available space to drop the new scenes, and a small box appears below the pointer (**Figure 7.15**).

3. Release the mouse button at the desired location.

   Studio inserts the scene in the specified location (**Figure 7.16**).

To see clip-related information in the Storyboard:

- In the Storyboard, hover the pointer over the clip for a moment.

  The scene name and duration appear in a small yellow box beneath the scene (**Figure 7.17**).

Figure 7.14 Decided to get the scenes back in order? Select the clip you want to move.

Figure 7.15 When you see that green line and the small box under the arrow, you can drag the clip to the desired location and drop it.

Figure 7.16 You're back in business. This ease of sequencing is why the Storyboard view is great for arranging your assets.

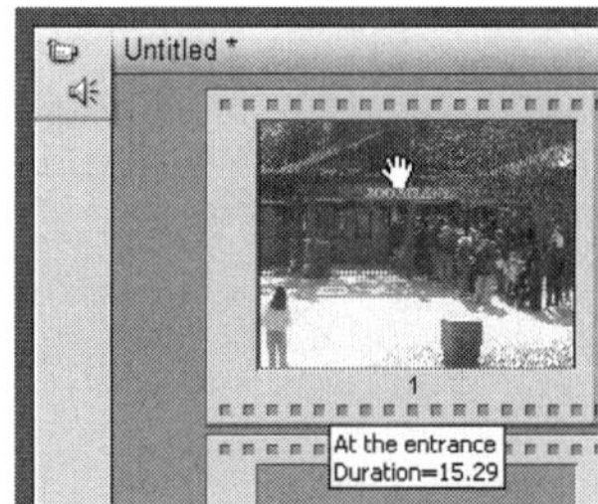

Figure 7.17 Since the Storyboard view doesn't visually convey duration-related information, Studio provides it when you hover your mouse over the asset.

Figure 7.18 The Player is your preview window. (Note that the real keyboard shortcut for Play is L, not K.)

To preview your video in the Storyboard:

1. Select the scene you wish to play back with your pointer.

   Studio highlights the clip in blue.

2. To start playback, do one of the following:
   - ▲ In the Player, click Play (**Figure 7.18**). The Play key switches to Pause mode, which you can click to stop playback.
   - ▲ Press the spacebar to stop and start playback.
   - ▲ Press the L key to start playback (ignore the tool tip). Press K to stop playback.

   Playback shifts automatically from scene to scene when multiple assets are present.

   During playback, Studio displays a progress bar beneath the scene.

   While the progress bar represents the playback position within each scene, the Player Scrubber represents the position within the entire video.

✔ Tips

- Here are some keyboard shortcuts:

  Press L for fast-forward (pressing multiple times accelerates the effect).

  Press J for fast-reverse (pressing multiple times accelerates the effect).

- You can always use the Player Scrubber to move around in the video file.

Getting Videos to the Timeline

The Timeline view is where you'll spend the bulk of your editing time. Although it's not quite as straightforward as the Storyboard view, its operational advantages quickly become very apparent.

This section identifies the various Timeline tracks and explains how to get video scenes to the Timeline. If your Timeline starts getting cramped or otherwise out of control, skip ahead one section to learn how to customize your Timeline view.

Once again, in default mode you'll notice that Studio automatically inserts the audio that was originally captured with the video file to the appropriate track when you transfer the video, so don't worry about manually moving the Audio track yourself.

Figure 7.19 highlights the components of the Timeline and other components of the Studio interface that are important in effectively using the Timeline.

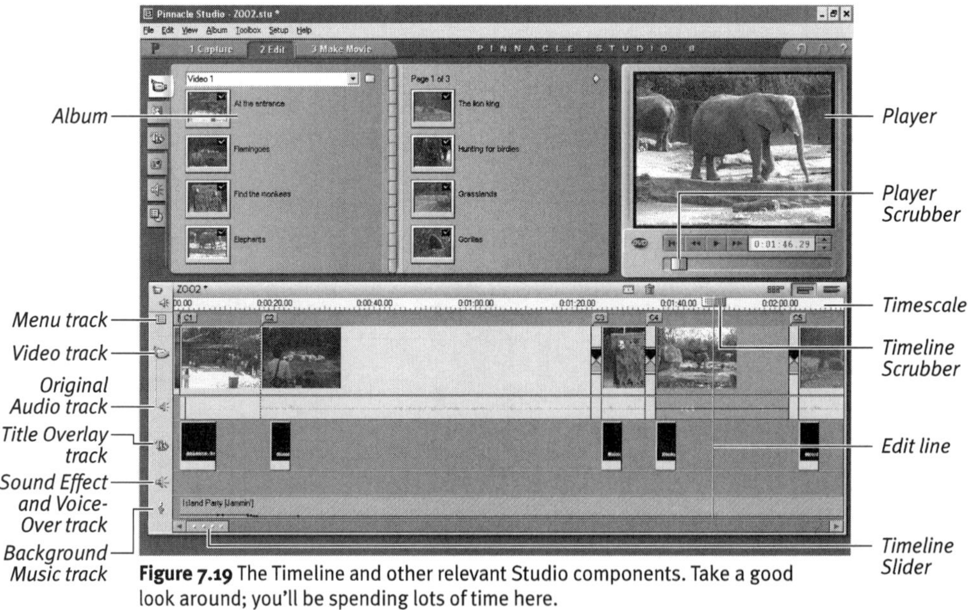

Figure 7.19 The Timeline and other relevant Studio components. Take a good look around; you'll be spending lots of time here.

- **Timescale.** Illustrates the absolute time of the assets displayed in the Timeline view. This can be modified to show more or less detail (see the following section).
- **Menu track.** Appears only after you add a DVD menu to the Timeline. (For details on DVD authoring, see Chapter 12.)
- **Video track.** The only track that can display video and can also display still images.
- **Original Audio track.** Contains only the audio that was captured with the video file.
- **Title Overlay track.** Contains titles and still image overlays (see Chapter 10).
- **Sound Effect and Voice-Over track.** Studio inserts all voice-over recordings in this track, or you can insert audio from any source. For example, to insert only the audio from a captured video file into the production, simply drag it to this track.
- **Background Music track.** Studio inserts background music produced by the SmartSound utility in this track. Or, as with the sound effect track, you can insert audio from any source. To learn how to set audio levels for the three Audio tracks, see Chapter 11.
- **Edit line.** The current editing position in the Timeline and the frame currently visible in the Player.
- **Timeline Scrubber.** A tool used to drag the edit line to different positions on the Timeline.
- **Player Scrubber.** A tool used to move the edit line through the project.
- **Timeline Slider.** A tool used to drag the visible area in the Timeline forward and backward through the project.

To drag videos to the Timeline:

1. In the Video Scenes tab, select one or more contiguous or noncontiguous scenes with the pointer, holding down the left mouse button.

   The outlines turn from white to blue, and a small hand appears over the scenes.

2. Do one of the following:
   - ▲ Drag the scene or scenes to the Video track.
   - ▲ Drag the scene or scenes to the Sound Effect and Voice-Over track.
   - ▲ Drag the scene or scenes to the Background Music track.

   A green box representing the duration of the clip appears in the first open space to the left of the Timeline, and a small plus sign appears below the pointer (**Figure 7.20**).

3. Release the mouse button.

   Studio inserts the scene or scenes into the selected track (**Figure 7.21**).

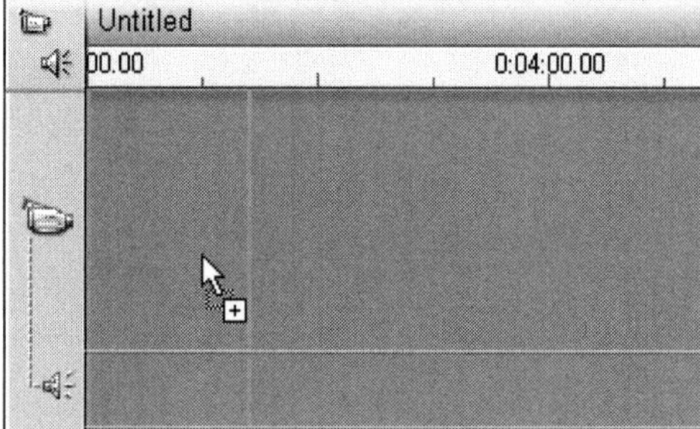

Figure 7.20 More placement cues. A green box defines the duration of the video on the Timeline, while the plus sign says it's OK to drop the file there.

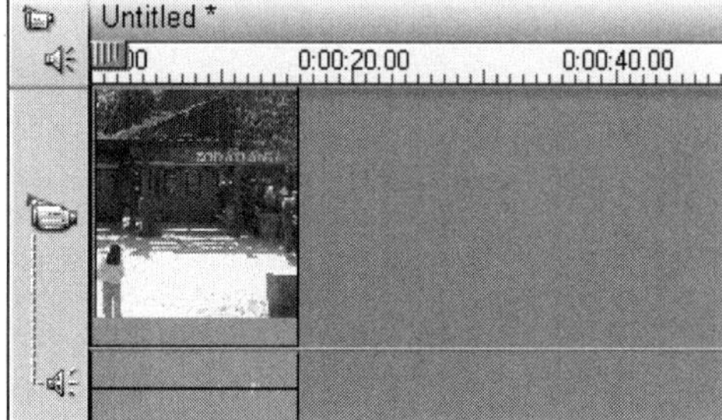

Figure 7.21 There's your scene, ready to go.

Figure 7.22 Danger, danger, Will Robinson—don't drop your clip there. See the prohibited sign and error message on the top line.

✔ Tips

- If you drop a video into the Video track, Studio always inserts the associated audio into the Original Audio track. To learn how to delete this audio track, see Chapter 11.
- If you drop the video file into either the Sound Effect and Voice-Over track or the Background Music track, only the audio, not the video, is inserted into the track.
- As with the Storyboard, Studio provides visual cues regarding where you can drop all assets. As shown in **Figure 7.22**, if you attempt to drop the scene or scenes in prohibited tracks, like the Title Overlay track, you'll see red lines instead of green, a "prohibited" sign, and the error message "Only titles, photos and transitions on graphic track" above the Timescale.
- As with the Storyboard, Studio always drops video and still image assets in the first available space at the beginning of a project. Although you can reorder assets at will once they're in the Storyboard, you can't create gaps in your projects in any of the Movie Window views.

To drag videos between one or more clips:

1. In the Video Scenes tab, select one or more scenes with the pointer, holding down the left mouse button.

   The outlines turn from white to blue, and a small hand appears over the scene or scenes.

2. Drag the scene or scenes to the desired location.

   Two vertical green lines appear between the two selected videos, and a small plus sign appears below the pointer (**Figure 7.23**).

3. Release the mouse button.

   Studio inserts the scene between the existing scenes (**Figure 7.24**).

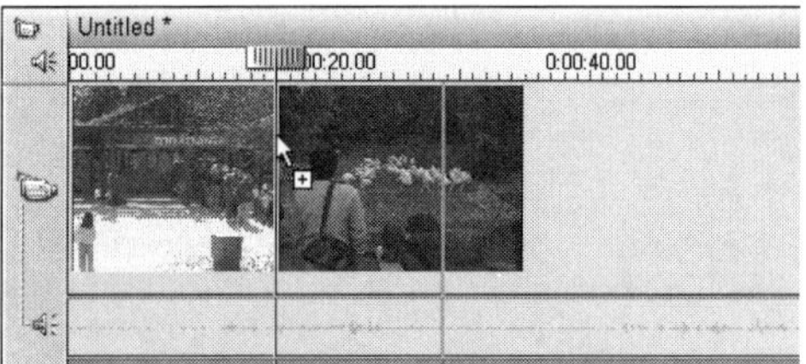

Figure 7.23 Studio won't let you drop a clip into the middle of another. Move the pointer until you see the green lines and plus sign.

Figure 7.24 Release the mouse button, and there you go.

✔ Tips

- Note that Studio inserts the new clip between the selected clips, pushing back all clips after the newly inserted clips (potentially out of your current frame of reference on the project). No clips are deleted or otherwise truncated.

- You can normally insert a clip only at the beginning or end of another clip, not in the middle of a clip. The steps "To perform an insert edit," later in this chapter, show you how to insert a clip in the middle of a different clip, a process called insert editing.

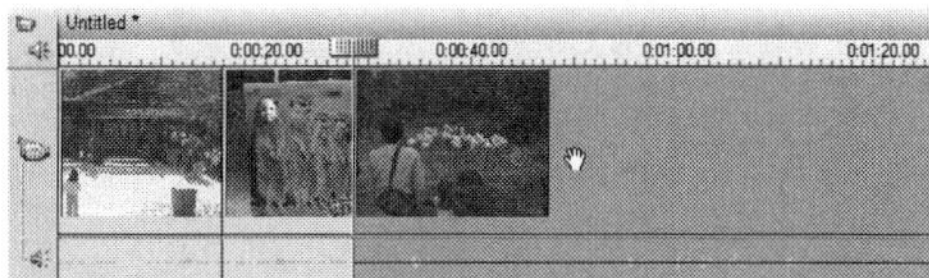

Figure 7.25 Moving clips is the same as in the Storyboard, just with different cues. Start by touching the clip.

Figure 7.26 Move it to the desired space, watching for the green lines and plus sign, then release the mouse button.

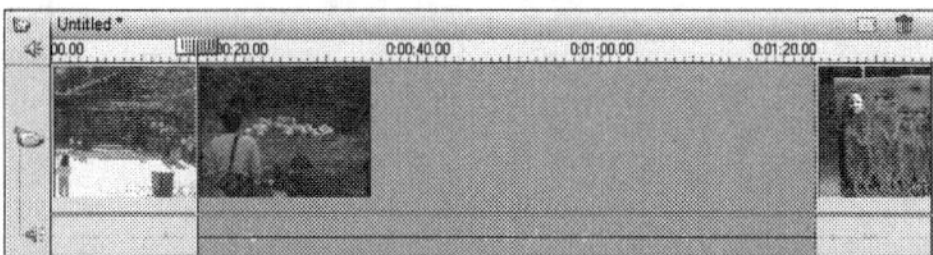

Figure 7.27 Studio inserts the clip, and pushes all clips behind it to the back of the line.

To arrange videos in the Timeline:

1. In the Video track, select one or more scenes with the pointer, holding down the left mouse button.

   Studio highlights the clip in blue, and a small hand appears over the scene (**Figure 7.25**).

2. Drag the clip to the desired location.

   Studio displays green lines at the beginning and end of the clip that you're arranging, and a small box appears below the pointer (**Figure 7.26**).

3. Release the mouse button.

   Studio inserts the scene in the specified location (**Figure 7.27**).

To preview your video in the Timeline:

1. To preview your video, do one of the following:
   - ▲ With the pointer, select the scene you wish to play back.

     Studio highlights the clip in blue and positions the Timeline Scrubber at the start of the scene.
   - ▲ Use the pointer to position the Timeline Scrubber to the desired start location (**Figure 7.28**).
2. To start playback, do one of the following:
   - ▲ In the Player, click Play.

     The Play key switches to Pause mode, which you can click to stop playback.
   - ▲ Press the spacebar to stop and start playback.
   - ▲ Press the L key to start playback (ignore the tool tip). Press K to stop playback.

   Playback shifts automatically from scene to scene when multiple assets are present.

   During playback, the Timeline and Player Scrubbers advance with the video.

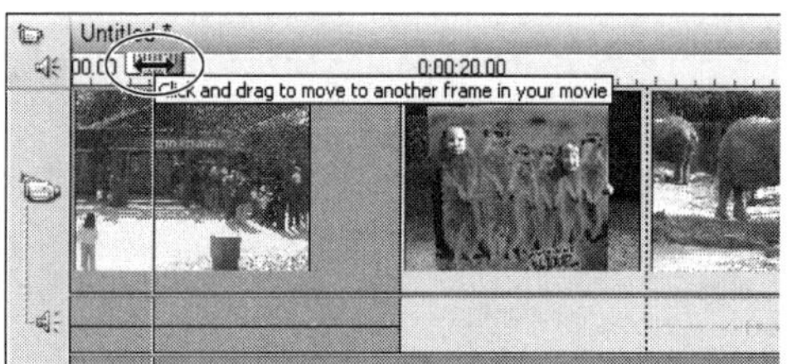

Figure 7.28 Get familiar with the Timeline Scrubber, which shifts the edit line and controls the frames viewed in the Player.

✔ Tips

- Here are some relevant keyboard shortcuts:

  Press L for fast-forward (pressing multiple times accelerates the effect).

  Press J for fast-reverse (pressing multiple times accelerates the effect).
- The keyboard shortcut K didn't work correctly as of version 8.5. (Pinnacle may have subsequently fixed this problem.)
- You can always use the Scrubber button in the Player to position video playback.

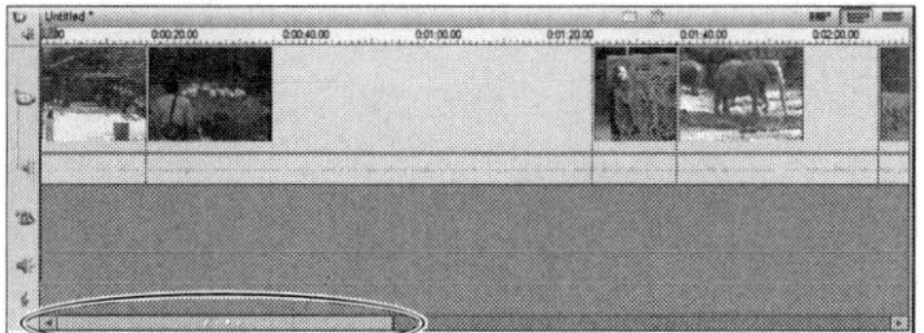

Figure 7.29 The Timeline Slider moves you around your production.

Customizing Your Timeline View

As you've probably already noticed, as you place additional videos on the Timeline, it gets more and more difficult to see the big picture. Fortunately, Studio supplies several tools that help you control your Timeline environment.

First, a slider bar at the bottom of the Timeline makes it easy to move through your production. In addition, Studio can stretch the Timeline so that it represents a longer period (and thus shows more videos, or longer stretches of a single video) to provide a high-level view. Or you can shrink down the Timeline to a frame-by-frame view, which is helpful when synchronizing production elements like a background audio track and the main video.

To move around in the Timeline:

- Do one of the following:
  - Touch the Timeline Slider at the bottom of the Timeline and drag it to the right to reveal the video inserted after the last visible track (**Figure 7.29**).
  - Press the Page Down key to move from the beginning to the end of the Timeline, or the Page Up key to move from the end to the beginning.
  - Press the right-arrow key to move forward to the next scene on the Timeline, and the left-arrow key to move backward from scene to scene.

✔ Tips

- Note that the Timeline Slider is not movable until the project assets exceed the space then visible on the Timeline.
- Also note that the Timeline Slider will shrink as the project gets longer, essentially representing the relative size of the video then visible in the Timeline to the entire project.

To adjust the Timescale of the Timeline:

- Do one of the following:
  - ▲ Place your pointer over the yellow Timescale on the Timeline and right-click.

    Studio opens a menu that lets you select the desired duration to be visible in the Timeline (**Figure 7.30**).
  - ▲ Press the plus sign (+) or minus sign (-) keys to make the Timescale larger or smaller.
  - ▲ On the yellow Timescale bar, place the pointer anywhere except directly over the edit line until a small clock with arrows appears (**Figure 7.31**). Drag the clock left to expand the Timescale and show more videos, or right to compress the Timescale and see more detail.

✔ Tips

- Choose Entire movie (Figure 7.30), and Studio places the entire movie in the visible area of the Timeline. It's the best way to see your whole production fast.
- When you set the Timescale at the highest magnification, each tick mark on the Timescale represents an individual video frame (although Studio shows only the initial frame on the Timeline). When performing precision trims on the Timeline, this level of detail can be extremely useful, though you'll have to view the frames in the Player, not on the Timeline.

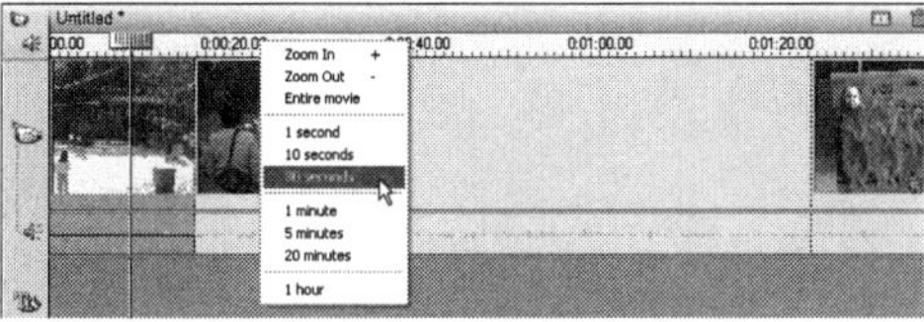

Figure 7.30 Working in the Timeline requires constant shuffling of the Timescale. Here's one way to adjust the Timescale, allowing you control over how many clips you can see on the Timeline at one time.

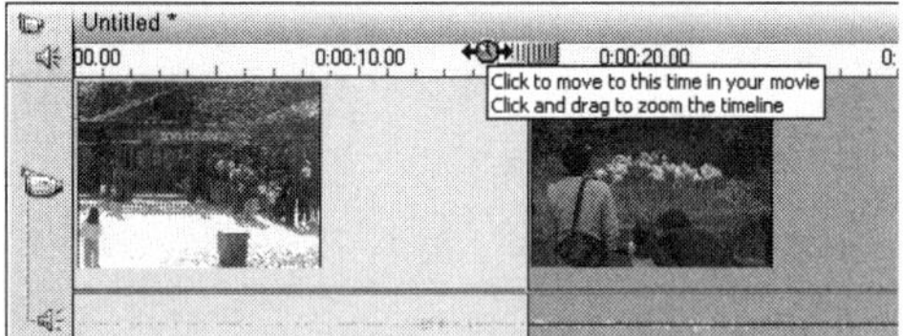

Figure 7.31 Here's another. Just click the yellow Timescale anywhere but on the Timeline Scrubber, and the clock appears. Drag to the left to show more videos, and to the right to see more detail. Don't forget the plus sign (+) and minus sign (-) keyboard shortcuts.

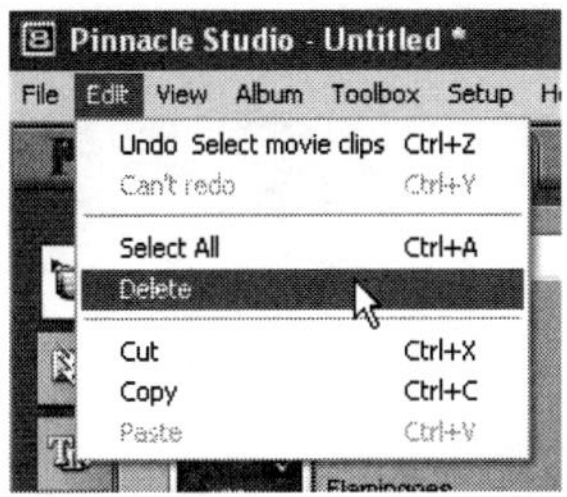

Figure 7.32 One way to delete a clip in the Movie Window.

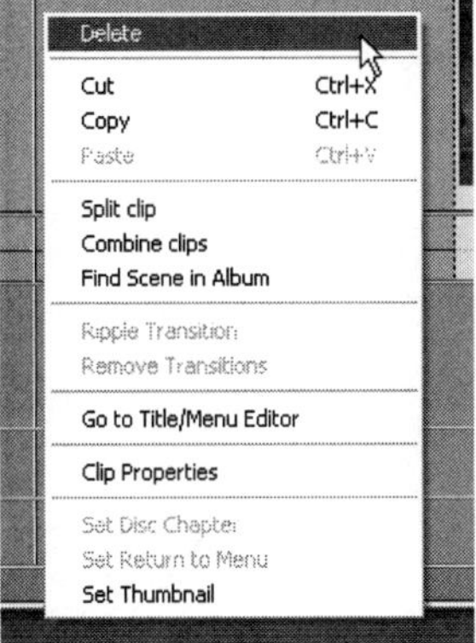

Figure 7.33 Another way, using the right-click command.

Common Tasks in Storyboard and Timeline Views

As you'd expect, Studio uses common commands for many housekeeping tasks you perform in the Storyboard and Timeline views. Here are the major ones, shown in the Timeline view for simplicity.

To delete assets:

1. With the pointer, select the asset you wish to delete.

   Studio highlights the clip in blue.

2. Do one of the following:
   - ▲ Press the Delete key.
   - ▲ From the Studio menu, choose Edit > Delete (**Figure 7.32**).
   - ▲ Right-click and choose Delete (**Figure 7.33**).

   Studio deletes the clip from the Timeline, but not from the Album or your disk.

✔ Tips

- If you delete any video scene, all scenes after the deleted clip automatically shift over to close the gap. This is called a ripple edit (see the section "Trimming Multiple Clips on the Timeline" later in this chapter). The only exception is when you lock the Video track (see the section "Advanced Timeline Editing" later in this chapter).
- In addition to the Edit menu and the right-click menu, you can use keyboard commands to cut (Ctrl+X), copy (Ctrl+C), and paste (Ctrl+V) files.

To split clips:

1. Use Player controls or the Timeline Scrubber to move the edit line to the initial frame of the desired second clip (**Figure 7.34**).
2. To split the clip, do one of the following:
   - ▲ Click the razorblade icon atop the Movie Window.
   - ▲ Positioning the pointer over the selected clip, right-click and choose Split clip (**Figure 7.35**).
   - ▲ Press the Insert key.

   Studio splits the clips at the edit line (**Figure 7.36**).

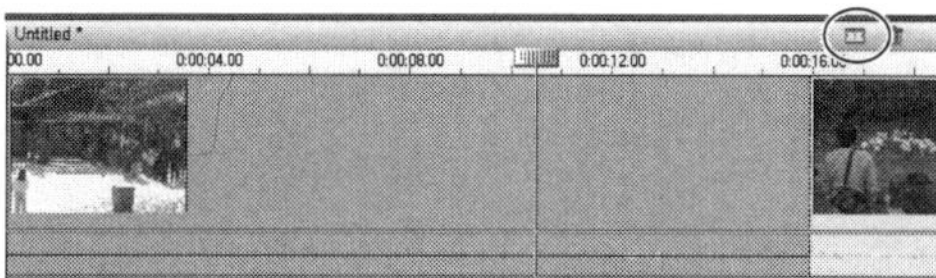

Figure 7.34 To split a clip, move the edit line to the desired location and click the razorblade icon.

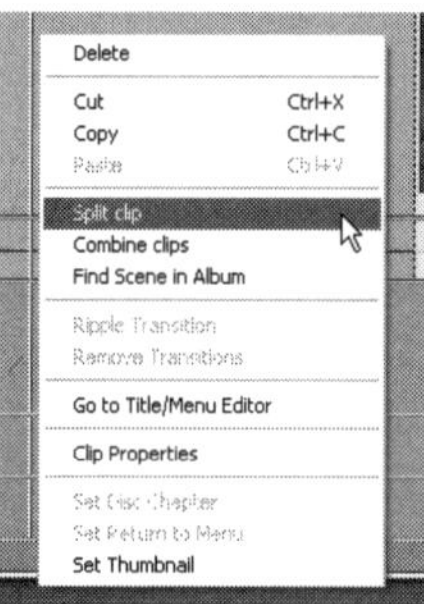

Figure 7.35 Or, for you right-click fans, choose Split clip.

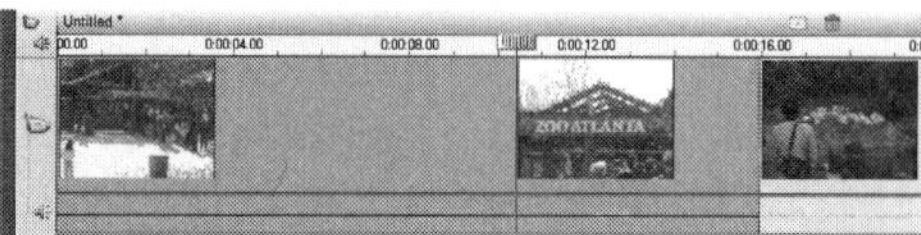

Figure 7.36 Either way, you now have two clips where formerly there was none.

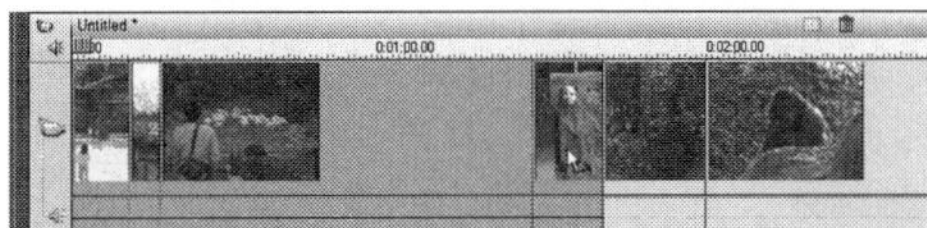

Figure 7.37 To combine scenes, hold down the Shift key while touching two (or more) clips.

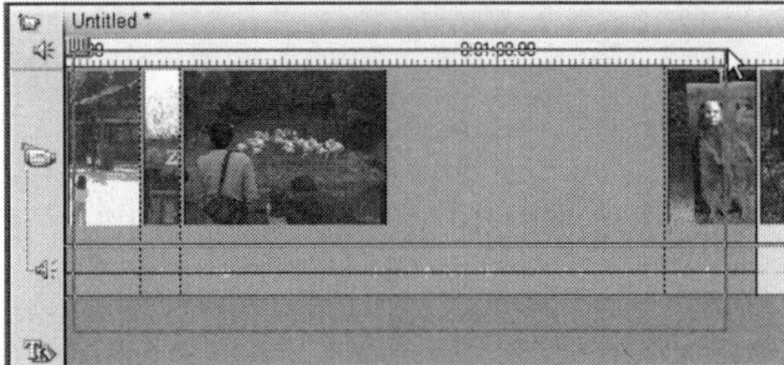

Figure 7.38 You can also drag on the Timeline to include the desired clips...

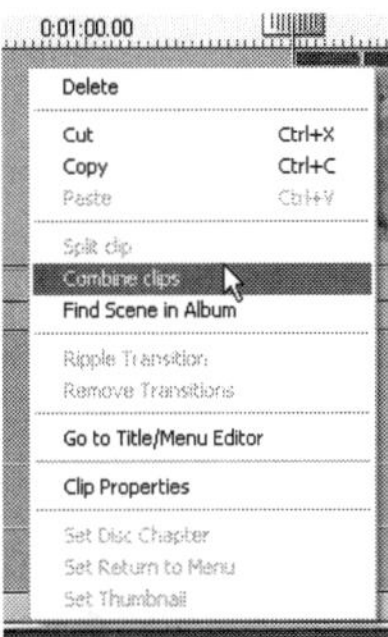

Figure 7.39 ...then right-click and choose Combine clips.

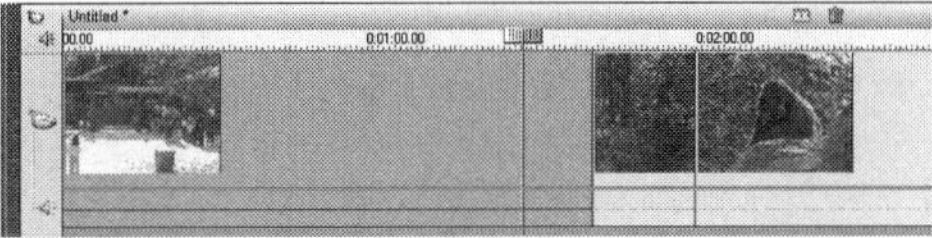

Figure 7.40 The clips are combined.

To combine scenes:

1. To select the scenes to combine, do one of the following:
   - ▲ Holding down the Shift or Ctrl key, use the pointer to select two or more scenes (**Figure 7.37**).
   - ▲ Starting with the pointer over a gray area (and not a scene) in the Storyboard or Timeline, click and drag to select all scenes under the marquee (**Figure 7.38**).
   - ▲ From the Studio menu, choose Edit > Select All to select all scenes in the Storyboard or the Timeline.
   - ▲ Press Ctrl+A to select all scenes on all pages of the Album.
2. Position the pointer over one of the selected scenes, then right-click and choose Combine clips (**Figure 7.39**).

   Studio combines all selected scenes (**Figure 7.40**).

✔ Tips

- If you select noncontiguous scenes from the same or different capture file, Studio ignores these selections and combines only the contiguous scenes. To help you in this process, Studio identifies contiguous scenes with a dotted vertical line between them on the Timeline (Figure 7.38).
- You can't combine two scenes if transitions have been inserted between them, even if they are contiguous. To combine them, delete the transition.
- You can't combine scenes if you've trimmed any frames from the beginning or end of either scene. To combine, restore each scene to its original length.

To change the thumbnail image:

1. Use Player controls or the Timeline Scrubber to move the edit line to the desired thumbnail image (**Figure 7.41**).
2. Position the pointer over the selected clip, then right-click and choose Set Thumbnail (**Figure 7.42**).

   Studio sets the new thumbnail image (**Figure 7.43**).

✔ Tips

- Setting a new thumbnail in the Movie Window doesn't reset the thumbnail in the Album. It also doesn't set it as the thumbnail for use when making your DVD.
- To reset the thumbnail to the original location, Undo doesn't work, even though it appears as an option in the usual spot, under Edit. You'll need to move the Scrubber to the original location and repeat Step 2.

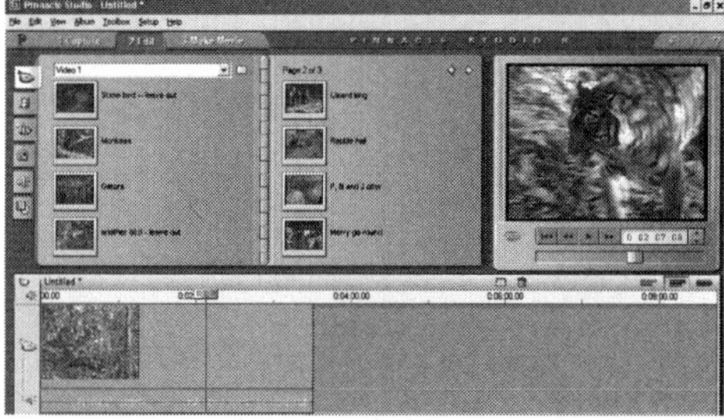

Figure 7.41 A thumbnail should tell you what's in a scene at a glance. If yours doesn't, change it by touching the clip with the pointer and moving to a better frame.

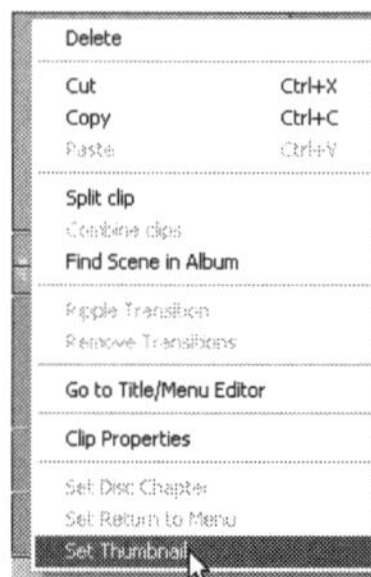

Figure 7.42 Then right-click and choose Set Thumbnail.

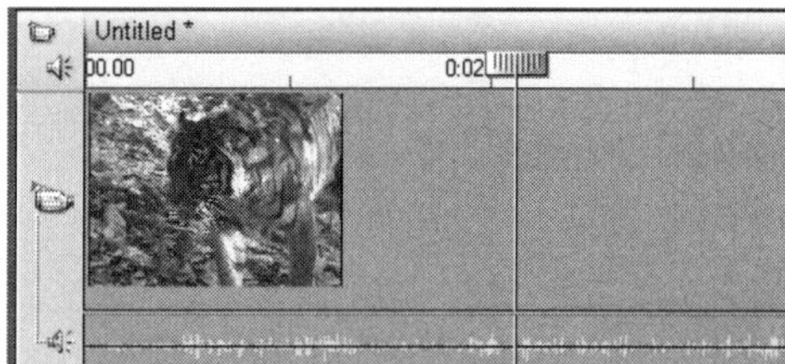

Figure 7.43 The new thumbnail. No problem telling what's in this video now.

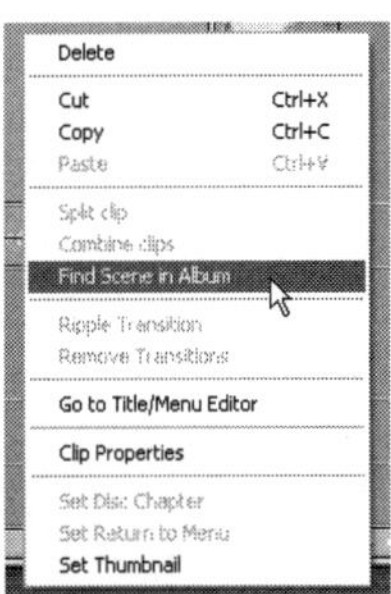

Figure 7.44 If you ever need to find the clip you're editing back in the Album, touch the clip, then right-click and choose Find Scene in Album.

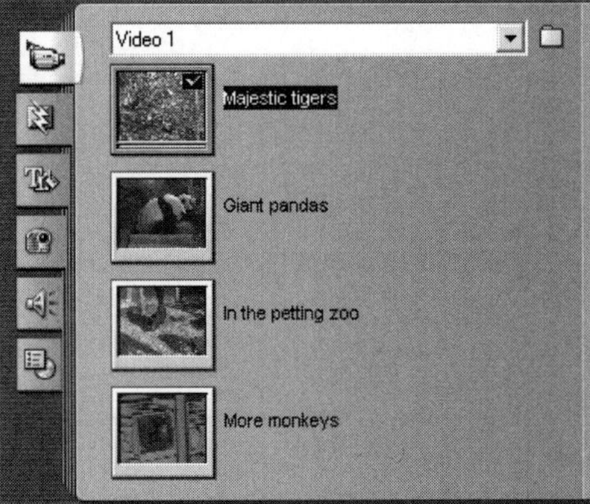

Figure 7.45 Studio locates the scene, even if it's in a different video clip.

To find a scene in the Album while in the Movie Window:

1. With the pointer, touch the scene you desire to locate.
2. Right-click and choose Find Scene in Album (**Figure 7.44**).

   Studio opens the Album to the page containing the scene and highlights the scene and scene comments (**Figure 7.45**). If another video file is loaded, Studio loads the necessary video clip to locate the scene.

Trimming with the Clip Properties Tool

Trimming video is the process of removing unwanted frames from the beginning and end of your captured scenes, often referred to as the *heads* and *tails*. Since this is probably the most common editing activity, Studio's Clip Properties tool (**Figure 7.46**), a mechanism for trimming your clips, is accessible in all three Movie Window views. See **Table 7.1** for a list of the controls of the Clip Properties tool.

As discussed later, you can also trim your videos directly on the Timeline, although generally you have greater precision with the Clip Properties tool.

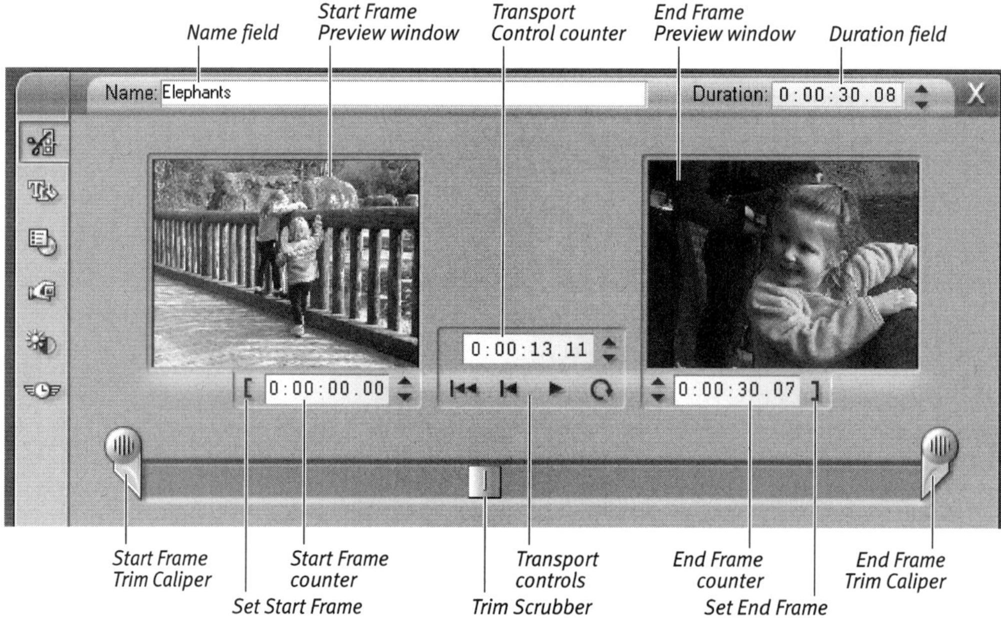

Figure 7.46 The Clip Properties tool is great for precision trimming of video, still image, and audio files.

Table 7.1

Controls in the Clip Properties Tool	
Name field	Contains the scene name specified in the Album.
Duration field	Displays video duration with new start and end frames.
Start Frame Preview Window	Displays the currently selected start frame.
End Frame Preview Window	Displays the currently selected end frame.
Transport controls	Like the Trim Scrubber, can be used to move loaded video to any desired frame, or can play back the trimmed clip.
Transport Control counter	Displays current edit point in video.
Set Start Frame	Sets the start frame to the current edit point.
Start Frame counter	In standard hours:minutes:seconds:frame format, displays the current start frame location. You can select the desired start frame by entering time code directly, or by adjusting the start frame position using the jog controls to the right.
Set End Frame	Sets the end frame to the current edit point.
End Frame counter	In standard hours:minutes:seconds:frame format, displays the current end frame location. You can select the desired end frame by entering time code directly, or by adjusting the end frame position using jog controls to the right.
Start Frame Trim Caliper	Shows the location of the currently selected start frame. Can be dragged to desired location.
Trim Scrubber	Reflects the edit point of the currently loaded video. Can be used to drag video to any desired frame, for setting as the start or end frame using the appropriate icon or keyboard command. As you scrub through the video, frames display in the Player window to the right of the Clip Properties tool, not in the Start or End Frame Preview windows. These displays only change as you move the Trim Calipers or the clocks beneath them.
End Frame Trim Caliper	Shows the location of the currently selected end frame. Can be dragged to desired location.

To open the Clip Properties tool:

- Do either of the following:
  - ▲ Double-click the video you wish to trim.
  - ▲ Select a clip with the pointer, and click the camcorder icon at the top left of the Movie Window (**Figure 7.47**).

  Studio opens the Video Toolbox, which contains the Clip Properties tool. If it doesn't open to the Clip Properties tool, click the scissors icon at the upper-left corner of the screen to open it.

  If you haven't yet trimmed the clips, the tool opens with the start frame time set to 0:00:00.00 and the end frame time set to the final frame of the clip. If you have trimmed the clip, the values will be those set in the previous session.

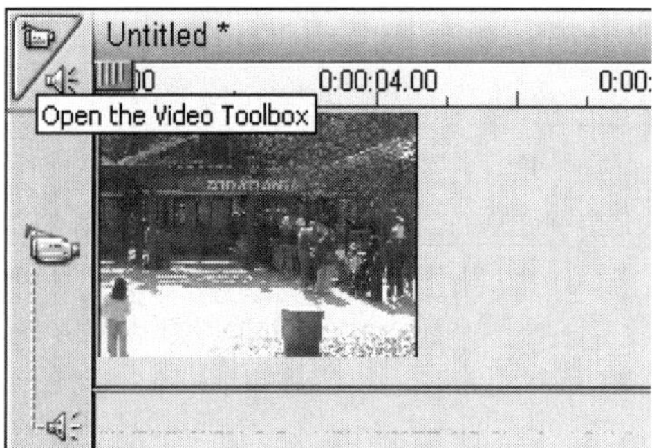

Figure 7.47 Click the camcorder icon to open the Clip Properties tool for video or still images.

Figure 7.48 The fastest way to set the start frame is with the Start Frame Trim Caliper.

Figure 7.49 Or, you can use the Transport controls to find the perfect frame and click the Set Start Frame icon.

To set a new start frame:

- To set a new start frame and trim frames from the beginning of a clip, do one of the following:
  - ▲ Click the Start Frame Trim Caliper and drag it to the desired start frame (**Figure 7.48**).
  - ▲ Enter the desired start frame in the Start Frame counter either manually or via the jog controls.

  Studio immediately sets the new start frame, shifting to the left all videos placed after the edited clip to close any gaps on the Timeline.

Or

1. Move the Trim Scrubber to the desired start frame by doing one of the following:
   - ▲ Manually drag the Trim Scrubber to the desired start frame.
   - ▲ Use the transport controls located in the center of the Clip Properties tool to play or advance the video until it reaches the frame you want.
2. Set the new start frame by doing one of the following:
   - ▲ Click the Set Start Frame icon to the left of the Start Frame counter (**Figure 7.49**).
   - ▲ Press the I (for *in*) key.

To set a new end frame:

- Set a new end frame and trim frames from the end of the clip by doing one of the following:
  - Click the End Frame Trim Caliper and drag it to the desired end frame (**Figure 7.50**).
  - Enter the desired end frame in the End Frame counter either manually or via the jog controls.
  - Enter a new duration in the duration field either manually or by using the jog controls.

  Studio sets the new end frame, shifting to the left all videos placed after the edited clip to close any gaps on the Timeline.

Or

1. Move the Trim Scrubber to the desired end frame by doing one of the following:
   - Click and manually drag it.
   - Use the Transport controls located in the center of the Clip Properties tool.
2. Set the new end frame time by doing one of the following:
   - Click the Set End Frame icon to the right of the End Frame counter.
   - Press the O (for *out*) key.

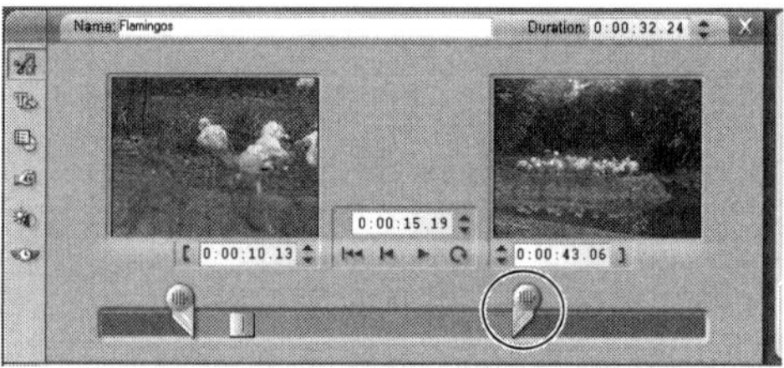

Figure 7.50 To set the end frame, drag the End Frame Trim Caliper to the desired shot.

✔ Tips

- Trimming doesn't impact the actual captured video file in any way. You're not really deleting any frames; you're just telling Studio to use a different start frame and end frame when incorporating the scene into your production. For this reason, you can easily reverse your trims by clicking the Undo icon, or using the steps above to locate new start and end frames.
- Once you're in the Clip Properties tool, you can select additional clips to trim by touching them with the pointer or moving the Timeline Scrubber to another clip.
- If you trim a scene that has many clips after it on the Timeline, Studio has to shift all subsequent clips to the left to eliminate any gaps in the Timeline. Depending on project length, this can cause perceptible delays. To avoid this, trim soon after you place the individual clips in the Timeline rather than waiting until all the clips are in place.
- The Clip Properties tool edits the original audio along with the video.

Planning Your Trimming Activities

Before trimming your clips, consider whether you intend to fade into the first scene, fade out of the final scene, and/or use transitions between the scenes. If you use any of these effects, you need to account for them in your trimming.

Briefly, transitions are animated effects inserted between video scenes to either smooth or emphasize the passage from one clip to the next (for details see Chapter 8). The most commonly used transition is a cut, which is actually the absence of a transition: The video simply jumps from the last frame of the first clip to the first frame of the second clip. Other frequently used transitions are dissolves, wipes, and fades, which you implement using frames that overlap between two clips.

If you were trimming two clips to be joined by a cut, the end frame for your first video would be the last frame you'd like to appear in the production. Similarly, the start frame for the second video would be the initial frame you'd want visible.

For example, in the video mockup shown in **Figure 7.51**, my daughter Whatley is about to start singing a song. In the final production, I want the first viewable frame to be the frame before she starts singing, marked the "Desired start frame" in the figure. Assume that this is the second scene in the video. If I use a cut transition between this and the clip, the desired start frame in Figure 7.51 would be identical to the start frame set in the Clip Properties tool.

Figure 7.51 If you cut between scenes, trim to the desired start frame. If you use a 3-second transition into the scene, add 3 seconds to the front so the desired start frame is the first post-transition frame.

(continued on next page)

Planning Your Trimming Activities *(continued)*

But what happens if I insert a 3-second transition between this and the first clip? If I use the same start frame, the desired start frame gets buried in the transition, and the first completely visible frame after the transition is actually 3 seconds into the scene (desired start plus 3 seconds).

To correct this, I have to leave 3 extra seconds at the front when trimming the clip. Then the desired start frame will be the first clip visible after the transition, which is what I want.

Similarly, if the last frame I wanted visible were the frame where she stopped singing, I would trim to this frame if I planned on using cuts between clips. Otherwise, I would find the desired end point, and then add the length of the transition to the clip before trimming. The same holds true for fading into videos at the start of your production or fading out at the end.

If you forget to plan ahead, it's no biggie, since trimming doesn't actually delete any frames, and you can easily retrim your video to the required lengths. Trimming considerations are more important during capture, because if you don't grab the necessary frames then, you'll have to fire up the old camcorder and recapture the desired scene.

Trimming a Clip on the Timeline

Where trimming with the Clip Properties tool is the ultimate in precision, trimming on the Timeline is generally much quicker and much more interactive with other elements (audio, video, etc.) in your project. Most producers use both tools extensively when crafting their videos.

To trim a single video on the Timeline:

1. Select the clip you wish to trim by placing the pointer over the right edge of the clip.

   The pointer becomes an arrow pointing left (**Figure 7.52**), or a bidirectional arrow if you previously trimmed the clip (**Figure 7.53**).

2. Holding down the left mouse button and watching the video frames displayed in the Player, drag the arrow to the desired end frame.

3. Release the mouse button to set the trim.

   Studio sets the end frame to the new location.

   As soon as you shift a single frame to the left, the single arrow becomes bidirectional, signifying that you can now drag the edge both ways.

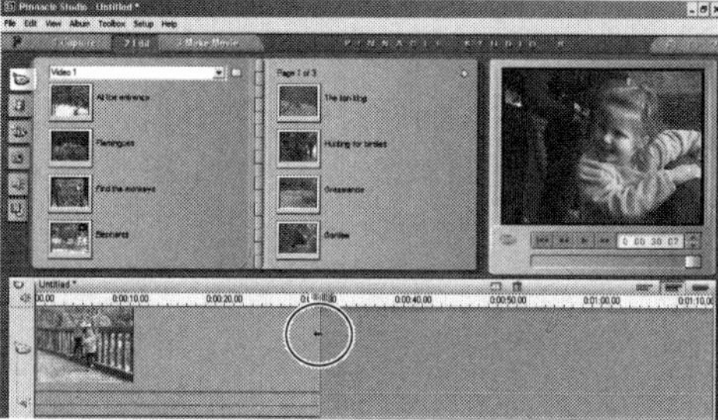

Figure 7.52 Trimming on the Timeline is much faster, but a touch more difficult to get to the desired start and end frames.

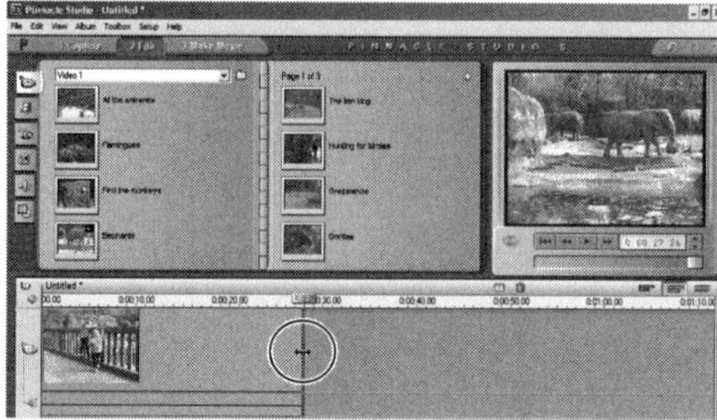

Figure 7.53 The arrow becomes bidirectional when you can edit in both directions.

✔ Tips

- Use the same procedure to trim unwanted frames from the start of a scene. The only difference is that the cursor arrow will initially point to the right.
- Trimming on the Timeline is generally easier when you're zoomed into the project and the Timescale covers a relatively short duration, since grabbing and moving the edge shifts only a few frames at a time. When long stretches of video are showing in the Timeline, grabbing and moving the edge may shift a few seconds at a time, making precise adjustments much more difficult. If you're going to trim on the Timeline, be sure to adjust the Timescale to a comfortable view (see the section "Customizing Your Timeline View" earlier in this chapter).

Trimming Multiple Clips on the Timeline

Studio offers two approaches for trimming when two scenes are adjacent on the Timeline: the ripple edit and the rolling edit. A ripple edit is very much like trimming a single clip on the Timeline; only that clip's duration is changed. However, the effect of the trimming *ripples* through the remainder of the project to compensate for the change in the trimmed clip. That is, if you trim 2 seconds from a clip, you shorten the entire project by 2 seconds. In contrast, in a rolling edit you trim two contiguous scenes simultaneously, such that the duration changes to both clips offset each other and there is no change in overall project duration.

Studio handles ripple editing, the program's default mode, very well, rippling not only the Video track but all other associated tracks as well. This ensures that titles, overlays, and sound effects remain synchronized with the underlying video.

Sometimes, however, you don't want project duration to change each time you trim a video. For example, if you create a narration or Background Music track closely synchronized to a video, a series of ripple edits would likely destroy synchronization. Or, if you committed to delivering exactly 2 minutes of video, ripple edits would make this difficult. For this reason, Studio supports both ripple and rolling edits. Here's how you perform each one.

Figure 7.54 You can also trim clips within the production.

Figure 7.55 The ripple trim affects all clips behind it on the Timeline, reducing duration from 30 minutes to 29 minutes in this example. This can wreak havoc on synchronization with other design elements.

To perform a ripple edit on the Timeline:

1. Select the clip you wish to trim and place the pointer over the right edge of the clip.

   The pointer becomes an arrow pointing left or, in this case, a bidirectional arrow because the clip was previously trimmed (**Figure 7.54**). The project duration is approximately 30 minutes.

2. Holding down the left mouse button and watching the video frames displayed in the Player, drag the arrow to the left to shorten the clip (**Figure 7.55**), or to the right to lengthen the clip.

3. Release the mouse button.

   Studio shortens the clip. The project duration is now approximately 29 minutes, as Studio shifted all clips to the left.

To perform a rolling edit on the Timeline:

1. Pressing either the Ctrl key or the Shift key, use the pointer to select two contiguous clips.
2. Position the pointer over the connection point between the two clips.

   The pointer becomes a bidirectional arrow with a vertical line in the middle (**Figure 7.56**).
3. Holding down the left mouse button, move the pointer to the desired location.
4. Release the mouse button.

   Studio shortens the first clip and extends the second clip backward to fill the gap. The overall project duration remains at approximately 30 minutes.

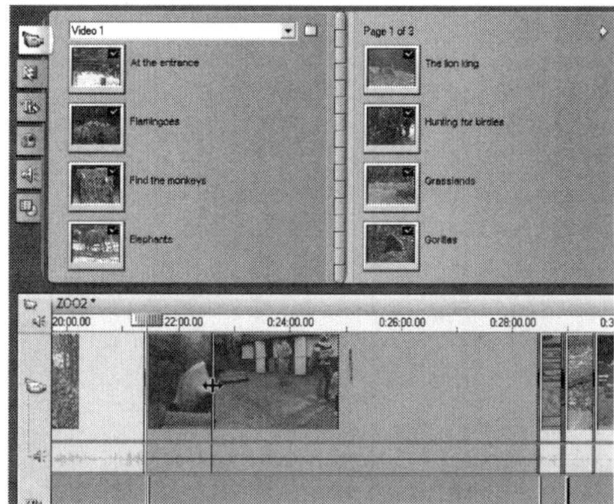

Figure 7.56 Avoid messing up synchronization by using the rolling edit tool, which trims without affecting overall video duration.

Figure 7.57 Like all video trims, your edit can't go beyond the starting or ending point of the original video.

✔ Tips

- Rolling edits are limited to the start and end of the original scene. When Studio reaches this limit, it displays a unidirectional arrow (**Figure 7.57**).
- When performing a rolling edit, Studio displays the start frame of the second video in the Player. Ideally, you would also see the final frame of the first video, but there's no way to display both simultaneously.
- Studio can't perform a rolling edit when there's a transition between the two target clips. To perform the rolling edit, delete the transition, perform the edit, and then reinsert the transition.

Advanced Timeline Editing

OK, you've worked through Timeline 101; now it's time for the advanced course. I've mentioned that in its default state, Studio maintains synchronization of the video file and the original audio file captured with the video, and also uses global ripple edits to maintain the relative position of assets on the Timeline. This works well in most common editing situations, but there are times when you want to undo both defaults. Fortunately, through the use of *locked tracks,* Studio allows just that.

When a track is locked, all the assets on the track are locked, and edits that would normally affect these assets have no effect on them. Lock the Video track, for example, and you can delete the Original Audio track and keep the Video track. Similarly, if you lock the Title Overlay track, you can add, trim, or delete video clips and the titles stay in place.

Locked tracks enable some interesting edits that can add a professional touch to any production. One example is the *insert edit.* Maintaining the same audio track for continuity, I could insert a short video of my children walking among some trees into a video of a tiger prowling through a different set of trees. Probably won't fool the grandparents into thinking my kids are at risk, but it could be fun to try. A more typical use of a locked track is the *cutaway shot,* where, for example, if you were filming a training session, you might insert a short shot of people in the audience laughing and applauding. Here's how it all works.

To lock a Timeline track:

1. Hold the pointer over any of the track indicators, such as the camcorder icon, at the left of the Timeline (**Figure 7.58**).

   The track indicator becomes a button.

2. Click the button.

   Studio locks the track, placing a small red padlock icon below the track indicator, as shown in the Title Overlay track in Figure 7.58.

   To unlock the track, simply press the button again.

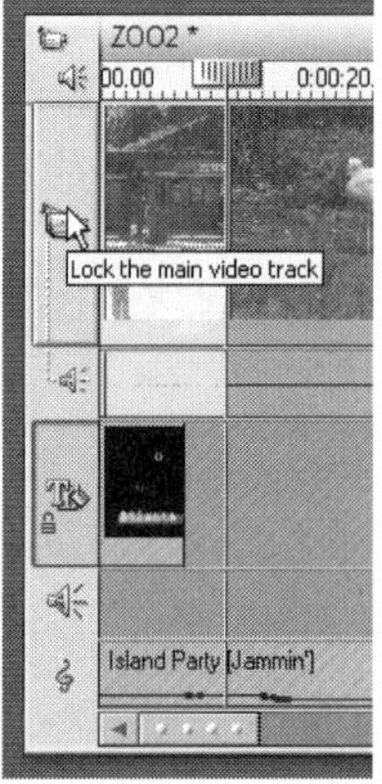

Figure 7.58 Lock the Video track by clicking the camcorder icon.

To delete the original audio from a video clip:

1. Lock the Video track (**Figure 7.59**).
2. Hold the pointer over the audio clip to select it, and delete it by doing one of the following:
   - ▲ Press the Delete key.
   - ▲ From the Studio menu, choose Edit > Delete.
   - ▲ Right-click and choose Delete.

   Studio deletes the original audio file, clearing the waveform from the track (**Figure 7.60**).

Figure 7.59 The red padlock indicates the track's locked status.

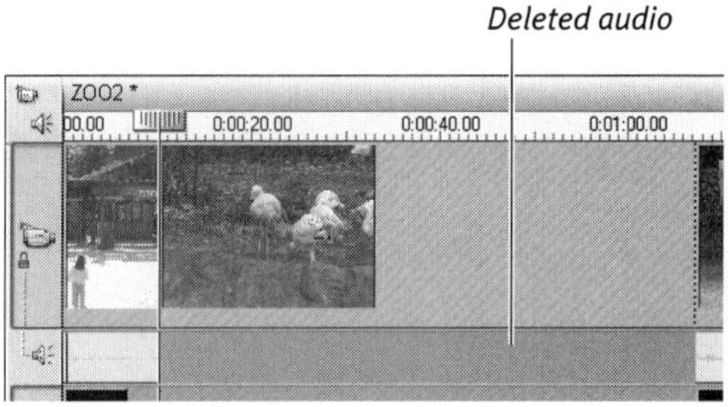

Deleted audio

Figure 7.60 Lock the Video track to delete the original audio from the project.

Figure 7.61 To insert video into another clip while retaining the same audio, start by locking the Audio track.

Figure 7.62 Then clear a gap for the new video. Position the edit line at the desired start point and click the razorblade icon to split the clip once.

Figure 7.63 Next, move to the desired end point, and split the clip again to create a section you can delete.

Figure 7.64 Hold the pointer over the unwanted segment and delete it. You should see a gap like that shown above.

To perform an insert edit:

1. To insert video into a clip without affecting audio, first lock the Audio track (**Figure 7.61**).
2. Move the edit line to the point you wish to insert the second video clip, and split the clip by doing one of the following:
   - ▲ Click the razorblade icon atop the Movie Window (Figure 7.34).
   - ▲ Positioning the pointer over the selected clip, right-click and choose Split clip (Figure 7.35).
   - ▲ Press the Insert key.

   Studio splits the clip into two parts (**Figure 7.62**).
3. Move the edit line to the approximate point you want the inserted clip to end, and create another split (**Figure 7.63**).
4. Hold the pointer over the segment you wish to replace, and delete it by doing one of the following:
   - ▲ Press the Delete key.
   - ▲ From the Studio menu, choose Edit > Delete.
   - ▲ Right-click and choose Delete.

   Studio deletes the segment (**Figure 7.64**).

(continued on next page)

5. Drag the segment you wish to insert from the Album into the gap created by the deleted segment.

   Studio inserts the segment (**Figure 7.65**).

   If the new segment is too large for the slot you created, Studio fits it into the slot. You can then use the trimming tools discussed earlier to resize all elements of the composite clip.

   If the new segment is too small for the slot you created, manually close the gap by dragging the original clip segments to the edge of the inserted scene.

Figure 7.65 Now drag in the desired segment. Oops, it's too small; just drag the edges from the original clip to close the gaps.

Figure 7.66 Oops. Track is locked. No can edit.

✔ Tips

- To insert audio in the Original Audio track, use the same procedure as with the Video track, except lock the Video track and cut the audio tracks. Of course, you can also drag the intended audio insertion to either of the other tracks, and then mute the Original Audio track (see Chapter 11).
- It's much easier to insert a still image into the video: Just drag it to the Title Overlay track and resize it as discussed later in "To change the duration of a still image on the Timeline." Unless the image is a specially prepared overlay image (see Chapter 9), the image will replace the video during playback.
- You can lock any track or combination of tracks except the Menu track that appears when you're creating DVD menus.
- It's good practice to unlock the track immediately after performing any edits that require locked tracks. Otherwise, when you try to select the Video track later, nothing will happen and you'll see an error message (**Figure 7.66**).

Figure 7.67 To create an L-cut, where the audio from the first video lingers when the video from the second video appears, trim the first video back to the last video frame you want to appear.

Producing Split Edits

Split edits are transitions where the audio and video start playing at different times. There are two basic types of split ends.

In an *L-cut*, the audio from the first video continues while the second video starts playing. The classic use is in newscasts, when the video switches from the anchor to a reporter on the scene. To make the transition feel seamless, the audio of the anchor asking a question continues to play while the video switches to a field reporter, usually nodding sagely to acknowledge the wisdom of the question.

In a *J-cut*, the audio from the second video precedes the appearance of the actual frames. In the example below, my daughter Whatley exclaimed at the start of the panda exhibit, "Look, there's a giant teddy bear." Using an L-cut, I played the audio to introduce the next scene while still playing the previous video. Though all this may sound complicated, Studio makes short work of both kinds of edits.

To create an L-cut:

1. Working with two contiguous clips on the Timeline, touch the first clip.
2. Move the pointer over the connection point between the two clips.

   The pointer becomes an arrow pointing left, or a bidirectional arrow if you previously trimmed the clip.
3. Holding down the left mouse button and watching the video frames displayed in the Player, drag the arrow to the left until you reach the last frame you wish to display (**Figure 7.67**).

(continued on next page)

4. Hold the pointer over the camcorder icon on the Video track, then click the camcorder button to lock the Video track.
5. Use the pointer to select the audio track from the first clip.
6. Hold the pointer over the connection line between the two clips, being careful to avoid the blue horizontal line (which is the volume control) in the middle of the audio clips; holding the pointer over the line converts the pointer to a speaker icon, which changes volume, something you don't want to do here (**Figure 7.68**).

   The pointer becomes a bidirectional arrow (**Figure 7.69**).
7. Drag the audio file to the right, to the desired start point of the audio from the second clip.

   Studio extends the audio from the first clip under the video of the second clip, forming the namesake *L* appearance (**Figure 7.70**).

✔ Tip

- If, during Step 6, you accidentally touch the blue horizontal volume control, you may inadvertently adjust the track volume. If so, you'll see a small blue dot in the middle of the line. You can undo this by choosing Undo from the Edit menu, or by using the Undo icon in the upper-right corner, or by pressing Ctrl+Z.

  If you've already performed some additional edits that you don't wish to undo, you can touch the blue dot with the pointer (which becomes a speaker icon when placed over the Audio track) and drag it straight down, thus deleting the dot. (See Chapter 11 for more on audio.)

Figure 7.68 When dragging the Audio track, select anywhere but the middle line, which is the volume control and produces a speaker icon.

Figure 7.69 To drag the audio to the right, select the audio at the connection line, converting the pointer into a bidirectional arrow.

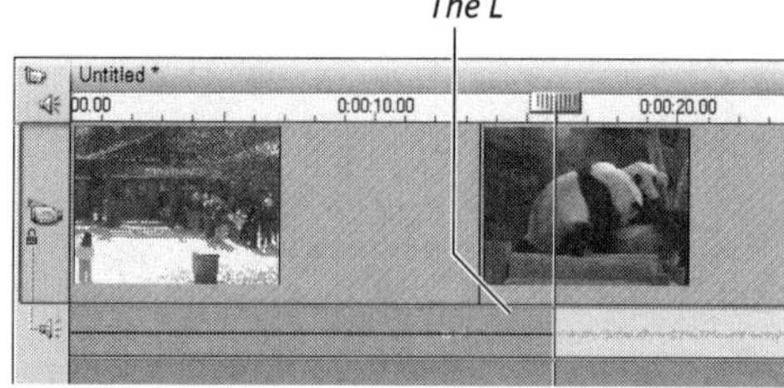

Figure 7.70 Then just drag the audio to the right, creating the *L* pattern.

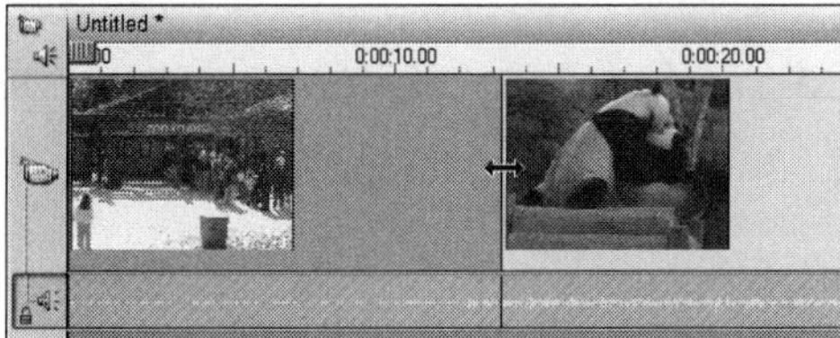

Figure 7.71 Lock the Audio track to produce the J-cut.

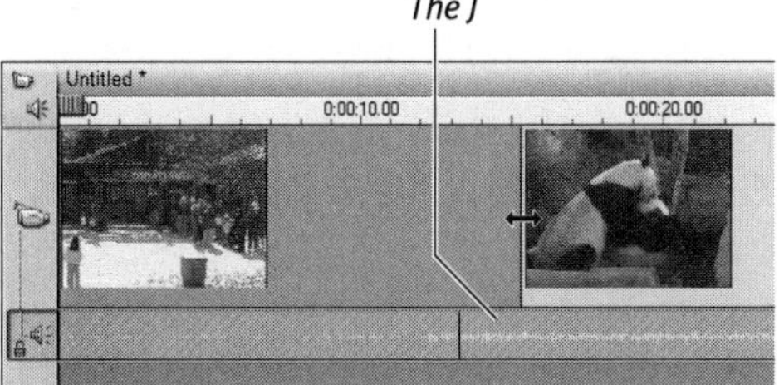

Figure 7.72 Then drag the first video to the right, producing the *J* pattern.

To create a J-cut:

1. Working with two contiguous clips on the Timeline, hold the pointer over the first clip.
2. Move the pointer over the connection point between the two clips.

   The pointer becomes an arrow pointing left, or a bidirectional arrow if you previously trimmed the clip.
3. Holding down the left mouse button and watching the video frames displayed in the Player, drag the arrow to the left until you reach the last frame you wish to display.
4. Click the speaker icon on the Original Audio track indicator to lock the track (**Figure 7.71**).
5. Use the pointer to select the first video clip.
6. Hold the pointer over the connection line between the two video clips.

   The pointer becomes a bidirectional arrow.
7. Drag the first video to the right, to the desired start point of the video from the second clip (**Figure 7.72**).

   Studio extends the video from the first clip over the audio from the second clip, forming the namesake *J* appearance.

Working with Still Images in the Movie Window

Studio handles images in two completely different ways depending on where you drop the file. Drop an image in the Title Overlay track, and it can serve as the background for a DVD menu or contain a logo or watermark to blend into the Video track. (Such uses are covered in Chapter 9 and Chapter 10.)

This section covers images that are dragged into the Video track to serve as the foreground video, usually in the form of a slide show. In this role, Studio treats image files almost identically to video files, except there are no duration limits or associated audio files. Accordingly, all the techniques described above for getting videos into the Movie Window, moving them around, trimming on the Timeline, and splitting and deleting them, apply equally to still images. There are just a couple of differences to note.

First, you set the default duration for all images inserted into your projects in the Pinnacle Studio Setup Options box, using a process described in Chapter 2 under "Setting Default Durations." This section also explains two ways to modify the default duration and how to create a slide show.

Figure 7.73 You can change the duration of a still image file.

To change the duration of a still image on the Timeline:

1. Do either of the following:
   - ▲ Trim on the Timeline using the techniques discussed for video files earlier in this chapter.
   - ▲ Launch the Clip Properties tool by selecting the still image with the pointer and clicking on the camcorder icon at the top left of the Movie Window (Figure 7.47).

   Studio opens the Video Toolbox.

   If you don't see the Clip Properties tool, click the scissors icon at the upper-left corner of the screen to open it.
2. At the upper-right corner of the tool, adjust duration by typing a new value in the duration field or by using the jog controls to the right (**Figure 7.73**).

To create a slide show:

1. Start with the Movie Window in Storyboard view and the Album window open to the Still Images tab.
2. Do one of the following:
   - ▲ Drag images one by one into the Storyboard.
   - ▲ To select all images in the Still Images tab and drag them to the Storyboard, choose Edit > Select All from the Studio menu or press Ctrl+A (**Figure 7.74**).

   A bug in Studio (through version 8.3.18) prevents the selection of multiple images by holding down the Shift or Ctrl key or by dragging a marquee.

   Once you're in the Storyboard, add, delete, and arrange the images as desired via drag and drop (see the steps under "To arrange assets in Storyboard view," earlier).

Figure 7.74 To select all the clips in the Still Images tab, choose Edit > Select All (or Ctrl+A).

✔ Tip

- For the ultimate in professional-looking slide shows, learn how to insert a ripple transition between images in Chapter 8.

Working with Audio Files in the Movie Window

Studio includes many different methods to capture and integrate audio into your production. Whether you're ripping music from a CD, adding a narration track, or creating background music from SmartSound, Studio places the results directly into the Timeline for you—no muss, no fuss. (These activities are covered in Chapter 11.) On the other hand, if you're using audio files you previously produced, you'll have to import them into the Album (see the section "Working in the Sound Effects Tab" in Chapter 6), and then get them to the Timeline.

Studio treats audio files almost identically to video files and still images, with exceptions noted in the sidebar, "Tracking the Audio Tracks." Otherwise, all the techniques described earlier for getting videos into the Movie Window, moving them around, trimming on the Timeline, and splitting and deleting them, apply to audio files.

This section takes a quick look at the Audio Clip Properties tool, demonstrates how to load only the Audio track from a captured video file into a project, and describes where to drag your audio files (see the sidebar, "Tracking the Audio Tracks").

To change the duration of an audio file on the Timeline:

1. Do one of the following:
   - ▲ Trim on the Timeline using the techniques for video files discussed earlier.
   - ▲ Launch the Clip Properties tool by selecting the audio file with the pointer and clicking on the speaker icon on the top left of the Movie Window (**Figure 7.75**).

   Studio opens the Video Toolbox.

   If you don't see the Audio Clip Properties tool, click the scissors icon at the upper-left corner of the screen to open it.
2. To adjust the start and end points of the audio file, use the controls described in the section "Trimming with the Clip Properties Tool" earlier in this chapter (Figure 7.46).

   Note in particular that most CDs have several seconds of blank space at the end of each clip. To avoid this gap in your production, trim this space as shown in **Figure 7.76**.

   For how to fade out of an audio clip, see Chapter 8.

Figure 7.75 Click here to open the Audio Clip Properties tool.

Figure 7.76 A little night music to add to our video project. Note the dead air at the end, present in many CD audio clips, that we're trimming out.

To add only the audio from a video file:

- ◆ From the Video Scenes tab in the Album window, drag a video file to either the Sound Effect and Voice-Over track or the Background Music track.

  Studio inserts only the audio from the video file. See Chapter 11 for more on audio.

✔ Tip

- ■ Studio lets you drag an audio file into a clip in Storyboard and Text views. However, since there is no indicator of duration, results are unpredictable, so you should work with audio in Timeline view.

Tracking the Audio Tracks

Here are some rules of the road for Studio's audio tracks. (Also see Chapter 11 for much more on audio.)

- To add an audio file to your production, drag it to either the Sound Effect and Voice-Over track or the Background Music track. Be careful, however, if you intend to use Studio's narration recording, CD-ripping, or SmartSound Background Music track features, which require that a specific track be open for the files they produce. For narration recording, the Sound Effect and Voice-Over track must be open; for CD-ripping and SmartSound, the Background Music track must be open.

  If you've dragged an audio file in the Sound Effect track, for example, you won't be able to record a narration track for that segment.
- To add the Audio track from a captured video file to your production—without the video—drag it to either the Sound Effect and Voice-Over track or the Background Music track.
- Studio prevents you from adding an audio file to the Original Audio track if the original audio is present. If you delete the original audio file, however, Studio lets you add the track (see "To delete the original audio from a video clip," earlier).
- Studio lets you place audio files anywhere in a production, even if it creates a gap in the playback audio. Be careful to avoid these unintended gaps when you place audio files.
- If you drag one audio file into another, Studio always trims the clip you're dragging. This makes it easy to accidentally truncate a clip by dragging it into another. (With video files, dragging doesn't trim a clip at all; you have to activate the trim handles.)

8

Using Transitions

Transitions are effects placed between video clips to help smooth the transition from one scene to another. We've all seen transitions, even if we didn't know them by that name. In movies, for example, when the screen fades to black at the end of a dramatic scene, then fades back in from black to the next scene, it's a *fade* transition. When two scenes blend together for a moment before the second scene appears clearly, it's a *dissolve* transition.

On *Monday Night Football,* when the halftime stats swing back, down, and under, revealing Al and John, that's a transition, too. However, in most film and television productions, the most frequent transition is a *cut,* which is actually the absence of a transition, or the instantaneous jump from the last frame of the first clip to the first frame of the second.

Studio 8 provides three transition collections: Standard Transitions, Alpha Magic, and Hollywood FX for Studio. This chapter describes each group, discusses when to use them, and then explains how to apply and customize them.

Looking in the Box

You access the three transition groups from the Transitions tab of the Album, opened by clicking the lightning bolt icon on the left panel of the Album (**Figure 8.1**). To define how these transitions work, the first video will be called Video A, and the second, Video B.

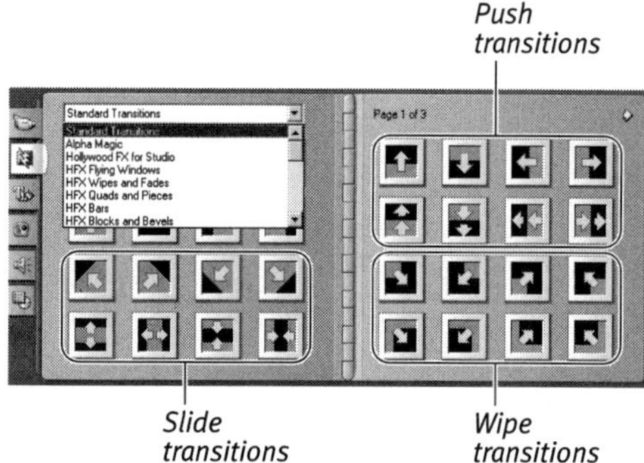

Figure 8.1 You access the Transitions tab by clicking the lightning bolt icon. Note how Studio differentiates between push, slide, and wipe transitions in the Standard Transitions group.

Standard Transitions. As you would expect, the Standard Transitions group includes the common transitions used in most video editing. In addition to the dissolves and fades discussed above, the Standard group includes the following types of transitions:

- *Wipes.* Both Videos A and B remain fixed, while an effect hides Video A and reveals Video B. Imagine you're pulling down a shade between two videos. With a wipe, both videos would remain static, and the shade would simply hide Video A and reveal Video B. In Studio's Transitions tab, any transition with an arrow that appears to be pulling Video B over Video A, with the arrow visible in both videos, is a wipe.
- *Slides.* Video B slides in over Video A. With the shade example, Video B would be playing on the shade and slowly appear, bottom first, as you pulled the shade down. As with a wipe, Video A remains static and is simply covered up by Video B. In Studio's Transitions tab, any transition with an arrow that appears to be pushing Video B over Video A, with the arrow contained completely in Video B, is a slide.

Figure 8.2 My favorite among the Alpha Magic wipes, the puzzle transition, is perfect for that murder-mystery movie you're planning to make.

Figure 8.3 Hollywood FX transitions are plentiful, but most aren't free. Those with *Plus* and *PRO* on them have watermarks that you can eliminate only by upgrading.

- *Pushes.* Video B pushes Video A off the screen. If you were pulling down a shade between two videos, Video B would push Video A down, very much like a slide, except that Video A doesn't get covered up; it gets pushed off the screen. In Studio's Transitions tab, any transition with two arrows moving in the same direction is a push.

The Standard Transitions collection includes many other transitions not characterized in these three major groups, so you should definitely explore what else is there. Just click the white arrows on the top of each page to navigate to the next page.

Alpha Magic. Technically, Alpha Magic transitions are wipes that use organic forms as masks to create the effect. In plain English, they're generally more artistic than the standard transitions and often more whimsical, like the puzzle transition shown in **Figure 8.2.**

Hollywood FX. All transitions in the Hollywood FX for Studio collection are yours to use as you wish. However, most transitions in the Hollywood FX collections below this are watermarked, meaning you can experiment with and potentially buy them to use them in a production. For example, in **Figure 8.3**, most of the transitions are marked with Plus/PRO or simply PRO, indicating that you'll have to upgrade to remove the watermarks.

Currently, the Plus upgrade costs $49.99, while the Pro upgrade, which includes all Plus effects, costs $99.99. The next section discusses when it makes sense to purchase these.

✔ Tip

- To see how a transition looks, touch it with your pointer and it will play in the Player window.

Understanding Transitions

Few things in life are more irritating than a production peppered with different transitions used frequently and randomly, exhibited the way an eight-year-old would show off his baseball card collection. Why do some video makers use transitions this way? Because they can.

Now that you know what to avoid, how do you get a sense of the right approach for using transitions? Probably the easiest way is to find a production that you'd like your project to emulate. If you're planning a serious production like a movie, note that few directors use any transitions other than cuts, dissolves, and fades.

Appropriately, the director lets the content tell the story, using transitions to move quickly between shots in a scene, to show the passage of time, or to highlight the end of one scene and the start of another. In this role, transitions are not content, but tools that enhance the footage.

At the other end of the spectrum, think of the old TV series *The Gong Show* or *Rowan and Martin's Laugh-In* (boy, am I dating myself), or, for you parents, the videos by The Wiggles. Here transitions are content, designed to promote and sustain the mood of the underlying video.

Somewhere in between are productions like *Monday Night Football* or the evening news, which use more exotic transitions to accomplish different editorial goals. For example, a news broadcast might have a transition between the anchor and a field reporter by showing both onscreen at the same time.

My Transition Usage Guide

I should start by stating that none of my movies have gone Hollywood, and I don't have a film school degree. In addition, most videos I create are family oriented, and my goal is making watchable videos, not artsy fare or an MTV-like production. My typical video might be six months in the life of the family Ozer, usually encompassing multiple events like a holiday, a birthday, and a significant visit.

All that said, here are the guidelines I follow to create coherent, enjoyable videos:

- I slowly fade into every major event, usually with a title identifying it.
- Each event may have multiple major scenes. For example, Thanksgiving may have Wednesday arrivals and festivities, then cooking for the big dinner, then the feast itself, then the party after the dinner. Within each scene, I use cuts between most shots.
- Between major scenes within an event, I use a transition to cue the viewer that a time shift is occurring. If the time shift is minor, like the break between eating time and after-dinner festivities, I would probably use a dissolve. I may also throw in a "motivated" transition or two, like a clock wipe between cooking and eating, just to let viewers know that time is passing. If the time shift is major, say from Wednesday night to Thursday morning, I may use a quick fade-out and then fade back in.
- I use a slow fade-out at the end of each event.
- For birthday parties and kid events, I get a bit more experimental and use the Hollywood FX transitions.

Similarly, when a *Monday Night Football* broadcast switches from the first-quarter stats back to the action, it detaches the stat graphic, then swings it out and under Video B to highlight the dramatic change from dry statistics to live play.

The trick in all these cases is to match the transition with the intended effect. Don't use a spiral wipe just because you have it; find the appropriate transition and use that.

This is where Hollywood FX comes in. Pinnacle offers some alluring transitions in the Basic pack, which is freely accessible to Studio 8 users. Some of my favorites are the *page peel*, perfect for showing the passage of time, and the *balloon* transition, which sucks the first scene into a balloon and floats it away—perfect for a birthday party.

However, as you'd expect, Pinnacle saves the best of Hollywood FX for the optional Plus and Pro packs. Not only do you get the dual onscreen news and *Monday Night Football*–type transitions discussed above, you get a boatload of other effects. Even better, Studio provides extraordinary fine-tuning options, enabling a high degree of customization.

If your productions warrant the frequent use of transitions, explore the Hollywood FX samples and consider upgrading to the Plus or Pro pack.

Using Transitions

The next few pages cover the basics of transitions. Once you've mastered these, you'll be ready to move on to the subsequent sections that illuminate advanced topics: customizing transitions, working with Hollywood FX transitions, and using ripple transitions for slide shows.

To set the default transition duration:

1. Choose Setup > Edit to open the Studio Setup Options screen to the Edit tab (**Figure 8.4**).
2. Change the Transitions default duration value to the desired setting by doing one of the following:
   - ▲ Use the jog controls (up and down triangles) to the right of the duration.
   - ▲ Touch the duration to make it editable and directly enter the desired setting.
3. Click OK to close the dialog.

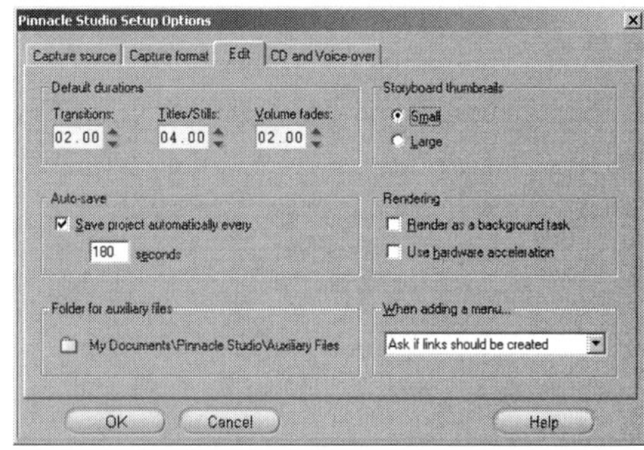

Figure 8.4 Here's where you change the default transition duration.

To identify and preview a transition effect in the Album:

1. If you're in a different panel, click the lightning bolt icon in Edit mode to open the Transitions tab in the Album (Figure 8.1).
2. Hover the pointer over the transition to preview.

   Studio displays the transition name in a callout window (**Figure 8.5**).
3. Touch the transition and it displays in the Player.

   A represents the first clip, while B represents the second. In Figure 8.5 you can see the heart-shaped transition, with Video B opening up into Video A. For use only for weddings and on Valentine's Day, please.

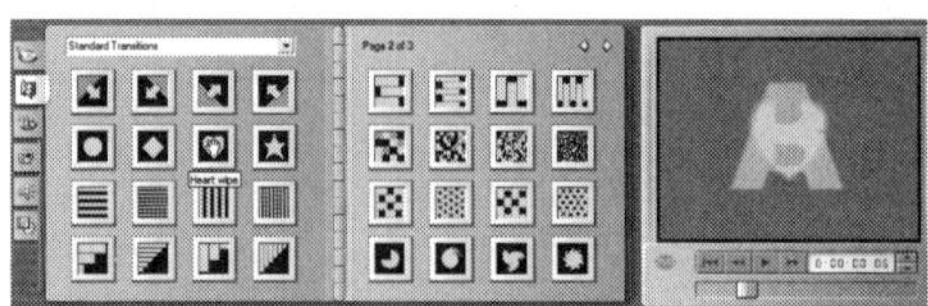

Figure 8.5 Hover your mouse over a transition and Studio tells you its name; touch it and Studio plays it in the Player. Note the Video A/Video B nomenclature in the Player.

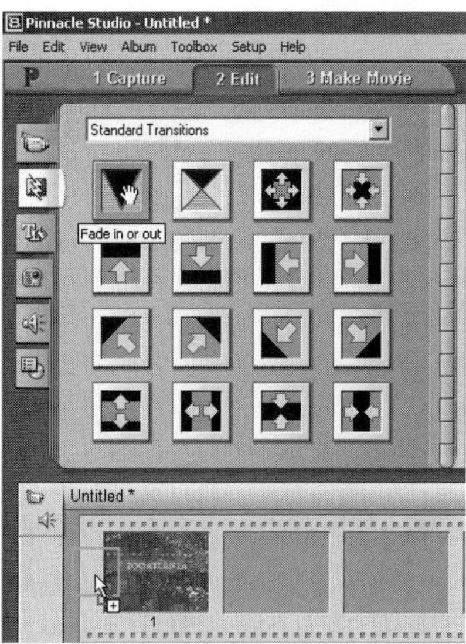

Figure 8.6 To use a transition in a production, just drag and drop it at the desired spot, aided by Studio's visual cues.

Figure 8.7 There you go, fading into a clip.

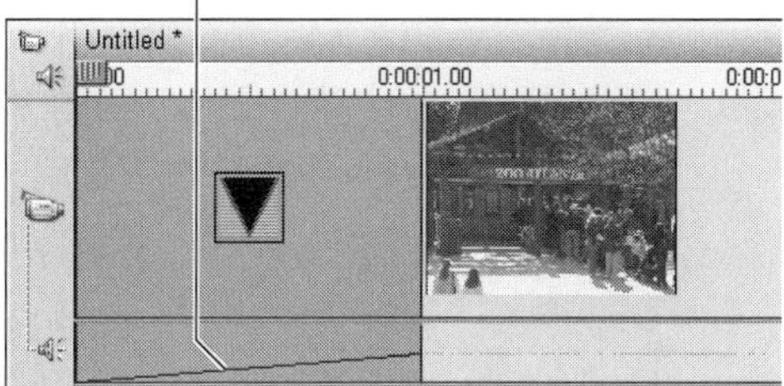

Figure 8.8 Here's the same transition in Timeline view. Note that Studio fades in the audio too, saving you some work.

To fade into or out of a clip:

1. With at least one clip in the Movie Window, drag the fade transition into the Timeline or Storyboard in front of the first clip (to fade in) or behind the last clip (to fade out).

   Studio displays a green box in the Storyboard (**Figure 8.6**), or two vertical green lines in the Timeline, to signify all safe areas for applying the effect. You'll also see a small transparent box and plus sign under the pointer.
2. Release the pointer.

   Studio inserts the fade effect (**Figure 8.7**).

✔ Tips

- You can apply transitions in any Movie Window, though the Storyboard and Timeline views are probably most appropriate. See **Figure 8.8** to see the fade transition shown in Figure 8.7 in the Timeline view.
- Studio also fades the audio component in when it applies a fade effect. This is a great convenience, but if you decide you'd like to do something different with your audio, Chapter 11 discusses how.

To insert a transition between two clips:

1. With at least two clips in the Movie Window, drag any transition between any two clips.

   Studio displays a green box in the Storyboard or two vertical green lines in the Timeline, signifying all the safe areas for applying the effect. Studio also adds a small transparent box and plus sign to the pointer (**Figure 8.9**).

2. Release the pointer.

   Studio inserts the transition (**Figure 8.10**).

Figure 8.9 When you drag a transition between two clips, a box and a plus sign let you know it's safe to drop the transition.

Figure 8.10 The completed dissolve transition.

✔ Tips

- Whenever Studio inserts a transition between two clips, it also inserts a cross-fade between the two audio clips, simultaneously reducing the volume on the first clip from 100 percent to 0 percent and boosting the volume on the second clip from 0 percent to 100 percent, changes reflected on the Audio track in **Figure 8.11**. This is appropriate, given that most transitions help you move smoothly from one scene to another, and audio treatment should follow the video. However, if you want to reverse this effect, and customize your audio treatment, see Chapter 11.

- The only exception to Studio's audio cross-fade approach is during the fade transition, where Studio fades the scene completely to black (or white) before starting to show the second scene. Here, Studio also fades out the old audio completely to zero before boosting audio on the second track (see Figure 8.19). This is appropriate given that fades are generally used to emphasize the ending of one scene and the beginning of another.

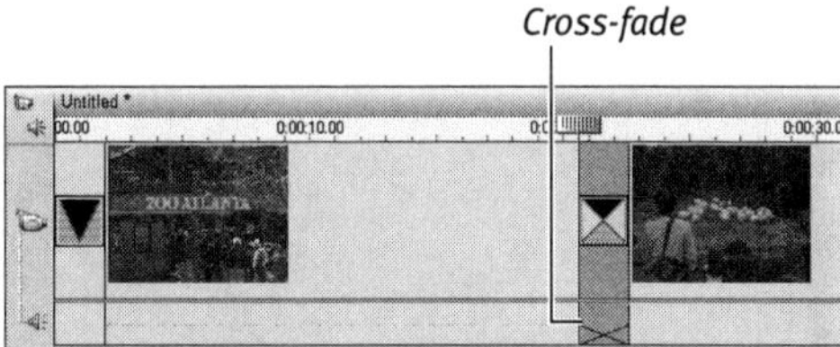

Figure 8.11 The same transition in Timeline view. Note the automatic audio cross-fade.

Figure 8.12 To preview the transition, touch it on the Timeline and click Play.

To preview a Standard or Alpha Magic transition:

1. Touch the transition to make it active.

   In the Storyboard view, the outside outline of the transition turns blue (Figure 8.10), and in the Timeline view the transition is colored blue (**Figure 8.12**), indicating that it's queued for immediate preview.

2. To start the preview, click the Play button in the Player (or press the spacebar or L).

✔ Tip

- Virtually all Standard and Alpha Magic transitions preview in real time, playing both audio and video, so you can immediately determine whether you like the effect. The Hollywood FX transitions are more complicated; many require rendering, which I address in a separate section later.

To fade into or out of a title or other element on the Title Overlay track:

1. With at least one title or other element on the Title Overlay track, drag the fade transition in front of the target (to fade in) or behind the target (to fade out).

   Studio displays a green box in the Storyboard or two vertical green lines in the Timeline, signifying all safe areas for applying the effect. Studio also adds a small transparent box and a plus sign to the pointer (**Figure 8.13**).

2. Release the pointer.

   Studio inserts the fade effect (**Figure 8.14**).

✔ Tips

- Previewing the fade-in works identically for effects dragged to the Video track.
- You can also apply a transition between titles or other elements on the Title Overlay track, as shown in **Figure 8.15**. The process is identical to inserting a transition between two clips on the Video track.

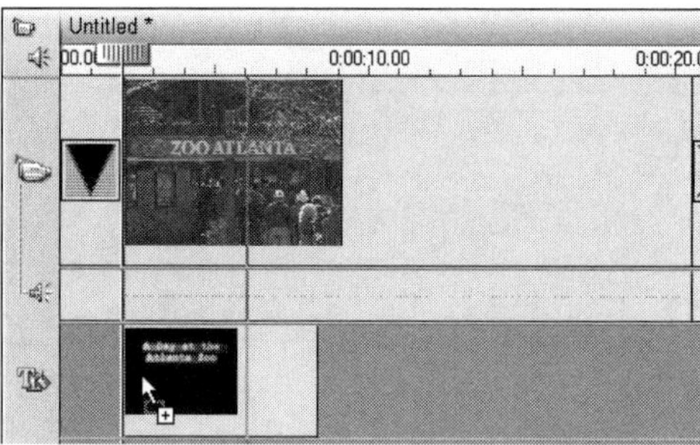

Figure 8.13 Inserting a fade into a title uses the same basic technique: drag it, drop it, move on to the next edit.

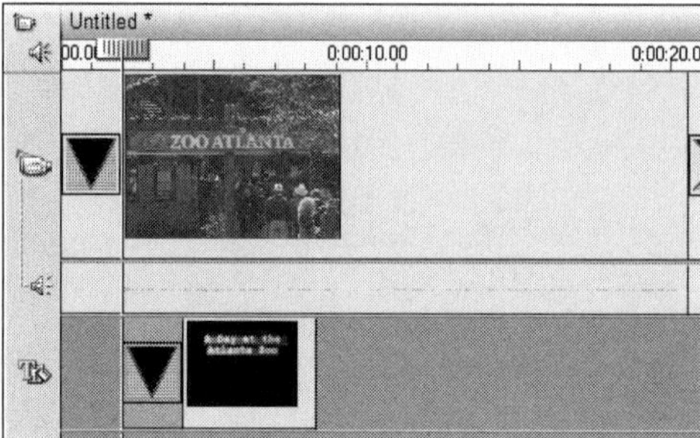

Figure 8.14 The completed fade.

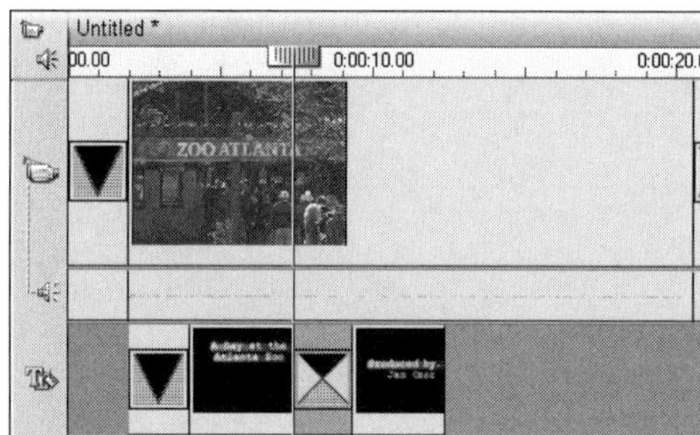

Figure 8.15 You can also insert transitions between titles and other images on the overlay track, following the same basic instructions as for video files.

To change transitions in the Video or Title Overlay track:

1. To try another transition, simply drag another on top of the previous effect.

   Studio shows the same green box or lines, and cursor with the box and plus sign (**Figure 8.16**).

2. Release the pointer.

   Studio replaces the previous effect, and you're ready to preview (**Figure 8.17**).

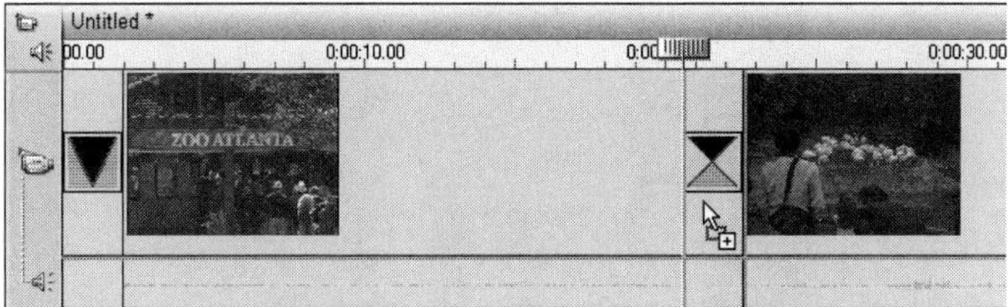

Figure 8.16 To use a different transition, simply drag and drop it over the old transition.

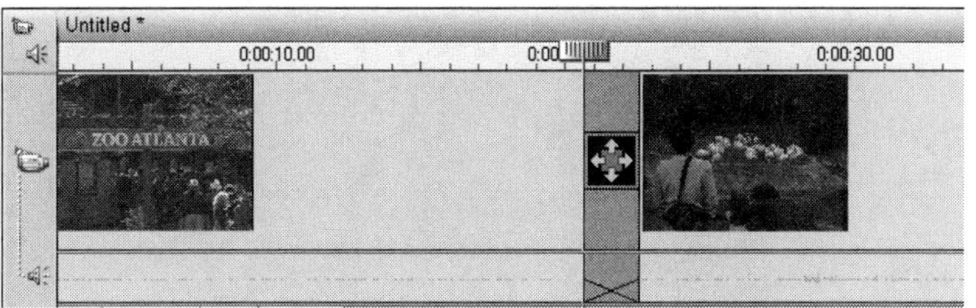

Figure 8.17 The replaced transition.

Transition Timing

Quick question: If you set your default transition time to 2 seconds, how many seconds of video does your transition take? Well, if you guessed 2 or 4, you're right (I'm trying to make this book a positive experience). But only part of the time (sorry).

The obvious answer is 2, since it should take 2 linear, real-time seconds to play the transition. That's true in every instance except for fade transitions, where Studio fades out for 2 seconds and then in for 2 seconds. In that case, the total transition time is 4 seconds.

For example, **Figure 8.18** shows two clips, each 6 seconds long, totaling 12 seconds. Then a 2-second dissolve is added between the two clips (**Figure 8.19**). However, if a fade is added, the entire transition takes 4 seconds: 2 seconds to fade out, 2 to fade in (**Figure 8.20**).

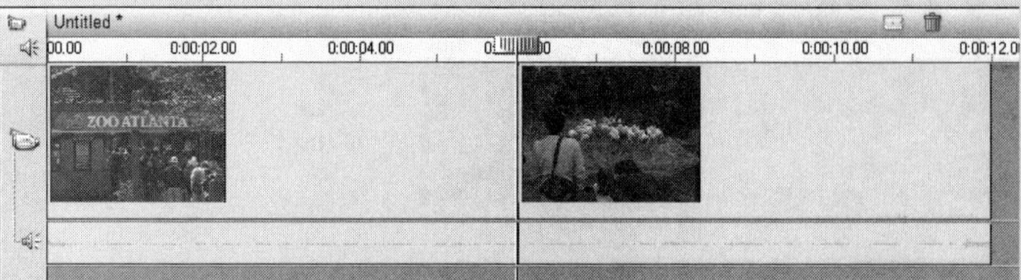

Figure 8.18 Two clips, 6 seconds each, 12 seconds total.

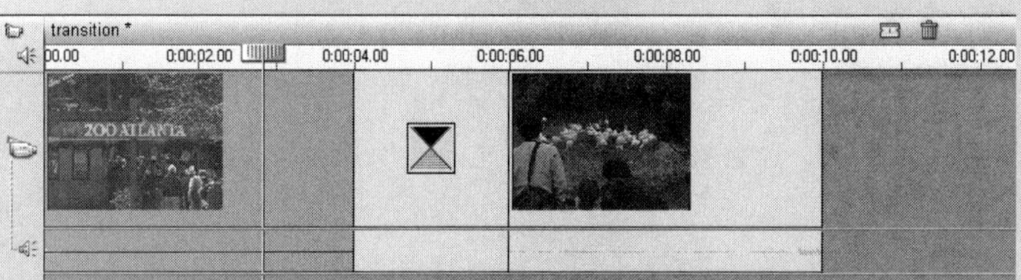

Figure 8.19 Insert a 2-second dissolve and we're down to 10 seconds. Hey, what happened? See Figure 8.21.

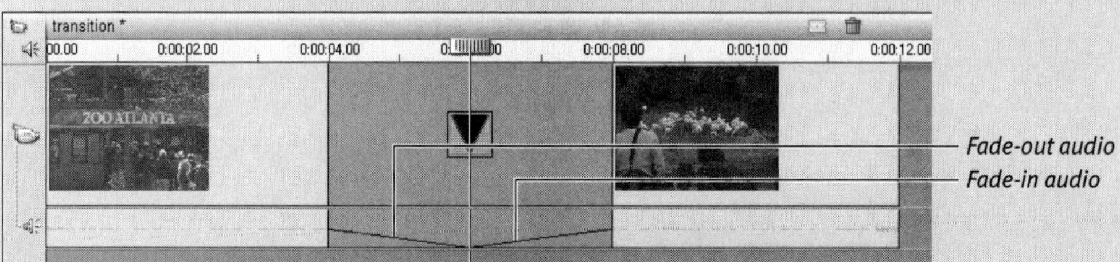

Figure 8.20 Insert the cross-fade and it takes 4 seconds, though the default is 2. Hey, at least the movie is still 12 seconds. Note the complete audio fade-out before the audio fades back in.

What's also intriguing about Figure 8.19 is that the transition starts at the 4-second point in the first clip, and that somehow the overall clip shortens from 12 to 10 seconds, (this didn't occur with the fade transition).

(continued on next page)

Transition Timing *(continued)*

What happened? To illustrate, I loaded the same clips into Adobe Premiere, which offers what's called an A/B editing view that shows both the clips on the Timeline and the transition (**Figure 8.21**). (This transition works the same in Premiere as in Studio; it's just presented differently in the Timeline.)

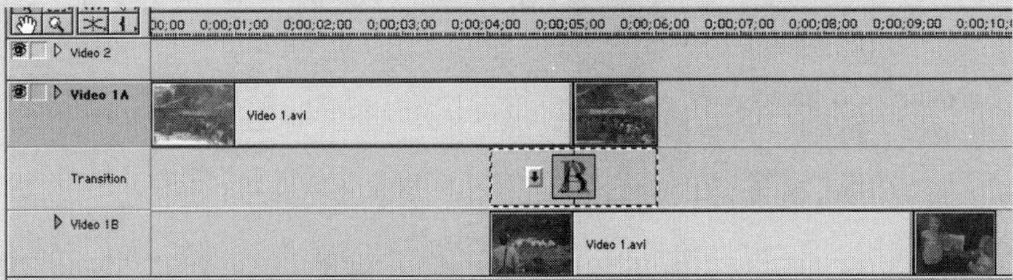

Figure 8.21 A screen shot from Premiere tells the story. The 2-second dissolve transition overlaps 2 seconds in each video, which is why it's shorter overall.

This screen shot reveals that during the 2-second dissolve transition, Studio uses the last 2 seconds of the first clip and the first 2 seconds of the second clip. Since segments from both clips are being used simultaneously, this shortens the video from 12 to 10 seconds.

In contrast, the fade transition—since it doesn't use simultaneous portions of the two clips—allows the clip to stay at 12 seconds (**Figure 8.22**). Obviously, if you used a cut, or no transition between the clips, there would be no overlap at all, and the video would still be 12 seconds long.

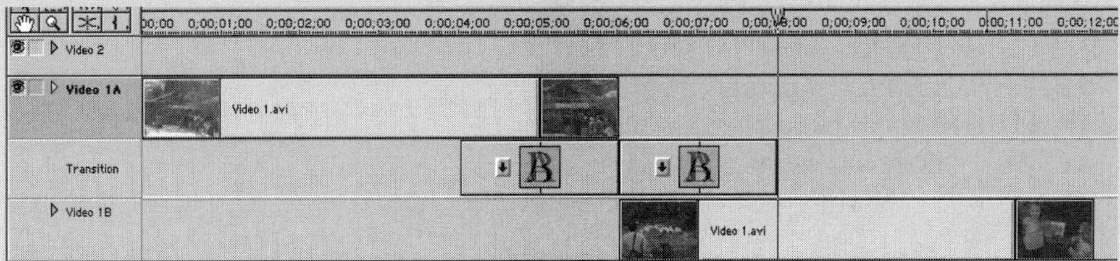

Figure 8.22 The clip isn't shortened with the fade-out and then fade-in, since there is no overlap.

Beyond the riddles, what are some practical ways to apply this information?

First, if you plan on using transitions other than cuts, be sure to trim your clips accordingly, leaving the planned durations of your transitions and fades at the beginning and end of each affected clip.

Second, if you're planning on a tight narration or Background Music track, remember that two 6-second clips don't add up to 12 seconds of video if you've got a 2-second dissolve between them. Though it's possible to do the math and compute the duration and precise starting points of each clip, it's generally easier to get the video lined up exactly the way you want it, and then produce your audio.

Customizing Transitions

This section explains how you can change duration by dragging it to the desired length on the Timeline, or by using the Clip Properties tool.

You can reverse the effect only in the Clip Properties tool.

To edit transition duration on the Timeline:

1. Select the target transition and place the pointer over either edge.

   The pointer becomes a bidirectional arrow (**Figure 8.23**).

2. Holding down the left mouse button and watching the video frames displayed in the Player, drag the arrow to the desired location.

3. Release the mouse button to set the new duration.

✔ Tip

- If you drag the transition to the right, the Player shows the *first* frame of the second clip that will appear after the transition finishes. If you drag it to the left, the Player shows the *last* frame in the first clip that will appear before the transition starts. This is a great way to fine-tune the starting and ending points of your transition.

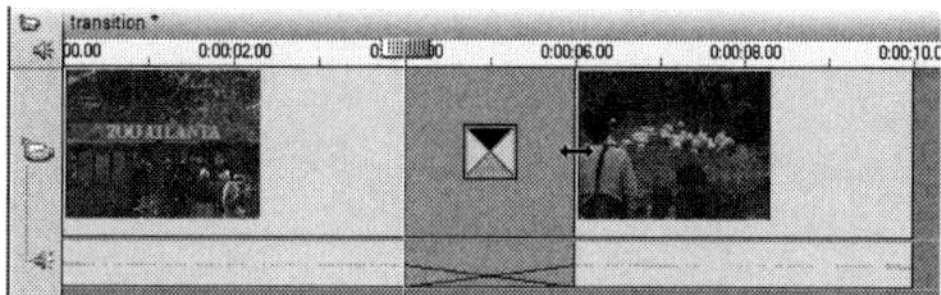

Figure 8.23 The easiest and most visual way to modify transition duration is on the Timeline, where you can see the key frames in the two affected videos.

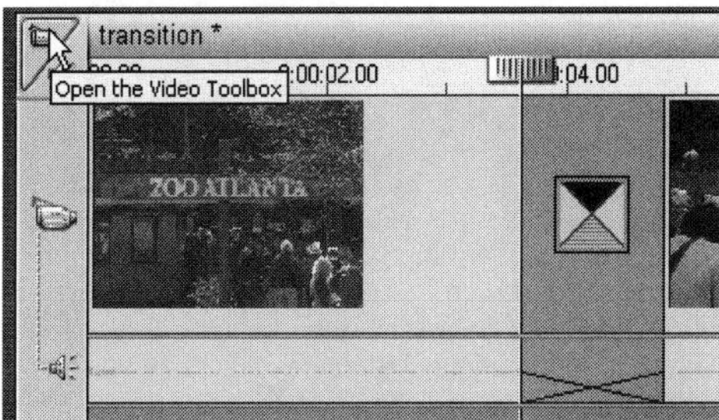

Figure 8.24 Or, you can open the Video Toolbox and use the Clip Properties tool.

To edit transition duration in the Clip Properties tool:

1. Open the Transitions Clip Properties tool by doing one of the following:
   - ▲ Double-click on the target transition (or right-click it and select Clip Properties from the pull-down that appears).
   - ▲ Select the target transition with the pointer and click the Video Toolbox icon at the top left of the Movie Window (**Figure 8.24**).

   The Video Toolbox opens to the Clip Properties tool for transitions (**Figure 8.25**).

2. In the upper-right corner, change the duration value to the desired setting by doing one of the following:
   - ▲ Use the jog controls to the right of the duration.
   - ▲ Touch the duration to make it editable and directly enter the desired setting.

(continued on next page)

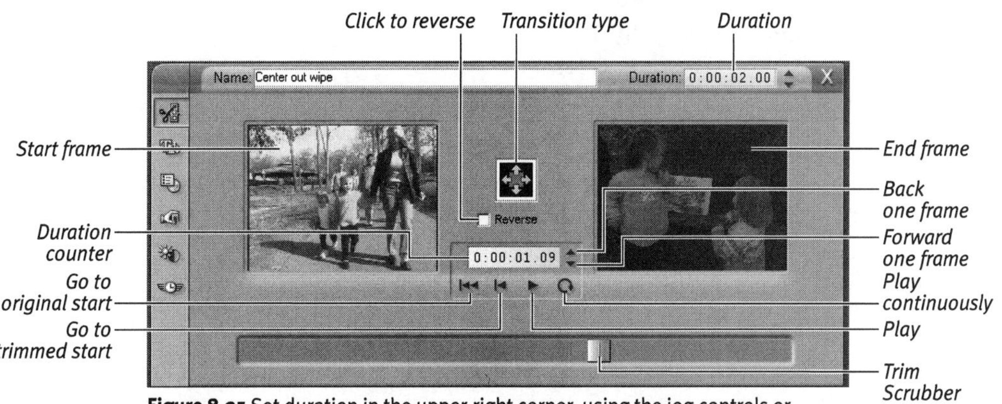

Figure 8.25 Set duration in the upper-right corner, using the jog controls or touching the duration number and entering a new one manually.

3. Use transport controls in the middle of the window to preview the transition.
4. Close the Video Toolbox by pressing X in the upper-right corner or by re-clicking the Video Toolbox icon you used to open the window (Figure 8.24).

✔ Tip

- The Video Toolbox is great when you want precise transition times, but the Timeline is more helpful when you're making artistic decisions, because it gives you a much better visual representation.

To reverse a transition effect:

- ◆ From the Transitions Clip Properties tool, click the Reverse checkbox (**Figure 8.26**).

  Studio reverses the transition effect. In this case, Studio converts the selected effect, the Center out wipe, to an outside-to-center wipe.

✔ Tip

- If you come across a Reverse checkbox that's grayed out for a particular transition, look for a transition in the library that performs the reverse of the selected transition.

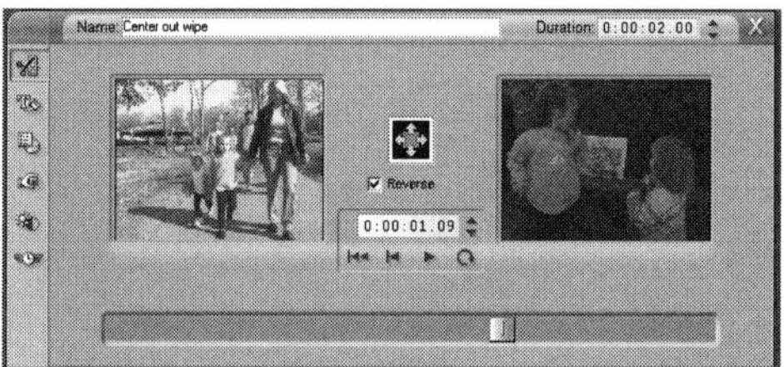

Figure 8.26 Checking the Reverse box gives you the predictably desired result.

Working with Hollywood FX Transitions

From a computer perspective, most Standard and Alpha Magic transitions are fairly simple. That's why you can get real-time previews on fairly old computers, like the Pentium IV 1.5 GHz computer I'm working on now.

However, Hollywood FX transitions, even some of the free ones, are much more complex, so Studio can't process them in real time. This makes it hard to view how the transition will really look in your final production.

Fortunately, Studio offers two options to get real-time previews. First, depending on the graphics card in your computer, you can enable what Studio calls "hardware acceleration" to view the effect. What happens here, in essence, is Studio sends the transition to the graphics card and says, "Here, you render this thing and display it."

If you have a reasonably current graphics card in your computer and the latest drivers, this should boost performance to real time. For example, on the desktop computer I'm using right now, I have a hot card from NVIDIA that accelerates everything Studio can throw at it in real time. On my IBM laptop, however, which has no three-dimensional capabilities, enabling hardware acceleration has no positive impact, and in fact makes the system a bit less stable.

In this case I can choose the other option, which is to render the transition as a background task. Here, Studio renders the actual frames that make up the transition, and stores them in a separate file. Although it takes a few moments, when it's done I can view my transition in real time.

Here's how to set the two options along with some caveats. Start by saving your project file (see "Saving Your Projects" in Chapter 1).

To enable hardware acceleration:

1. From the Studio menu, choose Setup > Edit.

   The Studio Setup Options screen appears, open to the Edit tab (**Figure 8.27**).

2. In the Rendering box on the right, check the "Use hardware acceleration" box (or press Alt+H).

   Studio opens the warning window (**Figure 8.28**).

   Operation can get unstable if your graphics card doesn't support this operation. So before you experiment, be sure to save your project file.

3. Close the warning window by clicking OK.

4. Close the Studio Setup Options dialog by clicking OK.

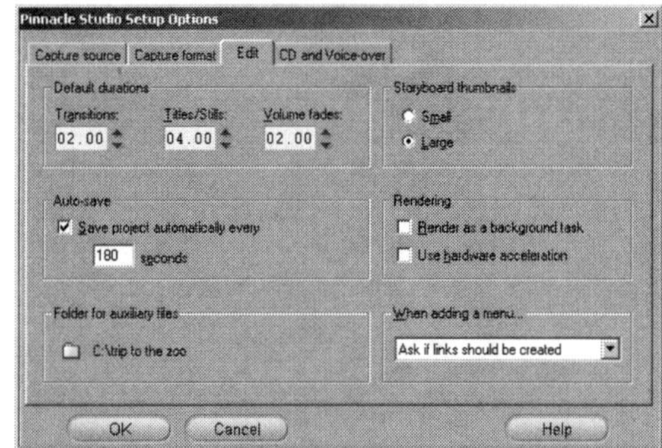

Figure 8.27 Select hardware acceleration and background rendering in the Studio Setup Options screen.

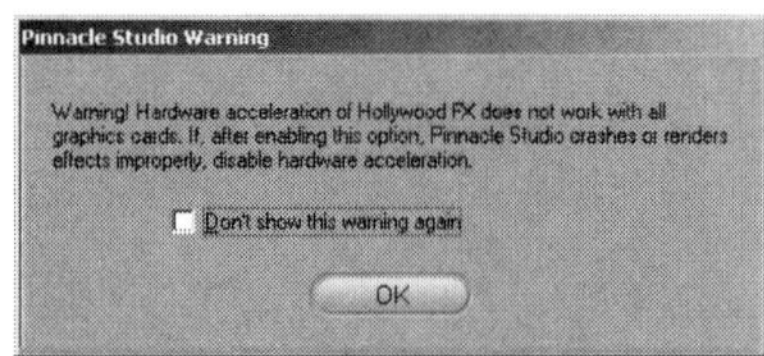

Figure 8.28 Heed this sign. If your system starts crashing after you enable hardware acceleration, go back and disable it. It should work with most current graphics cards, especially if the drivers are current.

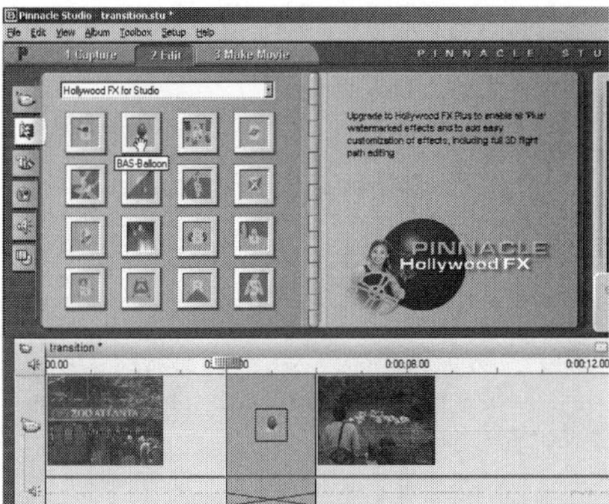
Figure 8.29 Hardware acceleration only affects Hollywood FX transitions like the balloon transition selected here.

5. Using the drop-down box in the Transitions tab in the Album, select the Hollywood FX for Studio transition group (**Figure 8.29**).
6. Drag the balloon transition down between two clips.
7. Preview the transition by clicking Play in the Player (or press the spacebar or L).

   If the transition plays in real time, it's likely that your graphics hardware is compatible with Studio, and you should stay in this mode.

   If the transition stops and starts like your car on a cold morning, your graphics card is not compatible with Studio, and you should reenter the Studio Setup Options screen as described in Step 1 and uncheck the "Use hardware acceleration" box.

✔ Tip

- If hardware acceleration is working, it probably doesn't make sense to render as a background task, since you're seeing the transition in real time anyway. If it's not working, enabling rendering as a background task is the only way (short of actually producing your video) to see the transition in real time.

To render as a background task:

1. From the Studio menu, choose Setup > Edit.

   The Studio Setup Options screen appears, open to the Edit tab (Figure 8.27).

2. In the Rendering box on the right, check the "Render as a background task" box (or press Alt+R).

3. Close the Studio Setup Options dialog by clicking OK.

   Studio will now render all transitions as background tasks.

4. Using the drop-down box in the Transitions tab, select the HFX Real World Basics transition group (Figure 8.29).

5. Drag the balloon transition down between two clips.

6. Preview the transition by clicking Play in the Player (or press the spacebar or L).

   Above the transition in the Timescale, you'll see a small bar over the top of the transition (**Figure 8.30**), at first completely light blue, and then a more transparent shade as Studio renders the video. Once the entire bar is transparent, Studio has finished rendering and you can preview your transition in real time.

Figure 8.30 Background rendering at work. The transparent bar indicates how much has been rendered, while the blue bar shows how much still needs to be rendered.

Figure 8.31 Start the ripple transition by dragging the desired transition between the first and second images.

Ripple Transitions for Slide Shows

As discussed in Chapter 5, you can create a slide show from still images by dragging multiple images to the Timeline. A lovely touch for slide shows is adding transitions between images, a process that Studio simplifies with a feature called ripple transitions.

Here's how it works.

To insert a ripple transition between slide show images:

1. With your slide show on the Timeline, drag the desired transition between the first and second images (**Figure 8.31**).

   Studio inserts the transition.

2. Select all slides in the slide show by doing one of the following:
   - ▲ If your entire presentation is a slide show, choose Edit > Select all (or Ctrl+A) from the Studio menu.
   - ▲ If you have other assets on the Timeline that you don't want included in the ripple transition, hold down the Shift key and select the first image and then the last image in the slide show with your pointer.

   Studio highlights all the images in the slide show.

(continued on next page)

3. Holding your pointer over any of the selected images, right-click to reveal the menu, then select Ripple Transition (**Figure 8.32**).

   Studio inserts the transition between all still images (**Figure 8.33**).

✔ Tips

- For most video clips, 2-second transitions—the default setting for video—are fine. But for still images, a 2-second transition can be a bit long, especially at the default 4-second duration for stills. You may consider changing the default transition time for the slide show, then change it back after applying the ripple transition.
- After applying the ripple transition, you're free to customize the duration for each and any transition as described above.

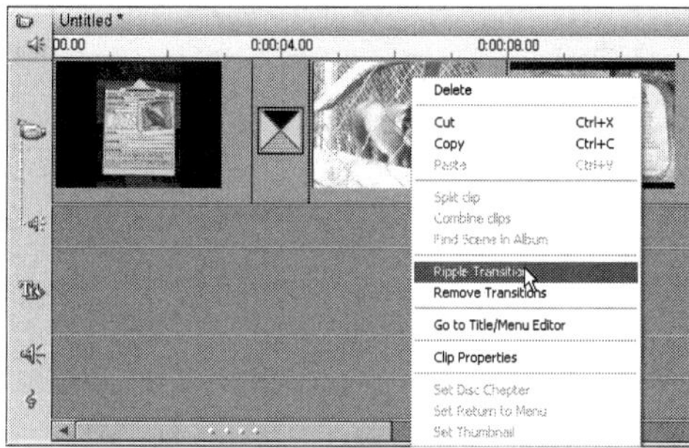

Figure 8.32 Then highlight all images in the slide show, right-click, and select Ripple Transition.

Figure 8.33 Voilà! Multiple transitions, neatly inserted. When I'm feeling really frisky, I'll use page curls instead of dissolves, creating the appearance of physically scrolling through the images.

9

Applying Special Effects

Studio's video effects fall neatly into two classes: curative effects, which fix underlying problems with the video, and artistic effects, which modify or enhance the footage. Curative filters include brightness and color adjustments, while artistic enhancements include the ability to convert your video to black and white, or create slow-motion or fast-motion effects.

Studio rounds out its effects with a strobe filter perfect for re-creating that Tony Manero disco look from *Saturday Night Fever.* White suits, anyone?

Fixing Problems with Your Videos

No matter how carefully you shoot your videos, problems are going to crop up. Take the Zoo Atlanta video that's been the working example in this book. The video was shot with a digital camera that required frequent white balancing to adjust for indoor and outdoor scenes, and to adjust for lighting changes that occurred when the late-December sun kept peeking in and out of the clouds.

As I learned that day, chasing two little ones around a public zoo is not conducive to frequent white balancing, and my failure to perform the necessary adjustments produced a number of scenes with overly bluish hues and some that were simply too dark. When working with an analog camera, Studio provides color and brightness controls during capture. However, if your source footage is DV, fixing the problem in the Movie Window after capture is your only option.

For addressing color issues, your primary tools are the *hue* and *saturation* sliders. When your video is too dark or too light, you'll work mostly with the *brightness* and *contrast* sliders. (The sidebar, "Adjustments Defined," provides the definition for each of these terms.) The starting point for all adjustments discussed in this chapter is the Movie Window with the clip selected.

Figure 9.1 Open the Video Toolbox to gain access to the tool for adjusting color and adding visual effects.

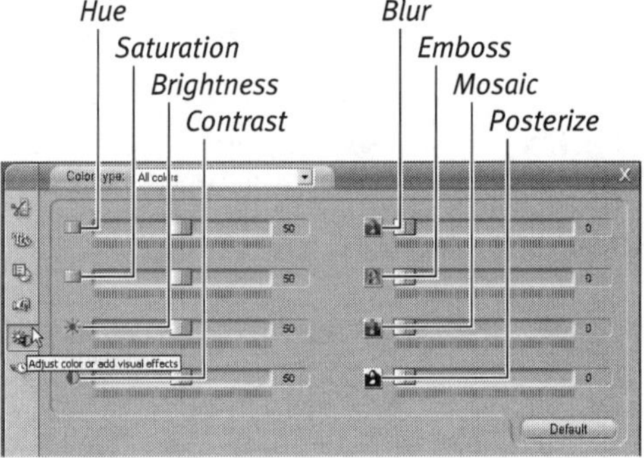

Figure 9.2 Click the sun icon to open the Visual Effects tool panel.

To fix color problems:

1. With the target clip in the Movie Window and selected, click the Video Toolbox icon at the upper-left corner of the Movie Window (**Figure 9.1**).

   The Video Toolbox opens.

2. Click the Sun icon (second from the bottom) to open the tool that adjusts color or adds visual effects.

   The tool opens (**Figure 9.2**).

(continued on next page)

Adjustments Defined

Studio provides four curative adjustments: two for color, two for brightness. Here are the technical definitions from the Pinnacle Studio manual. I'm also throwing in a definition of sharpness, which you can't adjust here but can during analog capture.

Hue. This is the visual property that allows you to distinguish colors. The slider biases all the colors in a clip toward red (left) or green (right). This can be especially useful for correcting flesh tones.

Saturation. This is the quantity of pure color, ranging from zero (no color at all, or gray scale) to fully saturated (the maximum color intensity your output system can deliver). Move the slider to the left for a tonally reduced, washed-out look, or to the right for extra vibrancy.

Brightness. This is the relative intensity of light, without regard to color. Try adjusting both brightness and contrast to correct video that is underexposed or overexposed.

Contrast. This is the range of light and dark values in a picture or the ratio between the maximum and minimum brightness values. Moving the slider to the left lowers contrast, forcing all areas of the image toward medium brightness values. Moving the slider to the right increases contrast, making dark areas darker and bright areas brighter.

Sharpness. Increases the contrast of edges in the image, making them appear sharper.

3. Use Player controls to move the video to a frame containing content with known colors, like a face, clothing, or a painted wall (**Figure 9.3**).

4. To adjust color, do one or both of the following while watching the real-time preview in the Player (**Figure 9.4**):
   - ▲ If color is incorrect, adjust the hue slider until the color is correct.
   - ▲ If color is oversaturated or undersaturated (reds are too red or blues aren't blue enough), adjust the saturation slider until the color is correct.

5. To accept the changes, do one of the following:
   - ▲ Press an icon for another tool in the Video Toolbox.
   - ▲ Click the X in the upper-right corner to close the Video Toolbox.

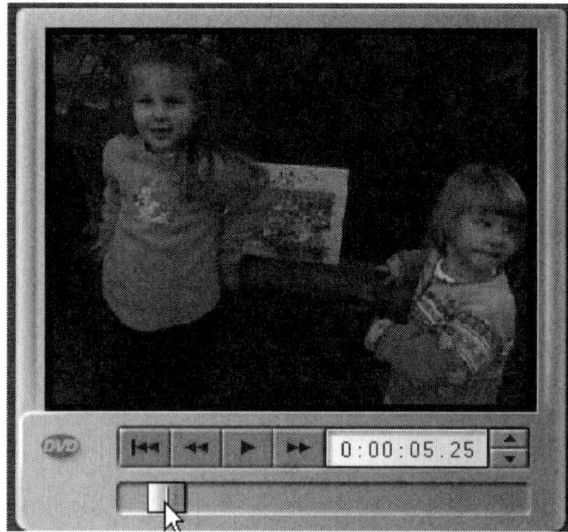

Figure 9.3 Tough to see in black and white, but the girls are looking a bit blue, courtesy of a videographer who forgot to white-balance his DV camera.

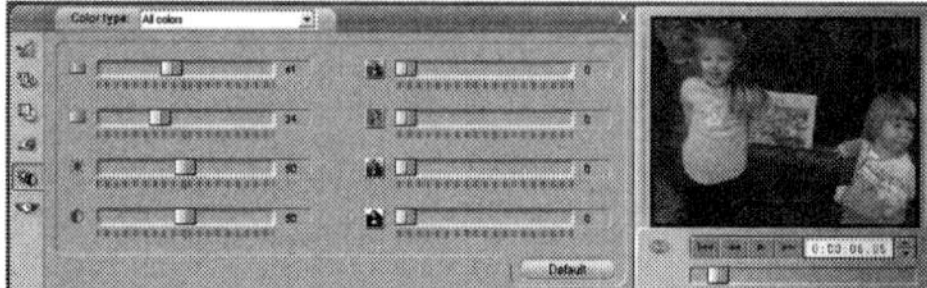

Figure 9.4 Find a frame with a known color, and start adjusting the hue and saturation controls until you get a good result.

✔ Tips

- If you have multiple clips requiring similar corrections, note the position of the sliders used to make the correction so you can easily adjust other clips.
- Despite how simple this five-step solution seems, color correction is typically a very difficult pursuit—especially in a business setting where quick-and-dirty solutions won't do (bosses and coworkers are typically less forgiving than grateful grandparents). In short, it usually takes several tries to get the video right. For critical videos, consider rendering a short portion of the corrected video into your final intended format so you can view the video in a larger screen than Studio's Player window.

Figure 9.5 Atlanta's Komodo dragon was a touch too dark to see easily.

To fix brightness and contrast problems:

1. With the target clip in the Movie Window and selected, click the Video Toolbox icon at the upper-left corner of the Movie Window (Figure 9.1).

   The Video Toolbox opens.

2. Click the sun icon, second from the bottom, to open the tool that adjusts color or adds visual effects.

   The tool opens (Figure 9.2).

3. Use Player controls to move the video to a frame exhibiting the brightness and contrast problems you're seeking to address (**Figure 9.5**).

4. To adjust the clip, do one or both of the following while watching the real-time preview in the Player (**Figure 9.6**):

   ▲ Use the brightness slider to adjust the picture until the brightness levels are appropriate.

   ▲ Use the contrast slider to sharpen edges lost when adjusting brightness.

5. To accept the changes, do one of the following:

   ▲ Press an icon for another tool in the Video Toolbox.

   ▲ Click the X in the upper-right corner to close the Video Toolbox.

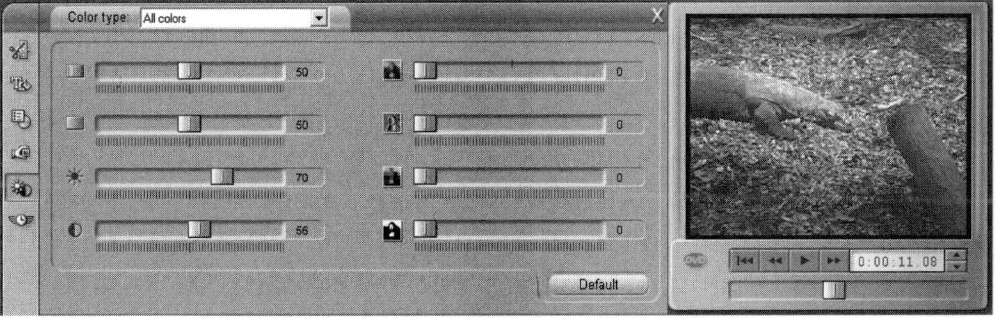

Figure 9.6 A quick boost to brightness and contrast dramatically improves the reptile's visibility.

Applying Artistic Video Effects

Your first artistic option is to convert your videos to black and white, a single hue, or sepia—all performed with the same control. Then Studio's more exotic effects take center stage; here are the definitions of these effects from the Studio manual:

- **Blur.** This is an effect akin to defocusing a camera. Studio offers ten steps of blur.
- **Emboss.** This specialized effect emulates the look of an embossed or bas-relief carving. Studio offers ten steps of emboss.
- **Mosaic.** This effect breaks an image into increasingly large colored squares as you move the slider to the right. The mosaic effect has 64 levels.
- **Posterize.** This effect progressively reduces the number of colors used to render an image, with the effect that regions of similar color are coalesced into larger flat areas. Studio offers seven steps of posterization.

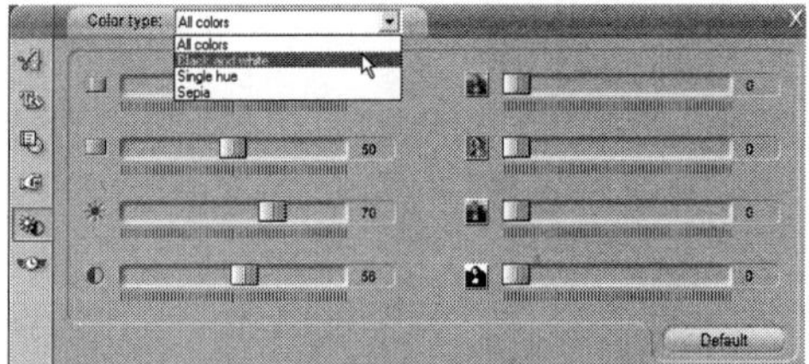

Figure 9.7 This control converts your video to black and white, a single adjustable hue, or sepia.

To convert to black and white, single hue, or sepia:

1. With the target clip in the Movie Window and selected, click the Video Toolbox icon at the upper-left corner of the Movie Window (Figure 9.1).

   The Video Toolbox opens.

2. Click the sun icon, second from the bottom, to open the tool that adjusts color or adds visual effects.

   The tool opens (Figure 9.2).

3. In the tool at the top left, click the Color type drop-down box and choose the desired effect (**Figure 9.7**).

4. To accept the changes, do one of the following:

   ▲ Press an icon for another tool in the Video Toolbox.

   ▲ Click the X in the upper-right corner to close the Video Toolbox.

✔ Tip

■ Once you've changed the basic color, you can adjust color and brightness values as described earlier.

To apply blur, emboss, mosaic, or posterize effects:

1. With the target clip in the Movie Window and selected, click the Video Toolbox icon at the upper-left corner of the Movie Window (Figure 9.1).

   The Video Toolbox opens.

2. Click the sun icon, second from the bottom, to open the tool that adjusts color or adds visual effects.

   The tool opens (Figure 9.2).

3. Select and apply the desired effect or effects by dragging the appropriate sliders to the right to the desired value (**Figure 9.8**).

4. To accept the changes, do one of the following:

   ▲ Press an icon for another tool in the Video Toolbox.

   ▲ Click the X in the upper-right corner to close the Video Toolbox.

Figure 9.8 The proud lion, feeling a bit mosaic.

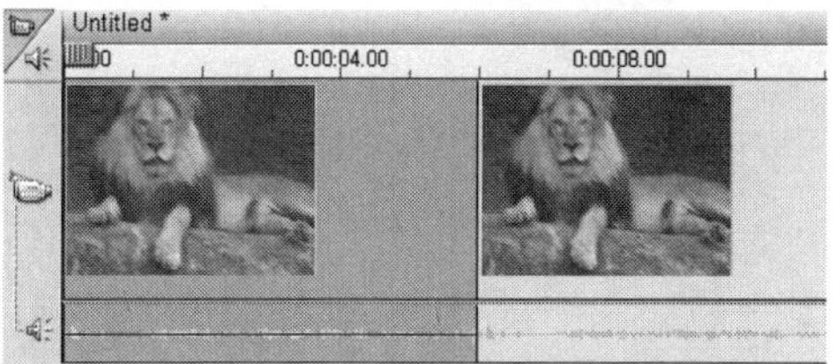

Figure 9.9 Studio doesn't provide an easy route to graduated effects, but you can jury-rig your way there. Start by placing the clip on the Timeline twice. Each clip is 6 seconds long; the entire project, 12 seconds.

Applying Visual Effects over Time

Studio provides no direct ability to apply a visual effect over time—a shame, since many effects are best used when applied gradually. There is a workaround, though it's a bit of a mindbender.

At a high level, it works like this: Say you have a 6-second clip you'd like to gradually emboss. The procedure is to place the clip on the Timeline twice in a row and apply the emboss effect to the second clip. Then you insert a dissolve transition between the two clips, and stretch the dissolve so it's the same length as the original clip.

You've effectively dissolved the first clip, without the effect, into the second clip, with the effect. Since the dissolve transition is gradual, it looks like the effect is applied gradually, thus getting the desired look. I'd love to say I thought of this creative idea but must give the credit to Studio's product manager. Here's the procedure.

To apply a visual effect over time:

1. Drag the desired clip into the Timeline twice (**Figure 9.9**).

   Note that the original clip is 6 seconds long, so the two clips combined are 12 seconds.

2. Select the second clip.

3. Click the Video Toolbox icon at the upper-left corner of the Movie Window (Figure 9.1).

   The Video Toolbox opens.

4. Click the sun icon, second from the bottom, to open the tool that adjusts color or adds visual effects.

   The tool opens (Figure 9.2).

(continued on next page)

5. Select and apply the desired effect or effects by dragging the slider to the right to the desired value (**Figure 9.10**).
6. Click the X in the upper-right corner to close the Video Toolbox.
7. On the left of the Album, open to the Edit tab, click the lightning bolt icon to open the Transitions tab.
8. If the Album isn't open to the Standard Transitions, choose them from the drop-down box at the upper left of the Transitions tab.
9. Drag the dissolve transition between the two clips (**Figure 9.11**).

   Studio places the transition between the two clips, and adjusts the total duration to 10 seconds to account for the 2-second overlap from the transition (**Figure 9.12**).

   Note that if you've changed the default transition duration from 2 seconds to another value, the total length of the two videos will be decreased by the new default.

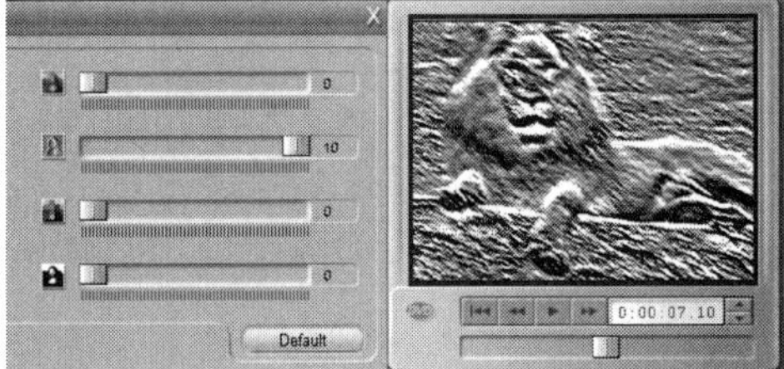

Figure 9.10 Apply the emboss effect to the second clip. What could be more appropriate for the king of the jungle?

Figure 9.11 Insert the dissolve transition between the two clips.

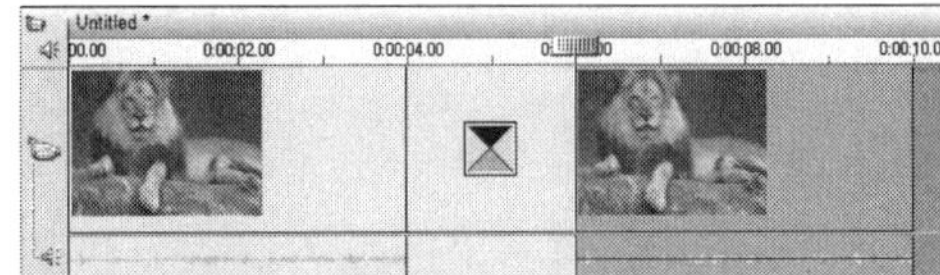

Figure 9.12 Dissolve inserted, the clips are down to 10 seconds overall.

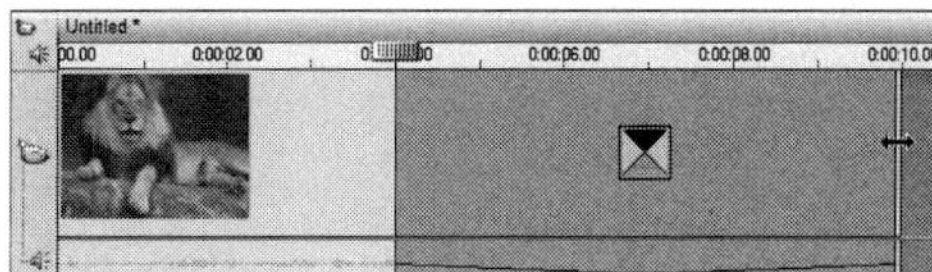

Figure 9.13 Stretch the dissolve transition over to the end of the second clip.

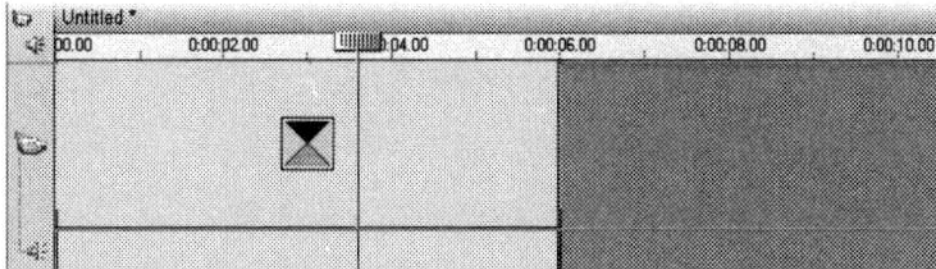

Figure 9.14 Voilà. The clip is down to the desired 6 seconds, with the first, unedited clip dissolving into the second, embossed clip.

10. Click and drag the transition to the right edge of the second clip (**Figure 9.13**).

    You could also perform this adjustment by double-clicking on the transition, which opens the Clip Properties window, and changing the value in the duration field. (See "Customizing Transitions" in Chapter 8.)

11. Release the mouse button.

    Studio expands the transition to 6 seconds, shrinking the combined two clips down to the desired 6 seconds (**Figure 9.14**).

✔ Tips

- If the clip to which you want to gradually apply the effect is a portion of another clip, isolate that portion by splitting the clip as described in the steps under "To split clips" in Chapter 7.
- This procedure works well for all color adjustments and artistic effects other than mosaic.

Reversing Visual Effects

So you've decided that sepia just isn't the right tone for your child's fifth birthday party video, even though it worked great for Butch and Sundance? Well, to reverse the effect—if your creative revelation comes right after you've applied it—you can always simply undo. However, if there's a bunch of intervening edits that you don't want to blow away, use this procedure.

To reverse visual effects:

1. With the target clip in the Movie Window and selected, click the Video Toolbox icon at the upper-left corner of the Movie Window (see Figure 9.1).

   The Video Toolbox opens.

2. Click the sun icon, second from the bottom, to open the tool that adjusts color or adds visual effects.

   The tool opens (see Figure 9.2).

3. To reverse visual effects, do one or both of the following:
   - ▲ If you've changed your clip to black and white, a single hue, or sepia, click the Color type drop-down box and choose All colors (**Figure 9.15**).
   - ▲ If you've changed any other values in the tool, click the Default button.

   Studio restores all values to their default settings.

4. Click the X in the upper-right corner to close the Video Toolbox.

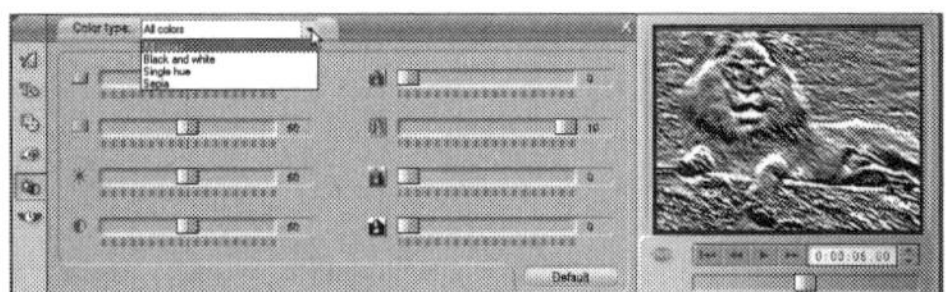

Figure 9.15 To change your mind, just click the Default button, but make sure you choose "All colors" in the Color type box to reverse black and white, single hue, and sepia effects.

Figure 9.16 The Vary Playback Speed tool shows that the clip of a sauntering tiger is originally 20 seconds long.

Varying Playback Speed

Changing the playback speed of your clips is useful in a variety of circumstances, whether it's to showcase a child's look of delight or slow your golf swing to better reveal its flaws. Studio offers two modes of resetting playback speed. First, by using a slider control, you can specify any speed from 1⁄10 the original to five times faster. Or, you can drag the clip to the desired duration, a useful method during insert edits or any time you need a clip to fill a defined space.

Studio also offers a *strobe* mode, which essentially displays the same frame multiple times, producing a stuttering strobe-light effect without those distracting flashes. This can be used in conjunction with changes in playback speed, or as a stand-alone effect.

Note that whenever Studio changes playback speed, it automatically mutes the audio from the Video track, since playback speed changes produce disturbing audio distortion. (You can prevent the audio-muting by locking the audio track before implementing playback speed variations, though you'll have an overlap if you make the clip faster, or gap if you make it slower.)

To change playback speed via slider control:

1. With the target clip in the Movie Window and selected, click the Video Toolbox icon at the upper-left corner of the Movie Window (Figure 9.1).

   The Video Toolbox opens.

2. Click the winged clock icon at the bottom of the icon panel on the left to open the Vary Playback Speed tool.

   The tool opens (**Figure 9.16**). Note the original clip duration of 20 seconds.

(continued on next page)

3. To adjust video speed, do one of the following:
   - ▲ To decrease playback speed and produce a slow-motion effect, drag the playback speed slider to the left, reducing speed to a fraction of the original (**Figure 9.17**).

     By reducing speed to $^{5}/_{10}$ the original, playback duration doubles to 40 seconds.
   - ▲ To increase playback speed and produce a fast-motion effect, drag the playback slider to the right, accelerating speed to a multiple of the original (**Figure 9.18**).

     Note that by doubling the playback speed, Studio has cut playback duration to 10 seconds.
4. Use Player controls to preview playback speed at the selected settings.
5. To accept the changes, do one of the following:
   - ▲ Press an icon for another tool in the Video Toolbox.
   - ▲ Click the X in the upper-right corner to close the Video Toolbox.

✔ Tip

- Whenever you slow clip speed below 1X, be sure to check the "Smooth motion between frames" checkbox, which produces interpolated frames between the original frames, smoothing overall motion. This control has no effect when you increase playback speed, so you might as well leave it checked all the time.

Figure 9.17 Now down to half the speed (5/10X), the clip is 40 seconds long. Click the "Smooth motion between frames" checkbox to create interpolated frames, which smooth the appearance of the resulting video.

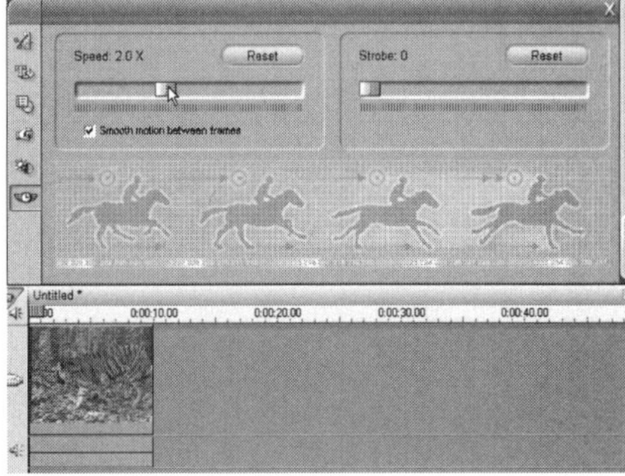

Figure 9.18 At 2.0X speed, duration is down to 10 seconds, and the tiger is hustling through those woods.

Figure 9.19 Drag the clip to fit a custom duration by opening the Vary Playback Speed tool, which converts the pointer to the Speed Change cursor.

To change playback speed on the Timeline:

1. With the target clip in the Movie Window and selected, click the Video Toolbox icon at the upper-left corner of the Movie Window (Figure 9.1).

   The Video Toolbox opens.

2. Click the winged clock icon at the bottom of the icon panel to open the Vary Playback Speed tool.

   The tool opens (Figure 9.16). Note the original clip duration of 20 seconds.

3. Move the pointer to the right edge of the clip.

   The pointer changes to the Speed Change cursor (**Figure 9.19**).

4. Drag the clip left or right to the intended duration, either longer or shorter than the original clip.

5. Use Player controls to preview playback speed at the selected settings.

6. To accept the changes, do one of the following:
   - Press an icon for another tool in the Video Toolbox.
   - Click the X at the upper-right corner to close the Video Toolbox.

To produce the strobe effect:

1. With the target clip in the Movie Window and selected, click the Video Toolbox icon at the upper-left corner of the Movie Window (Figure 9.1).

   The Video Toolbox opens.
2. Click the winged clock icon at the bottom of the icon panel to open the Vary Playback Speed tool.
3. Use the strobe slider to drag the strobe to the desired value (**Figure 9.20**).

   The Strobe setting is the number of times a frame is displayed.
4. Use Player controls to preview playback at the selected settings.
5. To accept the changes, press an icon for another tool in the Video Toolbox or click the X at the upper-right corner to close the Video Toolbox.

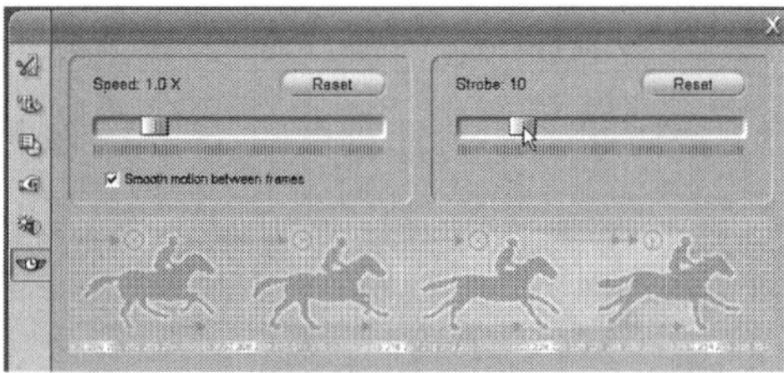

Figure 9.20 A Strobe setting of 10 means that Studio will display each frame 10 times, producing a strobe-like effect without all those annoying flashes. Click one or both of the Reset buttons if you want to start over.

To reverse playback speed or strobe effects:

1. With the target clip in the Movie Window and selected, click the Video Toolbox icon at the upper-left corner of the Movie Window (Figure 9.1).

   The Video Toolbox opens.
2. Click the winged clock icon at the bottom of the icon panel to open the Vary Playback Speed tool.

   The tool opens (Figure 9.16).
3. Click the Reset button in one or both boxes.
4. To accept the changes, press an icon for another tool in the Video Toolbox or click the X at the upper-right corner to close the Video Toolbox.

10 Designing Titles and Menus

Studio's Title Editor has always been a great tool for quickly and easily producing attractive titles. With Studio 8, Pinnacle adds the ability to create DVD menus and buttons, merging video editing and DVD authoring into one interface and simplifying DVD production immensely.

To start, here's a quick function flyover. First, for all video productions, DVD or otherwise, the Title Editor creates full-screen titles, positioned on the Video track, that introduce the movie or new sections, or show final credits. If you want to add full-screen credits at the end of the movie, this is where you produce them.

Second, again for all video productions, the Title Editor produces *overlay* titles, positioned on the Title Overlay track, which display over your videos. These are useful for adding logos or descriptions that enhance the video. For example, you could have the title "Billy's First Birthday" running along the bottom of a clip showing the happy child with chocolate cake all over his face. Finally, the Title Editor also produces the menus needed to navigate through and around your DVD titles.

Opening the Title Editor

At last count, there were approximately 6,583 ways to open the Title Editor, but I'm sure I missed a few. Just joking, of course, but here are the easy ways to get the job done.

To open the Title Editor:

1. Position the Timeline Scrubber to the desired title insertion point (**Figure 10.1**).
2. From the Studio menu, choose Toolbox > Create Title (**Figure 10.2**).

   The title creation screen opens (**Figure 10.3**).

Figure 10.1 You can open the Title Editor from either the Video track or the Title Overlay track. First position the Timeline Scrubber where you want the title inserted.

Figure 10.2 One of the many ways to open the Title Editor.

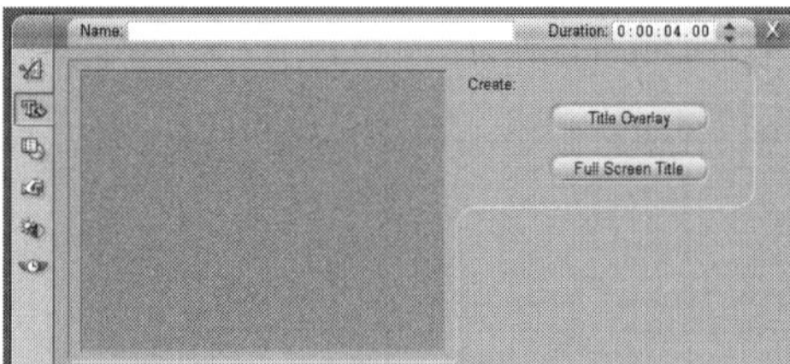

Figure 10.3 Here's where you choose between a title overlay and a full-screen title.

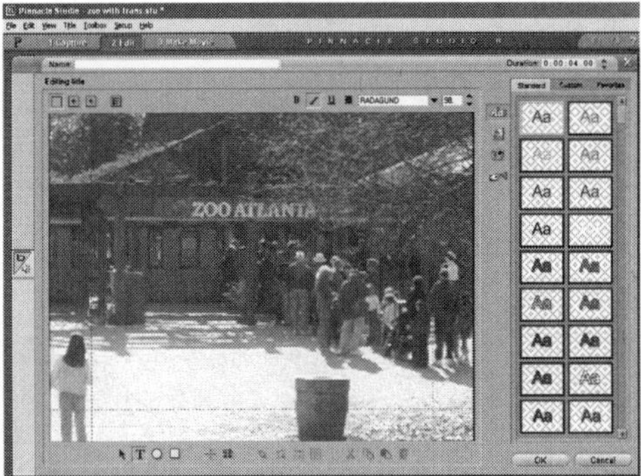

Figure 10.4 The Title Editor for a title overlay, with the underlying video showing through. Get comfortable, you're going to be here for a while.

3. Do one of the following:
   - Click the Title Overlay button to create a title that appears *over* your video on the Title Overlay track.

     The Title Editor opens, displaying the video underneath the title to assist design and placement (**Figure 10.4**).
   - Click the Full Screen Title button to create a title that appears *instead* of video.

     The Title Editor opens, with no video displayed underneath since the full-screen title displaces video on the Video track (see Figure 10.12).

To open the Title Editor (easier):

1. From the Edit screen, click the show titles icon on the left side of the Album (**Figure 10.5**).

   The Titles tab opens (**Figure 10.6**).

2. Select the desired title with the pointer and do one of the following:
   - ▲ Drag the title to the Video track and release to create a full-screen title (**Figure 10.7**).
   - ▲ Drag the title to the Title Overlay track and release to create an overlay title (**Figure 10.8**).

3. Once the selected title is on the track, double-click the title (**Figure 10.9**, with overlay title shown).

   The Title Editor opens with the selected title (**Figure 10.10**).

Or

- Double-click the Title Overlay track at the desired location for the title overlay.

  The Title Editor opens, displaying the underlying video (Figure 10.4).

  Note that this way (the easiest method) works only for overlay titles.

Figure 10.5 Studio includes an album of very useful titles. Here's where you find them.

Figure 10.6 Three pages of time-savers and idea generators.

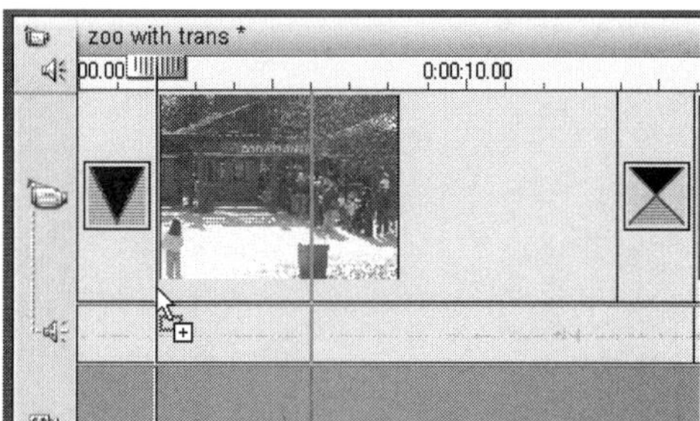

Figure 10.7 Placing the title on the Video track.

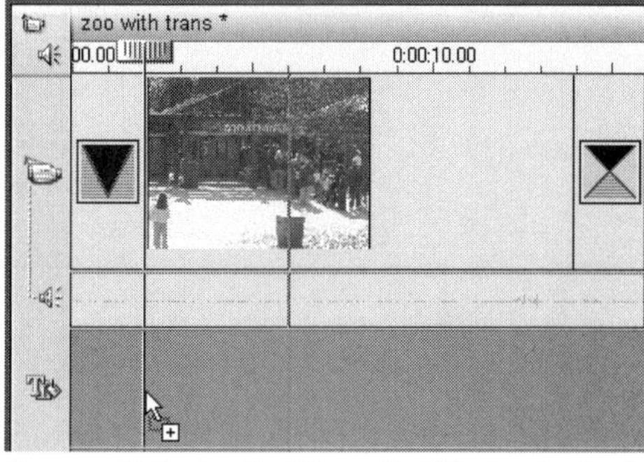

Figure 10.8 Placing the title on the Title Overlay track.

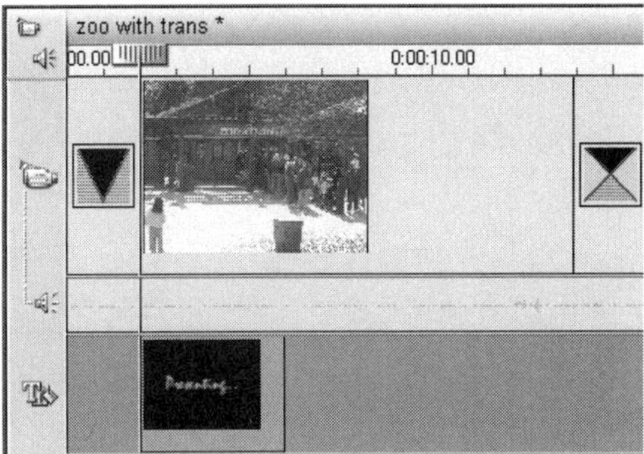

Figure 10.9 Double-click an existing title to open the Title Editor.

Figure 10.10 Here you go, ready to edit.

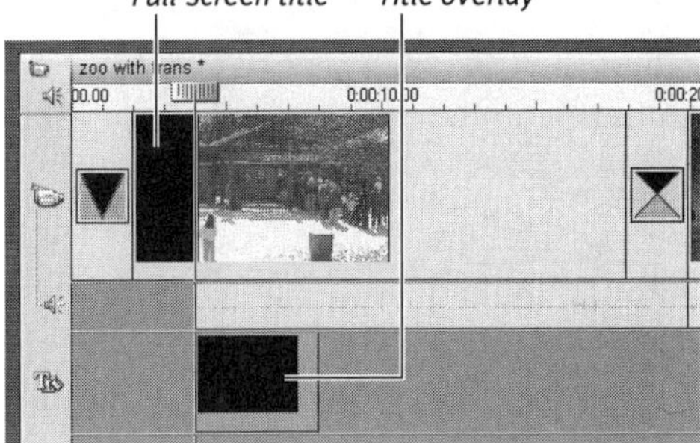

Figure 10.11 Where full-screen and title overlays end up on the Timeline.

✔ Tips

- Note that the Title Overlay track is beneath the Video track. To make Studio display a title "over" the video, you actually place it "under" the Video track.
- If you work with titles a lot (and who doesn't), the F11 (don't save) and F12 (save title) keys become pretty handy. Often it's easier to deep-six a title by pressing F11 and starting over than it is to attempt the multiple undos necessary to get back to square one.
- **Figure 10.11** illustrates the positioning of full-screen and overlay titles. As mentioned above, Studio places full-screen titles on the Video track, where they *displace* the video for their duration. In contrast, Studio places overlay titles on the Title Overlay track, where they appear *over* other videos. If you change your mind about whether you want your title to appear in overlay or full-screen mode, but don't want to redo your design, simply drag the title into the other track at the same position in the Timeline.

To close the Title Editor:

- ◆ To close the Title Editor and *save* your title or edits, do one of the following:
  - ▲ Click OK at the bottom right corner.
  - ▲ Choose File > Close Title Tool (or press F12).
  - ▲ Click the X at the upper right of the Title Editor (Figure 10.4).

Or

- ◆ To close the Title Editor *without saving* your title or edits, do one of the following:
  - ▲ Click the Cancel button at the bottom-right corner.
  - ▲ Choose File > Cancel Title tool (or press F11).

Looking at the Title Editor

Once you've opened the Title Editor, take a look at its interface and tool sets (**Figure 10.12**). Note that many of these functions are available from the Studio menu as well as the onscreen icons.

Design window. Studio's Design window is a WYSIWYG design area (what you see is what you get). When designing title overlays, you'll see the underlying video in the Design window (Figure 10.4); but with full-screen titles the Design window starts out empty.

Title-safe zones. When creating titles for DVD and other productions viewed primarily on a TV, keep all title elements inside these zones. Otherwise, they may be truncated.

Title-type buttons. These buttons control the type of title, whether static, rolling up and down, crawling sideways, or DVD menu.

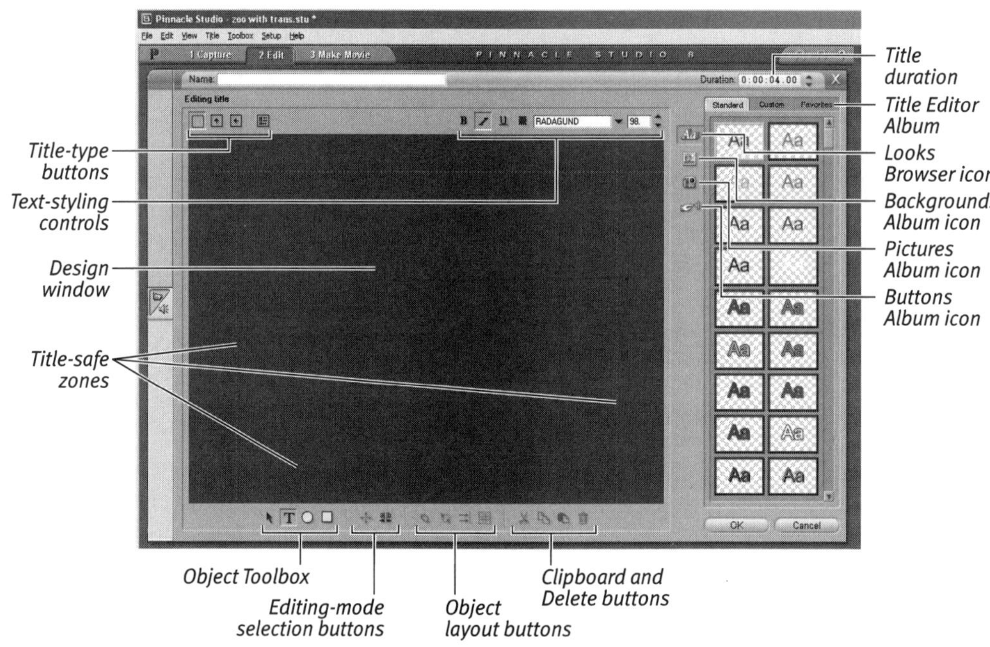

Figure 10.12 The Title Editor for a full-screen title, which takes over the entire screen.

Text-styling controls. These controls are similar to those in most word processing programs, with the addition of some excellent aligning and word-wrapping tools.

Object Toolbox. These controls allow you to create and position text, circle, and square-based objects that serve as either design elements or menu buttons.

Editing-mode selection buttons. Switch into and out of advanced editing modes for kerning text and deforming objects.

Object layout buttons. My favorite. Nothing is more irritating than menu components that are out of alignment or not quite the right size. These tools let you group, align, and resize objects for a more uniform appearance.

Clipboard and Delete buttons. When designing titles and menus, operation is often simplest when you copy and paste text attributes and other labels. These tools simplify these common tasks.

Title Editor Album. Studio includes libraries of looks, backgrounds, pictures, and menu elements to use in your productions. Generally, you can customize these, add your own, and save them in a Favorites Album.

Title duration. Here's where you can customize the duration of your title or, similar to how Studio treats still images, accomplish the same goal by dragging the menu to the desired length on the Timeline.

Adding and Editing Text

Studio's titles can be comprised of text and imported images, as well as circles, squares, and derivatives thereof drawn with the Title Editor's own drawing tools.

I'll start with text, and then examine other components and how they all work together.

To add menu text:

1. Open the Title Editor using any of the techniques described earlier in this chapter.

   An "I" should be adjacent to the pointer, indicating that the Text tool is active. If not, click the *T* in the Object Toolbox at the bottom of the screen (**Figure 10.13**).
2. In the Design window, click where you would like the text to display.

   Studio displays a bounding box for your text (**Figure 10.14**).
3. Type the desired text.
4. Click anywhere outside the box to set the text (**Figure 10.15**).

Figure 10.13 Click the Text tool to insert text. Studio rewards you with a special text-insert pointer.

Figure 10.14 The bounding box is ready to receive your text.

Figure 10.15 Pretty bland, eh? We'll spice it up in a minute.

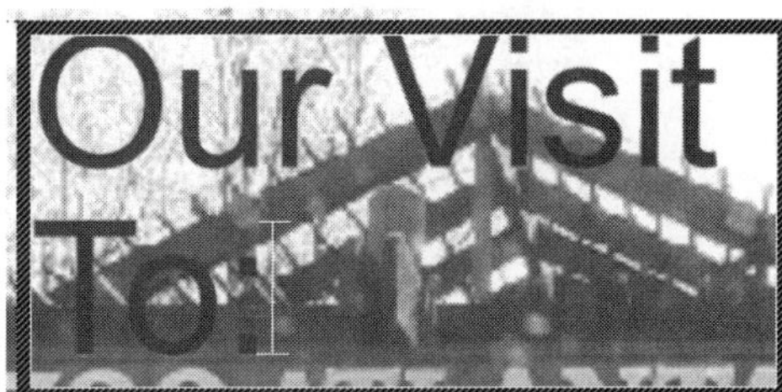

Figure 10.16 Select the box to edit the text. See the thin text-insert icon after the colon?

Figure 10.17 Studio highlights text you're about to replace.

Figure 10.18 The new text.

To change menu text:

1. Select the menu text with the pointer.

   A bounding box appears around the text (**Figure 10.16**). The thin insert bar after the colon is the text-entry pointer.
2. Move the text-entry pointer to the desired location using arrow keys or by clicking the pointer in the desired spot.
3. Type the desired text.

   Studio adds the text.
4. To set your changes, click anywhere outside the box.

To replace menu text:

1. Select the menu text with the pointer.
2. While holding down the left mouse button, drag over the text to replace. Or, while holding down the Shift key, use the arrow keys to select the text to replace.

   Studio highlights the selected text (**Figure 10.17**).
3. Type the desired text.

   Studio replaces the text (**Figure 10.18**).
4. To set your changes, click anywhere outside the box.

To move text:

1. Select the text.

   A gray bounding box appears around the text object (Figure 10.18).

2. Click the bounding box.

   Yellow control points appear around the box, a green dot appears above the box, and the pointer turns into the *move-object* pointer (**Figure 10.19**).

   The move-object pointer will disappear if it's moved outside the bounding box.

3. Hold down the left mouse button and drag the text to the desired location.

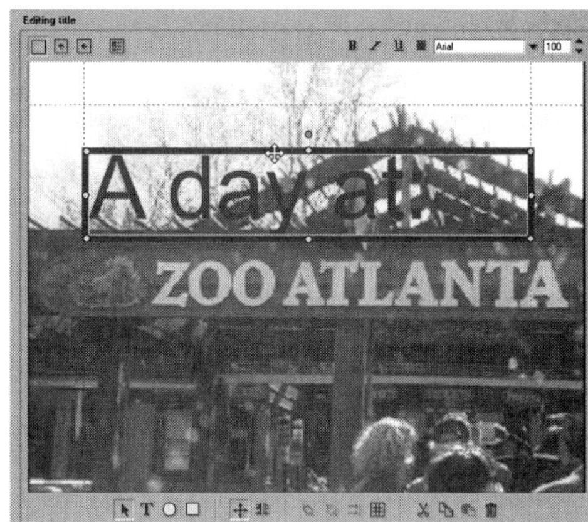

Figure 10.19 Select the text twice to move or resize it. First you get the gray bounding box, then these control points.

✔ Tip

- You can use your arrow keys to move text (and all objects) one pixel in any direction, a great way to fine-tune your positioning.

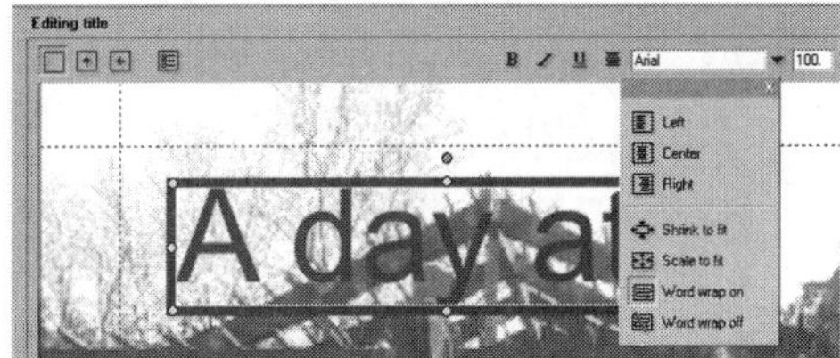

Figure 10.20 Studio's alignment controls work like those in most programs.

Figure 10.21 Studio prevents you from changing font attributes for selected text, but you can get around this by changing the attributes and then entering more text.

To change font, text attributes, and alignment:

1. Select the text.

   A gray bounding box appears around the text object (Figure 10.18).

2. Click the bounding box.

   Yellow control points appear around the box, a green dot appears above the box, and the pointer turns into the move-object pointer.

   All text-styling controls are now active. You know the drill for bold, italics, underlining, and changing font and font size.

3. To change alignment, do one of the following:

   ▲ Click the text justify icon at the top, and select Left, Center, or Right alignment (**Figure 10.20**).

   ▲ From the Studio menu, choose Title > Justify Text. Then choose the desired alignment.

✔ Tips

- Studio grays out all text-styling options once you select one or more letters, preventing you from changing these options for entered letters. However, you can change all but the alignment characteristics for any new text added by changing the characteristics first, and then entering the new text (**Figure 10.21**).

- The shrinking, scaling, and word-wrap options in Figure 10.20 are discussed later in this chapter, since most users should pick their styles before fine-tuning their text.

Using Studio's Styles

There are more extensive text-editing capabilities to explore, but if you're like me, you'll produce the most professional-looking titles by using styles contained in Studio's Looks Browser.

When you create your first text title, Studio applies the default style at the top left of the Looks Browser (**Figure 10.22**), which is open by default when you open the Title Editor. Otherwise, to open the Looks Browser, click the Looks icon on the left of the browser window or go to the Studio menu and choose Title > Album > Looks.

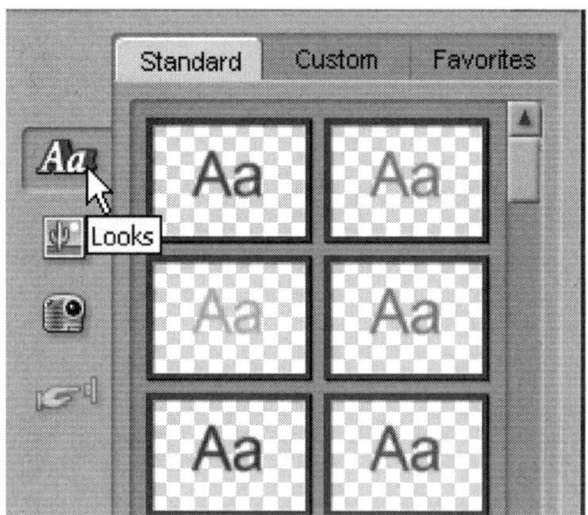

Figure 10.22 Studio's styles are a real blessing for creatively challenged individuals (like me), and can be applied to text and other objects.

As you scroll down the Looks Browser, you'll see increasingly creative title presets. This section deals with how to apply and customize Studio's looks. Note that changing styles doesn't affect font, font size, alignment, or any other text attribute. Just for the record, I've changed my font in the figures to Casmira because Arial was getting depressing.

Figure 10.23 Select the text to change, then select a new style and you're done. Use the scroll bar on the right for scrolling down the browser.

To apply a new look to text:

1. Select the text to adjust, and click the gray bounding box to see the control points (Figure 10.19)
2. Using the scroll bar on the right of the Looks Browser, scroll down to the desired style (**Figure 10.23**).
3. Select the style with the pointer.
   Studio applies the style to the selected text (Figure 10.23).

✔ Tip

- Note that you can apply different styles to different text in the same bounding box (though it looks pretty funky).

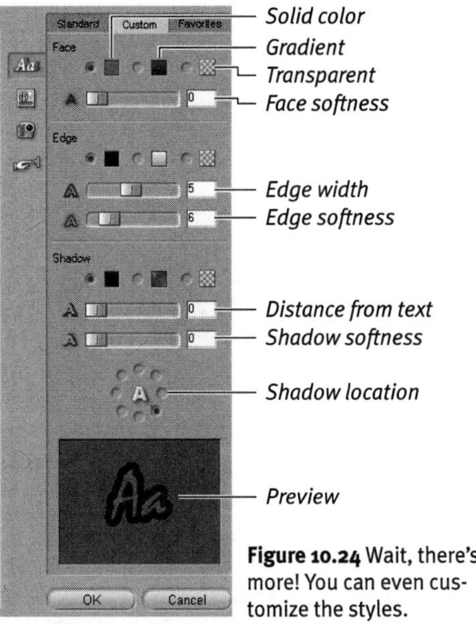

Figure 10.24 Wait, there's more! You can even customize the styles.

Figure 10.25 Throughout the Title Editor, you click the color swatch to edit the color.

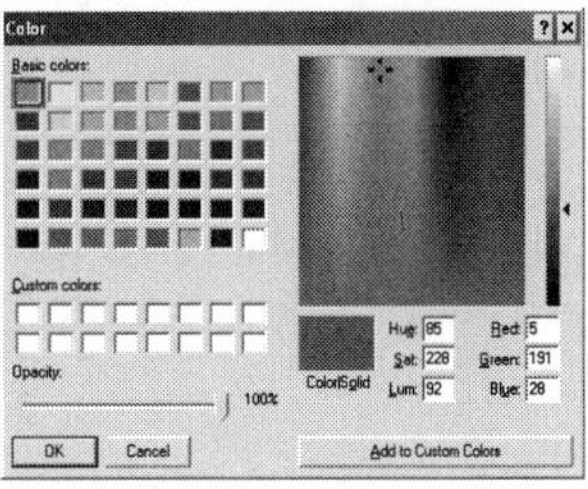

Figure 10.26 Studio's Color selection dialog. You can store your custom colors, a useful feature when you need to repeat them.

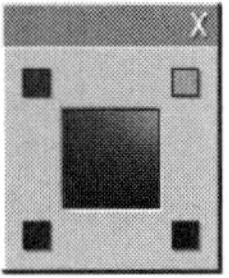

Figure 10.27 Here's how you edit the gradients. Each color dot opens the Color selection screen.

To customize a solid text color:

1. Select the style to customize (Figure 10.23).
2. In the Looks Browser, select the Custom tab (**Figure 10.24**).
3. Under Face, click the checkbox next to the solid-colored box (**Figure 10.25**).
4. Click the solid-colored box.

   Studio's Color selection dialog opens (**Figure 10.26**).
5. Select the desired color from Basic colors or Custom colors, or by selecting a different color from the spectrum.

   Studio lets you save custom colors by clicking the Add to Custom Colors button (Ctrl+A). Save the custom color to help maintain uniformity going forward.
6. Click OK to close the dialog.

To customize a gradient text color:

1. Select the style to customize.
2. In the Looks Browser, select the Custom tab.
3. Under Face, click the checkbox next to the gradient-colored box.
4. Click the gradient box.

   Studio's Gradient selection screen opens (**Figure 10.27**).
5. Click each box to open the appropriate Color selection dialog.

   You can configure each of the four colors independently.
6. Click the X in the upper-right corner to close the Gradient selection dialog.

To adjust text softness, edges, and shadows:

1. Select the style to customize.
2. In the Looks Browser, select the Custom tab.
3. Under Face, click the solid or gradient checkbox and adjust face softness with the Face slider, viewing the results in the Preview window (**Figure 10.28**).

   If you have text selected in the Title Editor, Studio applies these modifications to the title in near real time.
4. Select and modify edge appearance and color in the Edge section by clicking the solid or gradient checkbox and then following Steps 4 and 5 for changing text color, above.
5. Modify edge width and softness with the Edge sliders.
6. Select and modify shadow appearance and color in the Shadow section by clicking the solid or gradient checkbox and then following Steps 4 and 5 for changing text color, above.
7. Modify the distances of the shadow from the original text and shadow softness by using the Shadow sliders.
8. Change the position of the shadow by clicking a new button for the desired position.

   (See the difference in shadow position between Figure 10.28 and **Figure 10.29**.)

✔ Tip

- There are no customization options for the transparent text style.

Figure 10.28 Ruh, roh. Our day is fading into memory.

Figure 10.29 A much bolder look.

Figure 10.30 The Favorites Album comes in very handy, especially when you decide to change a style.

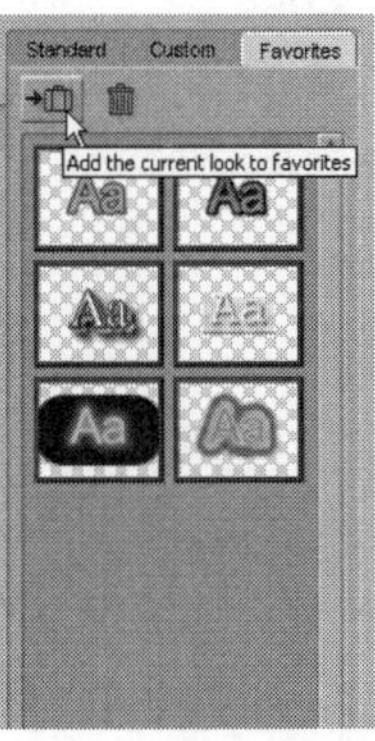

Figure 10.31 Click the suitcase icon to save the style.

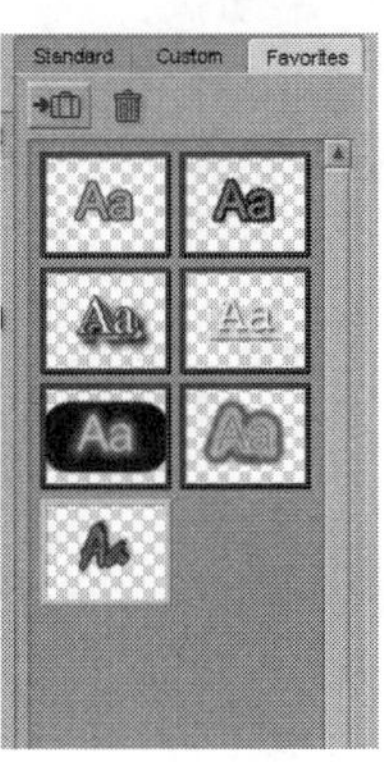

Figure 10.32 See the new style added to your Favorites.

To add a style to the Favorites Album:

1. Select the Favorites tab to open the Favorites Album (**Figure 10.30**).
2. Click the suitcase icon to add the currently selected style (**Figure 10.31**).

   Studio adds the style to the Favorites Album (**Figure 10.32**).

To delete a style from the Favorites Album:

1. From within the Favorites Album, select the offending style with the pointer.
2. Click the trash can icon to delete the style.

✔ Tips

- Saving styles to your Favorites Album is very convenient when you're changing the styles of multiple objects. Otherwise, you have to hunt through the style album each time you apply the style.
- You can save any style in the Favorites Album; it doesn't have to be one that you've edited.
- Think twice before deleting a style, because you cannot bring the style back with Undo.

Resizing and Justifying Text

Even after applying Pinnacle's wonderful styles, there may be some resizing and justifying to do to your text. Of course, you can resize your text by adjusting the font size, but that's just so non-WYSIWYG. Wouldn't you much rather push, pull, and drag than enter a dry number?

To justify text, you use a control to place the text in one of nine divided areas, a simple way to ensure consistency among menus.

To resize text:

1. Select the text to adjust, and click the gray bounding box to see the control points (**Figure 10.33**).
2. If the Move, Scale, and Rotate tool isn't selected, click the icon to enable the tool.
3. To shrink or expand the text, do one or more of the following:
   - Hold the pointer over a corner control point of the bounding box to convert it into a two-sided arrow (Figure 10.33). Press the left mouse button and shrink or expand the text.

     The text shrinks or expands proportionately.
   - Hold the pointer over the left- or right-side control point to convert it into a two-sided arrow (**Figure 10.34**). Press the left mouse button and shrink or expand the text.

     Text width shrinks or expands, and the height remains the same.
   - Hold the pointer over either the top or bottom control point to convert it into a two-sided arrow (**Figure 10.35**). Press the left mouse button and shrink or expand the text.

     Text height shrinks or expands, and the width remains the same.

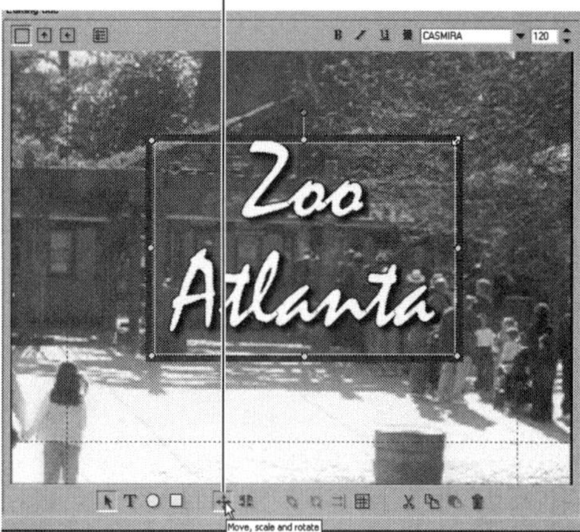

Figure 10.33 Here's our starting point for resizing. Click the Move, Scale, and Rotate tool to access the double-arrow pointer on the top-right control point, used to size the text proportionately.

Figure 10.34 Note the small double-arrow pointer on the right control point. Drag this to adjust width but not height.

Figure 10.35 You knew this was coming. The small double-arrow pointer on the bottom is used to adjust height but not width.

Figure 10.36 Use the Justify tool to place your text in one of nine positions.

Figure 10.37 Studio respects the title-safe zone—and changes your text justification when moving it. You can adjust it back to center if desired.

To justify text:

1. Select the text to adjust, and click the gray bounding box to see the control points.
2. Do one of the following:
   - ▲ On the bottom Title Editor toolbar, click the Justify tool, which looks like a tic-tac-toe board (**Figure 10.36**).
   - ▲ From the Studio menu, choose Title > Justify.
3. Select the desired area in the Justify tool.

   Studio aligns the text accordingly (**Figure 10.37**). Note that Studio also changes the text from center to right justification. You can change it back to center justification using the steps above under "To change font, text attributes, and alignment."

   After positioning your text, the Justify tool shows a little black dot in the selected spot (Figure 10.36), reflecting the current positioning.

✔ Tip

- The Justify tool is easily confused with the Text Justify (text alignment) tool discussed in "To change font, text attributes, and alignment," earlier. There, you justified or aligned the text within the text object. Here, you align the object itself within the title.

Managing Word Wrapping

Studio supplements the manual tools described earlier with specific tools for title word wrapping and resizing. This section examines them in the context of the title shown in **Figure 10.38**, which is too large and word wrapped, to boot. The goal is to get it smaller and all on one line.

Figure 10.38 Here's a starting point for examining Studio's scaling and word wrapping tools.

To disable word wrapping:

1. Select the text to adjust, and click the gray bounding box to see the control points (Figure 10.38).
2. Click the Text Justify tool at the top right of the Design window.

   Studio opens the Text Justify menu (**Figure 10.39**).
3. From the menu choose Word wrap off.

   Studio eliminates the word wrapping (**Figure 10.40**), but the title is still too large.

Text Justify tool

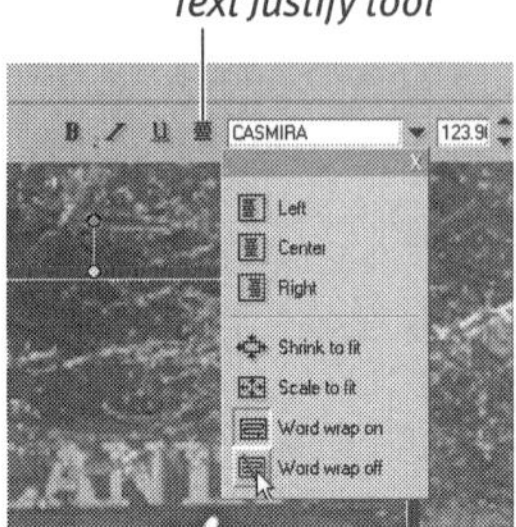

Figure 10.39 Select the Text Justify tool, to the left of the font box, to open the menu.

To shrink a title to a selected width:

1. Select the text to adjust, and click the gray bounding box to see the control points (Figure 10.38).
2. Click the Text Justify tool at the top right of the Design window.

   Studio opens the Text Justify menu.
3. From the menu choose Shrink to fit (Figure 10.39).

   Studio shrinks the menu to the selected width (**Figure 10.41**). This is probably the best result.

Figure 10.40 Word wrapping has been eliminated, but the title is still too big.

Figure 10.41 Here's what happens when you apply Shrink to fit—much better.

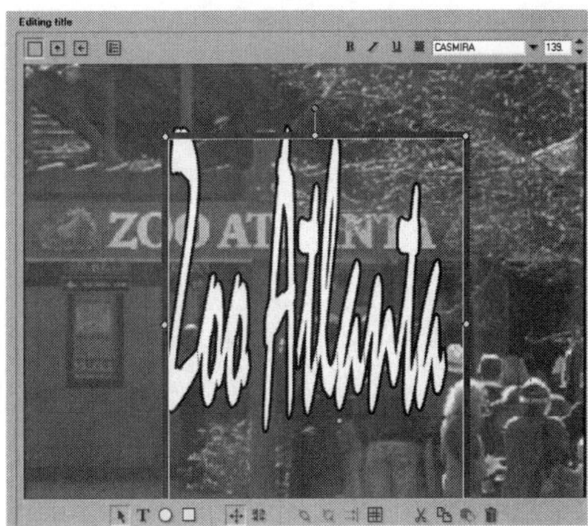

Figure 10.42 Here's the result of Scale to fit. Where's the Alka Seltzer?

To scale a title to a selected area:

1. Select the text to adjust, and click the gray bounding box to see the control points (Figure 10.38).
2. Click the Text Justify tool in the upper right of the Design window.

   Studio opens the Text Justify menu.
3. From the menu choose Scale to fit (Figure 10.39).

   Studio scales the text to fit the selected area (**Figure 10.42**).

✔ Tips

- Studio has word wrap turned on by default. Studio also turns it on each time you enter additional text.
- You can override word wrap controls by inserting your own line breaks in the text by pressing the Enter key.
- I find these word wrap and sizing controls a bit confusing and typically size my titles manually, using these tools as a last resort.
- These tools are also available from the Studio menu by choosing Title > Justify Text.

Kerning and Leading Text

Occasionally you may want to adjust the space between letters or characters, a process called *kerning*, or change the vertical space between words, called *leading*. Here's how.

To kern text:

1. Select the text to adjust, and click the gray bounding box to see the control points.
2. On the Title Editor toolbar at the bottom, click the Kern and Skew tool (**Figure 10.43**).
3. Position the pointer over one of the side control points.

   The pointer changes to the kern pointer (**Figure 10.44**).
4. Hold down the left mouse button and drag the pointer in or out to the desired width.

   Studio changes the distance between the letters (Figure 10.44).

To change leading between text:

1. Select the text to adjust, and click the gray bounding box to see the control points.
2. On the Title Editor toolbar at the bottom, click the Kern and Skew tool (Figure 10.43).
3. Position the pointer over either the top or bottom control points (not the corner).

   The pointer changes to the kern pointer (**Figure 10.45**).
4. Hold down the left mouse button and drag the pointer up or down to the desired height.

   Studio changes the distance between the words (Figure 10.45).

Figure 10.43 This font is too compressed for my taste. Fix it by clicking the Kern and Skew tool.

Figure 10.44 Place the kern pointer over a control point on the right or left and stretch out the text.

Figure 10.45 Place the kern pointer over the top or bottom control point to change the leading.

KERNING AND LEADING TEXT

Figure 10.46 Use the top control point to rotate the text.

Figure 10.47 Rotate your text to the desired location.

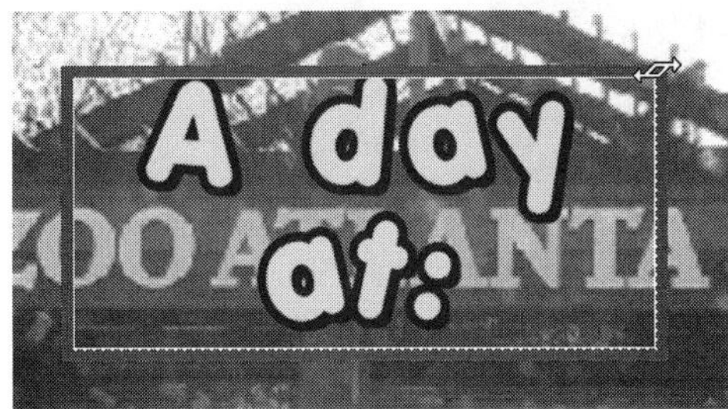

Figure 10.48 You can also skew your text. Just grab and stretch.

Figure 10.49 Here's what happens.

Rotating and Skewing Text

Here are two additional options for those pushing the design envelope: rotate and skew.

To rotate text:

1. Select the text to adjust, and click the gray bounding box to see the control points (Figure 10.43).
2. If the Move, Scale, and Rotate tool isn't selected, click the icon to enable the tool (Figure 10.33).
3. Move the pointer over the green control point atop the text object.

   The pointer changes to the rotate pointer (**Figure 10.46**).
4. Holding down the left mouse button, rotate the text to the desired location.

   A bounding box shaped with dotted lines follows your progress.
5. Release the pointer when your text is in the desired position (**Figure 10.47**).

To skew text:

1. Select the text to adjust, and click the gray bounding box to see the control points.
2. On the Title Editor toolbar at the bottom, click the Kern and Skew tool (Figure 10.43).
3. Position the pointer over one of the control point corners.

   The pointer changes to the skew pointer (**Figure 10.48**).
4. Holding down the left mouse button, drag the text to the desired location.

   A bounding box shaped with dotted lines follows your progress.
5. Release the pointer when your text is in the desired position (**Figure 10.49**).

Using Full-Screen Titles

As you may recall, a full-screen title is any title that lives on the Video track, since it replaces the video completely and displays in full screen. All full-screen titles initially have transparent backgrounds—essentially black because there's nothing underneath to show through. You can go with that minimalist approach or add a background, which can be a solid color, gradient, or full-screen image.

You can choose from Studio's range of useful background images or use your own. Just remember, all images used as a background are full screen and can't be resized and used as foreground design elements like logos. This section describes how to use images as logos.

To create a single-color background:

1. In the Title Editor, do one of the following:
   - ▲ Click the backgrounds icon on the Title Editor Album icon panel (**Figure 10.50**).
   - ▲ From the Studio menu, choose Title > Album > Backgrounds.

   The Backgrounds Album opens (**Figure 10.51**).
2. Check the single-color background checkbox (Figure 10.51).
3. To change colors, click the colored box next to the checkbox (**Figure 10.52**).

   Studio's Color selection dialog opens (**Figure 10.53**).
4. Select the desired color from Basic colors or Custom colors, or by selecting a different color from the spectrum.

   Studio lets you save custom colors by clicking the Add to Custom Colors button (Ctrl+A). Save the custom color to help maintain uniformity going forward.
5. Click OK to close the dialog.

   Studio replaces the background with the selected color.

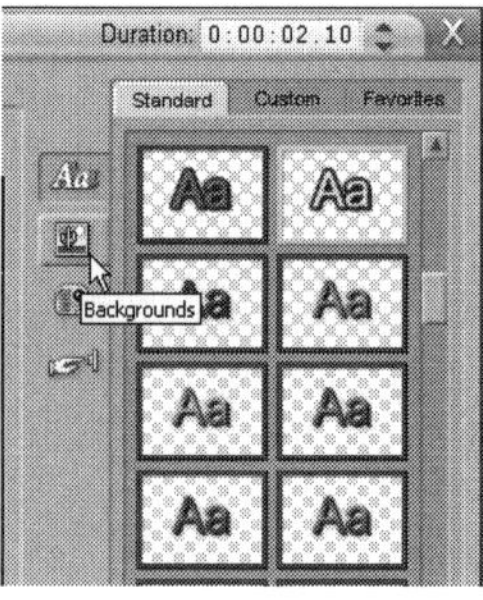

Figure 10.50 Getting to the Backgrounds Album.

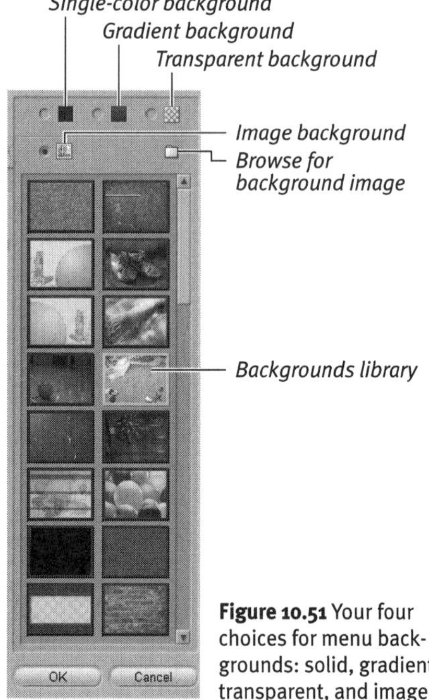

Figure 10.51 Your four choices for menu backgrounds: solid, gradient, transparent, and image.

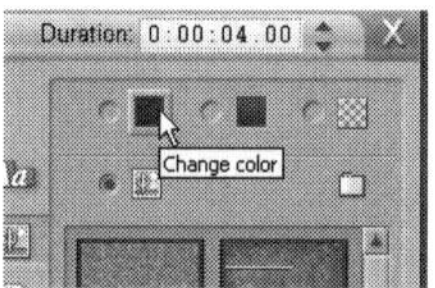

Figure 10.52 Click the colored box to pick another background color.

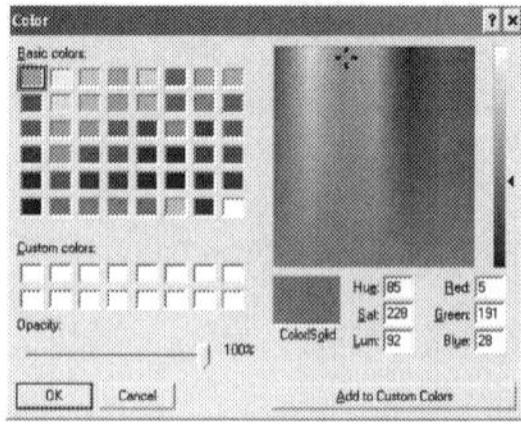

Figure 10.53 The familiar Color selection dialog.

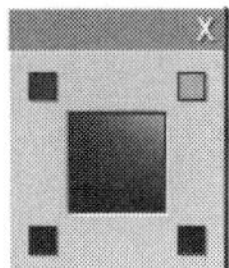

Figure 10.54 This is where you choose your gradient colors.

To create a gradient background:

1. In the Title Editor, click the backgrounds icon on the Title Editor Album icon panel (Figure 10.50).

   The Backgrounds Album opens (Figure 10.51).

2. Check the gradient background checkbox.
3. To change colors, click the colored box next to the gradient checkbox.

   Studio's Gradient selection screen opens (**Figure 10.54**).

4. Clicking any of the boxes opens the Color selection dialog (Figure 10.53). You can configure each of the four colors independently.
5. Click the X in the upper-right corner to close the Gradient selection dialog.

   Studio replaces the background with the selected gradient.

To create a transparent background:

1. In the Title Editor, click the backgrounds icon on the Title Editor Album icon panel (Figure 10.50).

   The Backgrounds Album opens (Figure 10.51).

2. Check the transparent background checkbox.

   This is actually the default setting, for which there are no options. The background simply appears as black behind the menu or title components.

To select an image background:

1. In the Title Editor, click the backgrounds icon on the Title Editor Album icon panel (Figure 10.50).

   The Backgrounds Album opens.
2. Check the image background checkbox (Figure 10.51).
3. Do one of the following:
   - ▲ To use an image from the Album, select the desired image with the pointer.

     Studio replaces the background with the selected image (**Figure 10.55**).
   - ▲ To use an image from another location, click the folder icon (Figure 10.51).

     Studio opens the standard Open dialog.

     Navigate to and select the desired image file.

     Studio replaces the background with the selected image and populates the Image Browser with the new files (**Figure 10.56**).

✔ Tips

- The original location for Studio's excellent background images is Program Files > Pinnacle > Studio 8 > Backgrounds, should you need to find these images again.
- If a selected image doesn't fill the screen in either height or width, Studio stretches the image proportionately (without distorting it) to fill either height or width, whichever is closer. For the most predictable results, prepare your background image files at your target output resolution, using 640 x 480 pixels for DVD, the resolution used for Pinnacle's background files.
- For a complete discussion of image preparation, see Chapter 5.

Figure 10.55 A quick break from the zoo project to illustrate some of the cool Studio-supplied backgrounds and fonts. To change backgrounds, just select the image you like with the pointer.

Figure 10.56 Or, use your own images as backgrounds. Somebody must have said "cheese."

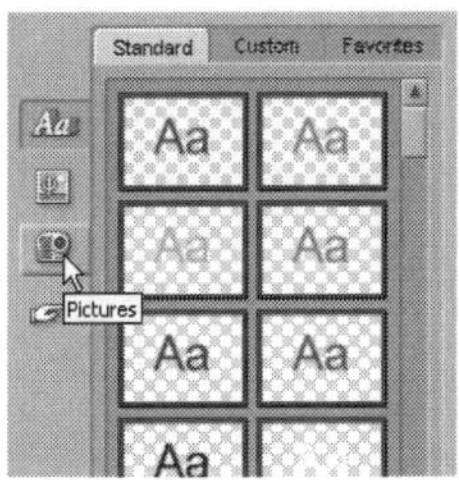

Figure 10.57 Click the pictures icon to open the Pictures Album.

Figure 10.58 The Pictures Album.

Figure 10.59 Drag the image into the Design window. Unlike a background image, an image dragged from the Pictures Album can be scaled or moved.

Adding Logos to Video

Placing logos over videos is a nice professional touch, though Studio presents a minor catch-22. Simply stated, from the Title Editor, you can place, move, and resize a logo over your video, but you can't make it transparent.

Alternatively, you can drag an image to the Title Overlay track from the Still Images tab in the Album and make it transparent (assuming you follow the rules discussed below), but you can't move or resize the image or it becomes a full-screen logo.

These are the general rules; this section covers how to work within them. It also discusses an exception in the sidebar "The Art of Being Transparent."

To overlay a logo on video:

1. Double-click the Title Overlay track at the desired location for the logo overlay.

   The Title Editor opens.

2. In the Title Editor, do one of the following:
   - ▲ Click the pictures icon on the Title Editor Album icon panel (**Figure 10.57**).
   - ▲ From the Studio menu, choose Title > Album > Pictures.

   The Pictures Album opens (**Figure 10.58**).

3. If necessary, click the folder icon to navigate to the directory containing your logos.

4. Drag the image into the Design window (**Figure 10.59**).

5. Move and resize the image as described earlier, under "To resize text."

   Note that you can't skew or rotate the image, only resize and move.

(continued on next page)

✔ Tips

- Although you can't argue with the sheer elegance of the logo shown in Figure 10.59 (pretty cheesy, eh?), you probably wish the black background would go away. The sidebar "The Art of Being Transparent" describes how to accomplish this.
- The program of choice for titling and logo creation is Ulead Systems' Cool 3D Studio, available at www.ulead.com. Using a supplied template, I created the logo shown in Figure 10.59 in about two minutes.

To make a logo transparent:

1. From the Still Images tab, drag the logo to the Title Overlay track (**Figure 10.60**).
   In the Player, Studio zooms the image to full screen and makes it transparent, so you can see segments of the video behind it (as in Figure 10.60).
2. Double-click the logo to open the Title Editor (**Figure 10.61**).
   The logo is full screen and shows no transparency in the Title Editor. In addition, selecting the logo raises no control points. The image looks fuzzy (though perhaps not in your small version of it) because the 160 x 120–resolution image was zoomed to full screen.

Figure 10.60 To make an image transparent, you must load it from the Album. See how this logo is transparent now.

Figure 10.61 Notice how the same logo shows no transparency in the Title Editor.

Figure 10.62 Since you can't resize images placed on the Title Overlay track from the Album, you have to premake your logo files like this.

Figure 10.63 Here's how the logo looks in use.

✔ Tips

- Studio assumes that the top-left pixel is the transparent color, and eliminates this color when displaying the logo. In the Ozer Productions logo, the top-left pixel is black, the same color as the background to be eliminated. When you want to make an image transparent, computer-generated images work the best, or real-world images carefully edited to produce a single, consistent background image.
- Since you can't resize the logo when pulling it down from the Album, the best solution is to create a full-screen (640 x 480) image with the logo as a small component in the desired location (**Figure 10.62**). Remember to observe the title-safe zones when creating images in this fashion. **Figure 10.63** shows the image after overlay.

The Art of Being Transparent

This section's introduction describes Studio's catch-22 when it comes to transparent logo overlay: If you drag in an image from the Title Editor, you can move and resize it, but not make it transparent. If you drag an image in from the Still Images tab of the Album, you can make it transparent, but not move or resize it.

There is one undocumented exception to this catch (Quick! Call Geraldo). If you create a 32-bit image with an alpha channel for the desired transparency region, Studio recognizes and eliminates this region from the Title Editor, allowing full moving and resizing control.

Figure 10.64 Contrary to what the manual says, the Title Editor can recognize transparency masks on 32-bit images with an alpha channel, providing the best of both worlds.

For example, of the three logos in **Figure 10.64**, two are transparent—including the Ozer Productions spinning globe that has active edit points, proving that the logo is both resizable and movable. These were produced as 32-bit video overlays in Targa format in Ulead's Cool 3D Studio. The third logo was output as a simple 24-bit bitmap file. Interestingly, Studio displays the two images as transparent in the Looks Browser, showing a checkered gray pattern behind them instead of the pure black backgrounds of the other images.

In retrospect, it's not surprising that Studio recognizes a transparent alpha channel in images, since the program uses this technique to recognize transparent areas in DVD buttons (see the section "Working with Buttons," later).

The net result is that if you understand how to produce 32-bit images with an alpha channel in programs like Adobe Photoshop, Cool 3D Studio, or Ulead's excellent image editor, PhotoImpact, you can easily make your images transparent in Studio so you can move and resize them at will in the Title Editor. Check the image editor's documentation for details.

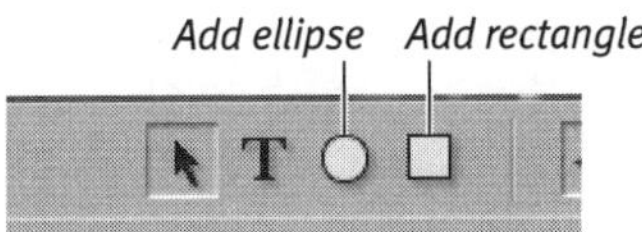

Figure 10.65 Studio lets you draw ellipses and rectangles on your titles.

Figure 10.66 You can manipulate an object at will once it's inserted.

Figure 10.67 You can even apply styles to the object.

Creating and Editing Title Objects

Now that you're comfortable with text, it's time to touch briefly on adding and editing ellipses and rectangles to your titles. Title objects serve quite nicely as text backgrounds or as stand-alone design components.

Studio's title objects are very flexible and can be assigned looks, customized, skewed, resized, and repositioned at will. You accomplish these tasks the same way you do for text, so this section refers back to these sections for customizing.

To create an ellipse or a rectangle:

1. From the Title Editor, click the add ellipse or add rectangle icon in the Object Toolbox (**Figure 10.65**).
2. Click and drag the pointer in the Design window while holding down the left mouse button (**Figure 10.66**).
   Studio creates the object (**Figure 10.67**).

To edit or customize a title object:

- Do one or more of the following:
  - To move the title object, see "To move text," in the "Adding and Editing Text" section earlier in this chapter.
  - To apply or customize a new style (Figure 10.67), see the section "Using Studio's Styles" earlier in this chapter.
  - To size or justify the object, see the section "Resizing and Justifying Text" earlier in this chapter.
  - To rotate or skew your object, see the section "Rotating and Skewing Text" earlier in this chapter.

Working with Buttons

Buttons are interactive links on a menu that let viewers play content like video or a slide show, or jump to other menus. Studio supplies an album of buttons, and you can convert any ungrouped object into a button. Once you add a button to a title, it magically becomes a menu. Like titles, menus can be either full screen or overlays displayed over an underlying video track.

Studio's Title Editor is a great place to produce attractive, custom menus, but you can also choose from an extensive range of customizable menus in the Disc Menus tab of the Album, accessible from the Edit menu. The easiest way to get started is to use the supplied templates, discussed in Chapter 12, a chapter that also describes how to link content to buttons. This chapter focuses exclusively on the mechanics of menu creation.

To add a button to a title:

1. In the Title Editor, do one of the following:
   - ▲ Click the buttons icon on the Title Editor Album icon panel (**Figure 10.68**).
   - ▲ From the Studio menu, choose Title > Album > Buttons.

   Studio opens the Buttons Album.
2. Drag the desired button into the Design window (**Figure 10.69**) and release the mouse button.

   Studio inserts the button into the title.

✔ Tip

- If you've created your own album of buttons, use the folder to the right of the drop-down box at the top of the Buttons Album (Figure 10.71) to navigate to the appropriate folder.

Figure 10.68 Time to start authoring! Step 1, open the Buttons Album.

Figure 10.69 Drag the button from the Buttons Album to the Design window.

Figure 10.70 Or, convert any menu object—text, ellipse, rectangle, image—to a button with this control.

Figure 10.71 The four button types: normal, thumbnail, previous, and next.

Figure 10.72 After converting text to a button, Studio highlights it with the selected color.

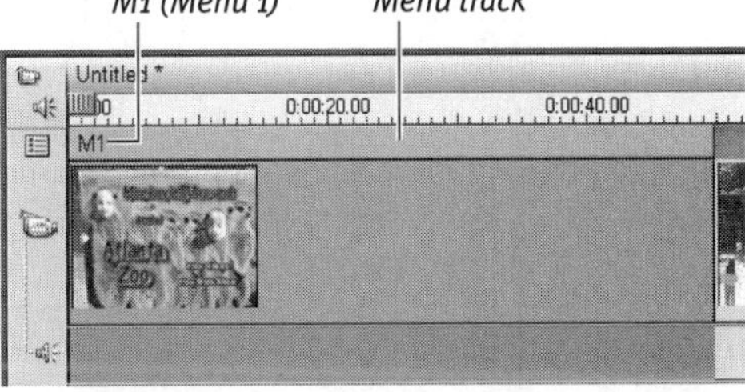

Figure 10.73 Adding a button converts a title to a menu. Now the Menu track is activated and Menu 1 in place.

To convert an object into a button:

1. Select the object to convert, and click the gray bounding box to see the control points (**Figure 10.70**).
2. At the top of the Buttons Album, select the drop-down box to reveal the menu (**Figure 10.71**).
3. Choose Normal button.

   Studio converts the text to a button, and highlights it with the selected color (**Figure 10.72**). When you return to the Menu view, you'll see that the Menu track is now active, and that the label M1, for *Menu 1,* appears atop the menu (**Figure 10.73**). Congratulations, you're now authoring a DVD!

To set a highlight style for a button:

1. Select the button to modify, and click the gray bounding box to see the control points (Figure 10.72).
2. At the top of the Buttons Album, choose one of the following three highlight styles (**Figure 10.74**):
   - ▲ *Follow shape.* When selected, the highlighting follows the object's shape.
   - ▲ *Box.* When selected, a box appears around the button.
   - ▲ *Underline.* When selected, the button is underlined.

   Figure 10.75 shows the styles.

✔ Tip

- Studio provides no feedback in the Title Editor after selecting the button style, so you have to preview the buttons in the Clip Properties tool.

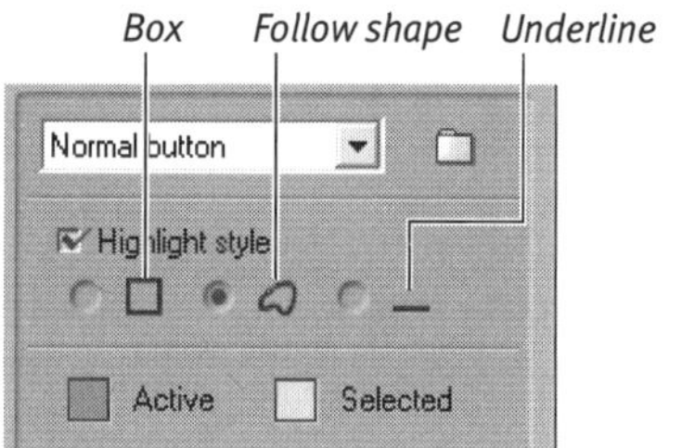

Figure 10.74 Buttons can have three highlight styles: box, follow shape, and underline.

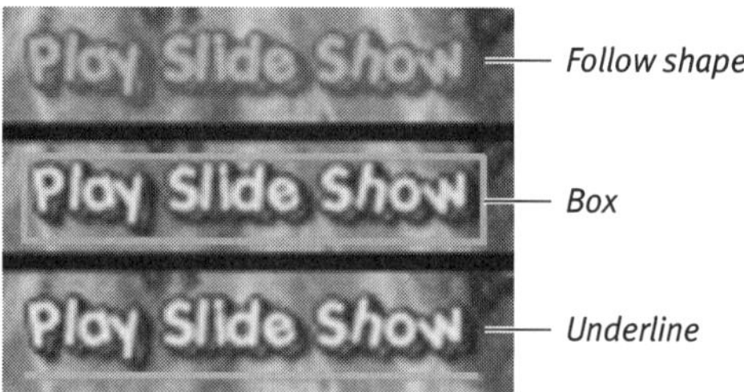

Figure 10.75 Here's what the three highlight styles look like.

A Taxonomy of Buttons

As shown in the drop-down box in Figure 10.71, Studio has the following four button types:

Normal. Links to video, slide shows, or another menu.

Thumbnail. Links to video or a slide show, and displays a thumbnail inside the button (usually shaped like a frame).

Next. Links to the following page. Appears on all but the final page of multimenu productions automatically created by Studio from menu templates.

Previous. Links to the previous page. Appears on second and subsequent pages of multimenu productions automatically created by Studio from menu templates.

If you're building your own menus one by one, always select either normal or thumbnail buttons, even when creating links to previous or next pages.

Use the Previous and Next buttons *only* when you're creating menu templates for Studio's auto-completion, covered below in the section "Creating DVD Menu Templates." Studio uses these buttons to enable navigation between menus that it automatically creates from these templates.

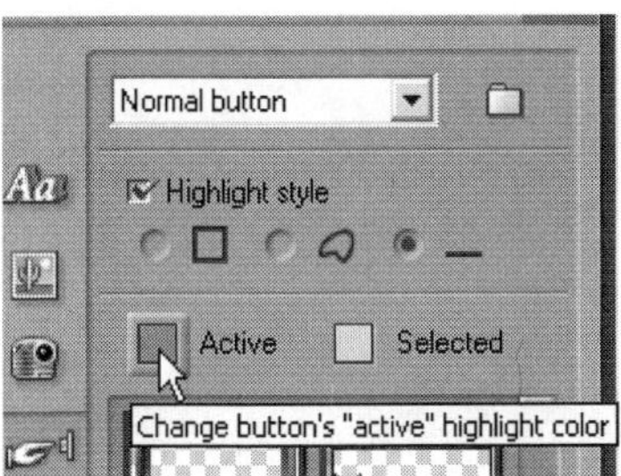

Figure 10.76 You can customize the highlight color for the active or selected state.

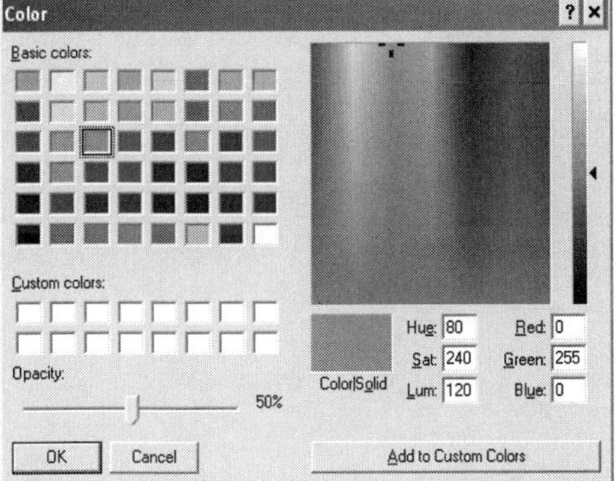

Figure 10.77 Once again, the Color selection dialog.

To set active and selected colors:

1. Select the button to modify, and click the gray bounding box to see the control points (Figure 10.72).
2. At the top of the Buttons Album, choose the color box next to the state (Active or Selected) you want to change (**Figure 10.76**).

   Studio's Color selection dialog opens (**Figure 10.77**).
3. Select the desired color from Basic colors or Custom colors, or by selecting a different color from the spectrum.

   Studio lets you save custom colors by clicking the Add to Custom Colors button (Ctrl+A). Save the custom color to help maintain uniformity going forward.
4. Click OK to close the dialog.

Working with Multiple Objects

Studio includes a wealth of grouping, alignment, sizing, and ordering tools that can be used with all text, figure, graphic, and other objects. However, they prove most helpful for DVD menu design, where they can shave countless minutes ordinarily spent ensuring that objects are similarly sized and properly sized, spaced, and aligned.

This section explores these features while creating a DVD menu ultimately saved as a Studio template.

To make objects the same size:

1. Select the objects to resize by doing one of the following:
   - ▲ Hold down the Ctrl key and select each object with the pointer.
   - ▲ Hold down the left mouse button and drag an area that includes only the objects to be resized.

   Studio places white highlights around each object, with yellow highlights around the final object selected (**Figure 10.78**). Studio will resize all objects to the dimensions of this object.

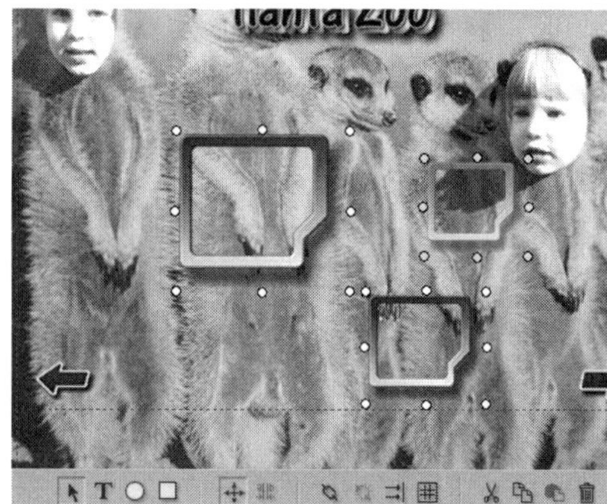

Figure 10.78 To make all objects the same size, select them, choosing last the one you want all the others to conform to (it should have a yellow bounding box around it).

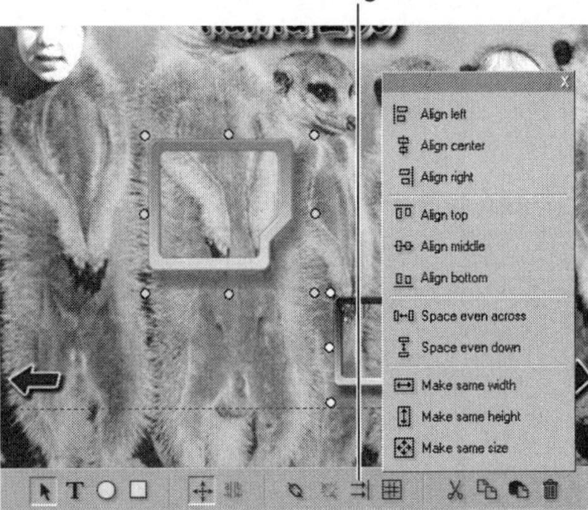

Figure 10.79 Click the align icon, then select Make same size at the bottom of the menu.

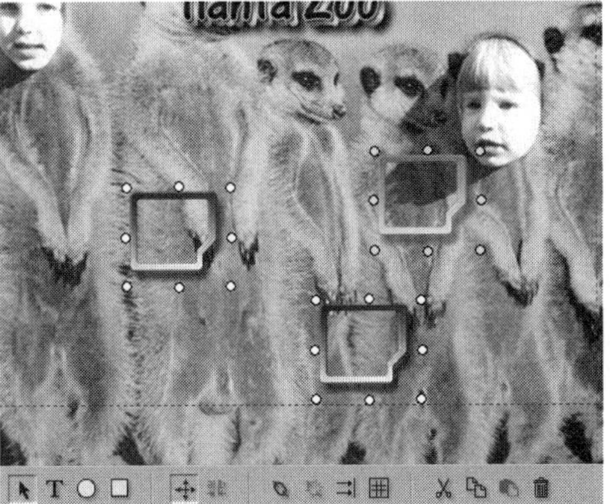

Figure 10.80 They're all the same size now!

2. Click the align icon at the bottom of the Design window.

   Studio displays the Align menu (**Figure 10.79**).

3. Select Make same size at the bottom of the Align menu.

   Studio resizes all objects to the size of the last object selected (**Figure 10.80**).

✔ Tips

- This method works best if you've already made your objects and need to resize them en masse. But often it's easier to copy and paste buttons and other objects to ensure they're identical (see "To copy and paste objects," later).
- There are icons in the Align menu for making objects the same height and width. Use the procedures described above to operate these functions.
- You can also access sizing functions from the Studio menu at Title > Align.
- In truth, these controls have worked sporadically for me in the past. If you find that they're not working for you, use the copy and paste method discussed in the first tip if you can; otherwise mutter (quietly) under your breath and resize them manually.

To space objects evenly vertically or horizontally:

1. Select the objects to space by doing one of the following:
   - ▲ Hold down the Ctrl key and select each object with the pointer.
   - ▲ Hold down the left mouse button and drag an area that includes only the objects to be spaced (**Figure 10.81**).
2. At the bottom of the Design window, click the align icon.
   Studio displays the Align menu (Figure 10.79).
3. Select Space even across.
   Studio spaces all objects evenly between the two objects at either extreme (**Figure 10.82**).

✔ Tips

- Studio does *not* space the objects evenly on the page, only between the objects at either extreme. To obtain the desired spacing, place the two outside objects at the desired location, and Studio spaces all other selected objects evenly between these two.
- Operation is identical when spacing objects vertically.
- You can also access spacing functions from the Studio menu at Title > Align.

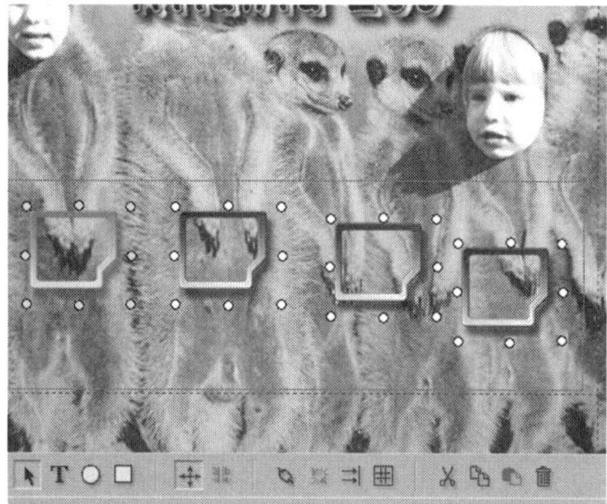

Figure 10.81 Now, to get them evenly spaced, first move the two outside boxes to the desired locations. Studio spaces the images inside these extremes.

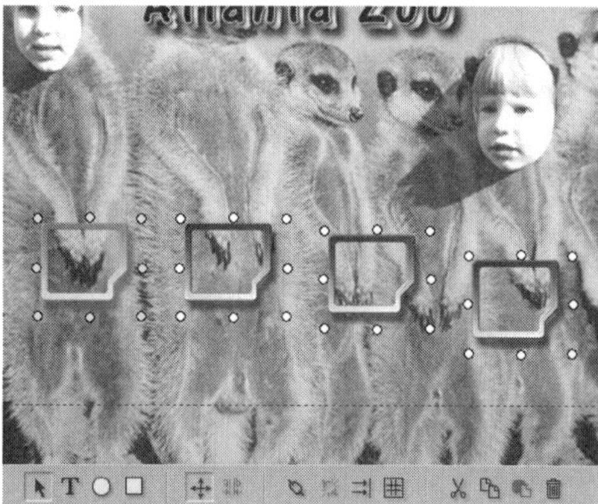

Figure 10.82 Now that the objects are spaced evenly, time to get them aligned. When selecting the images, choose the one in the desired position last (it should have a yellow bounding box).

Figure 10.83 Alignment achieved.

To align objects vertically or horizontally:

1. Select the objects to align by doing one of the following:
   - ▲ Hold down the Ctrl key and select each object with the pointer.
   - ▲ Hold down the left mouse button and drag an area that includes only the objects to be aligned (Figure 10.82).

   The object with the yellow control points becomes the reference: All other objects shift to the position of this object.
2. Click the align icon at the bottom of the Design window.

   Studio displays the Align menu (Figure 10.79).
3. Click the desired alignment—in this case, Align bottom.

   Studio spaces all objects evenly between the two objects at either extreme (**Figure 10.83**).

✔ Tips

- Operation is identical when using the other alignment functions.
- You can also access aligning functions from the Studio menu at Title > Align.

To group and ungroup objects:

1. Select the objects to group by doing one of the following:
   - ▲ Hold down the Ctrl key and select each object with the pointer.
   - ▲ Hold down the left mouse button and drag an area that includes only the objects to group.
2. Click the group icon at the bottom of the Design window (**Figure 10.84**).

   Studio groups the objects together. To ungroup the objects, click the ungroup object icon next to the group icon.

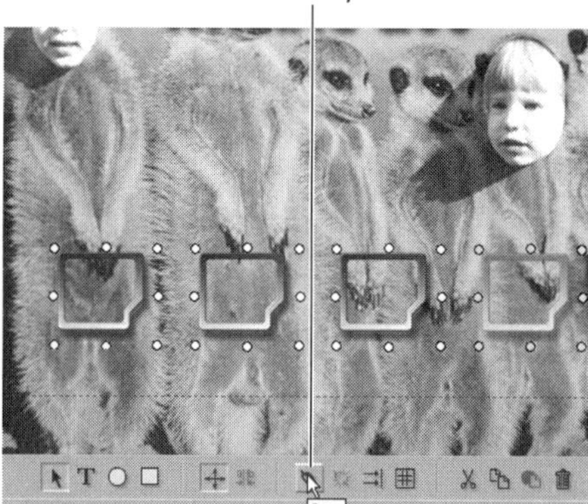

Figure 10.84 Now, group the objects so you can position them en masse. Use the group icon.

✔ Tip

- Once you've grouped the objects, you can perform extensive edits that impact all objects. For example, with the thumbnail buttons shown in Figure 10.84, Studio modified size, active color, and highlight style for all grouped icons—a very efficient editing mode.

To copy and paste objects:

1. Select the objects you wish to copy by doing one of the following:
   - ▲ Hold down the Ctrl key and select each object with the pointer.
   - ▲ Hold down the left mouse button and drag an area that includes only the objects to be copied (**Figure 10.85**).
2. Click the copy icon at the bottom of the Design window.
3. Click the paste icon to paste the objects.

   Studio pastes the objects directly on top of the original objects.
4. Drag the pasted objects to the desired location (**Figure 10.86**).

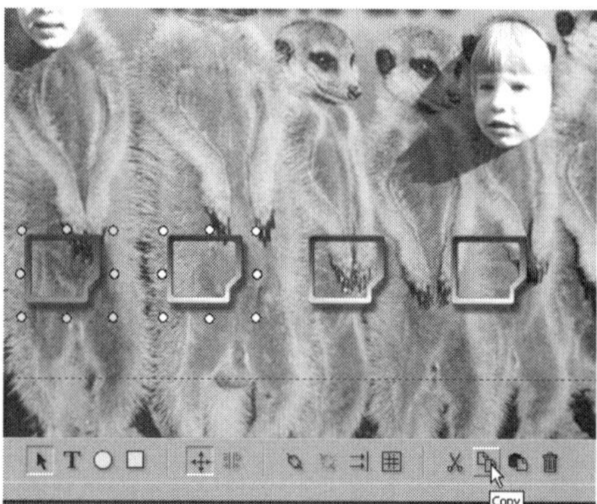

Figure 10.85 To copy two of the objects to move up to the top, select them and click the copy icon.

Figure 10.86 Next, paste them atop the originals using the paste icon. Then drag them to the desired location.

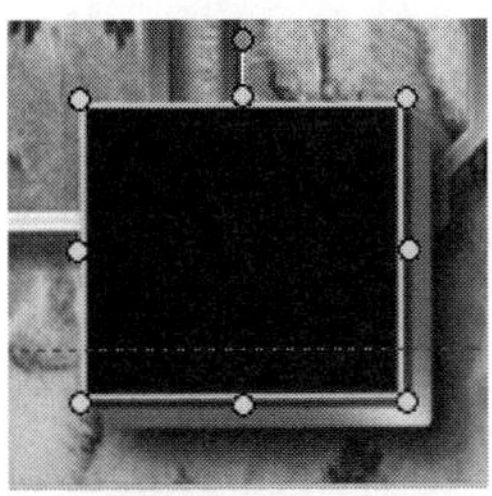

Figure 10.87 Suppose you wanted to use a rectangle as a frame for this thumbnail button. The problem is when you create the rectangle, it's placed over the thumbnail.

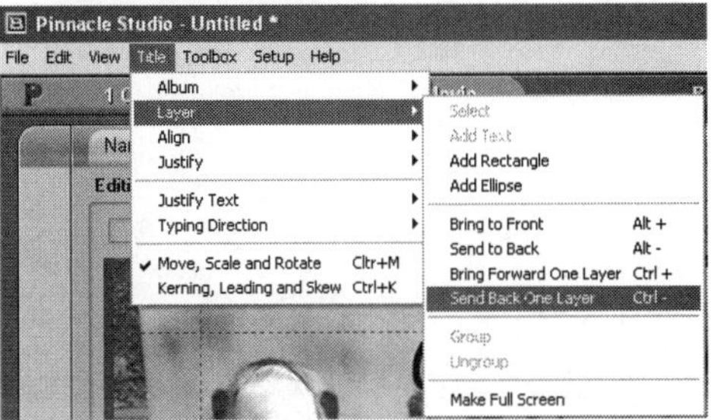

Figure 10.88 Use these controls to move objects to different layers.

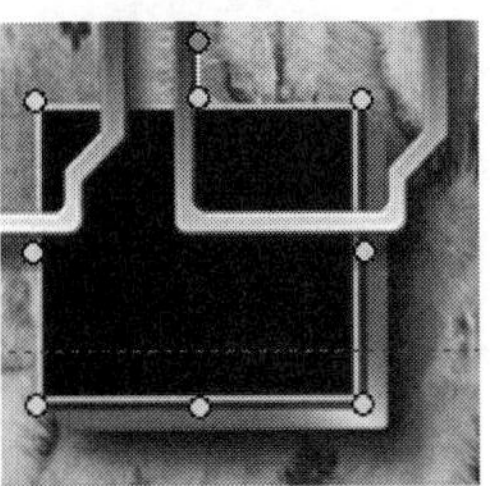

Figure 10.89 Now the frame is behind the button, where you can move it to serve as a frame for the thumbnail button.

In this example, a frame (a rectangle object) was created after the thumbnail button was created, and thus obscures the thumbnail when dragged to the same location. Here's how to place the frame behind the thumbnail.

To change object layers:

1. Select the object or objects to move forward or backward (**Figure 10.87**).
2. From the Studio menu, choose Title > Layer, then choose the desired action—in this case, Send Back One Layer (**Figure 10.88**).

   Studio moves the object back one layer, displaying the thumbnail button over the frame (**Figure 10.89**).

Creating DVD Menu Templates

One of Studio's coolest features is the ability to create menu templates that can be automatically populated just by adding videos to the Timeline. Through the work performed in the previous section, the template is almost complete.

A complete template has three components: buttons for linking content (which are already present on the template-in-progress) and the Next and Previous buttons, which allow Studio to create automatic menus and navigation controls between the menus. Text and a cute backgrounds are nice but not required.

See Chapter 12 for more on DVD menus.

To use existing Next and Previous buttons in your template:

1. Browse the Buttons Album until you find suitable buttons with the words *next* or *previous* in the name (**Figure 10.90**).
2. Drag the buttons to the desired locations (**Figure 10.91**).

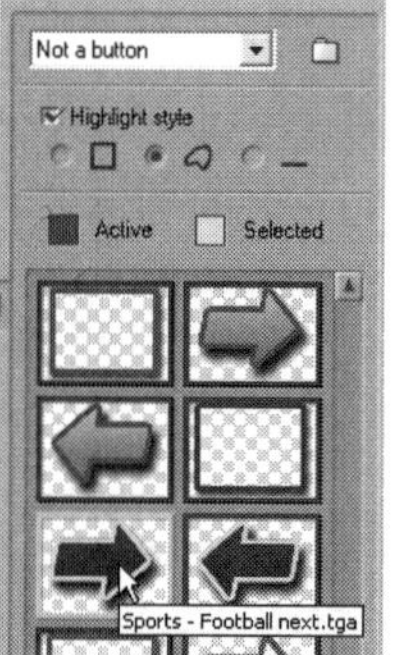

Figure 10.90 To complete the template menu, you need Next and Previous buttons.

Previous button

Next button

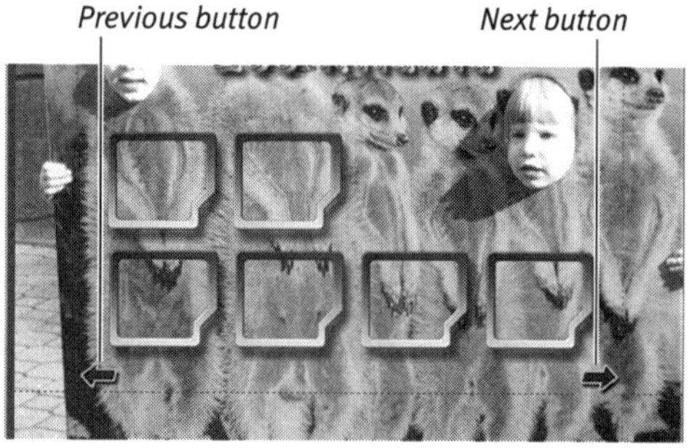

Figure 10.91 Drag the Next and Previous buttons to the desired locations.

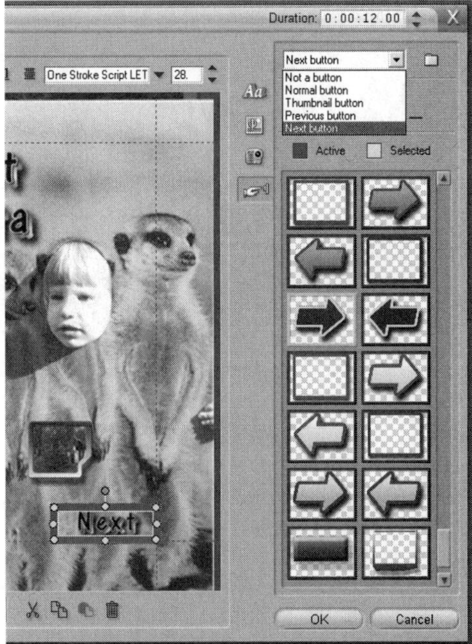

Figure 10.92 Or, you could use any object and simply assign it the necessary value.

Figure 10.93 Save the template.

To create your own Next and Previous buttons:

1. Create and/or input the desired text or object (**Figure 10.92**).
2. Select the drop-down menu atop the Buttons Album to activate the menu.
3. Choose Next button.
4. Repeat for the Previous button.

To save a menu as a template:

1. From the File menu, choose File > Save Menu As.

   Studio opens the Save Menu As dialog.
2. Name the file and save into the Program files > Pinnacle > Studio 8 > Menus folder (**Figure 10.93**).

Creating Rolls and Crawls

After all this work, there's only one way to close this chapter: with *The End* rolling onto the screen—or crawling across the screen. You pick. The grandparents are screaming for this DVD.

With rolls, you place the title object where you want it to end up, and Studio moves it from the off-screen bottom to the specified location.

With crawls, Studio moves the title object from off-screen on the right to off-screen on the left. You set the object at the desired height of the effect and Studio does the rest.

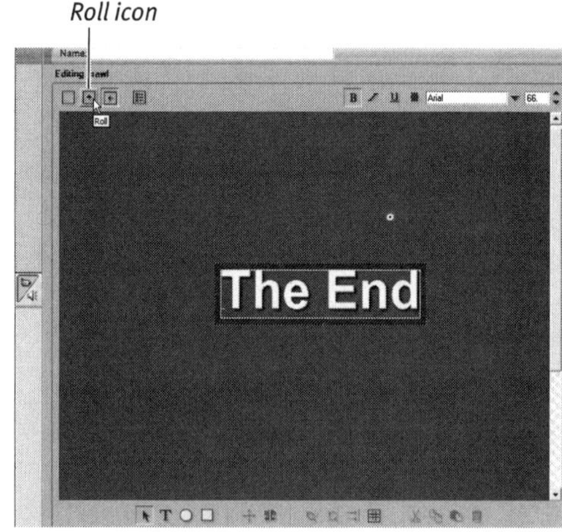

Figure 10.94 The perfect way to end this chapter: a rolling *The End* title, pulled from Studio's Album, of course.

To create a rolling title:

1. From the Title Editor, position the title object at the desired stopping point (**Figure 10.94**).
2. From the title-type buttons at the upper left, click the roll icon.

   Studio produces the effect, which you can preview only from the Movie Window.

Figure 10.95 You can make the title crawl across the screen.

To create a crawling title:

1. From the Title Editor, position the title object at the desired height.
2. From the title-type buttons at the upper left, click the crawl icon (**Figure 10.95**).

   Studio produces the effect, which you can preview only from the Movie Window.

✔ Tips

- Note that menus (i.e., titles with buttons) can't roll or crawl.
- Studio includes a *The End* title in the Titles Album, which is the easiest way to create this effect.
- To reverse a crawl or a roll and convert back to a static menu, click the first box in the title-type buttons (the square box).

11 Working with Audio

The last ten chapters have focused largely on video, perhaps leading the casual observer to believe that audio is less important. As serious producers will tell you, this just isn't so. The Internet experience is probably the best barometer. Many viewers will tolerate grainy, postage-stamp-size video, but let the audio break once or twice, and satisfaction quickly wanes. That's why streaming technologies from Apple, Microsoft, and RealNetworks all prioritize the delivery of audio over video.

Like most programs, Studio offers three audio tracks—for original audio, narration, and background music—plus tools for *ripping* CD tracks and recording narration (see "Setting Recording Options" later in this chapter). However, Studio's audio feature set is extraordinary in two respects.

First is SmartSound, which produces thematic background music of any customizable length. It's the same program Adobe includes with Premiere, a professional video editor that costs hundreds more. Also exceptional is Studio's Volume tool, a real-time mixer that lets you customize audio volume on all tracks simultaneously. Together, these tools let you easily create and integrate professional-quality audio into your productions.

About Audio Tracks and Workflow

Studio has three audio tracks, which operate as follows (**Figure 11.1**):

- **Original Audio track.** This track always starts with audio from the video file above it. If you lock the Video track, you can delete the original audio file and insert an audio file from the Album or drag one from any other track.
- **Sound Effect and Voice-Over track.** Studio places narrations created with the Voice-Over tool in this track. By designation, Pinnacle also suggests that sound effects should be placed in this track, but you can place the sound effects in any open track.
- **Background Music track.** Studio places files from both the CD Audio tool and SmartSound tool in this track, which can otherwise contain any audio file.

You can place any audio file from the Album in any track, but you should reserve the designated tracks for their namesake items if you plan to create narration or background audio files. Once Studio creates these files, it lets you move them to any track, thus providing additional design flexibility.

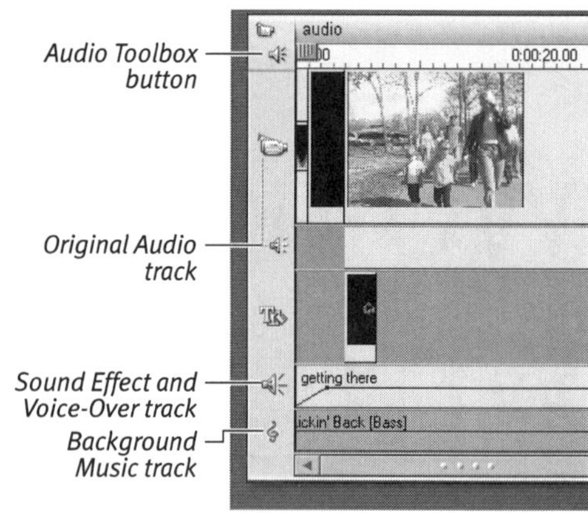

Figure 11.1 Studio has three audio tracks: one for the original audio included in the captured file, one for sound effects and voice-overs, and one for background music. At the top is the Audio Toolbox button.

Getting audio to the Timeline

As we've seen, the Original Audio track is populated with audio associated with the video file.

You can add just the audio from any video file by dragging the file from the Album to either the Voice-Over track or the Background Music track. (For details see Chapter 7.)

Studio can also import WAV and MP3 files for dragging to the audio tracks. (For details see the section "Working in the Sound Effects Tab" in Chapter 6.)

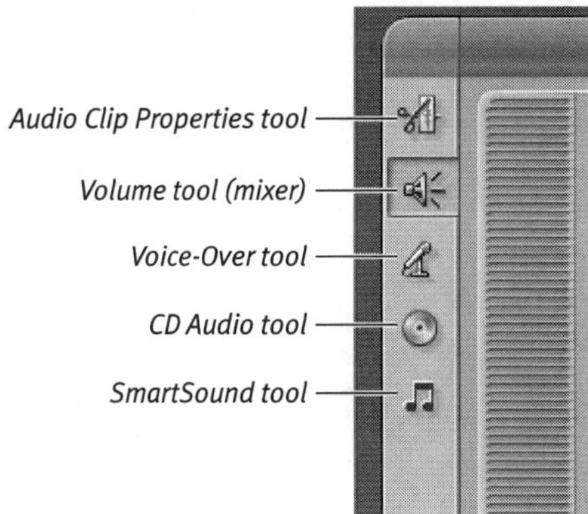

Figure 11.2 The Audio Toolbox contains five tools.

The Audio Toolbox

Studio's Audio Toolbox, accessed by clicking the namesake button at the top of the Movie Window (Figure 11.1), contains the various tools used to create, edit, and mix audio on the respective tracks (**Figure 11.2**). Here are those tools (top to bottom):

- **Audio Clip Properties tool.** For trimming audio files.
- **Volume tool (mixer).** For adjusting the volume of the various audio tracks.
- **Voice-Over tool.** For recording narration segments placed on the Voice-Over track.
- **CD Audio tool.** For ripping CD audio tracks that are placed on the Background Music track.
- **SmartSound tool.** For creating background music placed on the Background Music track.

✔ Tip

- Create your audio tracks last, after all your video edits are finalized. That way, adjustments to the video tracks won't throw off the synchronization of the Background Music and Voice-Over tracks with the video.

Setting Recording Options

There are two ways to capture audio from an audio CD. The better one is to pull off the tracks digitally, a process known as ripping—basically just a file transfer from the CD to your hard drive. Very much like DV capture, it's fast, high-quality, and simple, requiring no real options to set.

If that's not available, perhaps because you have an older computer or a missing cable, you can capture CD audio through your sound card, essentially performing an analog-to-digital conversion. You have to set some parameters for the conversion, but they're simple and described below.

To set CD-ripping options:

1. From the Studio menu, choose Setup > CD and Voice-over.

   The Pinnacle Studio Setup Options screen opens to the CD and Voice-over tab (**Figure 11.3**).

2. In the lower-left corner of the screen, select the drive containing the CD audio disc.

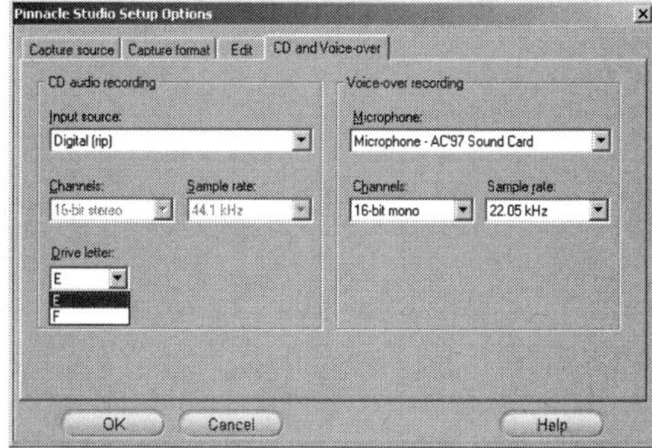

Figure 11.3 Here's where you select the drive for ripping CD tracks and set other recording options.

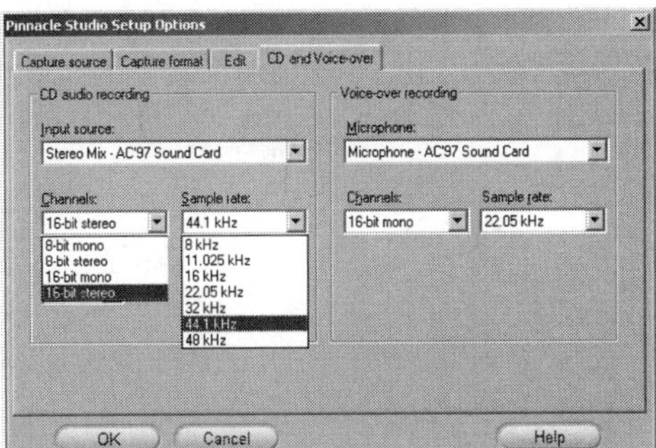

Figure 11.4 Most people rip audio digitally. If this option isn't available, select the appropriate input source and digitize at 16-bit stereo, 44.1 kHz.

3. Do one of the following:
   - ▲ If your CD drive is set to Digital (rip) in the Input source drop-down box (Figure 11.3), you're all set. Just jump down to set your voice-over recording options.
   - ▲ If your CD drive is not set to Digital (rip), click the Input source drop-down menu and choose the appropriate recording option for your sound card (**Figure 11.4**).
   - ▲ Click the Channels drop-down menu (still in the CD audio recording area on the left) and choose 16-bit stereo.
   - ▲ Click the Sample rate drop-down menu and choose 44.1 kHz.

✔ Tips

- If you have multiple CD/DVD drives, try to find a drive that you can set to Digital (rip), and use that drive.
- If this option isn't available, it's typically because a small cable that connects your sound card (or audio on your computer's motherboard) to the drive is dislodged or disconnected. If you're the intrepid type, consult the documentation for your computer and/or sound card and see if you can fix this problem.
- Unfortunately, all sound cards are different, so it's impossible to tell which options are available on each individual card.

To set voice-over recording options:

1. In the same option screen, now under Voice-over recording on the right, make sure that the Microphone drop-down menu is set to the microphone input source (**Figure 11.5**).
2. Click the Channels drop-down menu (still under Voice-over recording) and choose 16-bit mono (Figure 11.4).
3. Click the Sample rate drop-down menu and choose 22.05 kHz.
4. Click OK to close the dialog.

✔ Tips

- Pinnacle recommends using 16-bit mono at 22.05 kHz for narration because speech is less complex than music, and this format saves space without any perceptible quality difference. If the quality isn't good enough for your ear, or if you record your audio with music in the background, bump it up to the 16-bit stereo, 44.1 kHz, used for ripping CD tracks. It'll cost you an extra 128 Kbytes per second, about 3.5 percent of what DV video costs you.
- If you're creating auxiliary audio files, it helps to know where they're going so you can reuse or delete them. See Chapter 2 for details.

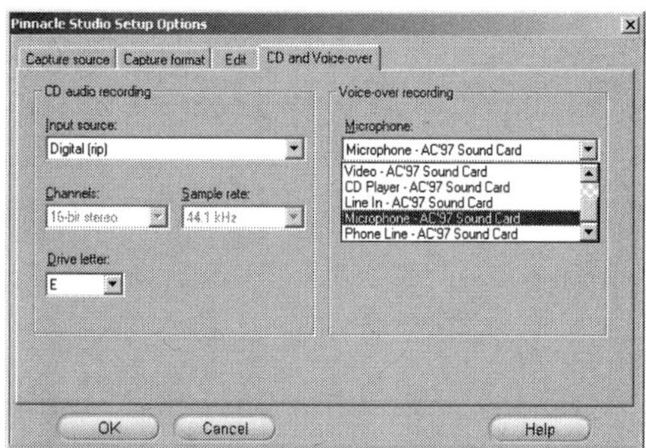

Figure 11.5 Studio does a pretty good job finding the microphone input, but if it doesn't on your computer, here's how you select it.

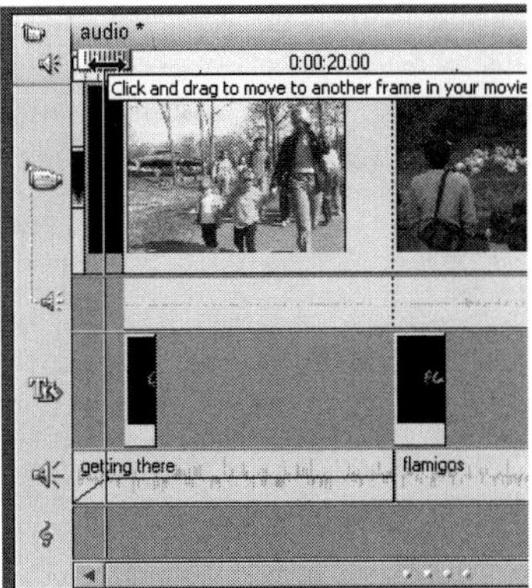

Figure 11.6 Position the Timeline Scrubber where you want Studio to place the ripped CD audio.

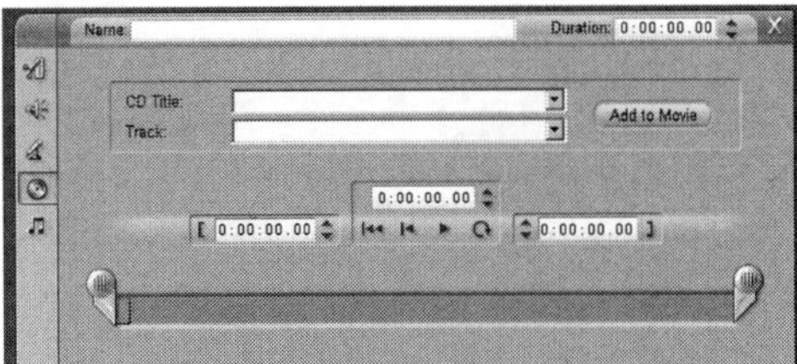

Figure 11.7 The CD Audio tool.

Ripping CD Audio

If you're used to fully functional jukebox products like those from MusicMatch, Microsoft, and RealNetworks, Studio's CD Audio tool will seem mundane. Although it may lack in flash and features, you know the files created will be compatible with Studio, and that's good enough for me.

To rip a CD audio track:

1. Place the Timeline Scrubber where the audio should be inserted (**Figure 11.6**).
2. To open the CD Audio tool, do one of the following:
   - ▲ Click the Audio Toolbox icon (Figure 11.1), then click the CD to switch to the CD Audio tool.
   - ▲ In the Studio menu, choose Toolbox > Add CD Music.

   The Audio Toolbox opens to the CD Audio tool (**Figure 11.7**).

(continued on next page)

3. Place a CD in the CD audio drive.

   Studio performs one of the following actions:

   ▲ If the CD is new, Studio prompts you to enter the name of the CD (**Figure 11.8**). Enter the appropriate name.

   ▲ If you've ripped tracks from this CD previously, Studio automatically recognizes the CD and inserts the name (**Figure 11.9**).

4. Select the desired track.

5. If desired, select the Start and End locations by doing one of the following:

   ▲ Slide the Trim Calipers to the desired location.

   ▲ Type the desired setting in the transport controls or use the Trim Scrubber to move to the desired location, then click the controls that set your Start and End locations.

   ▲ Use the jog buttons next to the Start and End Location counters.

6. Click the Add to Movie button.

   Studio adds the track to the selected location (**Figure 11.10**).

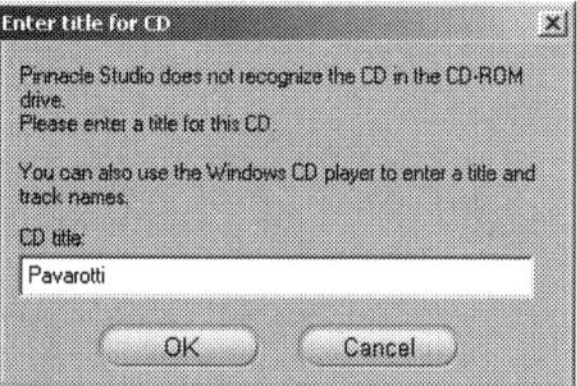

Figure 11.8 Studio tracks your CDs by the title you enter here. Pavarotti is appropriate for the zoo, don't you think?

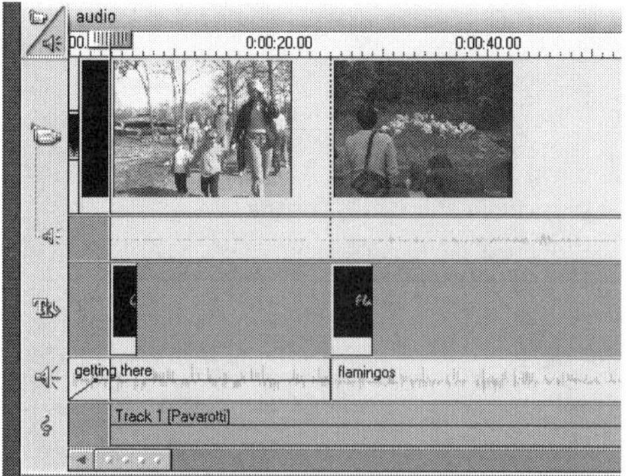

Figure 11.10 Studio adds the track. Note that Studio doesn't actually rip the track until you preview, so preview as soon as you place the track, or you'll have to find the CD again during final rendering.

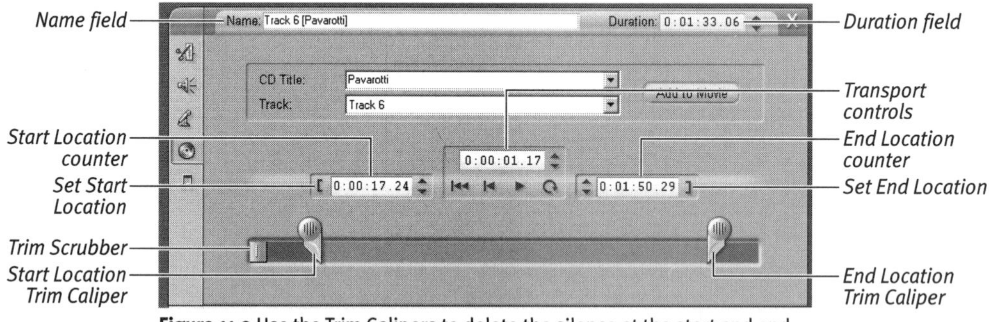

Figure 11.9 Use the Trim Calipers to delete the silence at the start and end of the track.

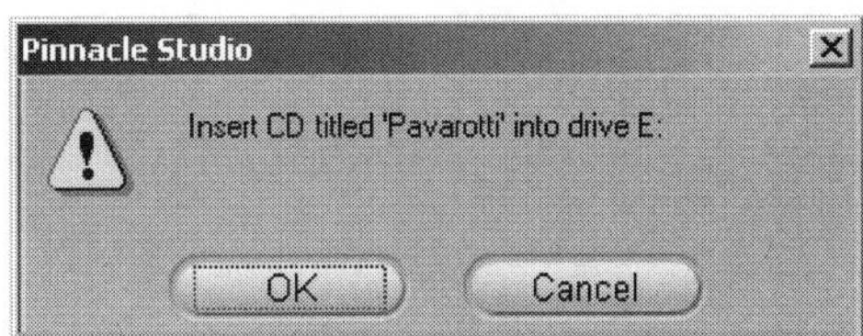

Figure 11.11 Here's Studio asking for that Pavarotti CD.

✔ Tips

- There's usually some silence at both the start and end of a CD audio clip. It's a good idea to eliminate this before you rip a track; otherwise it's another step with the Audio Toolbox.
- Studio doesn't actually rip the track until you preview the video at that location. At that time, if the CD is not in the drive, Studio prompts you to insert the CD-ROM (**Figure 11.11**). To keep things simple, you should preview right after inserting the track; that way Studio rips and inserts the audio right away, and you won't have to track down the CD later.
- On second thought, Studio really isn't the best tool for ripping tracks from your CD-ROM; you're better off with any of the players suggested above (MusicMatch's Jukebox, Microsoft's Media Player, or RealNetworks' RealOne), especially if you're a digital audio aficionado. All these programs can search the Internet and name your CDs and tracks, and rip the files for instant use and later reuse.
- If you use a third-party player, note that Studio can be finicky during import, and might fail to load MP3 files that are not 128 Kbps, or WAV files that are not 16-bit stereo at 44.1 kHz (the standard for CD audio). If you use another tool, rip a track or two and see if Studio can load it before ripping your entire collection. And remember, Studio can't load Windows Media files or QuickTime, so don't even think about it.

Creating Background Tracks with SmartSound

With the buildup I gave it in the intro, SmartSound can't possibly live up to its billing. So, I'll try the low-key approach, walk you through the tool quickly, and let you decide for yourself.

Note that you can't have CD audio and SmartSound files in the same location on the Background Music track (though you can certainly have both at different locations). Having impressed all you opera fans already, I'll delete Pavarotti and start with a clean background audio track.

To add SmartSound background music:

1. Do one of the following to select the scenes for SmartSound to synchronize to:
   - ▲ Holding down the Shift key, select contiguous scenes with the pointer (**Figure 11.12**).
   - ▲ Starting with any unpopulated area on the Timeline, drag a box around the scenes.
   - ▲ From the Studio menu, choose Edit > Select All (Ctrl+A) to select the entire Timeline.
2. To open the SmartSound tool, do one of the following:
   - ▲ Click the Audio Toolbox icon (Figure 11.1), then click the SmartSound tool icon on the left of the Audio Toolbox panel (Figure 11.2).
   - ▲ From the Studio menu, choose Toolbox > Generate Background Music.

   The SmartSound tool opens (**Figure 11.13**).

   If you didn't install SmartSound during installation, Studio prompts you to insert the setup disk.

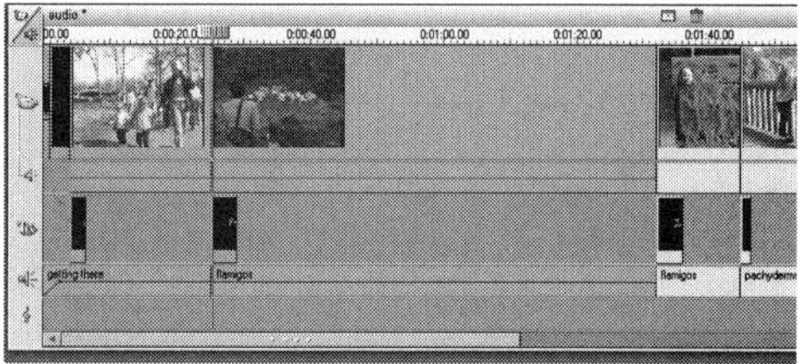

Figure 11.12 Studio's SmartSound creates background music for all selected tracks, so start by selecting the tracks.

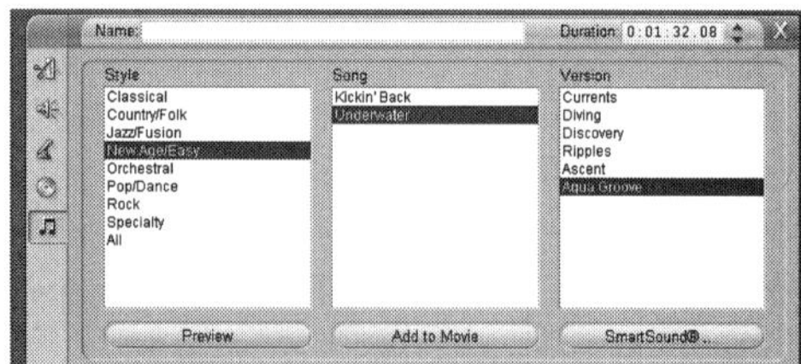

Figure 11.13 The SmartSound tool. Studio ships a lot of choices, and you can buy additional tracks at www.smartsound.com.

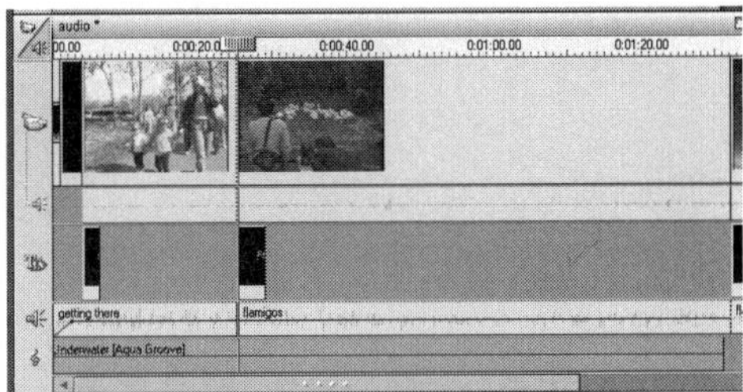

Figure 11.14 Studio adds the track to the selected videos.

3. Choose a style from the Style list.
4. Choose a song from the Song list.
5. Choose a version from the Version list.
6. Click the Preview button anytime to listen to your selection.

   You can change your selection and preview again anytime.
7. When complete, click the Add to Movie button.

   Studio adds the background audio track to the selected clips (**Figure 11.14**).

✔ Tips

- As with CD audio, Studio doesn't create the track until you preview.
- Each time you change the duration of the videos on the Timeline, Studio adjusts the duration of the SmartSound track, creating noticeable delays on longer projects as Studio creates the new audio track. This is another reason to add audio as the last editing step.
- Click the SmartSound button (Figure 11.13) to see more about SmartSound, including the URL for the SmartSound Software (formerly Sonic Desktop) Web site (www.smartsound.com), which offers an excellent selection of additional audio tracks.

Recording Narrations

Narrating your videos and slide shows is a great way to add context to the visual presentation, and Studio makes narrations simple to create and use. Even with an inexpensive microphone, you can create high-quality audio, but with the wrong gear or wrong setup, you'll be disappointed with the quality. For more details, see the sidebar "Getting the Most from Your Narrations."

To connect for narration:

1. Connect your microphone to the microphone port on your sound card or computer.

   Note that the internal settings for *line-in* are different from those of the microphone, so you're not likely to get good results using this connector.

2. Connect your headphones (if available) to the speaker port on your sound card or computer.

✔ Tip

- Many computers (like my Sony VAIO) designate the microphone connector with a red plug, which sometimes matches the plug on the microphone itself.

Getting the Most from Your Narrations

There are two aspects to a good narration: technical and artistic.

From a technical perspective, you can achieve great results with an inexpensive microphone, but I recommend that you use a microphone that's part of a headset. They are often sold together for use in Internet videoconferencing. If you're using a stand-alone microphone, ditch your external speakers for a set of headphones during recording, or you'll produce *feedback*—an annoying screeching sound caused by the microphone picking up output from the speakers.

From an artistic standpoint, you'll get the best results by scripting your narration and taking the time to try multiple takes until you get it right. Keep your comments short and to the point, or you'll complicate both the scripting and the performance.

If you're going to wing it without a script, adjust your expectations downward. While you may strive to emulate the baritone splendor of James Earl Jones, the mellifluous tones of yoga maven Tracey Rich, or the fluidity of Bryant Gumble, you'll never get finished if you insist on that level of perfection.

Finally, note that there are tools out there that can stretch or compress your narration to the duration of the corresponding video with minimal distortion, which can save oodles of time compared to re-recording a four-minute track to shave 15 seconds either way. Sonic Foundry's CD Architect is a good place to start (www.sonicfoundry.com).

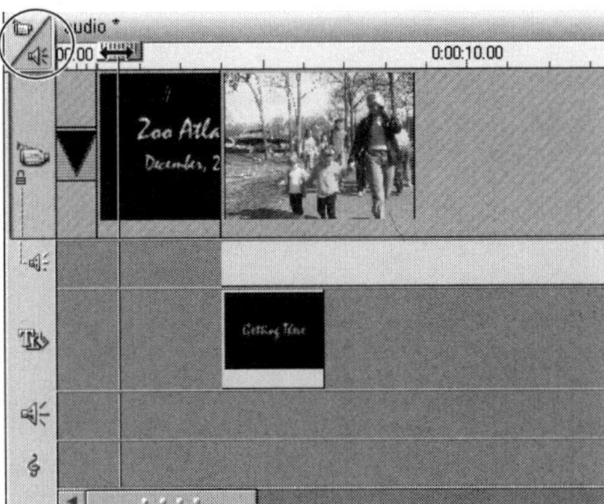

Figure 11.15 As with CD audio, start your narration by placing the Timeline Scrubber at the desired location.

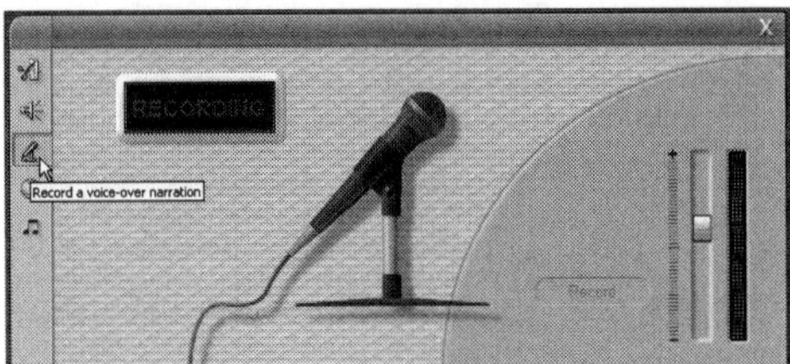

Figure 11.16 The Voice-Over Narration tool.

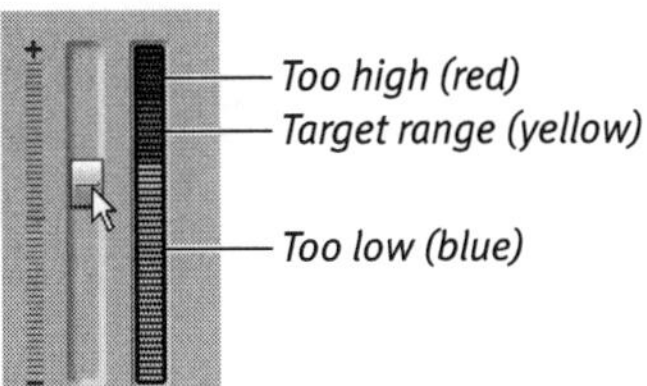

Figure 11.17 Use the Volume Adjustment tool to customize recording volume.

To record your narration:

1. Position the Timeline Scrubber to the desired insert point (**Figure 11.15**).

   There must be at least one video or still image on the Timeline to record a narration, and there can't be audio in the Voice-Over track at the desired insert point.

2. To open the Voice-Over Narration tool, do one of the following:
   - ▲ Click the Audio Toolbox icon (Figure 11.1), then click the icon for recording a voice-over narration (**Figure 11.16**).
   - ▲ From the Studio menu, choose Toolbox > Record Voice-over.

   The Voice-Over Narration tool opens.

   The volume meter on the right is completely unlit, meaning the microphone is hearing no audio—a good thing. When you have a noisy room or a poor microphone, the meter jumps, signifying noisy audio.

3. Speak into the microphone, and use the Volume Adjustment tool on the right (**Figure 11.17**) to position the audio level so that it is at the top of the blue level or into the yellow level, but never touches the red.

   Touching the red may clause *clipping,* which often sounds like a mechanical click on the audio, or it can distort your voice.

(continued on next page)

4. After setting the appropriate level, click the Record button (Figure 11.16) to start the recording.

   Studio first lights a "Standby" sign in the Recording box, then numbers count down from three, to two, to one. Then the Recording light turns on, and blinks slowly during the recording (**Figure 11.18**).

   While recording, watch the audio levels to maintain the appropriate volume.

   If the Recording button doesn't light up, it's most likely because the Timeline Scrubber is positioned above a point in the Voice-Over track that already contains audio. So move, edit, or delete the old audio, or change locations to a blank place in the track.

5. Press Stop to stop recording (Figure 11.18).

   When Studio stops recording, it creates and stores the audio file (you'll see the word *Standby* light for a moment), then posts the file in the Voice-Over track (**Figure 11.19**).

6. In the Player, press Play to hear your recorded audio.

   Since the proper levels haven't yet been set for the narration and other tracks, it may be difficult to hear the narration over the other tracks. For how to set the respective volumes, see "Using the Volume Tool" later in this chapter.

   After you've finished recording, the narration track becomes just like any file that you can trim, split, move, or delete. For example, if you don't like the recorded track, simply select it, press Delete, and it's gone.

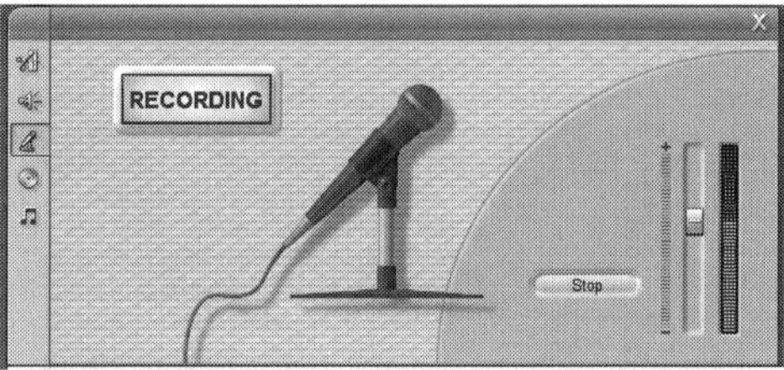

Figure 11.18 Once you're recording, try to keep the level predominantly in the yellow, avoiding the red at all costs.

Figure 11.19 The completed narration track.

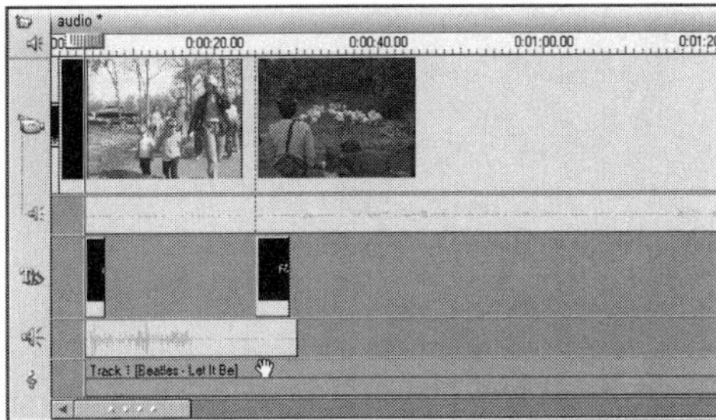
Figure 11.20 OK, so I ditched Pavarotti for the Beatles. To edit the track, double-click it. What opens?

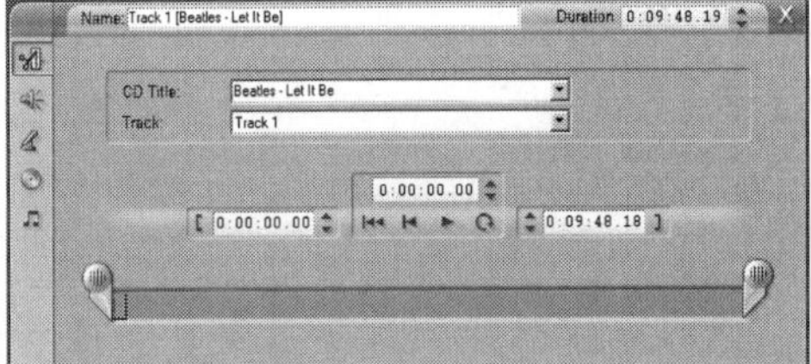

Figure 11.21 The Clip Properties tool for CD audio.

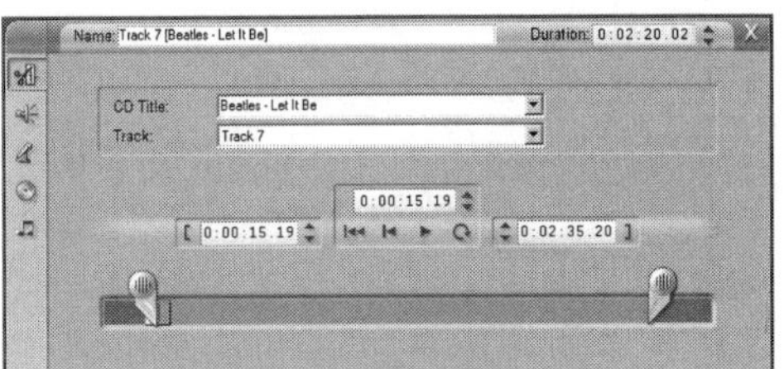

Figure 11.22 Make the desired edits.

Figure 11.23 Then preview, and Studio rips the track.

Figure 11.24 Once again, if the audio CD isn't present, Studio prompts you.

Editing Audio Clips

Chapter 7 described how to edit audio files on the Timeline. All of those principles apply equally to audio files created by the three tools discussed earlier.

In addition, you can edit audio files with Studio's Clip Properties tool, also discussed in Chapter 7. Since the Audio Clip Properties tool presents a slightly different face when editing a CD-Audio clip and a SmartSound clip, I'll address each separately below.

To edit a CD-ROM clip:

1. Double-click the Audio track to edit (**Figure 11.20**).

   Studio opens the CD Audio Clip Properties tool (**Figure 11.21**).

   Studio stores the track-related information, so you don't need the CD-ROM right away. However, Studio will need it if you make any changes and preview, so don't let the disc get too far away.
2. Make the desired edits (**Figure 11.22**).
3. To save edits, click the X to close the Clip Properties tool or touch another tool.
4. Click Preview in the Player to rip the CD track immediately.

   Studio rips the track (**Figure 11.23**) and then plays the clip. If the CD isn't in the drive, Studio prompts you to insert the disc (**Figure 11.24**).

To edit a SmartSound clip:

1. Double-click the track to edit (**Figure 11.25**).

   Studio opens the SmartSound tool (**Figure 11.26**).

2. Make the desired changes and click the Accept Changes button (**Figure 11.27**).

   Studio makes the changes.

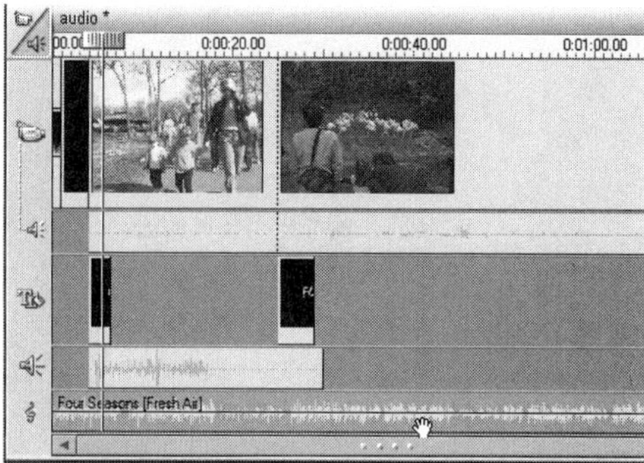

Figure 11.25 Editing SmartSound is pretty similar. Start by double-clicking on the track.

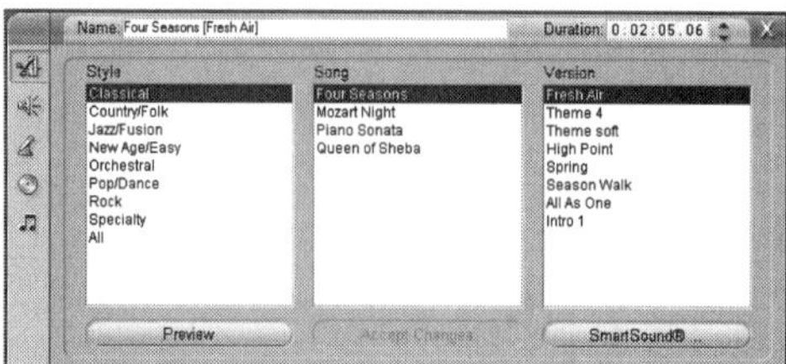

Figure 11.26 The SmartSound tool opens.

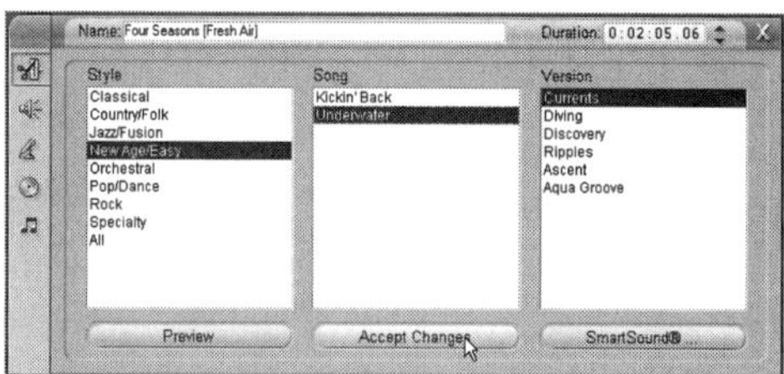

Figure 11.27 Make the desired changes and click Accept Changes.

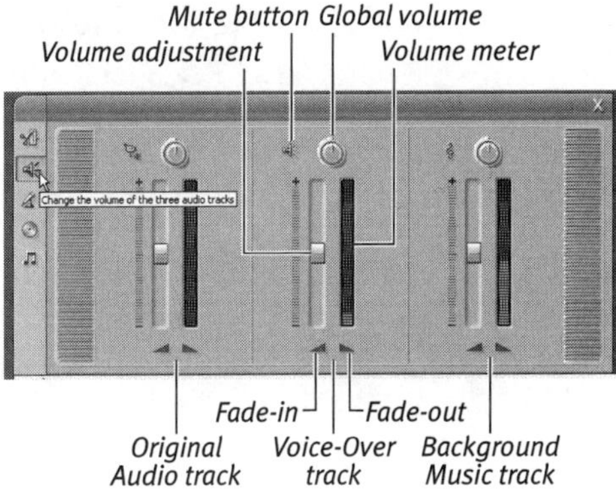

Figure 11.28 Studio's cool volume mixer. Each of the three tracks has a complete set of controls.

Using the Volume Tool

Now that you've created these multiple audio tracks, it's time to blend them into a synergistic audio experience by adjusting their relative volume. Studio offers two tools, the Volume tool discussed here, and the adjustment handles on the Timeline discussed in the next section.

There are three sets of volume controls, one each for the Original Audio track, the Voice-Over track, and the Background Music track. Here's how they operate:

- **Mute tool.** Mutes the *entire* track.
- **Global volume.** Adjusts the volume of the *entire* track.
- **Volume adjust.** Adjusts the volume *at the current edit location.* This tool is best used in real time with the audio playing, so you can listen to the volume and adjust as necessary.
- **Volume meter.** Reflects track volume at that location.
- **Fade-in** and **Fade-out.** Perform their namesake tasks at the current edit location.

To open the Volume tool:

- Do one of the following:
  - ▲ Click the Audio Toolbox icon (Figure 11.1), then click the speaker icon on the left of the Audio Toolbox panel (**Figure 11.28**).
  - ▲ In the Studio menu, choose Toolbox > Change Volume.

  The Volume tool opens (Figure 11.28).

To mute a track:

- Click the Mute button for the respective track.

  Studio places a red line over the mute button and adjusts track volume to zero, placing a red line at the bottom of the track (**Figure 11.29**).

To adjust track global volume:

- Adjust the global volume tool to the desired level (**Figure 11.30**).

  Studio adjusts the volume of the entire track and places a blue line at the adjusted level (**Figure 11.31**).

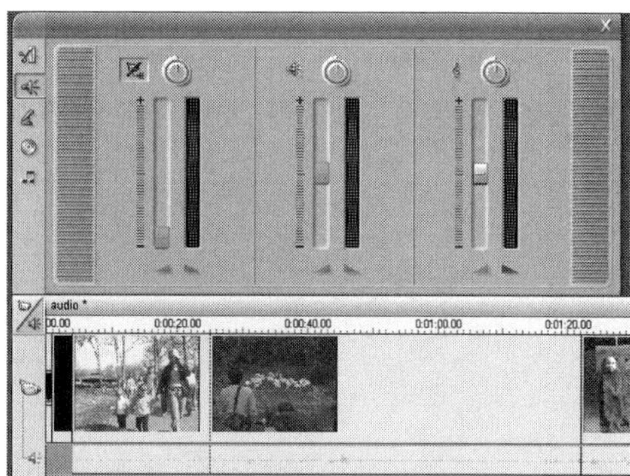

Figure 11.29 A muted track. Note the line at the bottom of the Original Audio track.

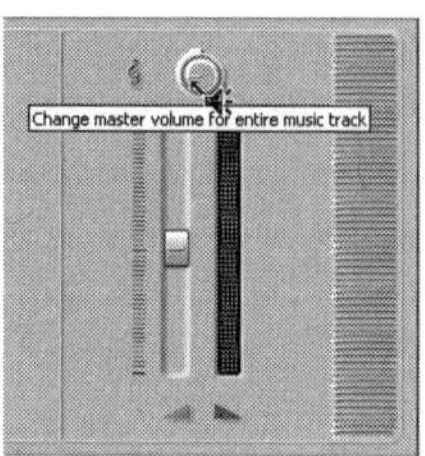

Figure 11.30 This control adjusts volume for the entire audio clip.

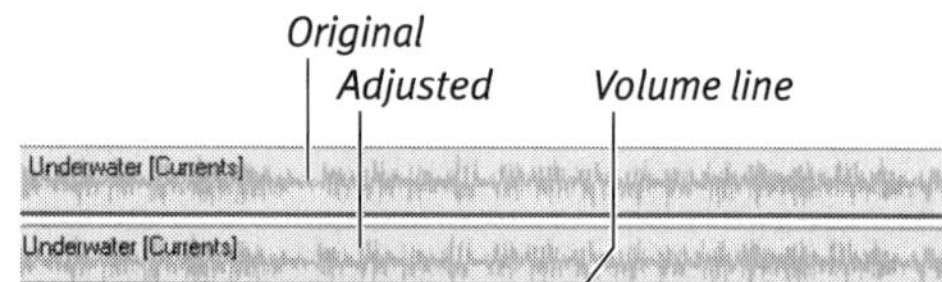

Figure 11.31 The adjusted audio track. Note the uniform level of the volume line, especially compared with Figure 11.33, where I created adjustment handles to edit track regions, rather than the entire track.

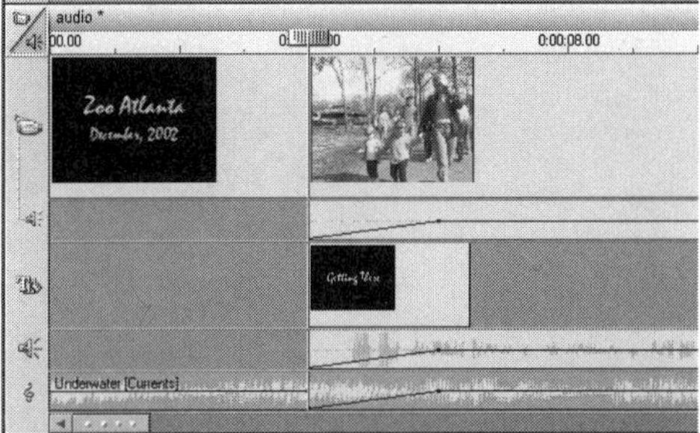

Figure 11.37 If you fade-in from this location, you get the weird effect on the Background Music track. You'll have to undo this one, and fade-in from a different location.

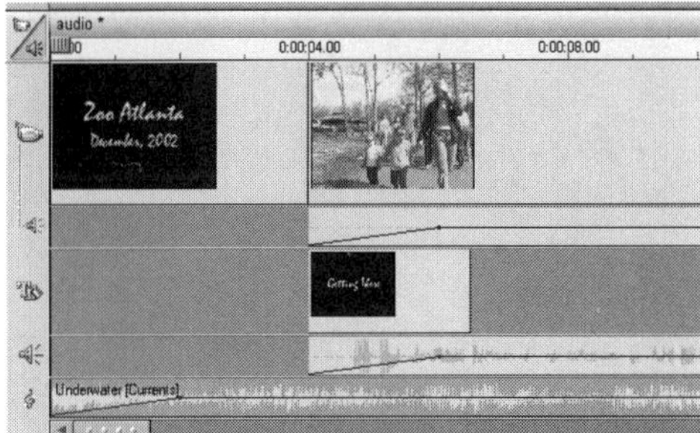

Figure 11.38 Here's a good place, the start of the clip. This looks better.

✔ Tips

- **Figure 11.37** illustrates what happens when you start the fade at a point other than the start of the clip. The fade-in looks normal for both the Original Audio track and the Voice-Over track, but it may not be the desired effect for the Background Audio track. To fade in from the beginning on this track, position the Timeline Scrubber at the absolute start of the clip (**Figure 11.38**) and click the fade-in icon.
- If your track has multiple files and you want each to fade in, you have to apply the effect separately to each audio file. For example, if you have multiple CD or narration tracks and want each to fade in, you must apply the fade-in to each file manually.
- When you apply transitions between clips, Studio automatically creates a cross-fade between the two original audio tracks, unless you apply the fade transition (in which case Studio fades the first track out and fades the second one in).

To fade out audio:

1. Position the Timeline Scrubber where the fade-out should end—that is, the point where volume should be set to zero (**Figure 11.39**).

   Normally, this is the absolute end of a scene.

2. Click the fade-out icon for the target audio track (**Figure 11.40**).

   Studio fades out the audio (**Figure 11.41**) using the default fade-in/fade-out duration. To set duration, see Chapter 2.

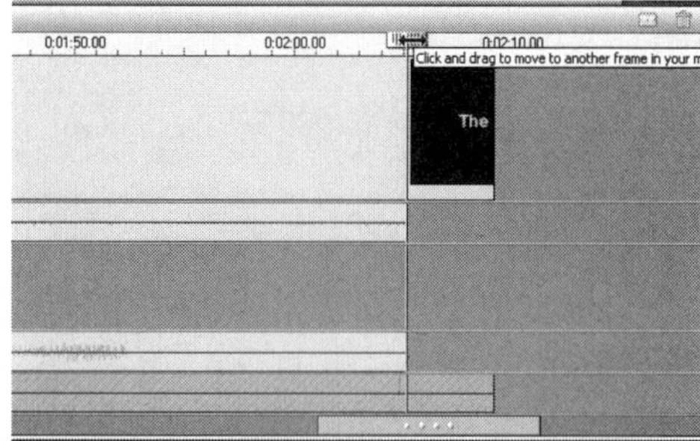

Figure 11.39 To fade out, place the Timeline Scrubber at the point you want volume to be set to zero—normally, the end of the clip.

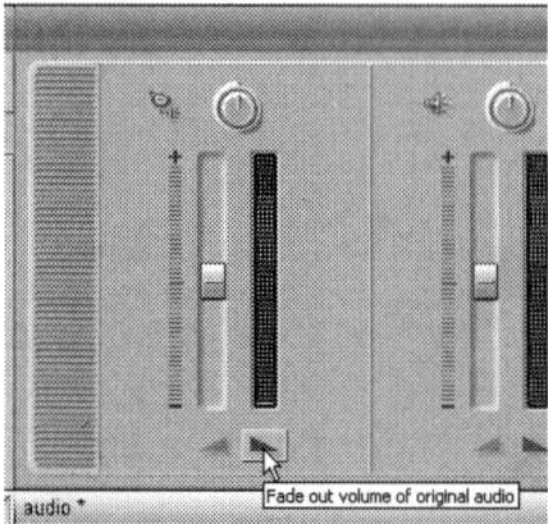

Figure 11.40 Here's the fade-out icon.

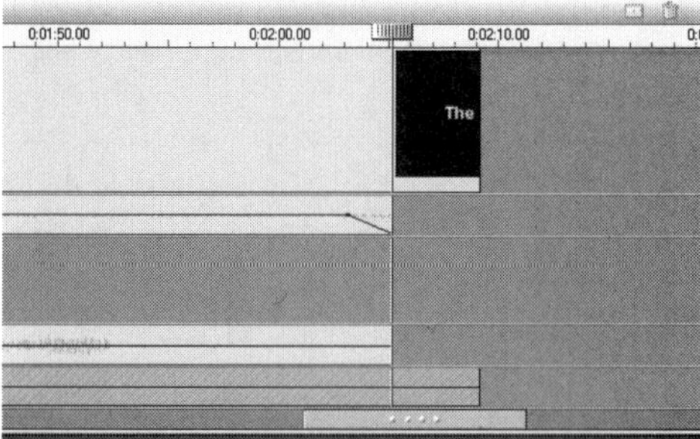

Figure 11.41 Fade-out accomplished.

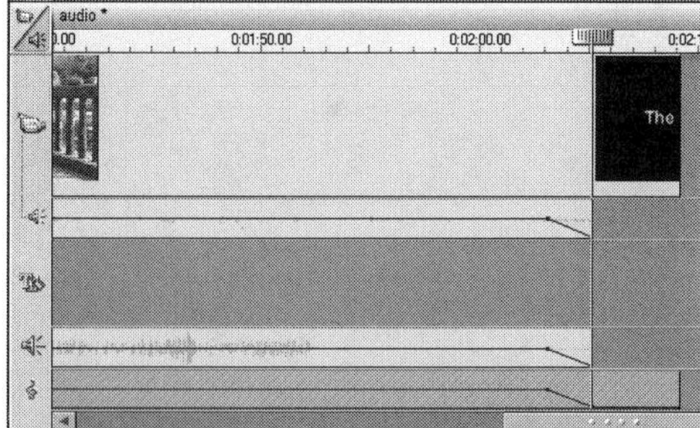

Figure 11.42 Oops, once again the bottom track looks funky because we started the fade at the wrong place. You want this track to fade out with *The End*.

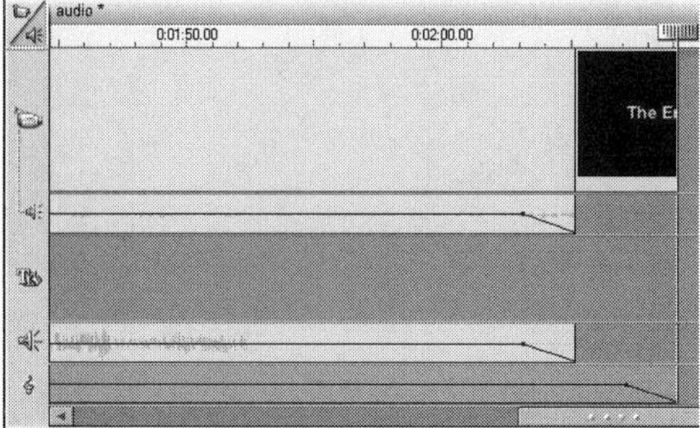

Figure 11.43 Place the pointer at the very end of the audio clip, then click the fade-out icon.

✔ Tips

- **Figure 11.42** illustrates what happens when you start the fade at a point other than the end of the clip. The fade-out looks normal for both the Original Audio track and the Voice-Over track, but it may not be the desired effect for the Background Audio track. To fade out to the end of this track, position the Timeline Scrubber at the absolute end of the clip (**Figure 11.43**) and click the fade-out icon.
- If your track has multiple files and you want each to fade out, you have to apply the effect separately to each audio file. For example, if you have multiple CD or narration tracks and want each to fade out, you must apply the fade-out to each file manually.

To perform real-time, multitrack audio mixing:

This is the main course: the activity for which this tool was designed and at which it excels. Because it's a real-time activity, it's tough to show in static screen shots, but here's my best shot.

1. Position the Timeline Scrubber where you'd like to start adjusting the volume (**Figure 11.44**).
2. In the Preview window, press Play.
3. As you listen to the audio, adjust the volume for each track using the appropriate volume adjustment (**Figure 11.45**).

   Studio creates adjustment handles and adjusts volumes in real time (**Figure 11.46**). Don't feel like you need to make this perfect; you'll learn how to manually fine-tune these settings in the next section.

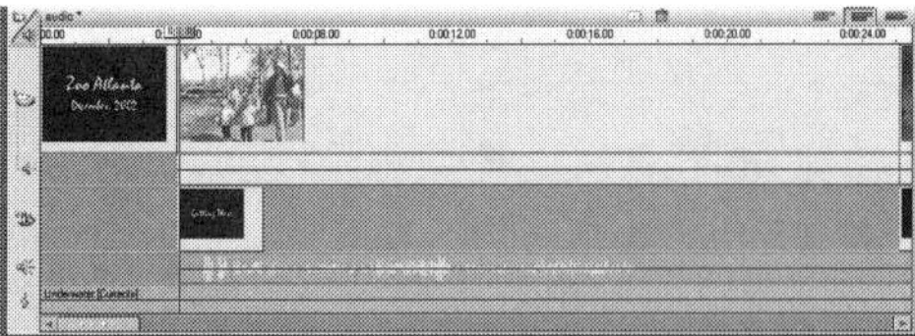

Figure 11.44 Now for some fun: real-time, multitrack mixing. Position the Timeline Scrubber at the starting point.

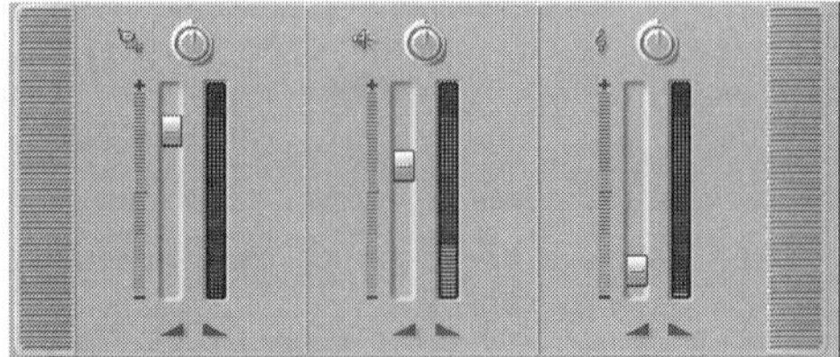

Figure 11.45 Wiggle the volume controls to set the desired levels for each track.

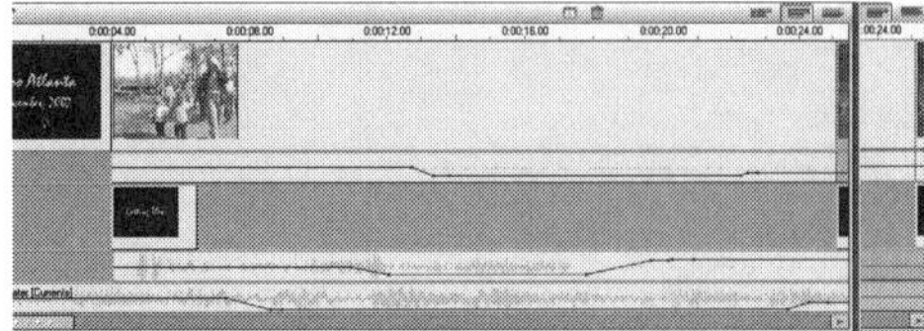

Figure 11.46 Here you go. Notice that I lowered the background music almost completely so I could hear the narration.

Figure 11.47 When the pointer looks like this hand, you can move the file to a different location on the track or a different track.

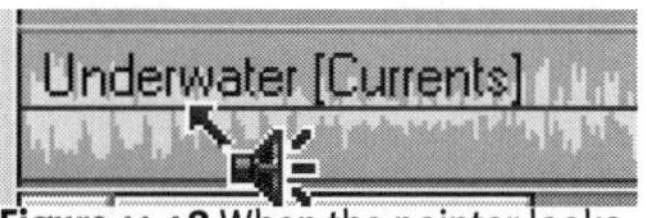

Figure 11.48 When the pointer looks like a speaker, you can create and move adjustment handles.

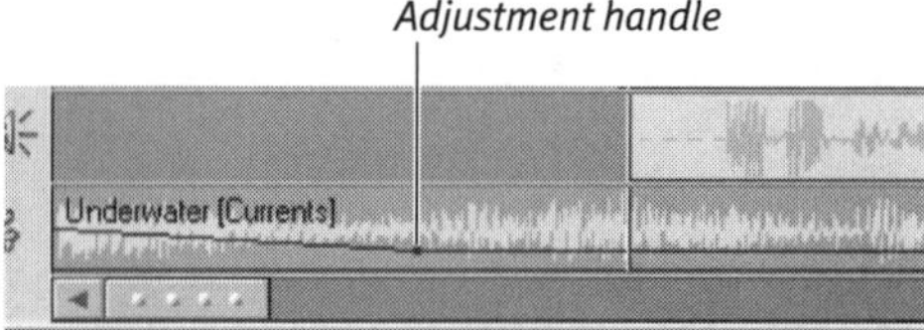

Figure 11.49 You can create an adjustment handle by touching the volume line, and dragging volume down.

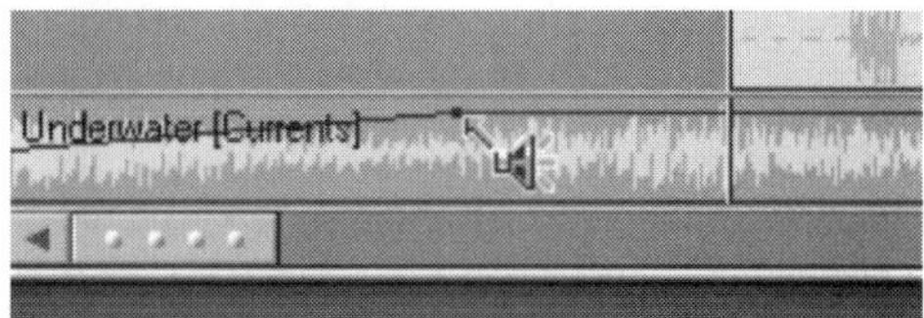

Figure 11.50 Here I'm grabbing the adjustment handle and increasing volume.

Adjusting Volume on the Timeline

As stated above, you can modify the adjustments created with the volume or fade tools, and create your own adjustment handles and edit manually. This section shows you how to do both (and how to delete unwanted adjustment handles).

To adjust audio volume:

1. Touch the target track.

   Studio turns the track blue. Note that the cursor has two states for audio editing. The cursor resembles a hand when hovering over any part of the audio track except the blue audio level line (**Figure 11.47**). In this state, when it's called the location adjustment cursor, you can move the track to a different location on the same track or to a different track.

   When you hover the pointer over the blue audio level line, it converts to a speaker and becomes the volume adjustment cursor, which you can use to create or adjust the levels of adjustment handles (**Figure 11.48**).

2. With the volume adjustment cursor, do one of the following:

   ▲ To create an adjustment handle and adjust volume, touch the audio line and move it to the desired volume level.

   Studio creates an adjustment handle and adjusts the level (**Figure 11.49**).

   ▲ To adjust a previously created adjustment handle, touch and drag it to the new volume level (**Figure 11.50**).

   You can drag the adjustment handle in all four directions: up, down, left, and right.

To delete an adjustment handle:

- With the cursor in volume adjustment mode, touch an adjustment handle, drag it straight down quickly, and release (**Figure 11.51**).

  Studio removes the adjustment handle.

To delete all volume changes:

1. Select the track or multiple tracks on the same Timeline to adjust back to pre-edited state (**Figure 11.52**).
2. Right-click and choose Remove Volume Changes (**Figure 11.53**).

   Studio removes all volume changes on the selected track (**Figure 11.54**).

✔ Tip

- Removing volume changes only works on a single track. Studio lets you select clips on different tracks and activate the tool via the right-click menu, but only removes volume changes from the top track.

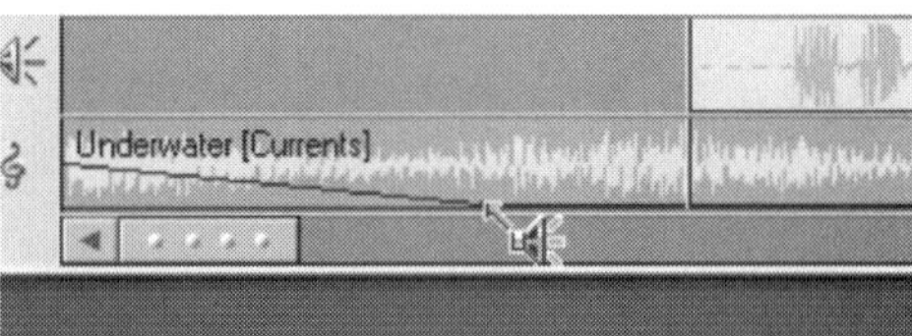

Figure 11.51 To delete an adjustment handle, just grab it and pull it down quickly.

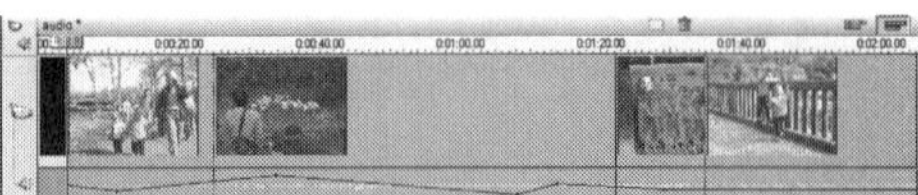

Figure 11.52 Say you don't like these adjustments and simply want to start over. First select all the affected clips.

Figure 11.53 Then choose Remove Volume Changes from the right-click menu.

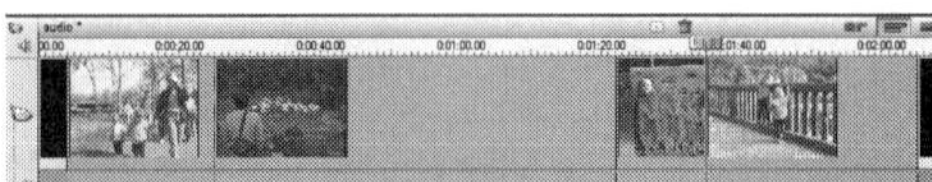

Figure 11.54 You're back at square one with a pristine volume line.

12

DVD Authoring

The problem with linear video is that it's so, well, linear. It can take roughly forever to create a 30-minute video from your four hours of vacation tapes, and then you still can't quickly find that cute spot where little Sally and cousin Johnny were holding hands, watching the July 4 parade.

That's the beauty of DVD. It's pretty much infinitely linkable, allowing you to find the most important scenes quickly. And, though you can dress your videos up as much as you like, you can also choose to break them into scenes (or let scene detection do the work for you) and create a menu with links to the good parts.

It's a parent's dream: simple, fast, and better than VHS quality, with tapelike playback simplicity. Just open up the drive and pop the disc in. With recordable drive and media prices dropping every time you turn around, it's also alluringly inexpensive.

Where Springsteen was "born to run," Studio 8 was born to author DVDs, the first program ever with an integrated editing and authoring environment. It's enough to get my creative juices flowing, how 'bout you?

About DVD Authoring

With a buildup like that, it's a letdown to start in tutorial mode, but you gotta walk before you can run. So spend some time learning about DVD authoring before diving in.

When planning your DVD, you have two basic issues to consider: video flow and menu structure.

Video flow

Video flow relates to how the video will play over the course of the DVD. There are two extremes with many points in the middle.

Linear production

At one extreme is a linear movie that simply happens to be on DVD. You've designed it to flow from beginning to end, like a Hollywood movie, and you're using DVD simply as a convenient distribution medium, perhaps in addition to dubbing to VHS tape. Maybe you want viewers to be able to jump in at certain points, but once the video starts, it will play from start to finish unless interrupted by the viewer.

Some Words of Advice

You may find this strange coming from me, but the best advice I can give to those new to DVD authoring is to be unambitious. In general, most DVD authoring tools, like Studio, offer a cornucopia of development options. Once you start to experiment, development time can go through the roof, and advanced options like video thumbnails and menus lengthen rendering time precipitously. With your first DVD projects, it's better to be unambitious and finished than inspired and still working.

And while Studio is a mature, eighth-generation video editor, it's a first-generation DVD authoring program. With all due respect to the obviously talented development and quality assurance staff at Pinnacle, this means that the farther you push the DVD authoring envelope, the more likely you are to move into untested waters.

The Two Faces of DVD

Recordable DVDs have two basic roles in life. The first is as a simple place to store data, like a CD-recordable disc but with 4.7 GB of capacity rather than 653 or 700 MB.

More to our interests, of course, is recordable DVD's second role, as a medium for playing back interactive productions on DVD players connected to TV sets and computers with DVD drives and the necessary player software.

Where any program capable of writing data to a disc can use DVD-R or DVD+R in their first capacity, only an authoring program like Studio 8 can produce titles that play on DVD players.

When planning a linear production, you have to build the entire movie on the Timeline first, then start adding the interactivity. When you first move a menu to the Timeline and tell Studio to automatically create the menus (as described later), you'll notice that Studio puts a flag at the start of every discrete scene, labeled sequentially, starting with C1 (**Figure 12.1**). These are chapter flags that you link to buttons on your menus, enabling direct access to any scene within your movie. Studio allows you to insert chapter flags at any point in any video and also remove them where you don't want them.

Disparate videos or slide shows

The opposite of linear productions are collections of related but essentially disparate videos that don't flow from start to finish. Perhaps you're converting your three-month tape from last summer, which covered little Johnny's trip to the Little League World Series, Sally's diving championship, and that ridiculously expensive trip to Disney World. In addition to the videotapes, you also shot pictures with a digital still image camera and you'd like to build them into a slide show viewable from the DVD.

Figure 12.1 Studio's DVD-authoring interface. Note the Menu track above the Video track, and the Menu Clip Properties tool, where you'll do most of your linking and customization.

You'll spend some time consolidating scenes from each event into a discrete movie, but you don't expect viewers to watch the video from start to finish. After each movie or slide show, you want the viewer to return back to the original menu so they can choose another sequence.

When planning this second type of production, you start by building all individual movies and slide shows on the Timeline. You again use chapter flags to link to the various movies and scenes within the movies. Then, using techniques discussed in this chapter, you'll insert Return to Menu flags (the M flags seen in Figure 12.1), which return the viewer to a menu after it finishes.

The net net is that two tools control video flow. Chapter flags allow you to jump to any spot in the video, while Return to Menu flags let you direct where the viewer goes after watching any particular video.

Irrespective of the production type you choose, it's best to get the video and slide show production done first, then start your DVD authoring.

Figure 12.2 Linear menus flow sequentially. Studio builds them automatically, making them easy, but not the best for navigation to content.

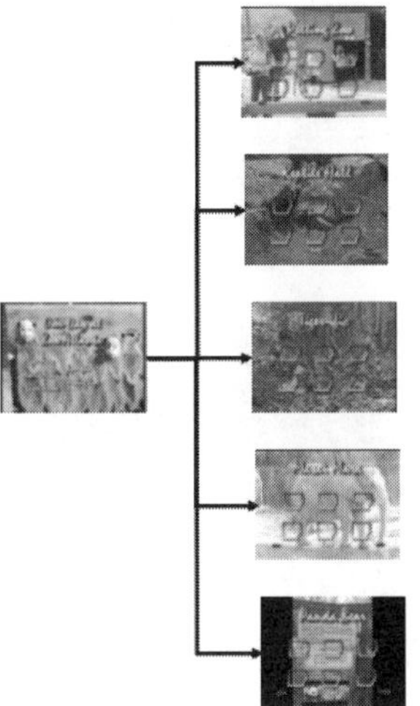

Figure 12.3 You build 'em, you link 'em: Custom menus are more work, but are customized for your content.

Menu structure

Menu structure refers to how the menus link to each other. Studio enables three basic types.

Linear menus

Linear menus flow sequentially backward and forward, as shown in **Figure 12.2**. You create these by using any Studio template or by building your own template, as described in Chapter 10.

When you use a linear menu, Studio automatically builds enough menus so that each chapter in your video has a link. Viewers move through the menus sequentially, using links between the menus that Studio automatically inserts. Because Studio does all the work for you, using linear menus is fast and easy.

However, though linear menus are acceptable for linear movies, they're poor choices for disparate collections of content. For example, if the trip to Disney World was the last event of the summer, you may have to toggle through ten menus to see that killer sunset from the hotel room balcony. Definitely not optimal.

Custom menus

When working with disparate collections, you may want to consider building your own custom menus, which have direct links from one to many menus, as shown in **Figure 12.3**. In my production, I created separate pages for different areas in Zoo Atlanta, and then linked these pages to the main menu. If viewers want to see the awesome Bengal tiger sequence, they only have to click twice, rather than multiple times.

Studio provides tremendous flexibility in this regard, allowing you to customize menus and link menu to menu at will. Though you'll get vastly improved navigation, the obvious downside is you have to build multiple menus and perform most of your linking manually. You'll also have to build links from these pages back to the home page, and, as discussed above, to insert Return to Menu flags at the end of each main sequence.

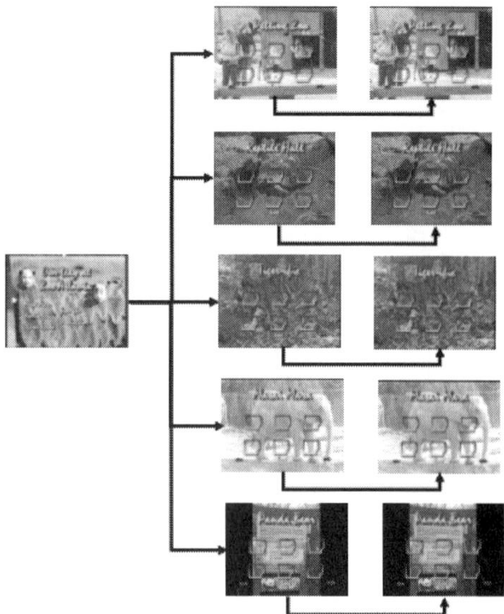

Figure 12.4 Hybrid menus are the best of both worlds—great navigation, and Studio handles some of the linking.

Hybrid menus

The third menu structure, shown in **Figure 12.4**, is a hybrid structure that includes both linear and custom menus. This is the structure used in my Zoo Atlanta project, because several of the menus had more sequences than I could fit on one page.

For example, the Masai Mara section contained nine videos, requiring two menu pages. Since I used a linear rather than custom menu, Studio built the second Masai Mara menu for me, along with links back and forth between the first and second Masai Mara menus.

If you study the custom menus in Figure 12.4, you'll notice they all look somewhat similar. That's because to speed production, I created the first menu by hand, saved it, then swapped background image and title by section, saving each menu as I went along. (Total production time for the five custom menus was about ten minutes.)

Figure 12.5 The linear menu template and the Preview window, showing only the populated buttons.

For a $100 program, Studio is surprisingly adept at authoring, with elegant touches like only displaying linked buttons on a menu and hiding those that are inactive, as shown in **Figure 12.5**.

In the figure, the Menu Clip Properties window on the left shows the linear menu template, while the Preview window on the right shows how the menu will look during playback. The five unpopulated video icons (those with ?? in the upper-left corner) are not displayed during playback, and neither are the Previous (left arrow) and Next (right arrow) buttons, which are unnecessary because there's only one menu in this section.

On the other hand, Studio also lacks link-checking capabilities and didn't notice the ?? in the middle bottom of the page, which is supposed to be a link back to the home page. Had this disc been produced without the link, navigation would have been awkward. To avoid this, you need to thoroughly preview and check links before burning the disc. All this and more later in this chapter.

Using Menu Templates

If you're a new Studio user, I recommend that you produce your first few DVD projects using templates. Note that the key ingredient to success here isn't what you'll learn on these pages, as production is largely automated, but how you've prepared your videos beforehand.

Specifically, Studio automatically inserts chapter flags at the start of each scene. If you have too many scenes, you'll have multiple menu pages that are cumbersome to navigable. To avoid this, combine scenes in the Album (Chapter 6) or Movie Window (Chapter 7) before starting your DVD. Also see Chapter 10 for more on menus.

For example, the Zoo Atlanta project started with 101 discrete scenes, ultimately consolidated down to 27 in the Album, of which 17 made it to the final production.

The one downside of this approach is that you can't trim or place transitions between scenes and then combine them. If this limitation prevents you from combining your scenes into useful chunks, you should tell Studio not to automatically create chapter links when you drag in your first menu, and simply create them manually (see below).

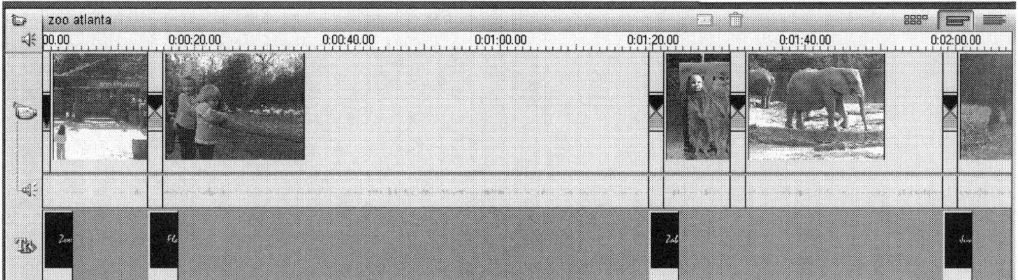

Figure 12.6 Finish your project before starting authoring.

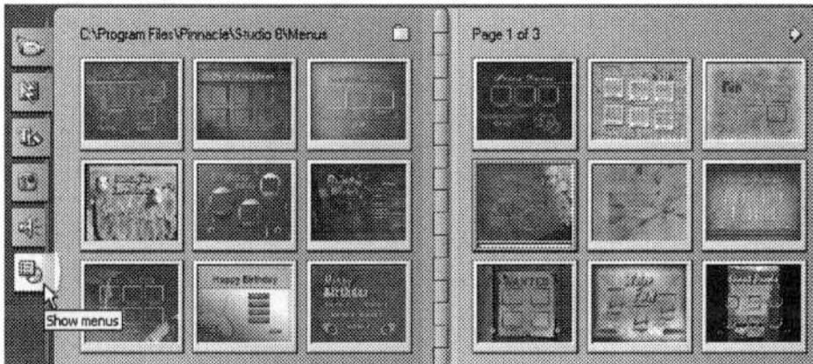

Figure 12.7 Welcome to the Menu store.

Figure 12.8 Click Yes and Studio practically builds the DVD for you.

To use a menu template:

1. In the Edit mode, place all project assets on the Timeline (**Figure 12.6**).
2. Click the show menus icon to open the Disc Menus tab of the Album (**Figure 12.7**).
3. Drag the desired menu to the front of the project, placing it on the Video track.

   Studio opens the Adding Menu to Movie dialog (**Figure 12.8**).
4. Click Yes to create links automatically to each scene after the menu.

   Studio automatically creates as many menus as necessary for all video scenes, inserts the Next and Previous buttons where necessary, and populates the thumbnail buttons with videos from the Timeline.

✔ Tips

- Studio automatically uses the first video frame as the menu thumbnail, not the thumbnail you've selected for either the Album or the Timeline (see Chapter 10).
- Note that when you use a menu template, Studio only shows one copy of the menu on the Timeline, even though the program may ultimately produce multiple menus. See "To select another menu page," later, on navigating through these pages in the Menu Clip Properties window.

To edit the menu:

1. Double-click on the menu.

   Studio opens the Menu Clip Properties tool (**Figure 12.9**).

2. In the upper-right corner, click Edit Menu.

   The Title Editor opens (**Figure 12.10**). See Chapter 10 for editing details.

3. After completing your edits, do one of the following:

   ▲ In the lower-right corner, click OK (or press F12) to save the menu and return to the Edit window.

   This overwrites the original menu.

   ▲ Choose File > Save Menu As (**Figure 12.11**) to save the file using a unique name, preserving the original Studio menu for reuse. Then click OK to return to the Edit window.

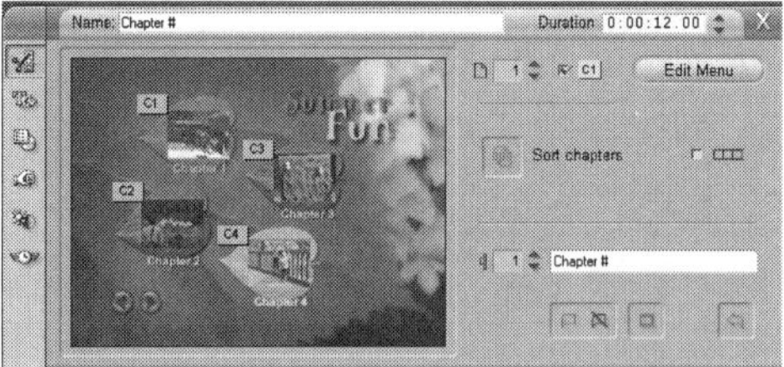

Figure 12.9 The initial menu showing the first four chapter links.

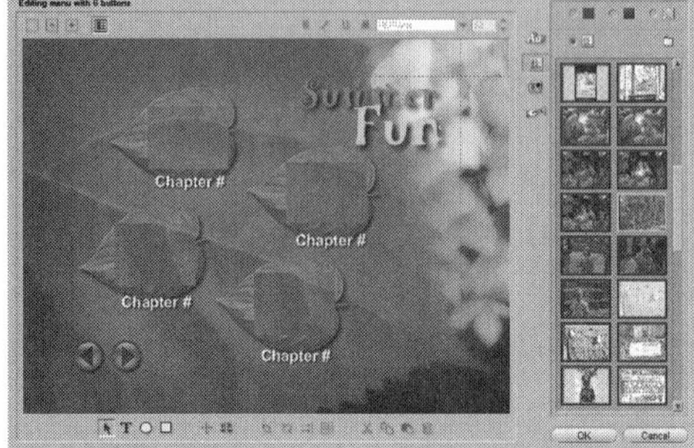

Figure 12.10 You can customize this template in the Title Editor.

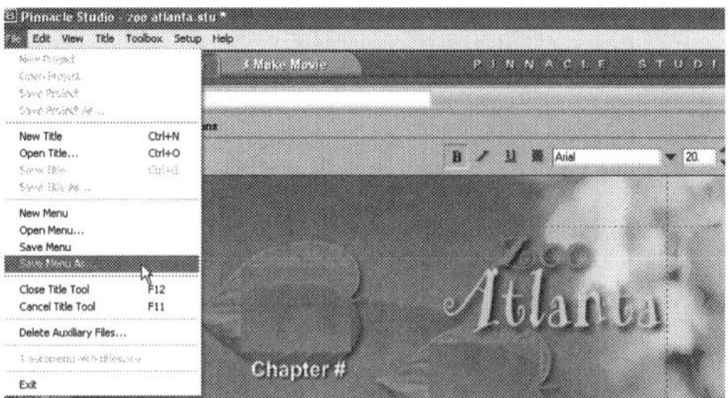

Figure 12.11 After changing Summer Fun to Zoo Atlanta, I saved the template for later use.

Figure 12.12 To create a chapter flag to link to from the menu, first choose the frame.

Figure 12.13 Use right-click commands from the Menu track...

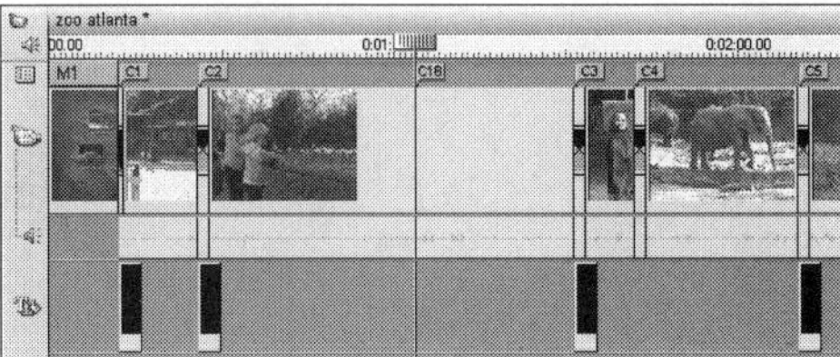

Figure 12.14 ...to set the new chapter link.

To create a chapter link:

1. Using the Timeline Scrubber or Player controls, navigate to the target starting point of the new chapter (**Figure 12.12**).
2. Do one of the following:
   - ▲ Right-click the Menu track and choose Set Disc Chapter (**Figure 12.13**).
   - ▲ Right-click the Video track and choose Set Disc Chapter.

Studio creates the new chapter link, in this case C18 (**Figure 12.14**).

✔ Tips

- Inserted chapter links are often out of order, which affects menu placement. For example, in Figure 12.14, the new chapter link (C18) is between C2 and C3. This means Studio will place it on the final menu, while the adjacent chapters, C2 and C3, will be on the first menu. See the following section to address this problem.
- You can move a chapter flag by dragging it with your pointer to any location on the Menu track. See "Previewing Your DVD," later in the chapter, for details.

To sort chapter flags:

◆ In the Menu Clip Properties tool, click Sort chapters (**Figure 12.15**).

Studio sorts the chapter flags sequentially (**Figure 12.16**).

Figure 12.15 To reorder the chapter flags after inserting, click Sort chapters.

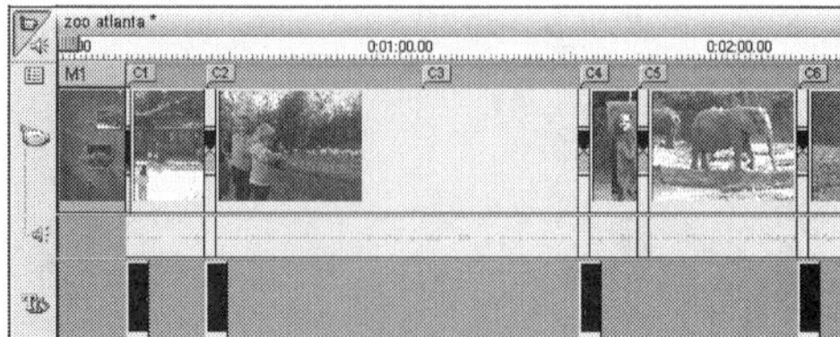

Figure 12.16 Order restored.

To delete chapter links:

◆ To delete chapter links, do one of the following:

- ▲ In the Menu Clip Properties tool, select the button linked to the target chapter link. Click Clear chapter link for selected button, or press V (**Figure 12.17**).
- ▲ In the Menu track, select the chapter flag with the pointer, right-click, and choose Delete.
- ▲ In the Menu track, select the chapter flag with the pointer and press the Delete key.

Studio deletes the chapter flag and clears the menu link (**Figure 12.18**).

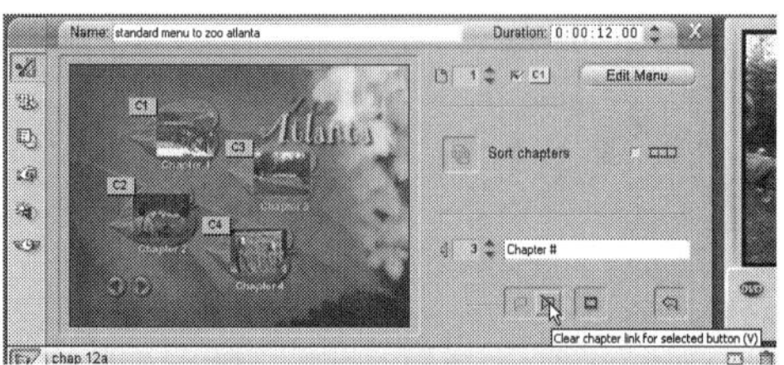

Figure 12.17 To clear chapter links (and delete chapters), select the chapter, and then click this button.

✔ Tip

■ After deleting a chapter link, you'll likely need to sort the chapter flags to restore order to your menu (see above).

Figure 12.18 Chapter flag and link created in Figure 12.14 are both gone.

Figure 12.19 Time to customize the captions for these snazzy menus.

Figure 12.20 Future Studio versions may pick up scene comments, but for now, it's data re-entry time.

Figure 12.21 To change the thumbnail, navigate to the target frame.

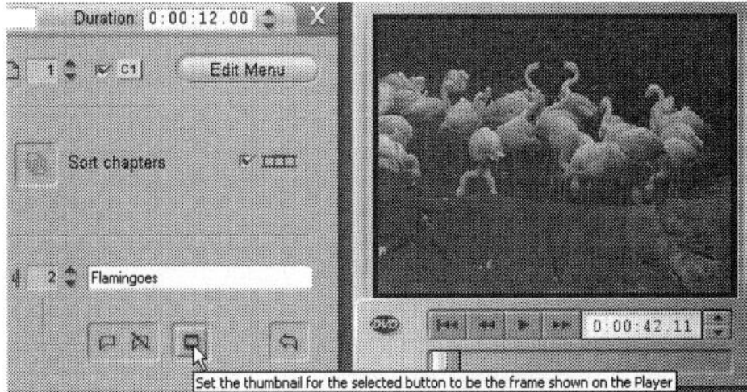

Figure 12.22 Or click here to set the new thumbnail. (Alternatively, use right-click controls.)

To change a button caption:

1. With the button highlighted in the Menu Clip Properties tool, select the button caption description to make the field active (**Figure 12.19**).
2. Insert the new text.
3. Press Enter to save the text (**Figure 12.20**).

   Studio saves the new description and changes the menu.

To change a button thumbnail:

1. With the button highlighted in the Menu Clip Properties tool, use the Timeline Scrubber or Player controls to navigate to a new thumbnail frame (**Figure 12.21**).
2. Do one of the following:
   - ▲ Right-click the Video track and choose Set Thumbnail.
   - ▲ In the Menu Clip Properties tool, click the set thumbnail icon (**Figure 12.22**).

Studio changes to the new thumbnail (**Figure 12.23**).

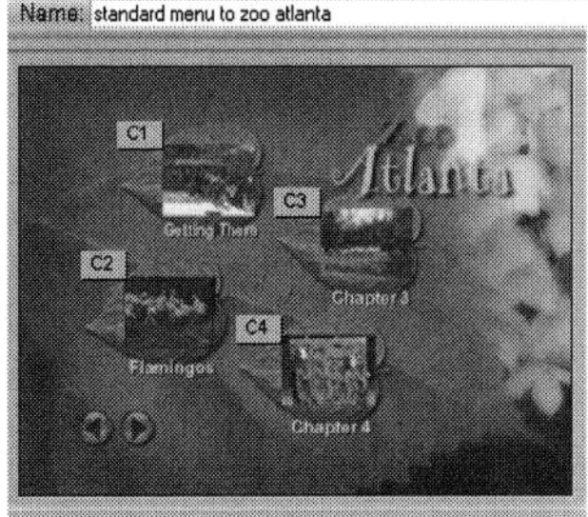

Figure 12.23 Mission accomplished.

To select another button to edit:

- In the Menu Clip Properties tool, do one of the following:
  - Click the button to edit.
  - Click the Select Button controls to move to the button you want to edit (**Figure 12.24**).

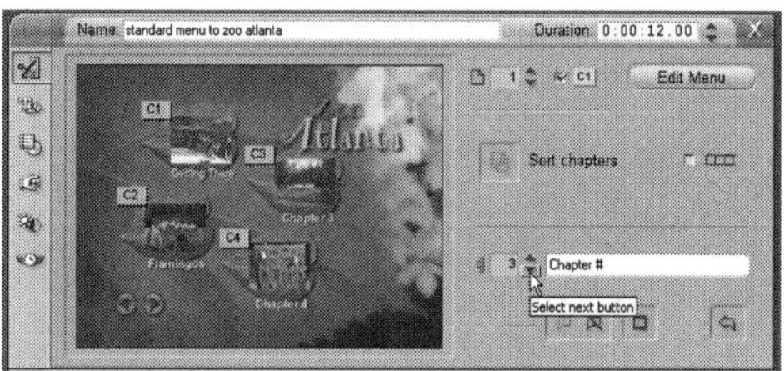

Figure 12.24 Use these controls to move from chapter to chapter.

To select the next menu page:

- In the Menu Clip Properties tool, click the show next page icon (**Figure 12.25**).

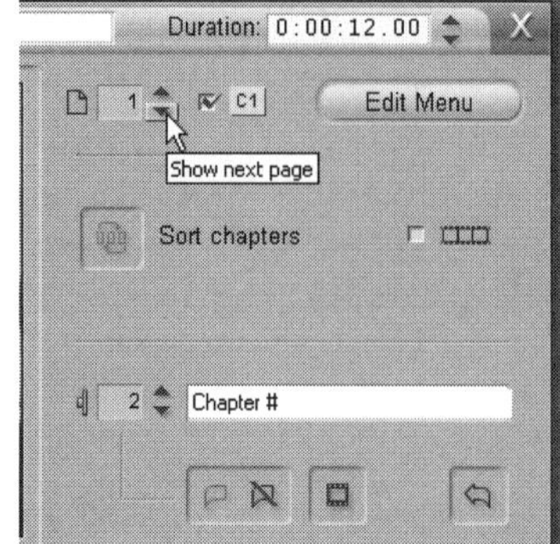

Figure 12.25 When populating multiple menu pages from a template, click from page to page with this key.

✔ Tips

- Use this procedure to move through the sequential menus automatically created by Studio to access all linked chapters.
- To select a completely different menu, double-click on that menu on the Timeline.

Figure 12.26 Click here to use moving videos for all buttons.

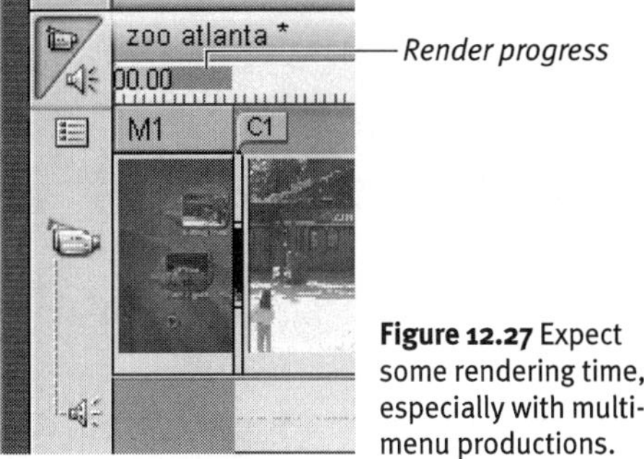

Figure 12.27 Expect some rendering time, especially with multi-menu productions.

To create video buttons:

- In the Menu Clip Properties tool, check the box next to the icon that says "Use moving video for all thumbnail buttons" (**Figure 12.26**).

  Studio replaces the still image thumbnail with a tiny version of the video, creating a video button.

✔ Tips

- The video button will last the duration of the menu and then restart. As discussed later with video and audio menus, this is most aesthetically pleasing when menus are at least one minute in duration. See "To change menu duration," later.
- Because video buttons must be separately rendered before displaying, these won't immediately show up when you preview your video. If you selected background rendering (see Chapter 8), you'll see your rendering progress atop the menu (**Figure 12.27**).
- Maybe it's just me, but video buttons are irritating, take a long time to render, and slow the computer when rendering in the background. These head my list of "don't try this at home" features.

To set Return to Menu links:

1. In the Menu track, double-click the target menu.

   Studio displays the menu in the Menu Clip Properties tool (**Figure 12.28**).

2. Click the video that, after playback, should return the viewer to the target menu (rather than automatically moving to the next scene on the Timeline).

3. Do one of the following:
   - ▲ In the Menu Clip Properties tool, click the Return to Menu icon (**Figure 12.29**).
   - ▲ Right-click the Menu track and choose Set Return to Menu.
   - ▲ Right-click the Video track and choose Set Return to Menu.

   Studio sets the Return to Menu flag (**Figure 12.30**).

✔ Tip

- Studio always sets the Return to Menu flag at the end of the video, figuring you'd probably never want to interrupt playback of a clip in the middle. If that's your intent, simply grab the flag with your pointer and move it to the desired location (**Figure 12.31**).

Figure 12.28 To set Return to Menu links, double-click on the menu to bring it up in the Menu Clip Properties tool.

Figure 12.29 Then click here (or press M).

Figure 12.30 Whatever method you use, look for the flag. It should be the same number as the menu you want to return to (in this case, M1 = Menu 1) and blue.

Figure 12.31 Studio automatically puts the flag at the end of the video, but you can manually override this placement. Move it with your pointer.

Figure 12.32 You can set duration here, or simply drag the menu to the desired length, just like a still image.

To change menu duration:

- To change menu duration, do one of the following:
  - ▲ Select the menu and drag it to the desired length (see Chapter 7 for details)
  - ▲ In the upper-right corner of the Menu Clip Properties tool, change the duration field by inserting the desired duration or using the controls to the right of the duration (**Figure 12.32**).

Using Custom Menus

Before starting work here, you should have at least two menus: a main menu (**Figure 12.33**) with links to your section menus and the section menu(s) themselves (**Figure 12.34**).

In the Zoo Atlanta production, all section menus were templates that could create additional pages and necessary links if there were more videos than available buttons on the page. As described in Chapter 10, this means they have Previous and Next links that Studio can populate automatically.

The only necessary addition is a page to take the viewer back to the main menu. This is the "home" link on the bottom of the menu shown in Figure 12.34. You must create this link in the Title Editor and then link this button back to the main menu.

Start by getting your main menu and section menus on the Timeline. Then link the menus to scenes on the Timeline and then to each other.

Figure 12.33 Here's the main menu for my custom DVD.

Links to scenes

Previous button *Home button (link to main menu)* *Next button*

Figure 12.34 Here's one of five section menus. Note the Next and Previous buttons, which handle navigation if Studio creates multiple menus, and the link to the main menu.

Figure 12.35 Clicking the Show Menus icon opens the Disc Menus tab.

Figure 12.36 Oops, look at all those question marks, representing open links. You'll fill them in a minute.

To insert the main menu:

1. In Edit mode, place all project assets on the Timeline (see Figure 12.6).
2. Click the show menus icon to open the Disc Menus tab in the Album (**Figure 12.35**).
3. Drag the main menu to the front of the project, placing it on the Video track.

   Studio opens the Adding Menu to Movie dialog (see Figure 12.8).
4. Click No to manually create all links.

   Studio inserts the menu and opens the Menu Clip Properties tool to the Set Menu Links window (**Figure 12.36**).

To insert and link a section menu:

1. From the Disc Menus tab, drag the section menu to the Timeline in front of the first video clip you will link to this menu (**Figure 12.37**).

   Studio opens the Adding Menu to Movie dialog.

2. Click No to manually create all links.

   Studio inserts the menu (**Figure 12.38**).

3. If Studio doesn't automatically open the Menu Clip Properties tool, double-click on the menu to open it.

Figure 12.37 Drag the section menu to the Timeline.

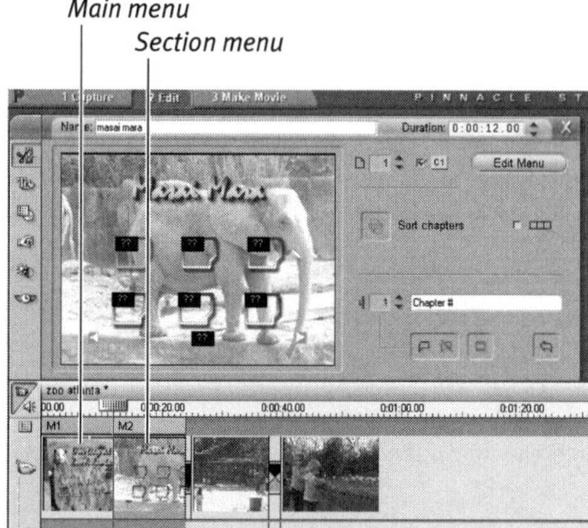

Figure 12.38 Bringing down the first section menu.

Figure 12.39 Drag the main menu into the Home link.

Figure 12.40 The M1 tells you that the link is accomplished.

4. Click the main menu, and holding down the left mouse button, drag it to the Home button in the section menu (**Figure 12.39**).

   Studio links the main menu to the section menu, allowing the viewer to navigate back to the main menu from the section menu (**Figure 12.40**).

(continued on next page)

5. To link project assets on the Timeline to the menu buttons, do one of the following:
   - ▲ Click a video, and holding down the left mouse button, drag it to a button in the Menu Clip Properties tool and release (**Figure 12.41**).
   - ▲ With a button highlighted in the Menu Clip Properties tool, right-click the Menu track at the desired location and choose Set Disc Chapter.
   - ▲ With a button highlighted in the Menu Clip Properties tool, right-click the Video track at the desired location and choose Set Disc Chapter.
   - ▲ With a button highlighted in the Menu Clip Properties tool, select the target video and click the set chapter link icon (**Figure 12.42**).

   Studio creates the new chapter flag, in this case C1 (**Figure 12.43**) and links the chapter flag to the selected button.
6. Populate the rest of the buttons on the section menu using these same procedures (**Figure 12.44**).
7. Add and populate other section menus.

Figure 12.41 Start dragging and dropping videos into the buttons.

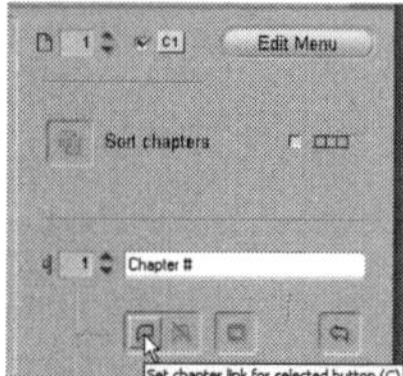

Figure 12.42 Or select a menu button, select a video, and click this button. This is the best method when Studio gets a bit balky and refuses to set the link.

Figure 12.43 Link accomplished. While you can't see it in this black-and-white image, the C1 link in the Menu Clip Properties tool is coded the same color as the menu.

Figure 12.44 First menu done.

Figure 12.45 When I used text for the home link, Studio saved a chapter link out of sequence.

Figure 12.46 Things looked a bit smoother when I used an image link.

✔ Tips

- At times, Studio gets a bit finicky about accepting a link via drag and drop. When this happens, highlight the target button, then the target scene, and click the set chapter link icon.
- Once you finish populating all buttons on the first menu page, you can move to the next page by clicking the Select Button controls (see Figure 12.24) or Show Next Page button (see Figure 12.25).
- Studio assigns each button on a menu a distinct number, but sometimes can't tell the difference between navigation and content-related buttons, which can interrupt the normal flow of chapter numbering.

  For example, in **Figure 12.45**, the menu uses a text link (the word "home", which you only see as the two question marks at the bottom middle of the page), and Studio jumps from C5 to C7, assigning C6 for the link to the home page. If the viewer was clicking from chapter to chapter using her DVD remote, she would click from the video at C5, to the Home button, to the video at C6, which makes no sense.

  However, if you use a graphic object rather than text (see Chapter 10) for the Home link, Studio assigns all of the asset-related buttons a number before assigning number 7 to the home link (**Figure 12.46**).
- If you change your menu to conform to this tip, remember to save the menu (see Chapter 10) before returning to the Timeline. This changes the menu template itself; otherwise, you've just changed the menu as used in the current project.
- Note that Studio resets the chapter flag number for each menu and color codes menus, chapter links, and Return to Menu links.

To link section menus to the main menu:

1. Double-click the main menu.
   Studio opens the main menu in the Menu Clip Properties tool (**Figure 12.47**).
2. Select the section menu and drag it to the appropriate link on the main menu and release the pointer (**Figure 12.48**).
   Studio creates the link (**Figure 12.49**), designated by the M2 above the text caption, in this case.
3. Repeat for all section menus (**Figure 12.50**).

✔ Tips

- If you're using a hybrid menu structure and your section menu has multiple pages, you'll have to link the first and all subsequent menus to the main menu to enable viewers to return to the main menu from each menu.
- Again, sometimes Studio gets a bit finicky about accepting a link via drag and drop. In these instances, make sure the target link is highlighted in the Menu Clip Properties tool, select the target asset, and then click the set chapter link icon (Figure 12.42).

Figure 12.47 Time to link the section menu to the main menu. Double-click on the main menu to open it in the Menu Clip Properties tool.

Figure 12.48 Drag the section menu to the target button.

Figure 12.49 Menu 2 linked and ready for duty.

Figure 12.50 All done. They look beautiful in color.

Figure 12.51 Choose the last video in the section.

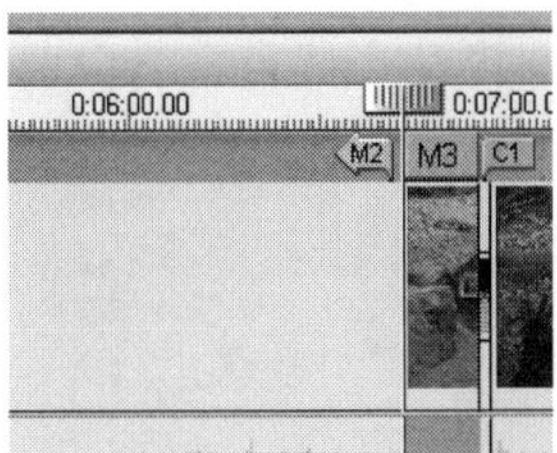

Figure 12.52 Return to Menu link set.

To set Return to Menu flags:

1. Double-click the target menu.

   Studio displays the menu in the Clip Properties tool.

2. On the Timeline, select the final video linked to that menu (**Figure 12.51**).

3. Set the Return to Menu link using one of the techniques described earlier under "Using Menu Templates."

   Studio sets the Return to Menu link for that menu (**Figure 12.52**).

4. Set Return to Menu links for all section menus.

✔ Tip

- If the Return to Menu flag has a different number than the menu number, you could be returning to the wrong menu—obviously OK if it's what you intended, but also a fairly common mistake.

Previewing Your DVD

Given Studio's DVD design flexibility, it's difficult to set rules for previewing your titles. Generally, I like to check the major inter-menu links first, because if these are wrong, viewers won't be able to access certain menu pages. Then I check the Return to Menu links, and finally the video links themselves.

Note, that even if you let Studio build the production for you from a template, you should check the inter-menu links, especially if you created your own template. That way, if you made a mistake creating the menu, you'll catch it before you burn.

Basically, the best practice is to go through each link on each menu. It's not so much the media cost that will get you if you have to reproduce, it's the rendering and production time, which can easily take hours even for short productions.

To preview your DVD:

1. In the Player window, click the Start DVD preview icon (**Figure 12.53**).

   The Player converts to DVD Preview mode with DVD-specific playback controls (**Figure 12.54**).

Figure 12.53 Click here to start the DVD preview (what *are* they looking at?).

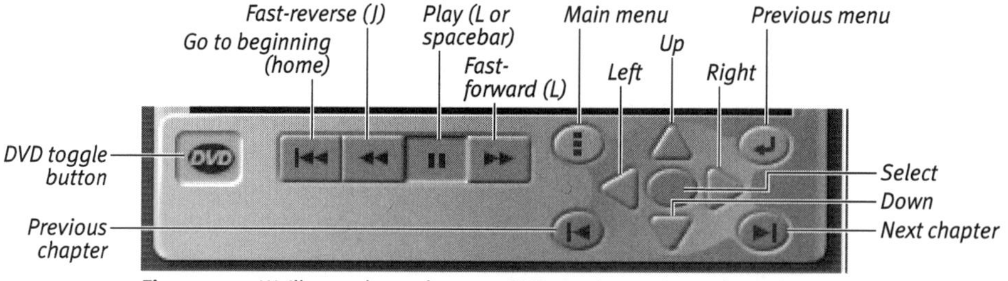

Figure 12.54 We'll never know, because DVD preview starts at the main menu. Who-wee, look at that DVD control. Makes me want to grab a beer and put my feet up!

Figure 12.55 Start by checking all links to section menus.

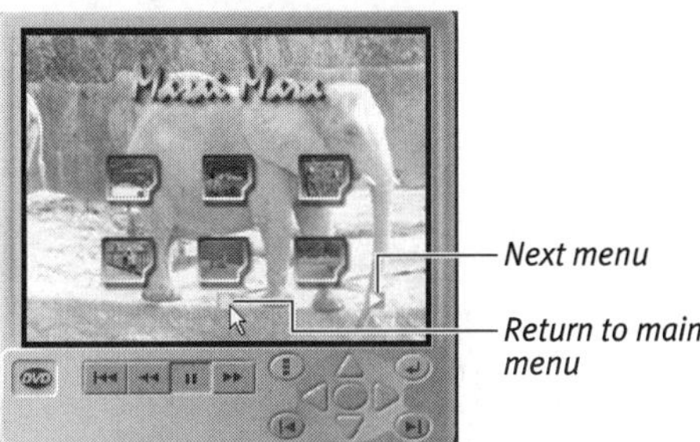

Figure 12.56 And then back to the main menu.

Figure 12.57 After clicking to the next menu, click here to return to the previous menu.

Figure 12.58 Drag the Timeline Scrubber along to the end of the video to speed things up.

2. Check all links from the main menu to section menus (**Figure 12.55**).
3. Check all links back to the main menu from the section menus (**Figure 12.56**).
4. From each section menu with multiple pages, check the links between each menu (Figure 12.56 and **Figure 12.57**).
5. If you inserted Return to Menu flags, play the last video in each section to test whether you return to the proper menu.

   You can use the Timeline Scrubber to move to near the Return to Menu flag and then click Play, which may be faster than waiting for the video to play (**Figure 12.58**).
6. Check each movie link in each menu.

✔ Tips

- If your chapter flags aren't in the desired location, you can click and drag them to any frame desired (**Figure 12.59**).
- Note that Studio may "stall" and simply stop playing during preview at times. If this occurs, simply toggle out of Preview mode by clicking the Start DVD preview icon (see Figure 12.53), and then toggle back in and try it again. If that doesn't work, try rebooting (saving your work first, of course).

Figure 12.59 You can grab chapter flags with the cursor and drag them to a new location, using the Player as a guide.

Creating Audio Menus

Many Hollywood DVDs play audio while displaying the menu, an effect that Studio can duplicate with ease. You can use any audio track you create or import into Studio (see Chapter 11) as background for your menu tracks.

For simplicity, this demonstration will use a CD audio track previously ripped to disk, but you can rip tracks at will or use SmartSound to create audio for your menus.

Few things are as irritating as music repeated over and over every 12 seconds. So if you're going to use audio menus, remember to extend the duration of your menus to at least one minute, preferably longer.

To insert an audio menu:

1. Double-click the target menu.

   Studio opens the menu in the Menu Clip Properties tool (**Figure 12.60**).

2. Extend the duration of the menu to at least one minute (**Figure 12.61**).

   (See "To change menu duration," above, for instructions.) The one-minute rule is for aesthetics, not any limitation in the Studio program.

3. In the upper-left corner of the Movie Window, click the camcorder icon to close the Video Toolbox (**Figure 12.62**), or click X in the upper-right corner of the Menu Clip Properties tool.

Figure 12.60 To add audio to your menu, start by double-clicking the menu to load it in the Menu Clip Properties tool.

Figure 12.61 Then extend the duration to at least one minute (for aesthetics, not due to a Studio limitation).

Figure 12.62 Close the Video Toolbox.

Figure 12.63 Mozart would be just perfect. Here he is in the Album.

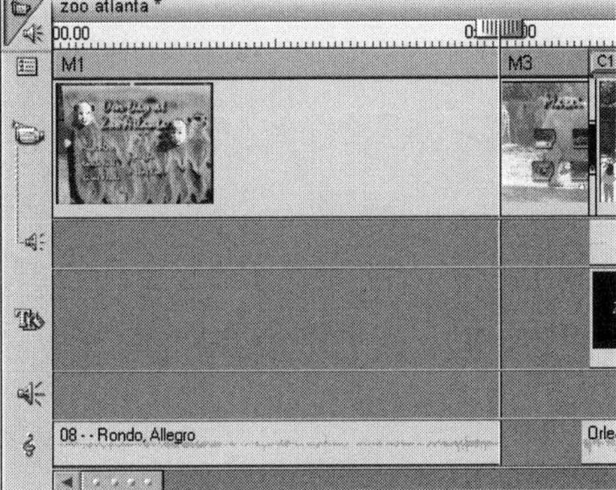

Figure 12.64 Match the length of the audio track to menu duration, lest the audio spill over into the production.

Figure 12.65 Before previewing, Studio has to load the audio track.

4. Click the show sound effects icon to open the Sound Effects tab in the Album (**Figure 12.63**).

5. Drag the desired audio track to either the Sound Effect and Voice-Over track or Background Music track (**Figure 12.64**) and trim to the desired length using techniques discussed in Chapter 11.

   When you first preview your DVD with background music enabled, Studio will load the audio file into memory before playing (**Figure 12.65**). Thereafter, preview should proceed just as it does with titles that don't have audio menus.

✔ Tips

- If you don't trim the audio track to the length of the menu, it will extend into your video segments. You can simply extend the duration of the menu by dragging it in the Timeline to the exact duration of the piece of music.
- Audio backgrounds work automatically with templates, inserting the audio into all sequential menus. The track won't start over when you jump to a new menu, but you will experience a brief blip in playback.
- Inserting an audio menu doesn't modify any menu settings, making it simple to insert audio backgrounds as the final development step. In contrast, video menus integrate most smoothly when planned from the start.

Creating Video Menus

Motion menus have video playing underneath the buttons to amuse viewers while they're making their menu selection. Note that video menus are easiest to use if you design them in from the start, since plugging them in at the end may break the links in the affected menus, forcing you to re-link.

Video menus are subject to the same caveat as audio menus; when they're short and repetitive, they get irritating. Plan on using video clips of at least one minute for your video menus.

Finally, like video buttons, video menus take time, add design complexity, and push the developmental envelop. Get a few successful DVDs under your belt before implementing these.

To create a video menu:

1. Drag the background video onto the Video track where the menu will be located (**Figure 12.66**).

   See Chapter 7 for details on how to drag videos to the Timeline.

2. If necessary, use tools described in Chapter 7 to trim the video to the desired length, which should be at least one minute (**Figure 12.67**).

   The one-minute rule is for aesthetics, not any limitation in the Studio program.

3. Click the show menus icon to open the Disc Menus tab in the Album (**Figure 12.68**).

Figure 12.66 Insert the background video on the Video track.

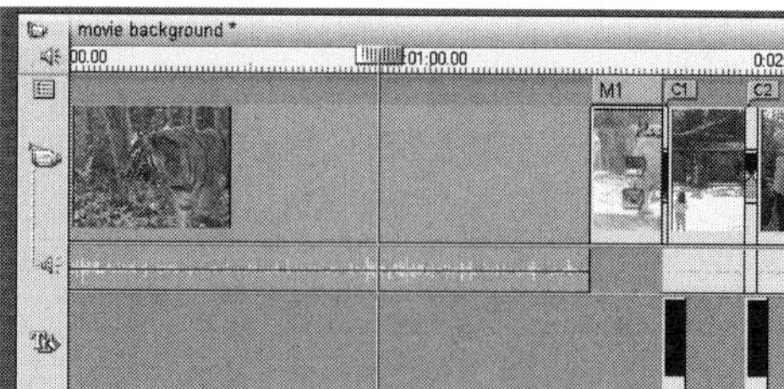

Figure 12.67 Trim the video to the desired length; once again, a minute or more works best.

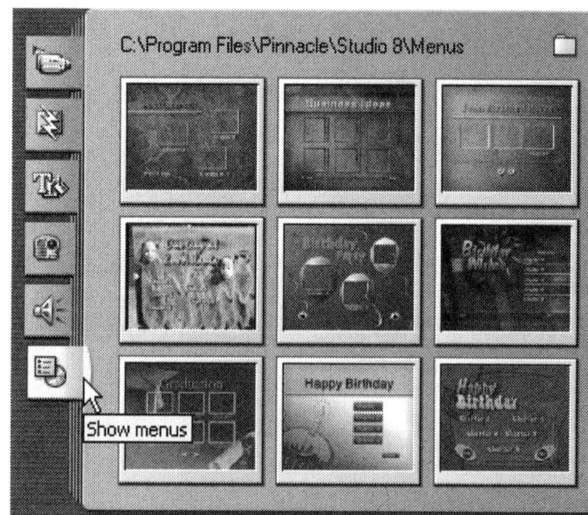

Figure 12.68 Locate the menu in the Album.

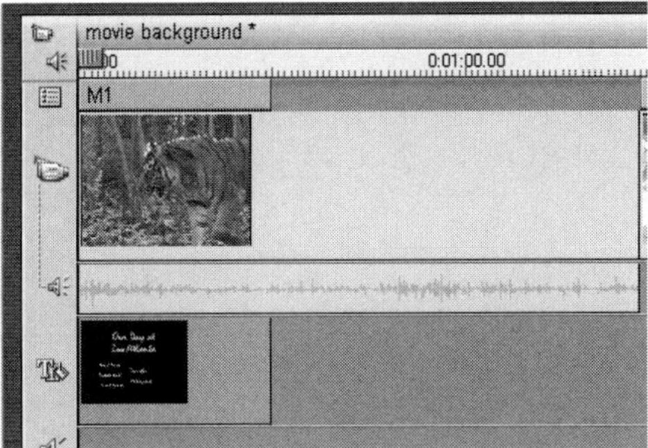

Figure 12.69 Drag it onto the Title Overlay track.

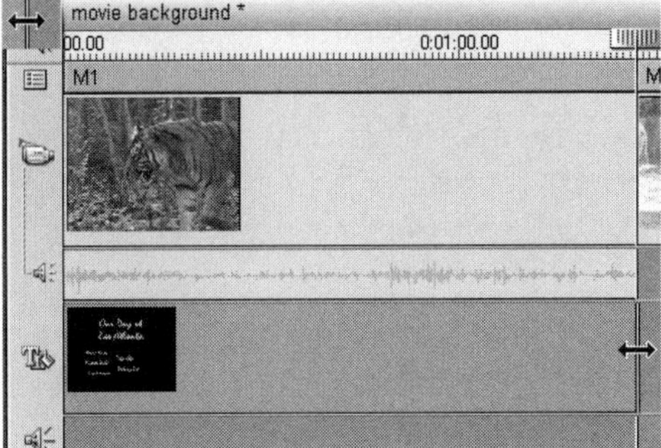

Figure 12.70 Drag it to the same length as the background video. That's it. Get ready to render!

4. Drag the desired menu to the Title Overlay track so it corresponds with the video background (**Figure 12.69**).

   Studio opens the Adding Menu to Movie dialog (see Figure 12.8).

5. Do one of the following:
   - ▲ Click Yes to automatically create links to each scene after the menu (see Figure 12.9).
   - ▲ Click No to link all videos and menus manually.

   Studio inserts the menu without the background image, making it transparent.

6. Drag the menu to the same duration as the background video (**Figure 12.70**).

7. If necessary, link the main menu to the section menus, and videos to the menus as described earlier in the chapter.

✔ Tips

- Video backgrounds work automatically with templates, inserting the video behind all sequential menus.
- Using your own videos as backgrounds works well for family shots, but not for professional videos that need a more muted and polished look. Red Plant Cinema offers several collections of media that are ideal in these instances. Check out www.redplanetcinema.com for details.

Choosing Your DVD Recorder

In the beginning, there was DVD, and it was good. Then DVD-RAM. Then DVD+RW. Then DVD-R, DVD-RW, and DVD+R/RW. Then DVD+R/RW/-R and DVD+RAM/-R. Or is it DVD-RAM/+R? I'm not sure.

This is not a misprint—in fact, I'm sure I've forgotten a few formats. Overall, if the DVD industry set out to confuse potential buyers of DVD recorders, it couldn't have done a better job.

But here are the details you need to know:

First, make sure whatever recorder you buy supports either -R or +R, the two formats most widely compatible with set-top DVD players. DVD-RAM or DVD+RW without an R option should be avoided at all costs. All DVD-RW drives support -R as well, and say so. To be completely sure, look for a statement like "compatible with DVD players" on the box or marketing literature, although this is not 100% true with any of the formats.

The other point is to make sure that whatever device you choose, you purchase the correct media. That is, a DVD+R drive can't write to DVD-R media, and vice versa. The only exceptions are "Dual RW" that support DVD-RW/-R and DVD+R/+RW, but most drives support one or the other.

I swear by my trusty DVD-R from Pioneer (the ancient but still working A03), but recent statistics published in *ExtremeTech* actually show that DVD+R discs may be more compatible with DVD players.

Other experts counter this by saying that the comparatively poor -R results were caused by the influx of cheap media from third-tier vendors, which hasn't yet happened in the newer +R market. In any event, compatibility is an issue. See the sidebar "The Dark Side of DVD-R" for details.

Figure 12.71 Click Make Movie to start the DVD production process.

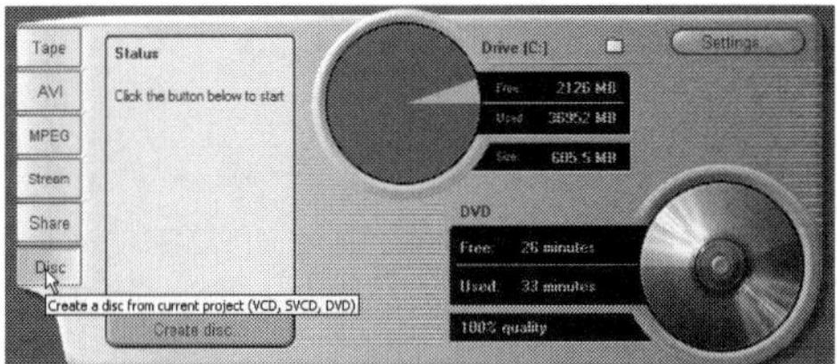

Figure 12.72 Click Disc to show the Diskometer.

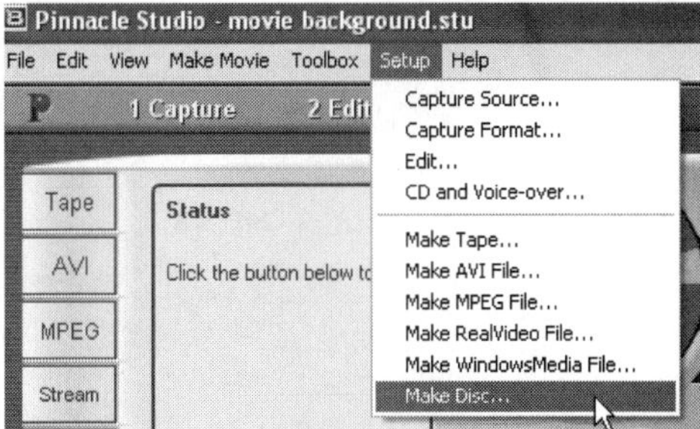

Figure 12.73 Or choose Setup > Make Disc.

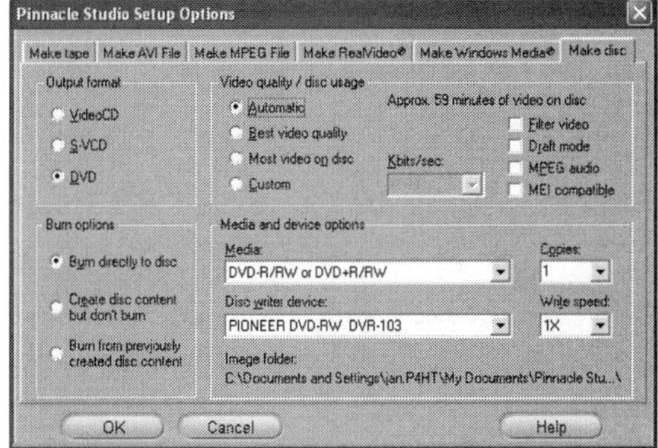

Figure 12.74 Decision central for DVD production.

Burning a DVD Title

The big moment has arrived; you've created, previewed, tinkered, and then tinkered some more. The babies are crying, the spouse complaining, and the grandparents doubting they'll ever see this DVD. It's time to shoot the videographer and ship the movie.

Let's burn, baby burn.

To burn a DVD title:

1. Put blank media in your DVD burner.
2. Do one of the following:
   - ▲ In the upper-left corner of the program, click Make Movie (**Figure 12.71**), then click Disk (**Figure 12.72**), then click Settings.
   - ▲ From the Studio menu, choose Setup > Make Disc (**Figure 12.73**).

   Studio enters Make Movie mode, and the Pinnacle Studio Setup Options dialog opens to the Make disc tab (**Figure 12.74**).
3. In the Output format section, choose DVD.
4. In the Burn options section, choose one of the following:
   - ▲ *Burn directly to disc*

     Choose this to render and burn the current project directly to DVD.
   - ▲ *Create disc content but don't burn*

     Choose this to render the current project and save it to your hard disk.
   - ▲ *Burn from previously created disc content*

     Choose this to burn from previously created content. Studio burns the content from the currently open project; this option is only available if the project was already burned to disc or saved as a disc image.

(continued on next page)

BURNING A DVD TITLE

5. On the left of the Video quality/ disc usage section, click Automatic.
6. On the right of the Video quality/disc usage section, choose one or more of the following:
   - Click *Filter video* if your input video is of poor quality.

     Studio uses a smoothing filter, which can improve quality but usually blurs the video.
   - Click *Draft mode* to encode more quickly, but at some sacrifice in quality.
   - Click *MPEG audio* to encode audio into MPEG format.

     Select this if you're getting short on disc space. If not selected, Studio will burn PCM (Pulse Code Modulated) audio to the disc, which is slightly better quality and may be more compatible.
   - Click *MEI compatible* only if you're creating a title to test with the MEI Verifier tool.

     Otherwise, do not check this box! Pinnacle inserted this command to improve its compatibility with the MEI Verifier tool developed by Matsushita Electronics, Inc. However, when checked, the Previous and Next commands are stripped out of menus generated from templates, crippling inter-menu navigation.

About VideoCD and Super VideoCD (S-VCD)

In theory, VideoCD and Super VideoCD (S-VCD) are CD-R-based formats that play on computers and DVD players. Sounds great, and sounded even better back in the day when DVD recorders cost $5000 or more.

In practice, however, using a variety of programs, I've had poor luck in creating VideoCDs or S-VCDs that played reliably on either computers or DVD players. And since DVD recorders dropped under $400, I have pretty much given up on the format.

If you're going to burn these discs, stick strictly to the default settings that Studio selects for you, which will optimize your chances for compatibility.

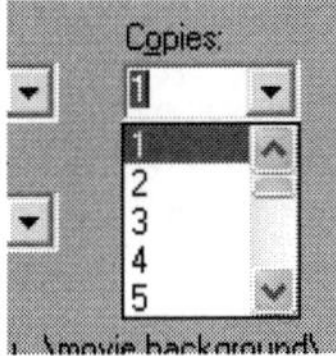

Figure 12.75 Setting the number of DVD copies.

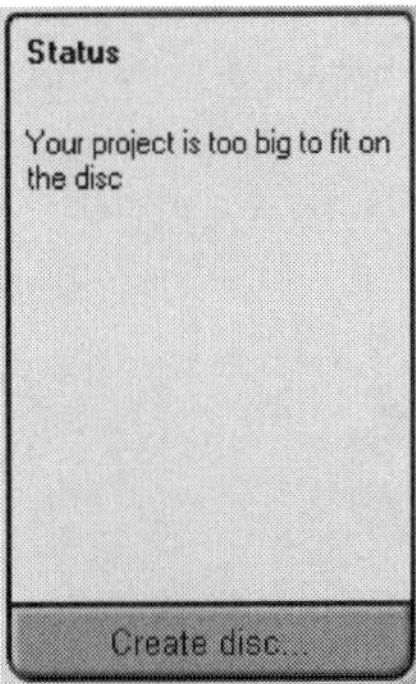

Figure 12.76 Studio isn't shy about letting you know there's a problem.

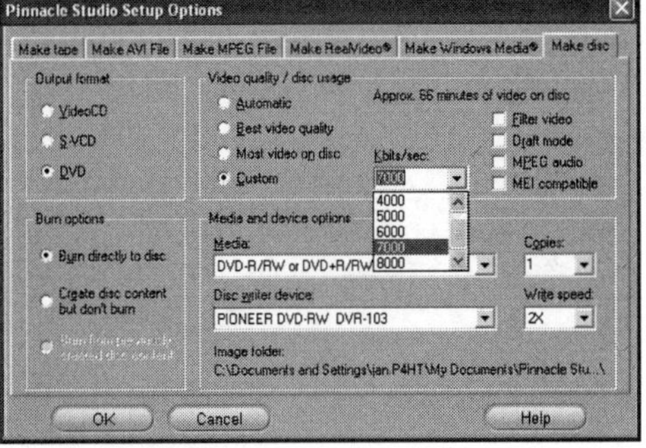

Figure 12.77 Encoding at a lower rate may resolve playback problems.

7. In the Media and device options section, do the following:
   - ▲ From the Media list box, choose DVD-R/RW or DVD+R/RW.
   - ▲ From the Disc writer device list box, choose your DVD recordable drive.
   - ▲ In the Copies list box, choose the number of copies you want to produce (**Figure 12.75**).

     Studio will create the set number of copies sequentially, prompting you for additional discs when required.
   - ▲ In the Write speed list box, choose 1X.

     See the sidebar "The Dark Side of DVD-R" for details.
8. Click OK to close the Setup Options dialog.

   Studio returns to the Make Movie window, and a Status box appears. You'll see an error message if the project is too large to fit on the recordable disc (**Figure 12.76**) or if there isn't sufficient hard disk space to stage the disc image.
9. Click Create disc to start encoding.

✔ Tips

- Though technically Studio can burn projects of any length, once you go over 80 minutes or so, Studio must increase compression to fit the video on the disk, degrading quality.
- If you're having problems playing your DVDs, particularly if they stutter and stop during playback, you may want to encode at a lower rate (see the sidebar "The Dark Side of DVD-R"). Try encoding between 6000 to 7000 kbits/second, using the controls shown in **Figure 12.77**.

The Dark Side of DVD-R

OK, so you work for ten hours getting your masterpiece on disc and then ship it off to the grandparents. What are the odds that it will play?

Well, anywhere from 63 to 90%, depending upon format and who's doing the figuring. These figures are according to Mark Hachman in an article entitled "DVD Compatibility: It's as Ugly as Ever" (*ExtremeTech*, October 29, 2002). The article described the results of studies by Pioneer and Intellikey. The Intellikey study tested 100 players manufactured between 1999 and 2002 and found compatibility issues at least 10% of the time across all media, though problems were less frequent on newer players. Both studies found -R and +R media more compatible than -RW and +RW.

What's a budding videographer to do? In addition to distributing your work on -R or +R media, an article by Ralph LaBarge entitled "DVD Compatibility Test" (*DV Magazine*, July 2002) offers two additional suggestions.

First, buy name-brand media, which Ralph found to produce lower error rates than off-brand. He also recommended burning videos at 7 megabits per second or below; at these rates, if there were some reading errors, the drive could re-read the segment and potentially play it back normally without a visible pause. (Normally, I let Studio pick the burn data rate, but I would try using a lower rate if I experienced compatibility problems with a particular player or were distributing discs widely.)

Interestingly, Ralph also found that off-brand media performed better when burning at slower speeds; since reading this, I've restricted all my burning to 1X speed.

To this I would add that once you find a solution that works, stick with it. My Pioneer A03 burning Verbatim media has long proven compatible with all players in my little circle, which is one reason I don't upgrade for a newer and faster burner or experiment with cheaper media. Of course, anyone starting out today will have a hard time finding the A03; my next-best choice would be subsequent Pioneer models like the A04 and A05.

Figure 12.78 Encoding is as slow as, well, an elephant, but Studio provides good feedback regarding your progress via bars under the Player.

Figure 12.79 Next is compiling.

Figure 12.80 Then burning. Getting close now.

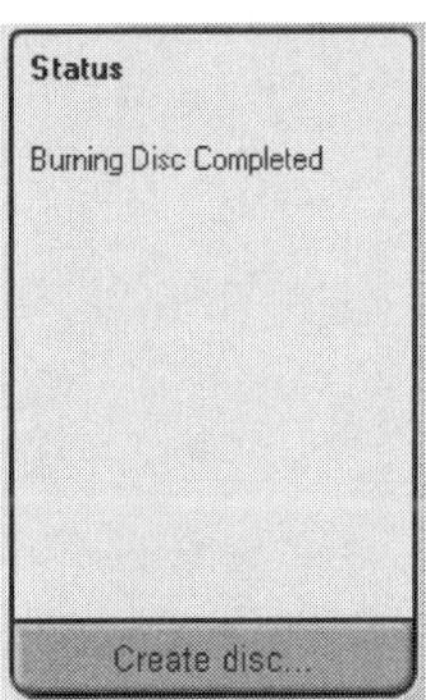

Figure 12.81 Success!

What's Happening?

After you start the process, Studio has three tasks to perform:

Encoding. Studio has to convert the video and other assets to the proper formats. Depending upon the length of content and speed of your computer, this can take anywhere from several minutes to several days. While encoding, Studio moves the Timeline Scrubber through the Timeline and updates the Player to show the video being encoded.

Two progress bars sit under the Player: the first showing progress for the current operation, in this case rendering, and the second showing overall progress (**Figure 12.78**). Hover your mouse over the drive Diskometer and you'll get additional progress-related information.

Compiling. Studio converts the encoded files into DVD-formatted files and stores the files to disk. Though the compiling phase has just started, **Figure 12.79** reports that overall, the project is about 50% completed. Once again, hover the mouse over the hard disk Diskometer and Studio will provide additional data.

Burning the DVD. Studio updates the Status screen and starts over on the top progress bar (**Figure 12.80**).

When completed (**Figure 12.81**), Studio ejects your freshly minted DVD. Time to address the envelope, lick the stamps, and get this disc off to the grandparents.

PART IV

OTHER OUTPUT

13

Writing to Tape

Most video producers render to tape to distribute or archive their productions. Working in DV, the workflow is typically to write to DV tape, then, if desired, dub to VHS or other widely supported analog formats for the grandparents.

If working in analog, you'll want to write each distribution tape directly from Studio, rather than dubbing one tape to VHS and then dubbing additional tapes from there. This avoids the quality loss associated with analog-to-analog copies, which is like photocopying a photocopy.

Writing to tape is a three-step process. First you set up your hardware, which is nearly identical to connecting for capture. Then, Studio renders the project, essentially implementing all of your editing work, inserting transitions, titles, mixing audio, and overlaying titles. Sounds like hard work, but it's all transparent; no user intervention required. When rendering is complete, you'll begin the final stage—actually writing the video to tape.

Setting Up Your Hardware

Hardware setup involves three discrete actions: getting connected to your camera or deck, getting the camera or deck ready, and getting your computer ready.

To set up your hardware:

1. Connect your camera or deck to the computer.

   For more information, see Chapter 3 for DV capture, or Chapter 4 for analog capture.

2. Make sure the camera or deck is in VTR, VCR, or Play mode.

3. If the camcorder has an LCD display, open the LCD and use camcorder controls to display all tape location and recording/playback information (if available).

   Sony camcorders usually have a "Display" button that reveals this information.

4. If the camera or deck has an input/output selector, select input.

   I haven't seen this in a while, but my venerable Sony Hi-8 CCD-TR81 had an input/output switch that needed to be set before writing to tape.

5. If there is no LCD, or you're writing to a stand-alone deck, connect a television or other analog monitor to the camera or deck.

   The only way to be sure you're actually writing to tape is to see the video in the camera or deck. If you don't have an LCD or TV you can connect, you should be able to track progress in the viewfinder.

6. Check that the tape in the deck has sufficient space for your production.

7. Check that any copy-protection features on the tape are disabled.

   Most DV tapes have a copy-protection tab on the back panel, a great way to make sure you don't overwrite your valuable video.

   In my tests, Studio didn't detect that copy protection was enabled, and played the video out to the DV camera anyway. No harm was done, as the camera didn't overwrite the video, but nothing got recorded either.

8. Close all extraneous programs from your computer, and don't perform any other tasks on the computer while writing to tape.

✔ Tip

- Like capture, writing to tape is extremely demanding, and one slip can ruin the tape. Try not to touch the computer or camera over the course of this procedure.

Writing to Tape

You may want to consider some minor adjustments when converting a DVD production to tape-based output (see the sidebar "Outputting DVD Projects to Tape"), but otherwise your project should be on the Timeline, complete, and itchin' to be written.

To write your project to tape:

1. Do one of the following:
   - ▲ In the upper-left corner of the Studio interface, click Make Movie (**Figure 13.1**). Then, in the upper-left of the Make Movie panel, click Tape.
   - ▲ From the Studio menu, choose Setup > Make Tape (**Figure 13.2**).

   Studio displays the Make Tape controls (**Figure 13.3**).

   Note that Studio will immediately compute the project's disk requirements and warn you in the Status box if you don't have the necessary disk space.

Figure 13.1 Click the Make Movie tab to get started.

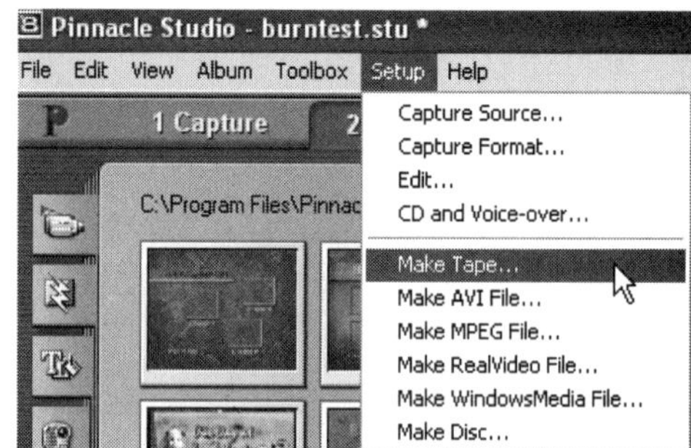

Figure 13.2 Another route to the Make Tape controls in the Make Movie screen.

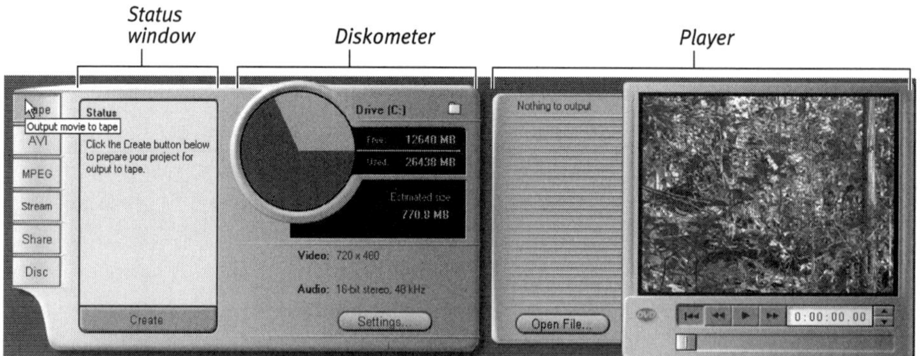

Figure 13.3 The Make Tape controls. Note the Status window, which delivers instructions and warnings; the Diskometer, which details disk requirements and capacity; and the Player, which controls writing to tape.

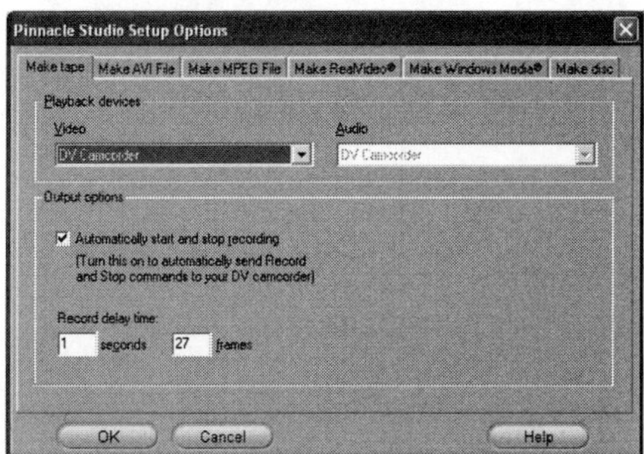

Figure 13.4 The Make tape tab in DV mode.

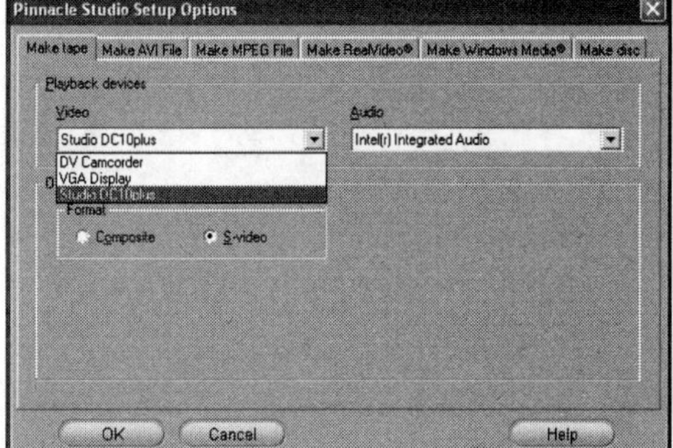

Figure 13.5 The Make tape tab in analog mode.

2. Below the Diskometer in the middle of the Make Movie window, click Settings.

   The Pinnacle Studio Setup Options dialog opens to the Make tape tab (**Figure 13.4**).

3. Choose the appropriate audio/video output device:
   - ▲ If outputting DV, as in Figure 13.4, choose DV.
   - ▲ If analog, choose both the device and the audio output (**Figure 13.5**), and the format (S-Video is preferred when available).

4. If DV, click the "Automatically start and stop recording" checkbox to allow Studio to control the DV camera, and adjust the numbers under Record delay time, if necessary.

   All DV camcorders have a short delay between the time they receive the Record command and when they start recording. Stick with the default (1 second, 27 frames), unless you notice your camcorder is not capturing the first few moments of the video; then you should extend the duration.

   If you're working with an analog camcorder or deck, this option won't be available (Figure 13.5), and you'll have to manually start the recording.

(continued on next page)

5. On the bottom of the Status box in the Make Movie window, click Create (see Figure 13.3).

   Studio starts to render the project. The Status box presents a "Rendering. Please wait" message (**Figure 13.6**), the Timeline Scrubber moves through the production as it's rendered, and the status bars under the Player reflect progress through the project (**Figure 13.7**).

   When rendering is complete, Studio displays the message shown in **Figure 13.8**.

6. If you have an analog camcorder or deck (or are manually cueing your DV deck), start your device recording now.

   If you clicked "Automatically start and stop recording," Studio will start and stop the DV tape automatically.

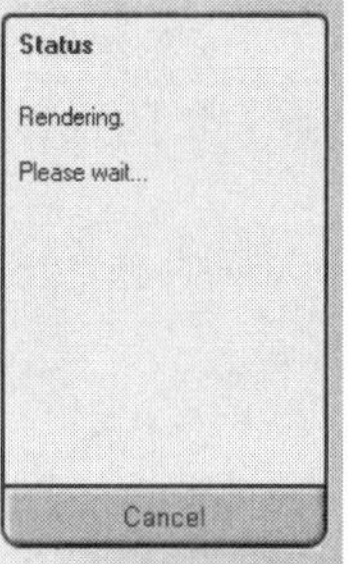

Figure 13.6 Studio tells you when it's rendering.

Figure 13.7 You can track your progress by watching the Timeline Scrubber, or watching the progress bars under the Player.

Figure 13.8 Itchin' to be written!

Figure 13.9 Studio preserves CPU resources and shows very little feedback during the actual writing, except updating the Player counter.

Figure 13.10 Your camcorder or deck should display the incoming video, with a red ball indicating the recording.

7. Click Play in the Player to start playback (**Figure 13.9**).

   Studio starts playing the video out the device selected in Step 3. The only progress you'll see on your computer is the Player counter advancing through the video.

   You should see video in the camcorder LCD panel (**Figure 13.10**) and/or on the television or other monitor attached to your analog device. You should generally also see a red light or other indication that the video is being recorded.

   If you don't see video, it's likely that you're not sending the video out to the device, so you should re-check your setup.

(continued on next page)

✔ Tips

- Don't go away during rendering. If Studio needs a CD-ROM to rip a track, or if you used SmartCapture and Studio needs to recapture video, you'll need to be there to respond.
- Studio saves all temporary files created during rendering, so if you want to write another tape, simply load the project, enter Make Movie mode, and everything should be rendered and ready to go.
- Some older DV cameras used nonstandard commands to start and stop recording, and may not recognize Studio's commands. If Studio doesn't automatically start your DV recorder, uncheck the "Automatically start and stop recording" checkbox and manually set the record function.
- Before recording a long segment to tape, try a one- or two-minute sequence, just to make sure it's working. Writing back to tape is one of those "tough to get it right the first time" activities, at least for me, so test your setup with a shorter project to catch any errors.

Intelligent Rendering

When working with DV source footage, Studio uses a process called Intelligent Rendering to produce the stream it sends out to tape. Rather than rendering the entire project into one huge file, Studio renders the edited portions of the project, like transitions, titles, and special effects, into discrete separate files, leaving unchanged segments alone. Then, when writing back to tape, Studio switches between the rendered files and the original captured files to dynamically create the stream.

This is much faster than rendering the entire project, and more disk-efficient, since fewer new files are created. It can be demanding on lower-powered computers, however.

If you experience problems writing back to tape, compile the project into one DV file (see Chapter 14), and then write this file back to tape, which should be a bit less strenuous on the computer.

The only caveat is that the size of the project file can't exceed the maximum file size for the operating system you're running and the way you've formatted your drives. (See "Windows File Size Limitations" in Chapter 3.)

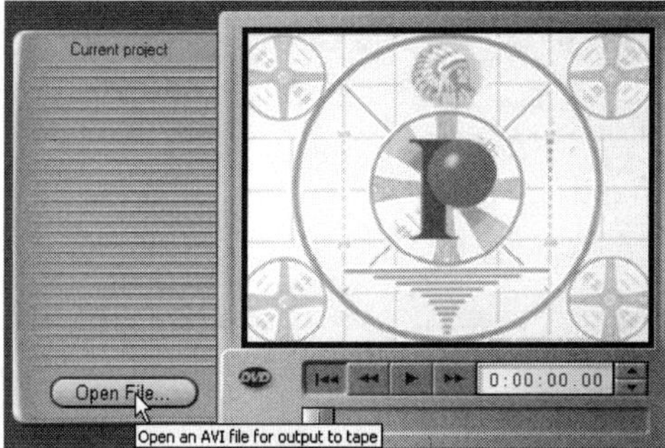

Figure 13.11 Start here to write a disk-based AVI file.

Writing Disk Files to Tape

Use this technique when writing disk-based AVI files to tape.

To write disk-based files back to tape:

1. Do one of the following:
   - ▲ In the upper-left corner of the Studio interface, click Make Movie (see Figure 13.1). Then, in the upper-left of the Make Movie interface, click Tape.
   - ▲ From the Studio menu, choose Setup > Make Tape (see Figure 13.2).

   Studio displays the Make Tape controls (see Figure 13.3).
2. To the left of the Player, click the Open File button (**Figure 13.11**).

(continued on next page)

Outputting DVD Projects to Tape

You've created this awesome DVD project and then realize Aunt Janie hasn't made the leap to DVD. VHS will just have to do.

What's the absolute bare minimum you have to do to convert your DVD project to tape output? Well, actually, nothing. You're in great shape. Studio simply treats the menus as still images and compiles them into the program normally.

Of course, the menus may look a bit bizarre, with all those windows and links and arrows and such (not that Aunt Janie would notice). So you may want to simply delete them and then write to tape. Remember to save your DVD project first so you don't lose any work.

3. Select and load the target file (**Figure 13.12**).

   Studio's status screen should tell you that the file is loaded and ready to play (**Figure 13.13**).

4. If you have an analog camcorder or deck (or are manually cueing your DV record), start your device recording now.

   If you clicked "Automatically start and stop recording," Studio will start and stop the DV tape automatically.

5. Click Play in the Player to start playback.

   The operation should proceed as described earlier under "Writing to Tape."

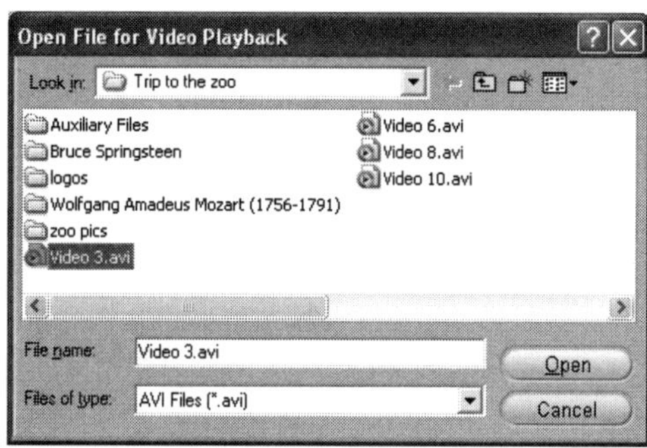

Figure 13.12 Then load the file.

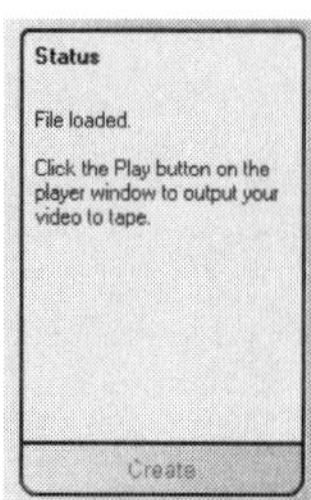

Figure 13.13 Studio's Status box tells you you're ready to go.

14

Creating Digital Output

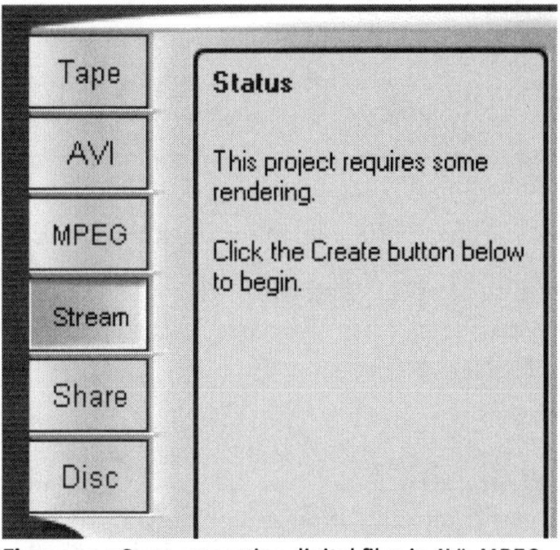

Figure 14.1 Start outputting digital files in AVI, MPEG, and streaming formats by clicking the appropriate button in the Make Movie window.

Chapter 12 addressed DVD creation, and Chapter 13 covered writing back to tape. Now I'll cover options for creating digital files for playback on your hard disk, copying to a CD-ROM or DVD, sending via email or posting to a Web site. This chapter deals with three options on the Studio output panel (**Figure 14.1**): AVI, MPEG, and Stream.

Choosing between these formats is simple; if outputting for disk-based playback or CD-ROM distribution, choose MPEG, which has largely supplanted AVI files as a distribution format. If posting your files to a Web site or sending via email, use a streaming format.

Note that this chapter discusses CD-ROM and DVDs as data-storage devices, not specialized formats that play in a player attached to your television. That is, if you want to produce an MPEG file to copy to CD/DVD to send to a friend to play from his computer, you're in the right place. If you want to author a production that can be viewed on a DVD player and TV set, go to Chapter 12.

A Brief Overview of Compression

Though compression sounds complicated, in use the concept is simple: video files are extremely large, and compression technologies, or *codecs*, make the files smaller. DV video is clean and pristine, but at 3.6 megabytes per second, you can only fit about three minutes on a 700 MB CD-ROM. The higher compression rates offered by technologies like MPEG, Real, and Microsoft make digital video distributable, and that's why compression is so important.

Back in 1994, when folks started distributing digital video, the most relevant distribution medium was CD-ROM, mostly played on the computers of the day, 80386 and Pentium computers with 1X CD drives that could only retrieve 150 kilobytes/second of data or 300 kilobytes/second at most. The only codecs that could play on these computers were Cinepak and Indeo, which sacrificed visual quality to achieve the 15 frames-per-second (or more) playback speed necessary to actually look like video.

MPEG-1 technology was around back then, and offered vastly superior visual quality, but the underpowered computers of the day couldn't play back the files without hardware assistance, so the technology never really caught on. On today's much-faster computers, MPEG-1 playback is a walk in the park, especially since both Microsoft and Apple ship MPEG-1 playback software with their operating systems. Since MPEG-1 offers better quality than all AVI codecs, and can play on virtually all computers, AVI files—as a format for distributing video—are seldom used.

However, the AVI file format is still tremendously vital as a capture and editing format, and is used by Studio and most other Windows-based programs to capture DV video. To distribute your video, however, MPEG formats are typically better choices.

MPEG-1 vs. MPEG-2

So, which do you use, MPEG-1 or MPEG-2? Well, MPEG-2 offers larger resolution, 720 x 480 vs. MPEG-1's 320 x 240, and better quality, though it generally requires about four times the disk space of MPEG-1. More importantly, however, where MPEG-1 players have been included free with every Windows and Mac computer shipped since the late 1990s, this isn't the case with MPEG-2 playback, which requires software that typically costs $10 to $20.

Not a huge deal, but while you can anticipate that everyone can play MPEG-1 files you send them, you can't make the same assumption with MPEG-2. If you're sending your CD-ROM to an audience that you know has MPEG-2 playback capabilities, and have sufficient space on your CD/DVD-ROM, use MPEG-2. If you're distributing your videos to a broader audience with unknown MPEG-2 capabilities, MPEG-1 is a safer choice.

Streaming media technologies

Streaming media technologies are advanced codecs that deliver much higher quality than their predecessors at fantastically reduced bit rates. That's what makes them ideal for email as well as essential for streaming video from a Web site. For casual users, both Real and Windows Media technologies are free, and qualitative differences between the two are minor. Both are great choices for email or posting to a Web site.

Decoding Your Compression Parameters

Before you start encoding, take a quick look at the parameters you'll be selecting.

Video resolution. Video resolution is the number of horizontal and vertical pixels in the video file. By way of reference, DV video starts life at 720 pixels across and 480 pixels north and south, or 720 x 480. You capture and edit in this format to maintain the best possible quality, and then generally *scale* to a lower resolution to distribute your videos. As seen in **Table 14.1**, the only exception is MPEG-2, which is encoded at 720 x 480 as well.

Why scale the other technologies to lower resolutions? Generally, when compressing video to lower and lower data rates (defined below), the individual frames look better when you start with smaller frames. That's why most Web-based videos are 320 x 240 resolution or lower, especially those distributed at modem speeds.

I discuss which resolutions to use and when in the individual compression sections. However, the general rule for video resolution is that if the video is bound for playback on computers, use a 4:3 aspect ratio, the same as that used for still image capture. In contrast, if the video is for viewing on a TV set, use 720 x 480, or an aspect ratio of 4:2.66.

Table 14.1

Common Compression Parameters

Technology	Resolution	Data Rate	Frame Rate (FPS)
MPEG-2	720 x 480	4000–8000 kilobits/second	29.97
MPEG-1	320 x 240	1150–2400 kilobits/second	29.97
AVI Codecs	320 x 240	200–300 kilobytes/second	15
Windows Media	160 x 120 and 320 x 240	22–500 kilobits/second	8–30
RealVideo	160 x 120 and 320 x 240	22–500 kilobits/second	8–30

Generally, choosing the correct aspect ratio is fairly easy using Studio's standard controls, with one exception: Windows Media still uses 176 x 144 as the target resolution for certain lower-bit-rate files, which will distort your videos. See below for how to work around this.

Data rate. Data rate is the amount of data associated with a specified duration of video, usually one second. For example, as seen in Table 14.1, MPEG-2 usually has a data rate of between 4000 and 8000 kilobits/second (kbps), while streaming formats like Real and Microsoft's Windows Media can go down to 22 kbps.

The most important factor in determining data rate is the capacity of the medium from which or over which the video is played. Exceed this capacity and the data can't keep up, and then playback is interrupted, something we've all experienced with Internet-based video.

DVDs are capable of retrieving more than 10 mbps, leaving a comfortable margin over the 4 to 8 mbps used for most DVDs. On the other hand, if connecting to a Web site via a 28.8 modem, retrieval capacity is down around 22 kbps, requiring the much lower rate. Real and Microsoft make it simple to select the right data rate by using presets for common devices, like dial-up modems, local area networks, or DSL modems.

Frame rate. The frame rate is the number of frames per second (fps) included in the encoded file. For both MPEG-1 and MPEG-2, this is always 29.97 fps, a parameter that Studio doesn't allow you to change. Both Real and Microsoft dynamically assign a frame rate to a file based on the target distribution medium (modem, broadband) and video content, so you won't see a frame rate option in either encoding interface.

This leaves the AVI format as the only place you need to make a frame rate choice. For the most part, if you've chosen AVI, it's to play back on older computers, which is why Table 14.1 shows 15 fps. If your target computer is more recent (e.g., Pentium II or above), MPEG-1 is probably a better choice.

With this as prologue, let's compress some video.

Compressing to AVI Format

Producing a DV-based AVI file may be a valuable workaround if your computer is having difficulty using Studio's Intelligent Rendering technique (see the "Intelligent Rendering" sidebar in Chapter 13). I cover this procedure first, then describe how to produce an AVI file to distribute your videos (but remember, MPEG-1 or MPEG-2 are almost always superior choices).

To encode a project in DV format:

1. After completing your project, do one of the following:
   - ▲ In the upper-left corner of the Studio interface, click Make Movie (**Figure 14.2**). Then, in the upper-left of the Make Movie panel, click AVI (see Figure 14.1).
   - ▲ From the Studio menu, choose Setup > Make AVI File (**Figure 14.3**).

   Studio enters Make Movie mode with AVI controls (**Figure 14.4**).

   Note that Studio immediately computes the project's disk requirements and warns you in the Status box if you don't have the necessary disk space.

   Studio also displays the currently selected encoding parameters for both audio and video.

2. Below the Diskometer, click the Settings button.

   The Pinnacle Studio Setup Options dialog opens to the Make AVI File tab (**Figure 14.5**).

Figure 14.2 The encoding process begins in the Make Movie window.

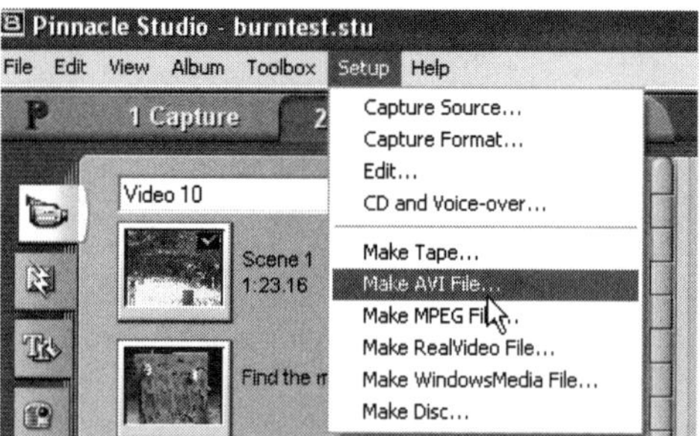

Figure 14.3 Another route to the Make AVI File tab.

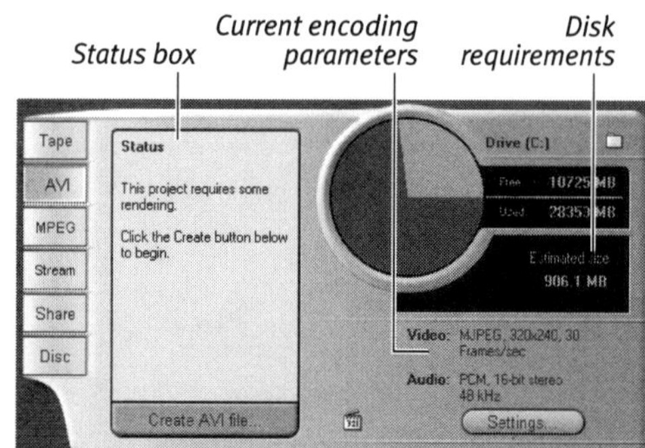

Figure 14.4 The AVI file screen. Note that Studio shows the estimated disk requirements and will alert you if you're short. The current encoding parameters are also displayed here.

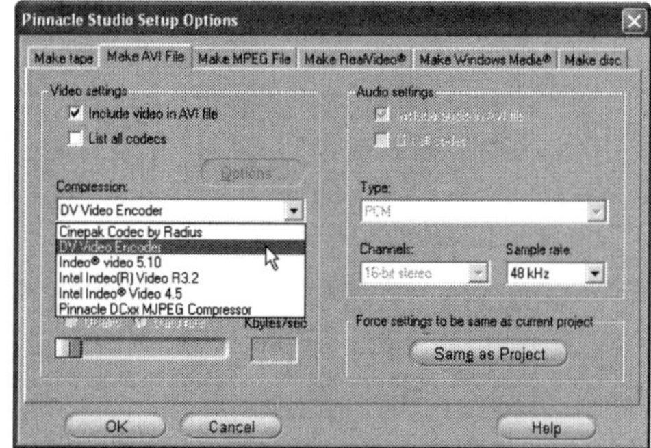

Figure 14.5 DV should be the default decoder, but select it here if it isn't.

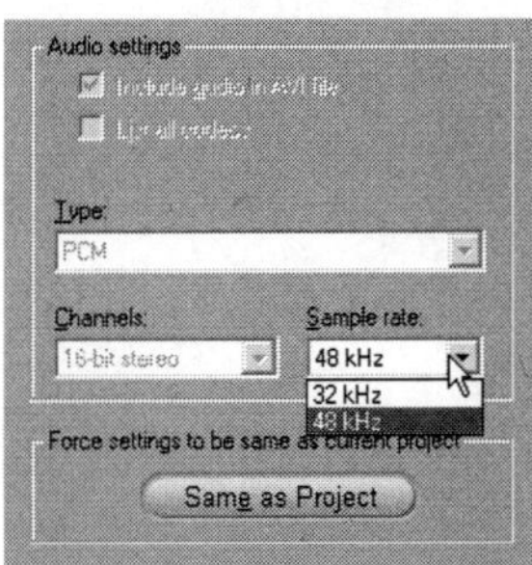

Figure 14.6 Choose your audio sample rate here.

Figure 14.7 You're ready to rumble. Press Create AVI file to get started.

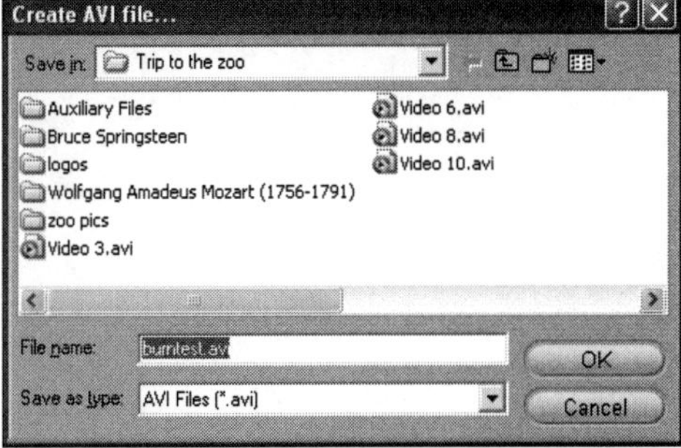

Figure 14.8 Choose a filename and target location.

3. In the Video settings section, click the Include video in AVI file checkbox.
4. In the Compression list box, choose DV Video Encoder.

   Once selected, all other video compression options should gray out. This reflects that DV is a highly standard format, which helps ensure compatibility between computer and camera.
5. In the Audio settings box, in the Sample rate list box, choose the sample rate used in the original DV video (**Figure 14.6**).

   If you don't know the sample rate, and the project contains DV videos originally captured from your camera, click the Same as Project button. Studio will scan the DV files on disk and determine the sample rate.

   If you're using disk-based assets, use 48 kHz.
6. Click OK to return to the Make Movie dialog.
7. At the bottom of the Status box, click Create AVI file (**Figure 14.7**).

   Studio opens the Create AVI file dialog (**Figure 14.8**).
8. Type the filename, and change the location if desired.

(continued on next page)

Figure 14.9 Encoding in progress. You'll see the Timeline Scrubber moving over the video being encoded, and can track progress under the Player window.

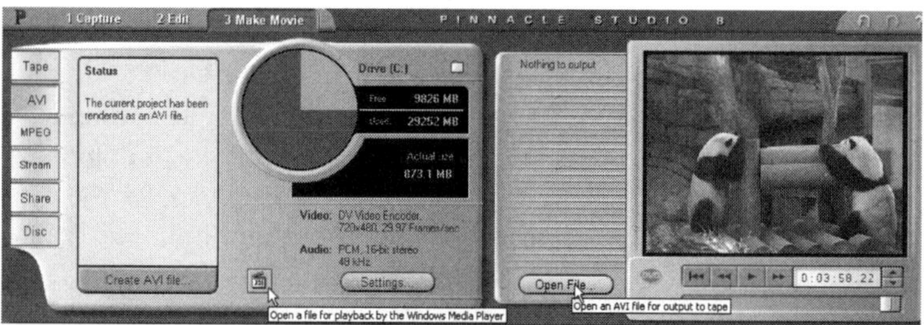

Figure 14.10 File encoded, ready to play or write back to tape.

9. Click OK to close the dialog.

   Studio starts encoding. You should see the Timeline Scrubber moving through the video, the video updating in the Player, and progress in the bars beneath the Player window (**Figure 14.9**).

   To play the video after encoding, click the Open File button on the Diskometer (**Figure 14.10**). To open the file for output to tape, click the Open File button on the Player, and follow the instructions in Chapter 13.

✔ Tip

- If you're working with an analog capture card and want to create an AVI file for output to tape, substitute the codec used by your capture card for DV in the above instructions. For example, in Figure 14.5, the Pinnacle DCxx MJPEG Compressor is the encoder used by the installed Pinnacle DC10 capture card.

Figure 14.11 The venerable Cinepak codec, choosing between color and black and white.

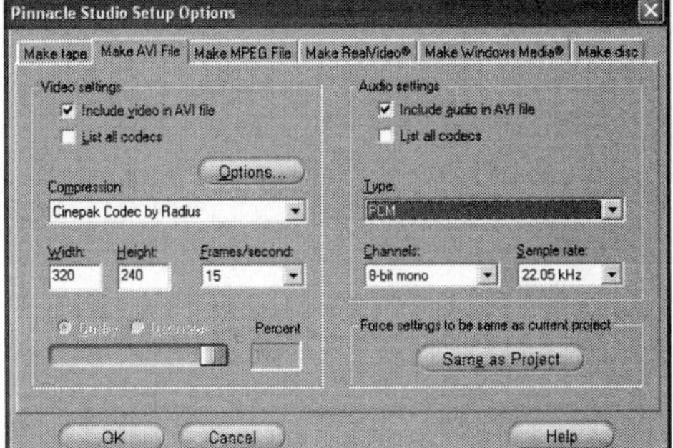

Figure 14.12 Choosing the right parameters for your AVI file. Note that the data rate option is grayed out, a significant issue for those placing AVI video on CD-ROM.

To encode a project in AVI format for distribution:

1. Follow Steps 1 through 3 above.
2. In the Compression list box, choose either the Cinepak Codec by Radius or Intel Indeo(R) Video R3.2 (see Figure 14.5).

   These two codecs provide the best playback on lower-power computers.
3. If you choose Cinepak, the Options button above the Compression list box will become active. Click Options to open the Cinepak for Windows 32 options box and click Compress to Color (**Figure 14.11**).
4. Click OK to close the Cinepak options box.
5. Change the resolution to 320 x 240 (**Figure 14.12**).
6. Change the frame rate under Frames/second to 15.
7. In the Audio settings box, click Include audio in AVI file if desired.
8. In the Type list box, choose PCM.
9. In the Channels list box, choose 8-bit mono.
10. In the Sample rate list box, choose 22.05 kHz.
11. Click OK to return to the Make Movie window.
12. At the bottom of the Status box, click Create AVI file.

    Studio opens the Create AVI file dialog.
13. Type the filename, and change the location if desired.
14. Click OK to close the dialog.

    Studio starts encoding. You should see the Timeline Scrubber moving through the video, the video updating in the Player, and progress in the bars beneath the Player window (see Figure 14.9).

(continued on next page)

To play the video after encoding, click the Open File button on the Diskometer (see Figure 14.10). The Open File button on the Player should be grayed out because you can't upload a Cinepak or Indeo file back to a camera.

✔ Tips

- Studio provides poor data-rate controls for encoding AVI files, forcing you to choose a quality percentage rather than a data rate when encoding with Indeo and most other formats (**Figure 14.13**). You'll have to experiment with different quality percentages to hit your data rate target.
- Even though most current CD-ROMs can retrieve data at 24X or higher rates, don't encode at data rates higher than 300 KB/second for two reasons: First, though you'll see dramatic quality improvements between 150 KB/s and 250 KB/s, improvements slow thereafter. Second, even a 24X drive may start to choke at data rates of 500 KB/s and higher, especially on lower-powered computers, resulting in choppy playback.
- The audio parameters listed above are conservative numbers for primarily speech-based audio. At full CD-ROM quality, audio comprises 176 KB/second, and this is in addition to video data rate. At the listed parameters, the audio data rate is approximately 44 KB/second, which is much more reasonable.
- If you click the List all codecs checkbox in the Video settings section, Studio will open the warning dialog shown in **Figure 14.14**. Basically, Studio only displays known and proven compatible codecs in both the audio and video sections. Unless you want to experiment, you should probably stick to these codecs.

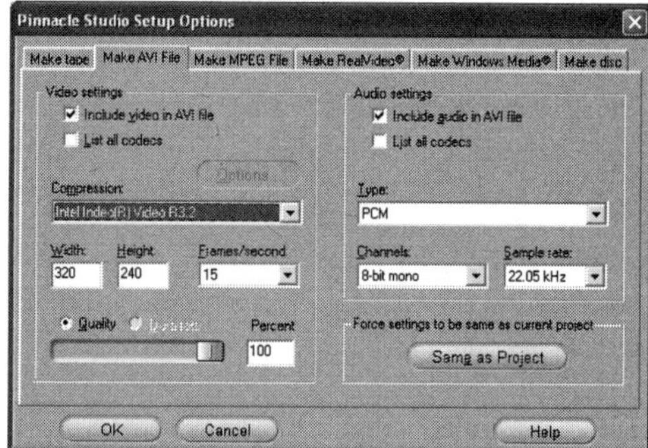

Figure 14.13 With Indeo 3.2, you have to adjust quality to arrive at your target data rate, which usually involves trial and error.

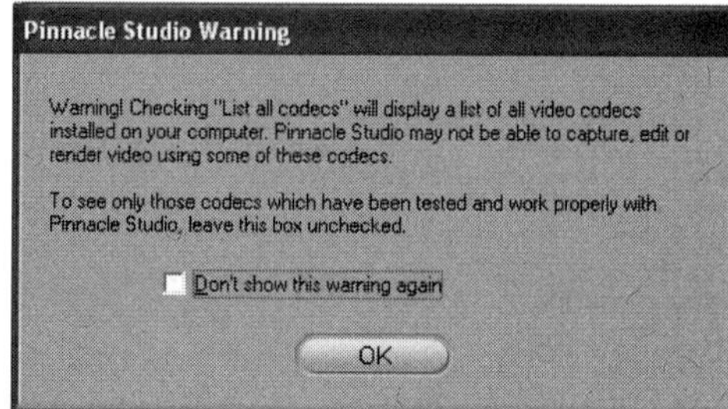

Figure 14.14 Studio recommends only working with tried and true codecs (I second that emotion).

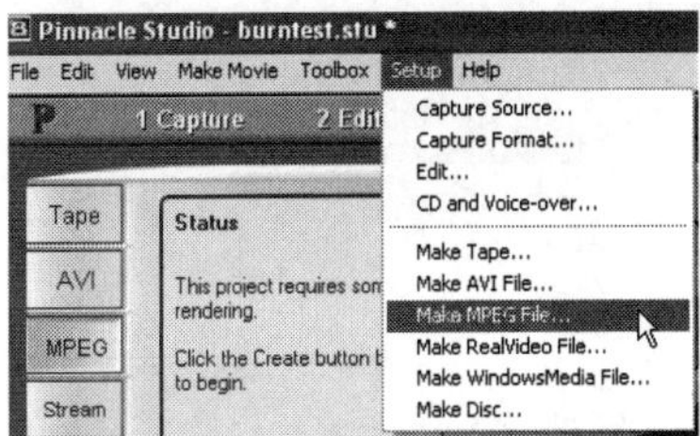

Figure 14.15 The direct route to the MPEG encoding tools.

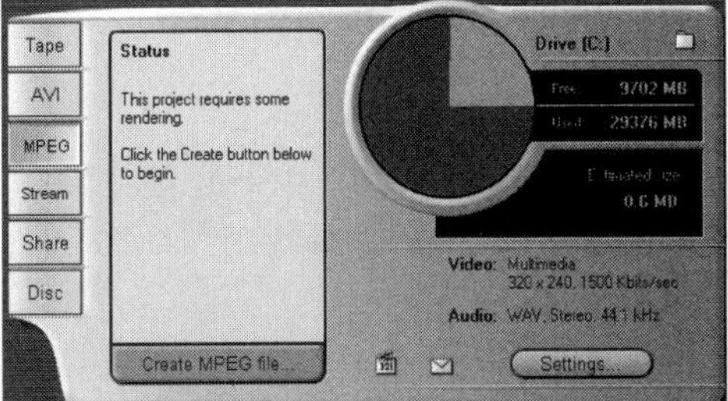

Figure 14.16 The MPEG encoding screen. Note the estimated file requirements and current encoding settings.

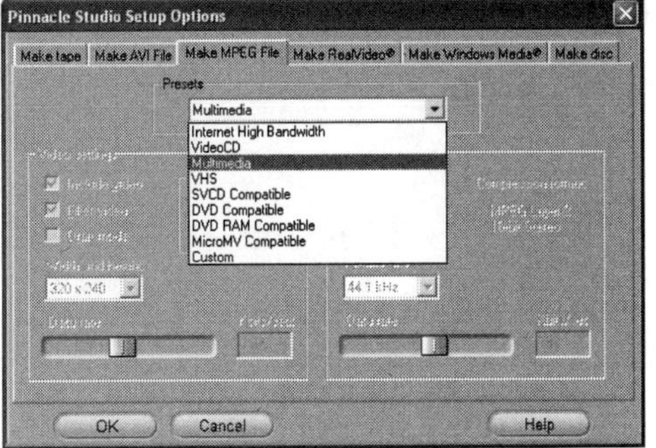

Figure 14.17 Stick with the Studio presets for MPEG encoding. This preset is appropriate for creating MPEG-1 files for playing from a hard disk or CD-ROM.

Producing MPEG Files

Studio simplifies the production of MPEG files with excellent presets for most common MPEG distribution situations. You can also customize your options completely, but most users are better off sticking with the presets.

To produce an MPEG file:

1. After completing your video project, do one of the following:
   - ▲ In the upper-left corner of the Studio interface, click Make Movie. Then, in the upper-left of the Make Movie window, click MPEG.
   - ▲ From the Studio menu, choose Setup > Make MPEG File (**Figure 14.15**).

   Studio enters Make Movie mode with MPEG controls (**Figure 14.16**).

   Note that Studio immediately computes the project's disk requirements and warns you in the Status box if you don't have the necessary disk space.

   Studio also displays the currently selected encoding parameters for both audio and video.

2. Below the Diskometer, Click the Settings button.

   The Pinnacle Studio Setup Options dialog opens to the Make MPEG File tab (**Figure 14.17**).

(continued on next page)

3. In the Presets list box, choose one of the following:
   - ▲ VideoCD, SVCD, or DVD for files intended for these disk-based projects
   - ▲ MicroMV for files to write to MicroMV-compatible devices
   - ▲ Multimedia for files to be played back on computers
   - ▲ Custom to create your own parameters (**Figure 14.18**).
4. Click OK to close the dialog and return to the Make Movie window.
5. At the bottom of the Status box, click Create MPEG file.

   Studio opens the Create MPEG file dialog (**Figure 14.19**).
6. Type the filename, and change the location if desired.
7. Click OK to close the dialog.

   Studio starts encoding. You should see the Timeline Scrubber moving through the video, the video updating in the Player, and progress in the bars beneath the Player window (see Figure 14.9).

   To play the video after encoding, click the Open File button on the Diskometer.

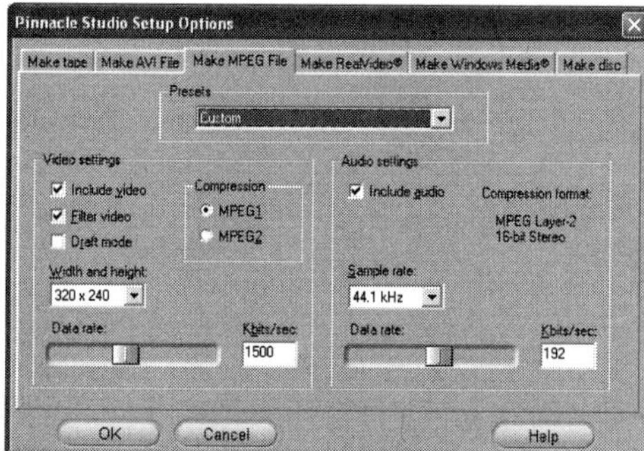

Figure 14.18 You may need to go Custom to disable filtering or boost the data rate.

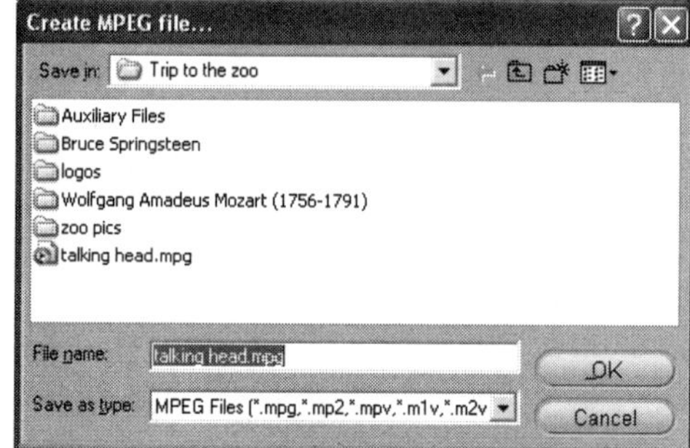

Figure 14.19 Choose a filename and target location.

✔ Tips

- Note that all presets use filtering, which can cause blurriness in certain videos. If quality is unacceptable, note the preset settings, select Custom encoding, and reenter all preset values, making sure not to check the Filter video checkbox.
- The Multimedia preset uses a data rate of approximately 1500 kbps, which may be inadequate for very-high-motion videos. If so, note the other preset settings, select Custom encoding, and reenter all preset values, boosting the data rate to no more than 2400 kbits/second.
- Do not use custom settings when creating files for DVD, VideoCD, or Super VideoCD (S-VCD) formats. These formats are specifically defined, and straying from the general guidelines could produce files incompatible with the specification.
- Check the Draft mode box to improve the encoding speed of your video, at some cost in quality.

Creating RealVideo Files

The RealVideo format is produced by RealNetworks. To view files encoded in this format, viewers need the RealOne Player, available for free download at www.realnetworks.com. Available in Macintosh and a number of Unix flavors, Real supports a broader audience than Microsoft's Windows Media, and low bit rate quality is considered slightly better.

Like Windows Media, RealNetworks can produce files that support multiple bit rate connections, but only when streaming from a RealNetworks server. Note that if you're creating a file with multiple bit rates, they share the same resolution (which is why so many sites displaying RealVideo content have links for modem and broadband connections).

Though functional, Studio's tools for RealVideo encoding lack filtering, variable bit rate encoding, and other advanced options available in Real's free encoding tools. Studio is great for encoding videos for email and for other casual projects, but for high-volume production and real-time encoding (which Studio doesn't perform), you're better off using other tools.

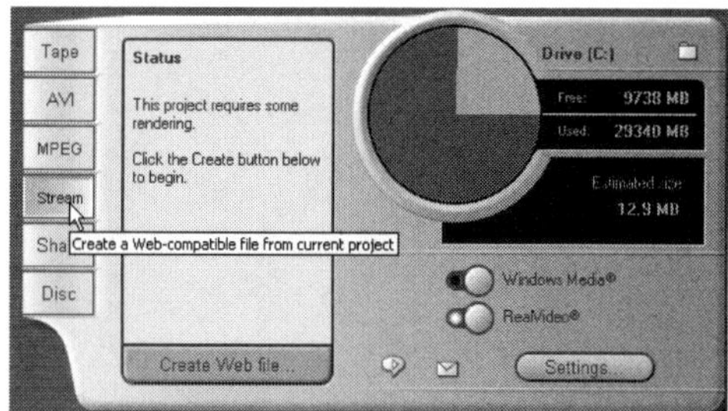

Figure 14.20 Ready to go streaming? Start here...

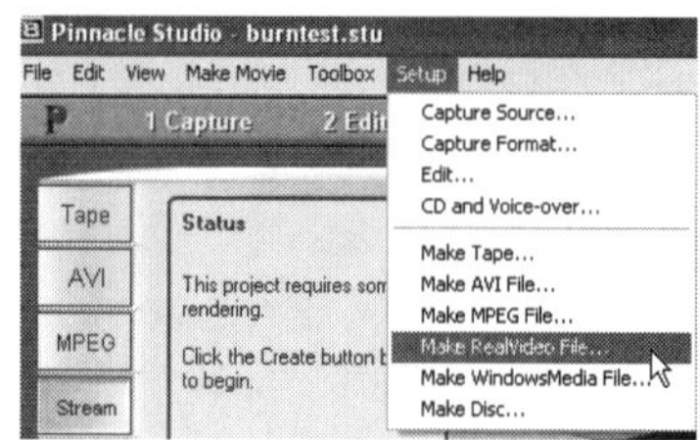

Figure 14.21 ...or here.

To create RealVideo files:

1. After completing your video project, do one of the following:
   - ▲ In the upper-left corner of the Studio interface, click Make Movie. Then, in the upper-left of the Make Movie window, click Stream (**Figure 14.20**). Below the Diskometer in the Make Movie window, click the RealVideo button.
   - ▲ From the Studio menu, choose Setup > Make RealVideo File (**Figure 14.21**).

   Studio enters Make Movie mode with Stream controls.

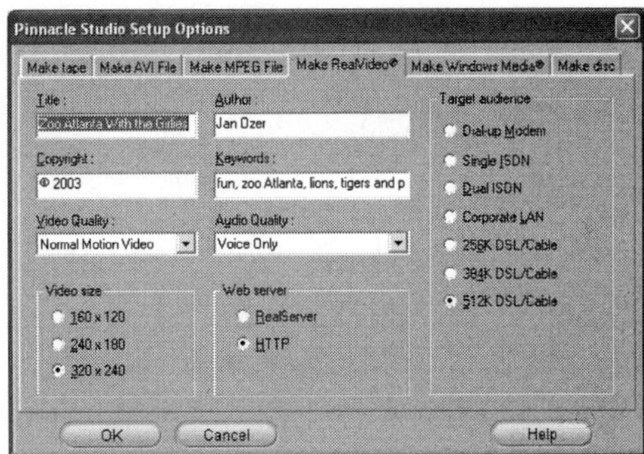

Figure 14.22 RealVideo encoding parameters.

Title and author information

Figure 14.23 Your title and author information shows up in the RealOne player.

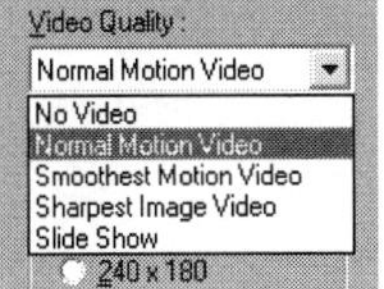

Figure 14.24 Customize video encoding for your footage.

Note that Studio immediately computes the project's disk requirements and warns you in the Status box if you don't have the necessary disk space.

2. Below the Diskometer, click the Settings button.

   The Pinnacle Studio Setup Options dialog opens to the Make RealVideo tab (**Figure 14.22**).

3. Type Title, Author, and Copyright information.

   This information will appear when the file is played by the remote viewer (**Figure 14.23**).

4. Type the desired keywords in the Keywords box.

   If the video is posted to a Web site, this information will be used to categorize the video by Internet search engines.

5. In the Video Quality list box (**Figure 14.24**), select one of the following:

   ▲ *Normal Motion Video* for clips with normal motion (no extremely high motion or low motion). During encoding, Real will balance frame rate and image clarity.

   ▲ *Smoothest Motion Video* for "talking head" and similar clips with very limited motion. During encoding, Real will produce a higher frame rate and smoother motion.

   ▲ *Sharpest Image Video* for high-action clips. During encoding, Real will reduce the frame rate and produce fewer frames of higher quality.

   ▲ *Slide show.* During encoding, Real will reduce the video to a series of high-quality still photos.

(continued on next page)

6. In the Audio Quality list box (**Figure 14.25**), select the description that best matches your audio content.

   During encoding, Studio will use the appropriate audio codec and data rate for your audio content.

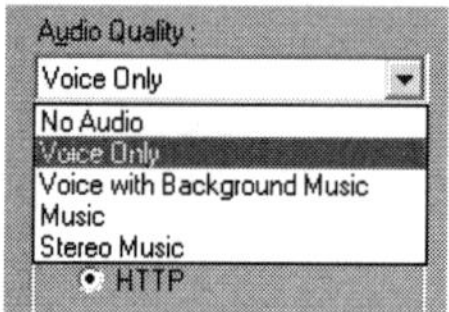

Figure 14.25 Customize your audio encoding for your soundtrack.

7. In the Video size section, click one of the following resolutions.
   - *160 x 120* for video to be streamed via dial-up modems
   - *240 x 180* for video to be streamed via single ISDN
   - *320 x 240* for all other available categories of video

8. In the Web server section, choose one of the following:
   - *RealServer* if the ISP hosting the video has a RealServer installed. Streaming files with the RealServer is the preferred method, since it provides several valuable options, including the ability to create files that serve multiple target audiences and the ability to adjust playback performance to changing line conditions. If you don't know if there is a RealServer installed, ask your ISP.
   - *HTTP.* You can still stream videos from an HTTP server without a RealServer installed, but you can only produce a file that will serve one connection speed. Also use this option for email.

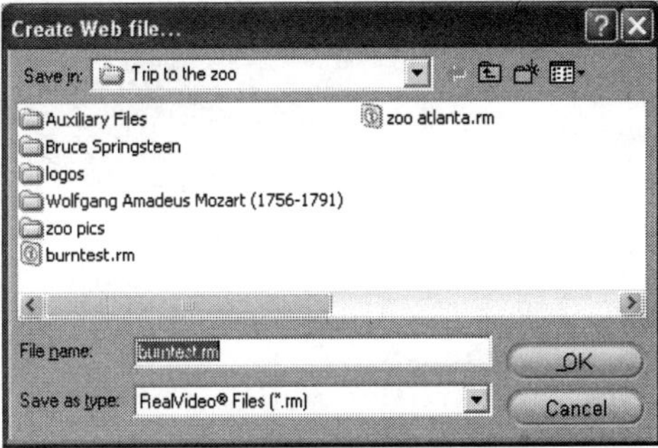

Figure 14.26 Choose a filename and target location.

9. In the Target audience setting, choose the connection or connections that your viewers will use to view the video.

   If you selected RealServer above, you can choose multiple options and produce a file that can serve a diverse range of connection speeds.

   If you selected the HTTP option, you can only select one profile.

10. Press OK to return to the Make Movie window.

11. At the bottom of the Status box, click Create Web file.

    Studio opens the Create Web file dialog (**Figure 14.26**).

12. Type the filename, and change the location if desired.

13. Click OK to close the dialog.

    Studio starts encoding. You should see the Timeline Scrubber moving through the video, the video updating in the Player, and progress in the bars beneath the Player window (see Figure 14.9).

To play RealVideo files:

1. At the bottom of the Diskometer, click the RealPlayer icon. (After encoding is completed, the RealPlayer icon at the bottom of the Make Movie window becomes active; see **Figure 14.27**.)

   Studio opens the Open Media Player dialog with the most recently encoded file selected (**Figure 14.28**).

2. Click Open.

   Studio opens RealOne (or whatever RealPlayer you have installed) and plays the file.

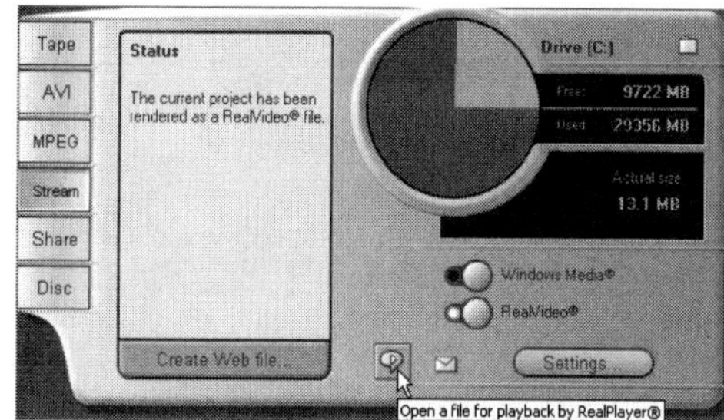

Figure 14.27 Click here to play the file in the RealOne player.

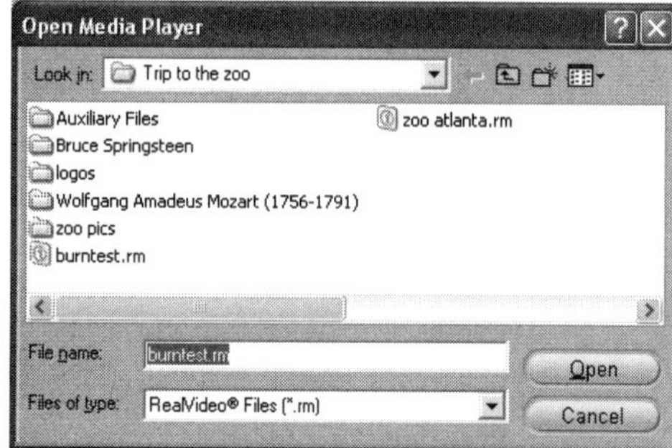

Figure 14.28 Select the file and click Open.

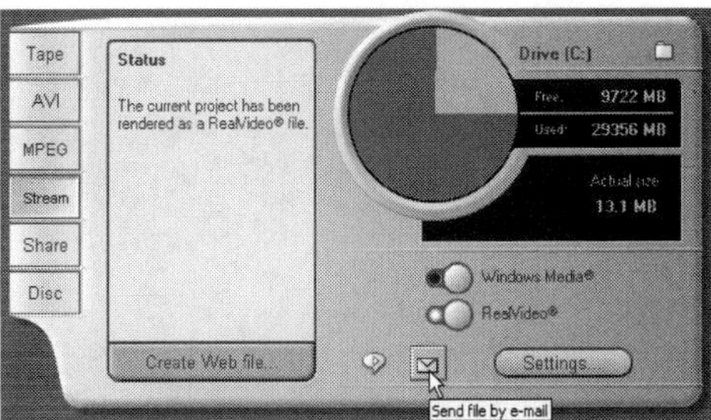

Figure 14.29 Click here to send the file via email.

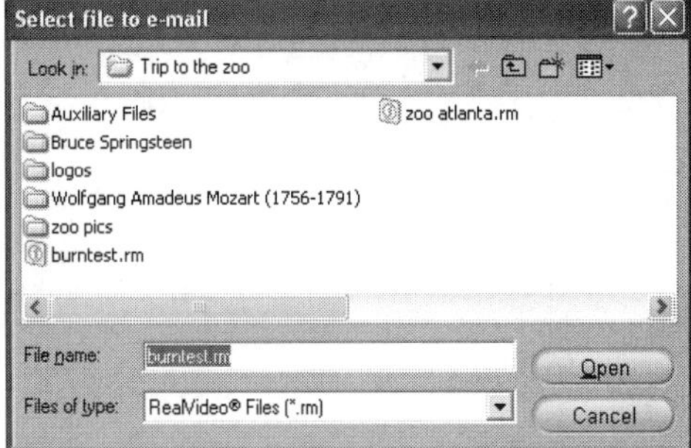

Figure 14.30 Choose the file and click open.

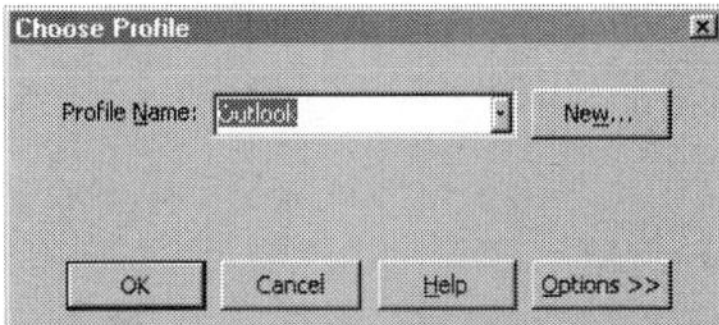

Figure 14.31 Choose the profile in Outlook or other MAPI-enabled email client.

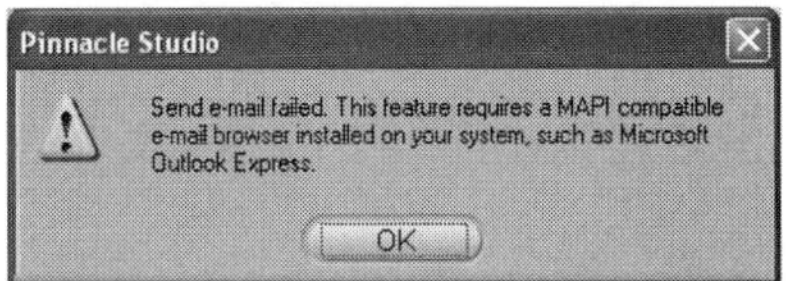

Figure 14.32 Oops. You'll have to send the file to another computer and mail it from there, or load a MAPI-compatible program.

To send RealVideo files via email:

1. At the bottom of the Diskometer, click the envelope icon. (After encoding is completed, the Send file by e-mail icon becomes active; see **Figure 14.29**.)

   Studio opens the Select file to e-mail dialog with the most recently encoded file selected (**Figure 14.30**).

2. Click Open.

   If you have a MAPI-compatible (Messaging Application Programming Interface) email client installed on your computer, such as Microsoft Outlook or Outlook Express, Studio opens the Choose Profile dialog (**Figure 14.31**). If not, Studio will open the error message shown in **Figure 14.32**).

3. Choose the correct profile and click OK.

   Your mail client takes over and opens a new message window with the newly compressed file attached. Enter the target address and send the email.

✔ Tip

- If you're sending the file via email, the bandwidth of the recipient shouldn't control how you encode it. Even if they have a slow connection, the recipient may be willing to wait to download the file. The only practical issue is the attached file limitation imposed by many Internet Service Providers (ISPs). For example, Earthlink allows attachments of only 5 MB, while Hotmail and Yahoo impose much smaller limitations. Be sure to consider this when producing your file.
- Remember, your recipient will need the RealPlayer installed to view the video, or the Windows Media player to view Windows Media videos.

Creating Windows Media Files

Microsoft's streaming technology is called Windows Media. To view files encoded in this format, viewers need Microsoft's Windows Media Player, which ships with all Windows computers and is freely downloadable at www.microsoft.com/windowsmedia. Microsoft offers players for all relevant Windows flavors, Macintosh (8.01 to OS X) and Sun Solaris, but no Linux version (quel surprise!).

Like RealNetworks, Microsoft can produce files that support multiple bit-rate connections, but only when streaming from a Windows Media server, which is available only for Windows XP, or from a RealNetworks Helix server. Microsoft's most recent release of Windows Media 9 supports multiple-resolution files within the multiple bit rates, but if you're working at this level, you should use the Windows Media Encoder, not Studio. Studio is a great tool for casual Windows Media encoding, but doesn't expose all relevant encoding controls and doesn't support real-time encoding.

To create Windows Media files:

1. After completing your video project, do one of the following:
   - ▲ In the upper-left corner of the Studio interface, click Make Movie. In the upper-left of the Make Movie window, click Stream (**Figure 14.33**). Below the Diskometer, click the Windows Media button.
   - ▲ From the Studio menu, choose Setup > Make WindowsMedia File (**Figure 14.34**).

   Studio enters Make Movie mode with streaming controls.

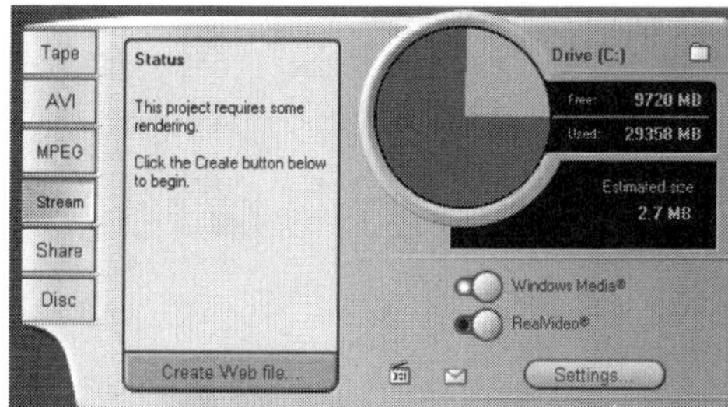

Figure 14.33 The starting point for creating Windows Media files.

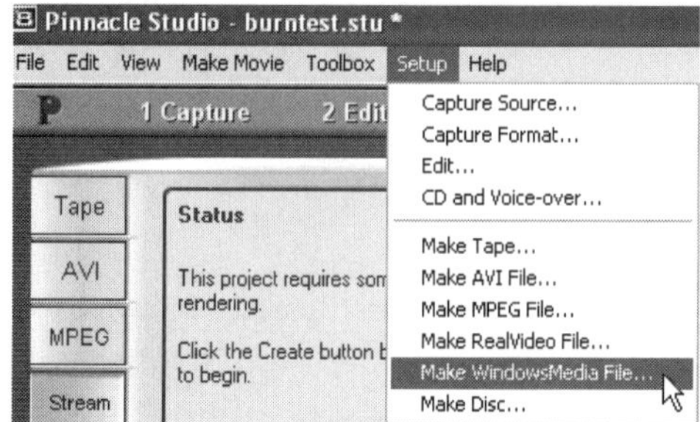

Figure 14.34 Another route to the Windows Media encoding screen.

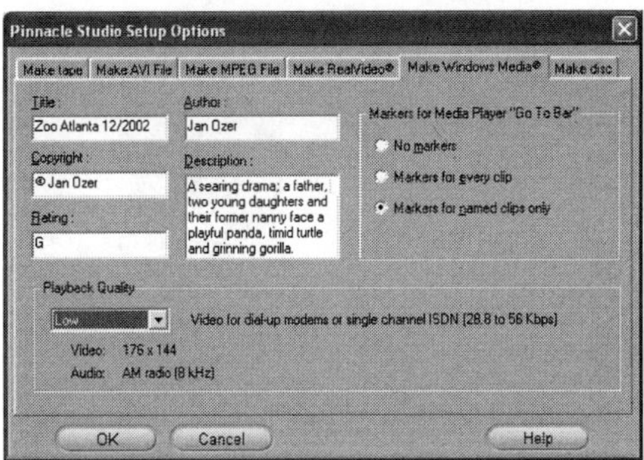

Figure 14.35 Windows Media encoding parameters.

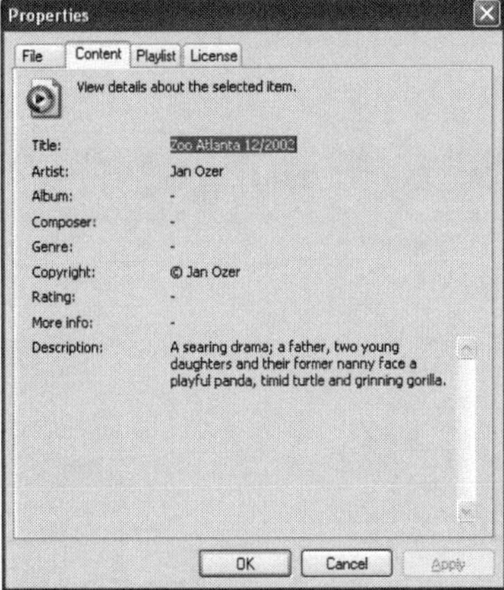

Figure 14.36 Here's where the viewer sees the title, author, and description.

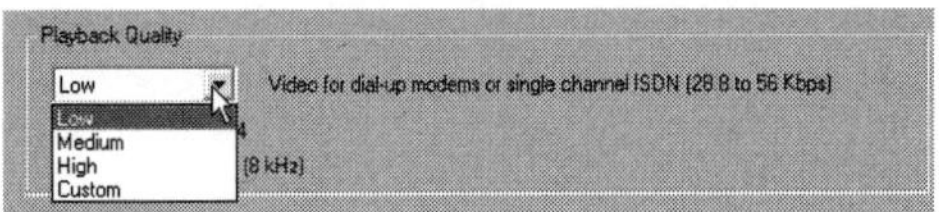

Figure 14.37 Choose your playback quality.

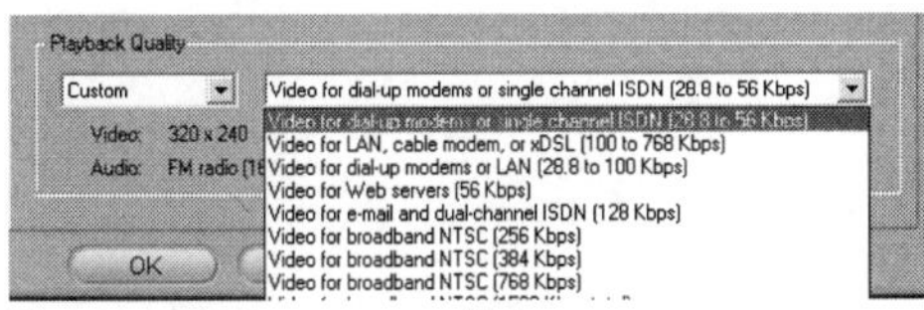

Figure 14.38 Custom encoding parameters.

Note that Studio immediately computes the project's disk requirements and warns you in the Status box if you don't have the necessary disk space.

2. Below the Diskometer, click the Settings button.

   The Pinnacle Studio Setup Options dialog opens to the Make Windows Media tab (**Figure 14.35**).

3. Type information in the Title, Author, Copyright, Rating, and Description boxes.

   This information will appear when the file is played by the remote viewer (**Figure 14.36**). If the video is posted to a Web site, the description will be used to categorize the video by Internet search engines.

4. In the Playback Quality list box (**Figure 14.37**), select one of the following:
   - ▲ *Low.* Studio encodes these files to a data rate appropriate for dial-up modems or single-channel ISDN.
   - ▲ *Medium.* For email and dual-channel ISDN, Studio encodes these files to a data rate of 128 kbps.
   - ▲ *High.* For broadband video, Studio encodes these files to a data rate of 384 kbps.
   - ▲ *Custom.* Offers a range of other encoding parameters (**Figure 14.38**).

(continued on next page)

5. In the Markers for Media Player "Go To Bar" section, select the desired option.

   If you insert markers in the clip, viewers can jump to these markers using controls in Microsoft's Media Player B (**Figure 14.39**).

   If you enable markers and don't name your clips, Studio will enter a default name based on project name and clip start point.

6. Click OK to return to the Make Movie window.

7. At the bottom of the Status box, click Create Web file.

   Studio opens the Create Web file dialog (**Figure 14.40**).

8. Type the filename, and change the location if desired.

9. Click OK to close the dialog.

   Studio starts encoding. You should see the Timeline Scrubber moving through the video, the video updating in the Player, and progress in the bars beneath the Player window (see Figure 14.9).

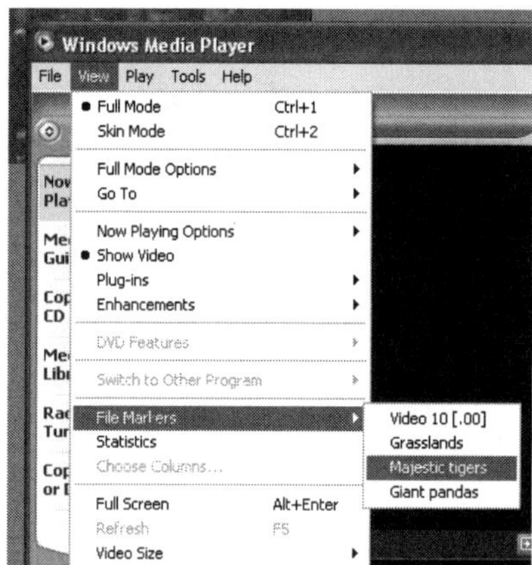

Figure 14.39 Here's how the viewer uses the file markers.

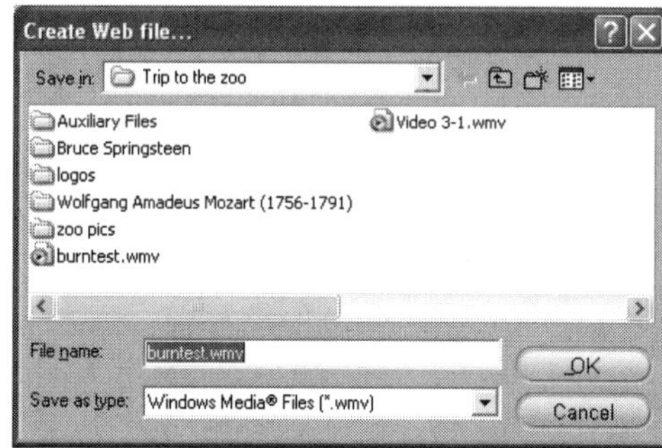

Figure 14.40 Choose a filename and target location.

✔ Tips

- If you use the Low Playback Quality setting, Studio encodes at 176 x 144 resolution, which is not a 4:3 aspect ratio (to fit 4:3, it should be 176 x 132, or 192 x 144). This will distort your video slightly. Note that Microsoft abandoned this resolution in its free Windows Media Encoder, providing an alternative to Studio for these low bit rates.
- To play or send your Windows Media files via email, see "To play RealVideo files" and "To send RealVideo files via email," earlier.

15

Using StudioOnline

The Internet is the ultimate mechanism for sharing videos, and Pinnacle makes it simple with StudioOnline, its Internet-based video distribution site. After you're done editing, Studio can automatically publish your videos to StudioOnline, or you can manually upload files yourself. StudioOnline can then send custom email messages to your intended audience, build an address book for frequently used contacts, and even schedule messages for later transmittal.

There are two major caveats: First, you only get 10 MB of storage on the site, which you can't upgrade. When you're working with video, that ain't much. More importantly, if you upload the video directly from Studio, StudioOnline converts it to relatively low bit rate files in Real and Microsoft formats, then distributes these files—often visually degraded—to your target viewers.

Pinnacle may change this procedure in a planned Web site upgrade that should hit soon after the publication of this book. Unless and until they do, you'll get better results encoding the file yourself and then manually uploading it to StudioOnline. The only downside to this approach is that you can't pick the thumbnail image used by StudioOnline to represent your video.

Uploading Videos to StudioOnline

There are two ways to get your files up to StudioOnline, directly from Studio or manually through a browser.

To upload to StudioOnline from Studio:

1. After completing your project, click Make Movie (**Figure 15.1**).

   Studio opens the Make Movie window.

2. On the left of the Make Movie panel, click Share (**Figure 15.2**).

3. To change the thumbnail image used to represent your video once uploaded to StudioOnline, navigate to the target frame using the Timeline Scrubber or Player controls and click the set thumbnail icon (**Figure 15.3**).

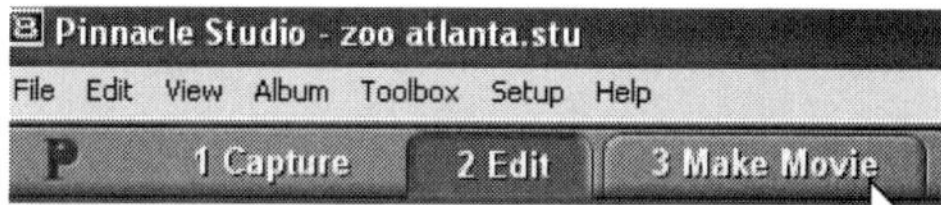

Figure 15.1 Once you're ready to transmit, click Make Movie.

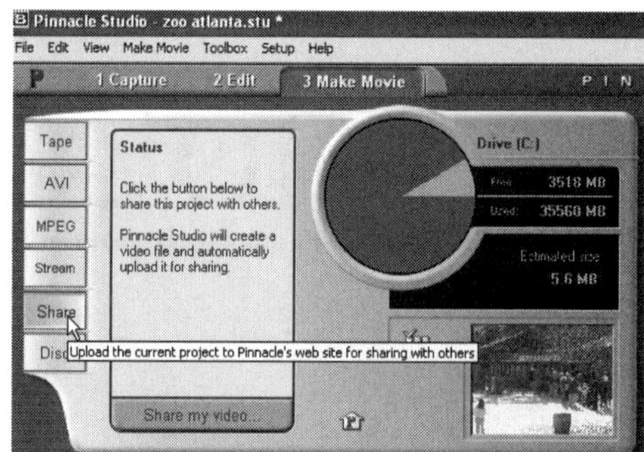

Figure 15.2 Then click Share to upload your video to StudioOnline.

Figure 15.3 When you upload from Studio, you can pick the thumbnail image.

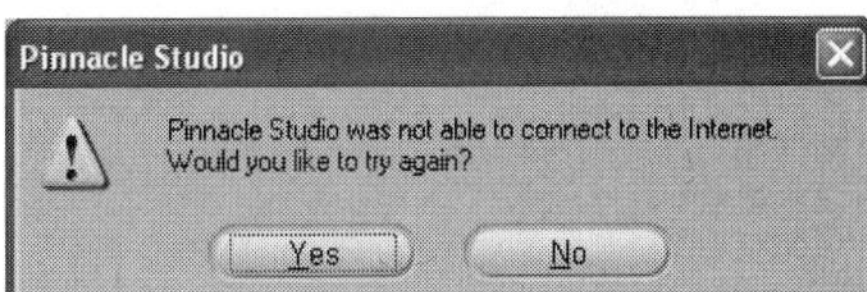

Figure 15.4 Oops. You can't upload a file if you're not online. If your video-editing station isn't connected to the Internet, you can encode and upload manually from another computer.

Figure 15.5 The Status box reports that my video file arrived safely.

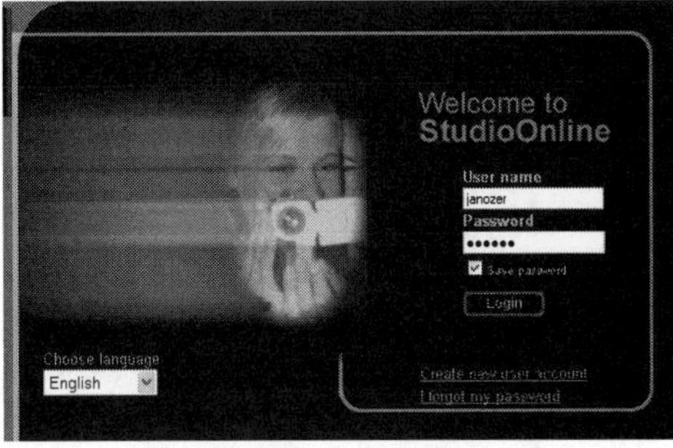

Figure 15.6 The StudioOnline login screen.

4. At the bottom of the Status box, click Share my video.

   Studio starts encoding the file. You should see the Timeline Scrubber moving through the video, the video updating in the Player, and progress in the bars beneath the Player window.

   If your computer is not connected to the Internet, Studio will prompt you to connect to the Internet with the message shown in **Figure 15.4**. You must be online to continue.

   If you are online, Studio will encode and automatically upload your file, letting you know when it's finished with the message shown in **Figure 15.5.**

   Studio will also open your default browser to the StudioOnline login screen (**Figure 15.6**).

(continued on next page)

5. Do one of the following:
   - ▲ If you've already registered, enter your User name and Password, and click Login.
   - ▲ If you haven't registered, click Create new user account, and register for your account. StudioOnline will send you an email and a link you can click to sign in and upload your video.

   You should see a screen that looks like **Figure 15.7**. Note that if you were already logged into StudioOnline, you would see a screen that looks like **Figure 15.8**.

✔ Tip

- If you attempt to produce a file longer than four minutes, expect an error message like that shown in **Figure 15.9**.
- I describe how to actually send the email notification later, in "Sending Videos from StudioOnline."

Figure 15.7 The StudioOnline My Videos screen.

Figure 15.8 Here's where you end up if you're already logged into StudioOnline when you start uploading the file.

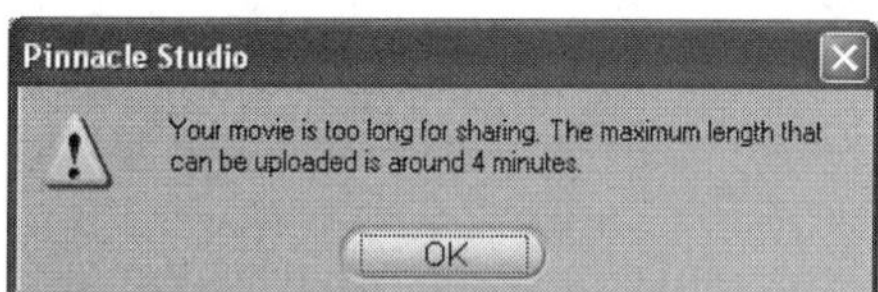

Figure 15.9 What you'll see if you try to send a video longer than about four minutes.

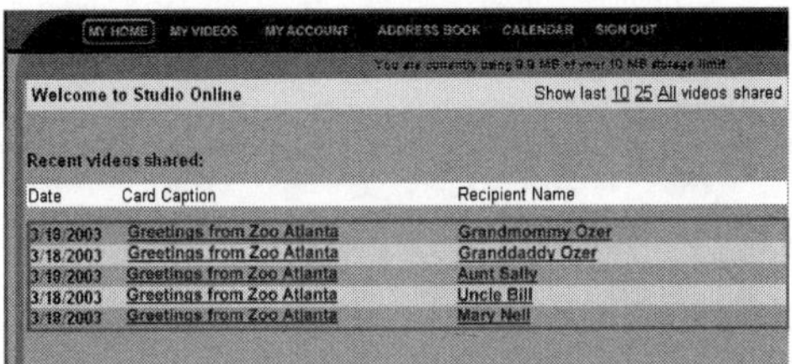

Figure 15.10 When you first enter StudioOnline, the first screen you'll see is a list of the most recent cards that you sent.

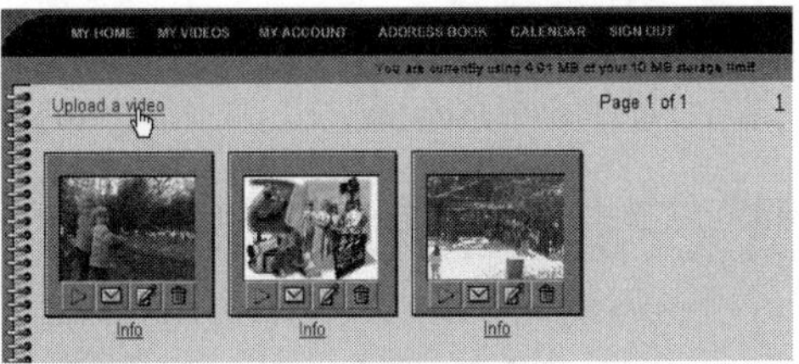

Figure 15.11 Click here to start manually uploading a video.

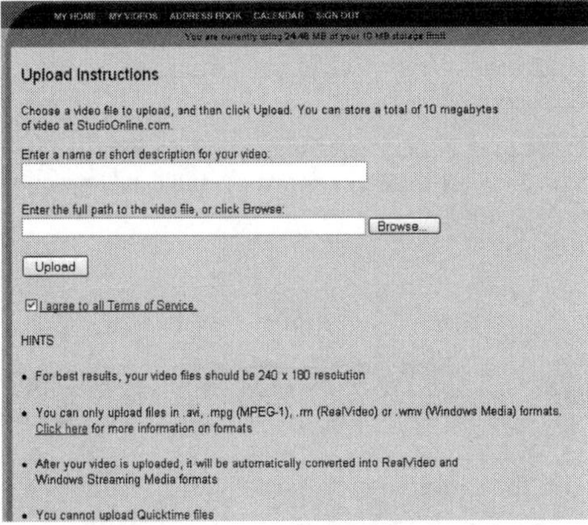

Figure 15.12 Upload instructions. Note the rules (particularly that QuickTime files need not apply).

To manually upload to StudioOnline:

1. From your browser, surf over to StudioOnline at www.studioonline.com and log in to your account.

   StudioOnline opens a screen similar to **Figure 15.10**.

2. On the top of the StudioOnline page, click My Videos.

   StudioOnline opens the My Videos page (**Figure 15.11**).

3. Click Upload a video.

   StudioOnline opens the Upload Instructions page (**Figure 15.12**). Note that StudioOnline recommends uploading files encoded at 240 x 180 resolution, in AVI, MPEG-1, RealVideo, or Windows Media formats.

   Contrary to the third bullet point on the screen, StudioOnline did not convert the files uploaded to RealVideo or Windows Media formats in my tests.

(continued on next page)

4. Click Browse.

   StudioOnline opens the Choose file dialog (**Figure 15.13**).

5. Choose the file to upload and click Open.

   Studio returns to the Upload Instructions page.

6. Type the desired description for your video, and click that you agree with the terms of service (**Figure 15.14**).

   StudioOnline gives you an error message if you don't enter a description or click in agreement.

7. Click Upload.

   StudioOnline uploads the file and adds it to the My Videos page (**Figure 15.15**). Note that videos uploaded by Studio have a thumbnail image, while those uploaded manually do not.

✔ Tip

- Though StudioOnline can accept AVI and MPEG-1 files, you'll get the best bang for your bandwidth buck (in English, the best quality for a particular file size) using RealVideo or Windows Media. See Chapter 14 to learn how to output digital files in all these formats.

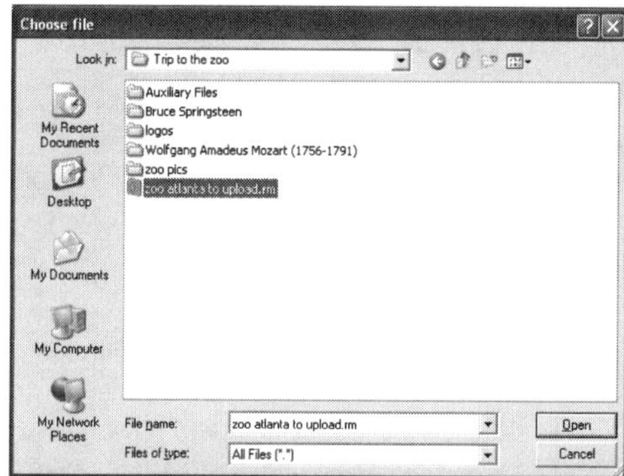

Figure 15.13 You know this drill. Select the file you want to upload and click Open.

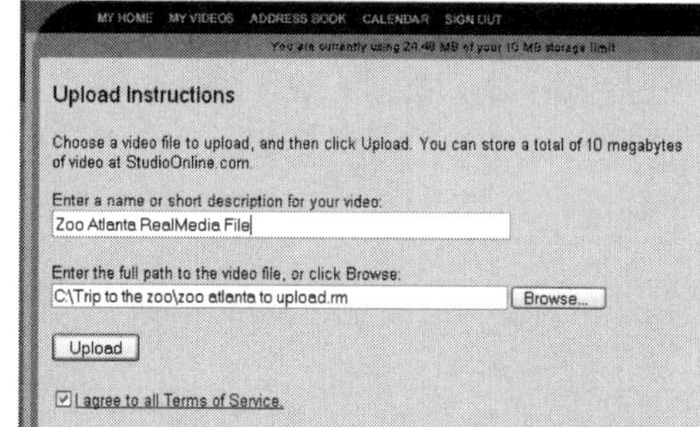

Figure 15.14 Enter a name or description and click that you agree to service terms or StudioOnline won't upload your file.

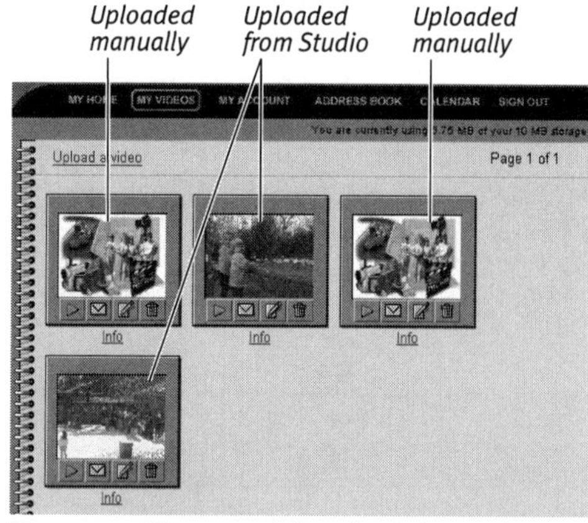

Figure 15.15 File successfully uploaded. Note that only the files uploaded via Studio have thumbnails, not the files you've uploaded manually.

Figure 15.16 Click the envelop to send an email announcement to the target recipient.

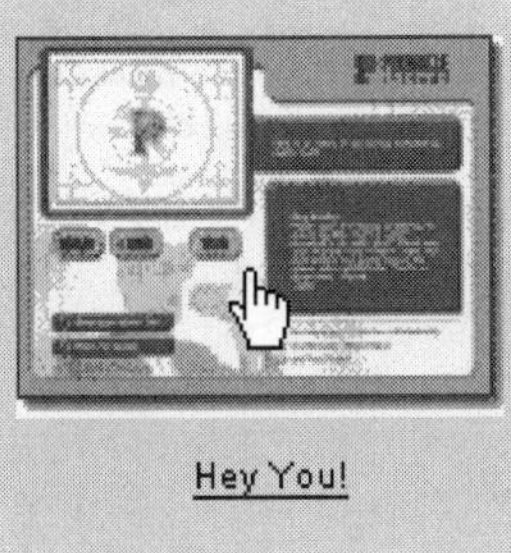

Figure 15.17 Since this message is to my father, I'll use the endearing Hey You! postcard.

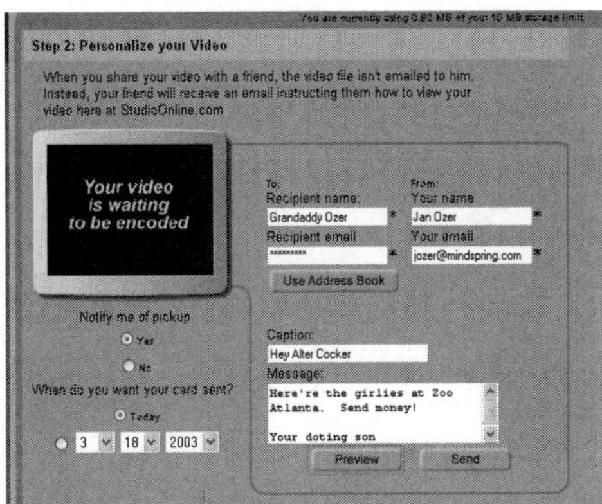

Figure 15.18 Note the ability to be notified when the video is viewed, and to schedule the email for later transmission. For you non-Yiddish-speaking folks, Alter Cocker is a term of utmost respect I reserve for my dear dad.

Sending Videos from StudioOnline

Once your file is available online, you can email people to let them know it's ready for viewing. Email recipients simply click a link to go online and watch the video.

To send a video from StudioOnline:

1. From your browser, surf over to StudioOnline at www.studioonline.com.

   StudioOnline opens a screen similar to Figure 15.10.

2. On the top of the StudioOnline page, click My Videos.

   StudioOnline opens the My Videos page.

3. Choose a video to send and click the envelope icon underneath the video (**Figure 15.16**) to open the screen shown in Figure 15.8.

4. Click the desired video postcard (**Figure 15.17**).

5. Complete the information shown in **Figure 15.18**.

(continued on next page)

6. Do one of the following:
   - ▲ Click Send to send the email. Studio sends the email.
   - ▲ Click Preview to preview video-screen appearance when accessed by the email recipient (**Figure 15.19**). Click Back to perform more edits, or Send to send the email.

   StudioOnline sends the email to the recipient (**Figure 15.20**), who will be instructed to click on a link to view the video, and let you know that the email has been sent (**Figure 15.21**).

   Once the remote viewer clicks to the page, the video starts playing automatically, and the remote viewer will have the option to play any of up to four streams, download the file, and/or send an email back to you (**Figure 15.22**).

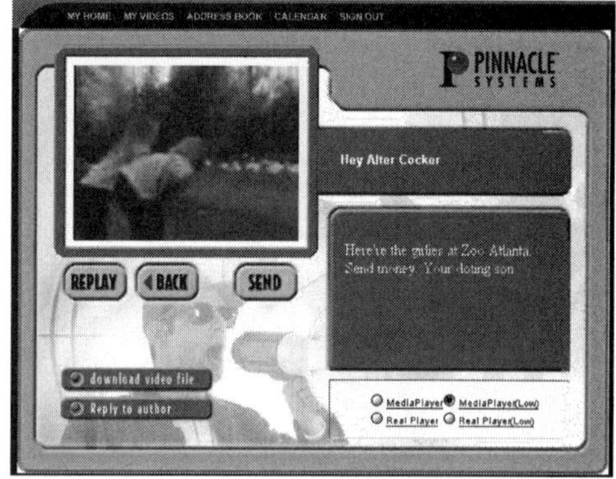

Figure 15.19 Here's a preview of what the email recipient will see.

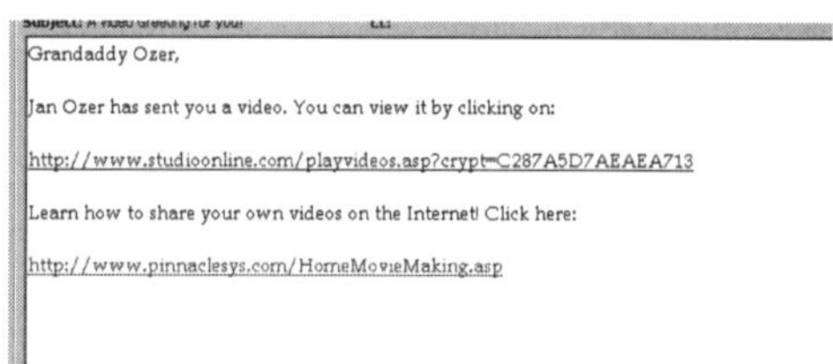

Grandaddy Ozer,

Jan Ozer has sent you a video. You can view it by clicking on:

http://www.studioonline.com/playvideos.asp?crypt=C287A5D7AEAEA713

Learn how to share your own videos on the Internet! Click here:

http://www.pinnaclesys.com/HomeMovieMaking.asp

Figure 15.20 Here's the actual email your recipient will see.

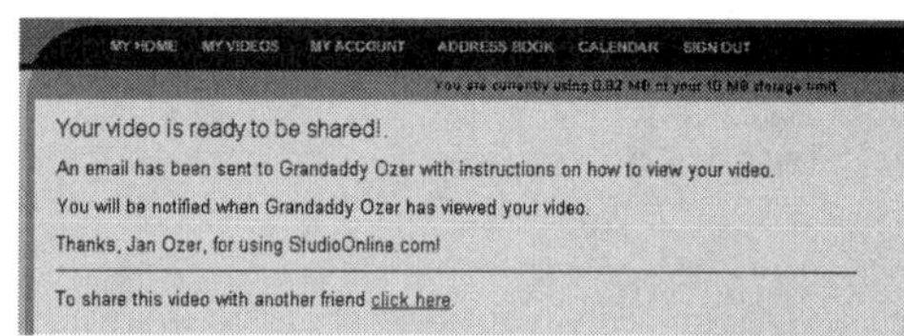

Figure 15.21 Here's your notice that it was sent.

Figure 15.22 Live playback of the file. Note that the recipient can download the file and send an email back at you.

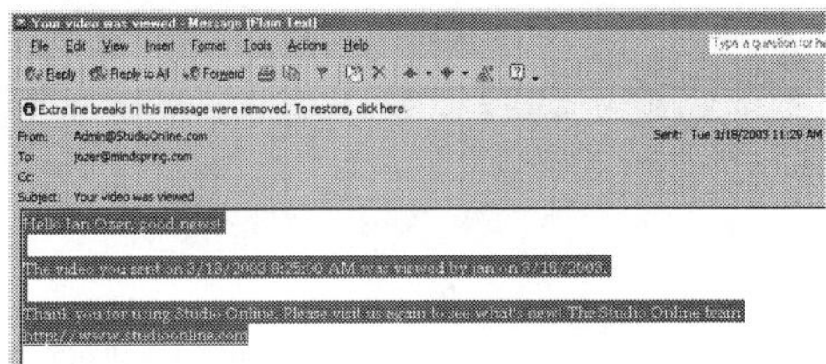

Figure 15.23 Here's notice that the video was actually viewed.

✔ Tips

- Note on Figure 15.18 that you can request notification that the email recipient actually watched the video (**Figure 15.23**) or schedule the card to be sent in the future.
- StudioOnline keeps a log of all videos you've sent in the My Home section that appears when you log in to your account (Figure 15.10). This is a convenient way to keep track of your email, and you can view the presentation by clicking on it under Card Caption.

Managing Videos in StudioOnline

StudioOnline will refuse to accept additional videos once you reach your 10 MB limit, making frequent maintenance critical.

To delete videos from StudioOnline:

1. From your browser, surf over to www.studioonline.com and log in to your account.

   StudioOnline opens a screen similar to Figure 15.10.

2. On the top of the StudioOnline page, click My Videos.

   StudioOnline opens the My Videos page.

3. Click the trash can icon on the video to be deleted (**Figure 15.24**).

4. Studio opens the Delete Video dialog (**Figure 15.25**).

5. Click Delete.

   Studio deletes the file and restores drive space.

✔ Tips

- You access StudioOnline's Address Book by clicking Address Book on the top menu bar (see Figure 15.10). Adding and deleting contacts is self-explanatory.
- You access StudioOnline's Calendar function by clicking Calendar on the top menu bar. Though you can enter events in the Calendar manually, you can only schedule the future transmission of an email by working through the process described in "To send a video from StudioOnline," using the controls found in Figure 15.18. In my tests, when I scheduled an email for later transmission, StudioOnline didn't show it on the Calendar, but did send it as scheduled.

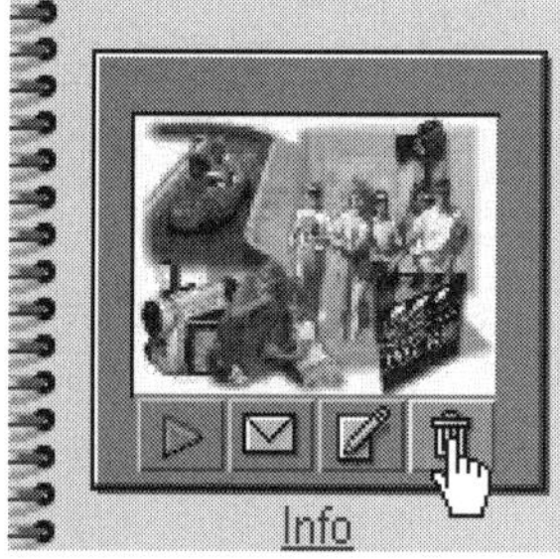

Figure 15.24 When you've only got 10 MB of space, spring cleaning is a year-round occupation. Click here to delete the file.

Figure 15.25 Yes, you really mean it. Click here to let StudioOnline know.

PART V

REFERENCE

Keyboard Shortcuts

A

The terms *Left, Right, Up* and *Down* in this table refer to the arrow (cursor) keys. *Plus* and *Minus* refer to the + and – keys. Note that Studio's manual and tool tips designate K as the key to press to start video playback. In my tests (as of Studio version 8.5), this didn't work, but pressing L did. So, if you have a version after 8.5, and L doesn't work, try K.

Table A.1

Main Studio Interface	
Spacebar	Play and stop
J	Fast-reverse (hit multiple times for faster playback)
K	Stop
L	Play or fast-forward (hit multiple times for faster playback)
X or Ctrl+Up	Step forward 1 frame
Y or Ctrl+Down	Step back 1 frame
A or I	Mark in
S or O	Mark out
Ctrl+Left	Trim in point by -1 frame
Ctrl+Right	Trim in point by +1 frame
Alt+Left	Trim out point by -1 frame
Alt+Right	Trim out point by +1 frame
Alt+Ctrl+Left	Rolling trim out point by -1 frame (trims following clip too)
Alt+Ctrl+Right	Rolling trim out point by +1 frame
G	Clear mark in and mark out
D	Go to mark in (in Clip Properties tool)
F	Go to mark out (in Clip Properties tool)
E or Home	Go to start
R or End	Go to end
Left	Select previous clip
Right	Select next clip
Delete	Delete selected clip(s)
Insert	Split clip at Scrubber position
Page Up	Go to next page of Storyboard or Timeline
Page Down	Go to previous page of Storyboard or Timeline

(continued on next page)

Table A.1 *(continued)*

Main Studio Interface *(continued)*	
+	Zoom in the Timeline
–	Zoom out the Timeline
C	Set menu chapter
V	Clear menu chapter
M	Set Return to Menu flag
Ctrl+Page Up	Go to previous menu chapter
Ctrl+Page Down	Go to next menu chapter

Table A.2

Title Editor	
Alt+Plus	Bring to front
Alt+Minus	Send to back
Ctrl+Plus	Bring forward one layer
Ctrl+Minus	Send back one layer
Ctrl+0	Text justification off
Ctrl+1	Text justification: bottom-left
Ctrl+2	Text justification: bottom-center
Ctrl+3	Text justification: bottom-right
Ctrl+4	Text justification: middle-left
Ctrl+5	Text justification: middle-center
Ctrl+6	Text justification: middle-right
Ctrl+7	Text justification: top-left
Ctrl+8	Text justification: top-center
Ctrl+9	Text justification: top-right
Ctrl+K	Kern, leading, and skew
Ctrl+M	Move, scale, and rotate
Shift+Left	Expand character selection left
Shift+Right	Expand character selection right
Ctrl+Left	Reduce horizontal scale of, or squeeze (kern), text selection depending on current edit mode (move/scale/rotate or kern/skew/leading)
Ctrl+Right	Increase horizontal scale of, or stretch (kern), text selection
Ctrl+Down	Reduce scale or leading of text selection depending on current edit mode
Ctrl+Up	Increase scale or leading of text selection
Shift+Ctrl+Left	Same as Ctrl+Left (larger adjustment)
Shift+Ctrl+Right	Same as Ctrl+Right (larger adjustment)
Shift+Ctrl+Down	Same as Ctrl+Down (larger adjustment)
Shift+Ctrl+Up	Same as Ctrl+Up (larger adjustment)
Alt+Left	*In text selection:* Move characters left *No selection:* Move left all text from cursor to end of line
Alt+Right	*In text selection:* Move characters right *No selection:* Move right all text from cursor to end of line
Shift+Alt+Left	Same as Alt+Left (larger adjustment)
Shift+Alt+Right	Same as Alt+Right (larger adjustment)

B

Troubleshooting

Video capture, editing, and output to tape are without question the most demanding activities most computers ever perform. For this reason, it's not surprising that video editing reveals more "imperfections" in computers than surfing the Web or word processing.

Though Studio works on computers running Windows 98 (Second Edition), if you're running this operating system, you're likely running at least three-year-old hardware and perhaps drivers. This is the computer equivalent of running the Paris to Dakar road race in that jalopy you drove back in college—you may get there, but you're likely to experience a breakdown or two.

While writing this book, I used four different computers, from an old ThinkPad running Windows 98 SE to the latest Intel 3.06 GHz Pentium IV with HT Technology running Windows XP Pro. All computers worked fine, but the process was more fun on the last.

Another thing to keep in mind: Not all programs run on all computers (something I've learned through testing hundreds of hardware and software products over the last few years). If you're having problems you can't resolve through techniques in this appendix, through Pinnacle's extensive online help facilities, or directly through technical support, cut your losses. Either try Studio on another computer or return the software. Life is way too short to make a quest of it.

Finally, a complete troubleshooting guide for all computers and operating systems Studio supports would be a book in its own right, and definitely not a book I care to write. These next sections will hopefully hit the high points, but this appendix is not intended to be comprehensive.

Optimizing Your Capture Computer

Since you can avoid most installation and operational hassles by using a new computer with current drivers, I'll start there, and then discuss how to give your current computer its best chance to make a good first impression with Studio. Then I'll move on to troubleshooting.

If a rich friend called and asked what kind of computer to buy to run Studio (i.e., price is no concern), this is what I would tell her to get:

- Intel Pentium IV 3.06 GHz with HT Technology
- 512 MB RAM
- Windows XP Professional
- Graphics card from ATI, Matrox, or NVIDIA; 32 MB RAM is more than sufficient, 3D gaming power not needed and not recommended, given that this would encourage her to play games on the computer. Dual monitor output is cool but wouldn't help with Studio, which doesn't support multiple monitors
- Any DirectX-compatible sound card

- Dual hard-disk drives, both UDMA ATA-100 drives, one for the system (at least 40 GB), one for video (at least 80 GB)
- Pinnacle DV card (Studio DV is fine) if one isn't embedded on the motherboard
- Pioneer DVD-R/RW burner (A05 is the most current model)
- 10/100/1000 gigabit (Gb) Ethernet

A bigger monitor is always better. Any three-button mouse should work just fine. The computer absolutely must be online, with broadband preferred, to manage the file downloading and uploading inherent to video production.

In terms of care and feeding of her powerful beast, I would recommend that my rich friend load as few extraneous programs as possible. Games and other multimedia programs in particular often ruin a perfectly functioning computer.

I know it's tough for many parents to dedicate a computer to editing, but the more programs you load on your computer, the greater chance you have of overwriting some critical driver or causing a conflict that hinders or interrupts Studio's performance. This is especially so with other video editors and DVD authoring programs. I've been fortunate, having tested many additional software programs on my primary Studio test bed, including many other video editors, with few problems. Still, computer issues seem to hit those least equipped to resolve them (e.g., my parents and certain friends), and each additional program loaded involves a small but real risk.

If you plan on installing Studio on your current computer, here are some steps you should take to smooth the transition.

To ensure a smooth installation:

1. If you're not running Windows XP Professional, consider upgrading.

   At the very least, check the Microsoft Web site to make sure you've installed the most current Service Pack and all critical updates of your current operating system (http://v4.windowsupdate.microsoft.com/en/default.asp).

2. Check the Web sites of your graphics card, motherboard, and sound card vendors and make sure you have the latest updates.

3. Make sure you have the latest update of Microsoft's Direct X installed (www.microsoft.com/directx).

4. Uninstall any extraneous programs on your computer, including games and other multimedia programs.

   If you're running Windows XP, you might even want to restore your system to its pristine state at a date before you installed those other applications. It won't affect any files or documents you've created in the meantime, and it will clear out unnecessary drivers you might not notice in your own cleaning efforts.

5. Defragment all hard disks (as described in Chapter 2).

   Consider buying a separate capture drive if you don't already have one.

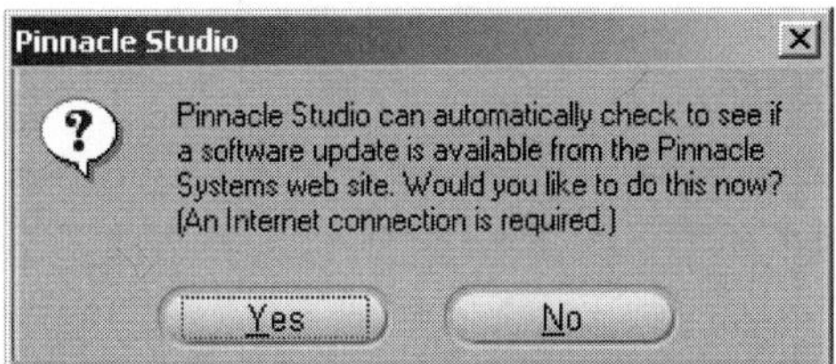

Figure B.1 Always let Studio check for updates after installing.

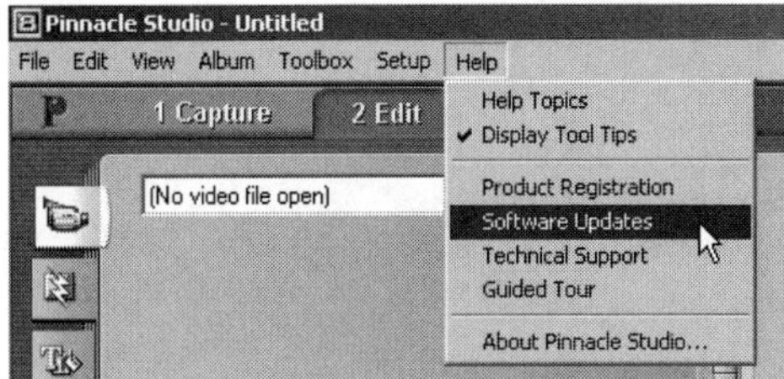

Figure B.2 If you start experiencing problems, search and load the latest update first.

6. Check that your CD or DVD drive is *not* on the same IDE cable as your video drive, which can slow operation.

   The optimal configuration is the video drive on its own cable.

7. Remove all extraneous programs from background operation (see the sidebar "Optimizing System Disk Performance" in Chapter 2).

8. Make sure there are no viruses on the system.

9. Install Studio.

   Studio should prompt you to see if there is an update available (**Figure B.1**).

10. Click Yes to see if there is an update.

    If so, download it (it's free). If Studio doesn't prompt you for some reason, choose Help > Software Updates (**Figure B.2**) to open the same dialog and check for an update. Note that you may have to register the program to download the upgrade.

11. After installing Studio and any updates, test your capture drive as described in Chapter 2.

    If performance is acceptable, your system should be ready.

Troubleshooting Common Problems

Again, the following section is by no means comprehensive. If you run into problems with Studio that aren't addressed here, check Pinnacle's Web site or technical support.

DV card and camera

Note that Studio doesn't interface with your capture card or camera directly; it does so through facilities provided by all Windows operating systems. If, during DV capture, you see the error message in **Figure B.3**, and the three suggested activities (turning the camera on and off, disconnecting and reconnecting the 1394 cable, and restarting Windows) don't resolve the issue, check whether Windows sees these components in the Windows Device Manager.

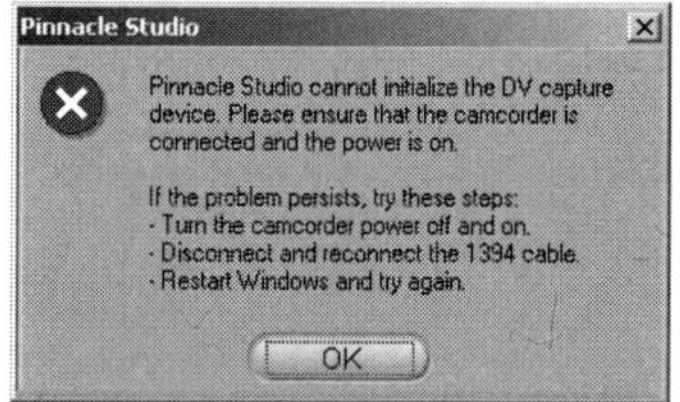

Figure B.3 Studio doesn't see your camera. Try the three suggestions.

To troubleshoot your DV card and camera:

1. From the Windows Taskbar, choose Start > Control Panel (**Figure B.4**).

   (In Windows 98 and Windows 2000, choose Start > Settings > Control Panel.)

   Windows opens the Control Panel (**Figure B.5**).

2. At the bottom of the Control Panel, click System.

   Windows opens the System Properties dialog (**Figure B.6**).

Figure B.4 Getting to the Windows Control Panel.

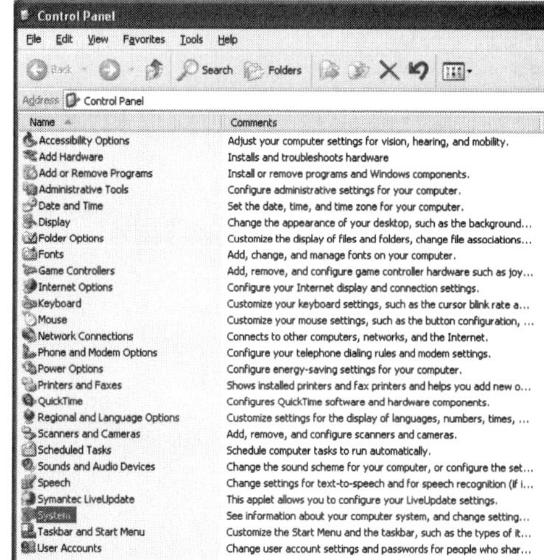

Figure B.5 Click here to open the System Properties window.

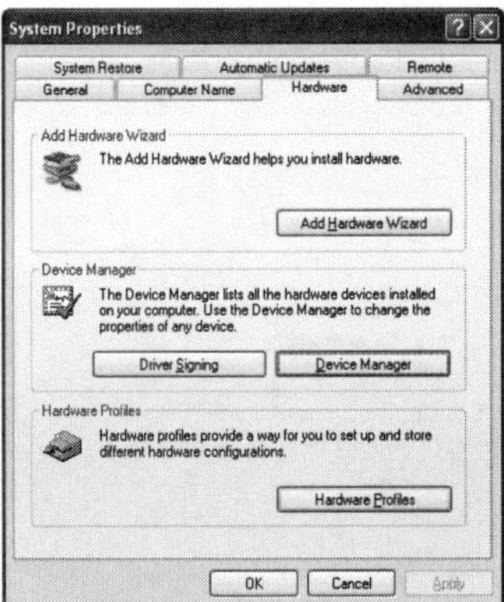

Figure B.6 Click here to open the Device Manager.

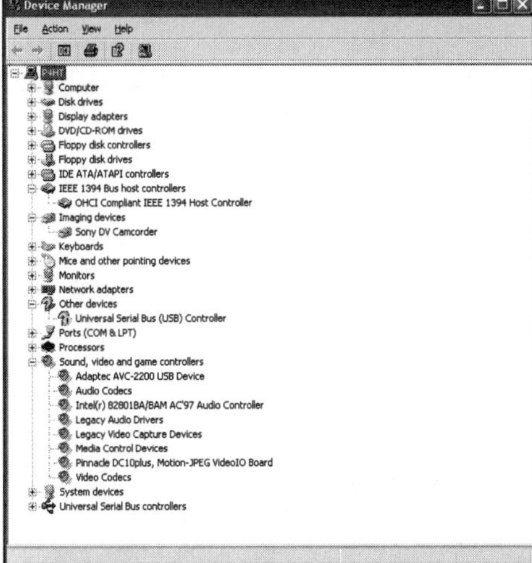

Figure B.7 The Device Manager details the status of all system hardware. Oops, looks like a problem with USB! Better diagnose this one before installing any USB devices.

3. At the top of the System Properties dialog, select the Hardware tab.

4. On the Hardware tab, click the Device Manager button.

   Windows opens the Device Manager dialog (**Figure B.7**).

5. Click the plus sign next to IEEE 1394 Bus host controller.

   You should see something close to the description shown in Figure B.7, a device listed with OHCI in the title. If such a device is present, and there is no yellow exclamation or question mark signifying a problem (like there is with the USB Controller), you have the necessary DV hardware and it is properly running.

   If there is no device present, or there is a yellow exclamation mark, check the documentation that came with your computer or DV card to troubleshoot further.

6. If the DV card is present, click the plus sign next to Imaging Devices.

   You should see something close to the description shown in Figure B.7, Sony DV Camcorder. If not, the camera is turned off, it's in the wrong mode (should be in Play mode), or the cable is bad.

(continued on next page)

✔ Tips

- If Windows doesn't see your FireWire card, shut the system down, remove the card, restart Windows, shut down again, reinsert the card, restart, and see if Windows recognizes the newly reinstalled card upon boot up. If Windows doesn't even try to install the card, try the same procedure in a different PCI slot. If this doesn't work, try a different FireWire card.
- If Windows sees the FireWire card, but Studio doesn't, uninstall the card by clicking the card in the Device Manager, then right-clicking and choosing Uninstall (**Figure B.8**). Then reboot, let Windows find the card, and reinstall all necessary driver software. (You may need your Windows disc handy to accomplish this, especially for Windows 98 SE. Don't uninstall unless you can locate the disc.)
- When troubleshooting an analog capture card, click the plus sign in front of Sound, video and game controllers, which is where Windows installs analog cards (see Figure B.7).
- Note that the route to the Device Manager is slightly different among all Windows flavors. If it doesn't work for you, check the Windows Help files (**Figure B.9**) for instructions on how to open this dialog.

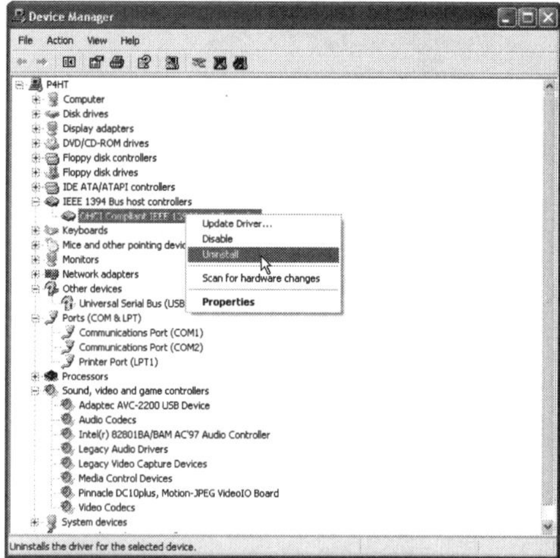

Figure B.8 Sometimes uninstalling and then reinstalling solves the problem.

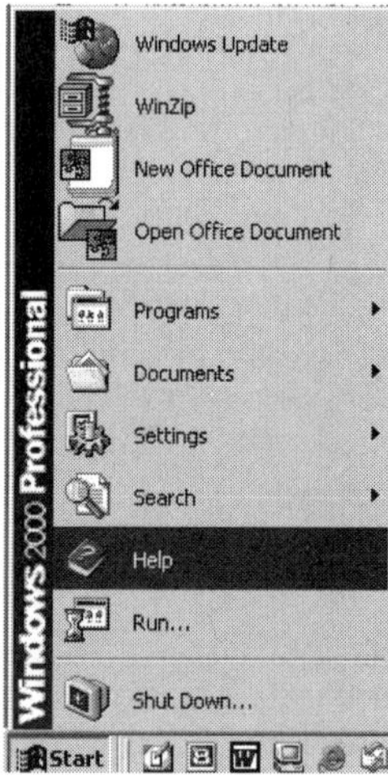

Figure B.9
If you're having trouble finding the Device Manager, check your Help files.

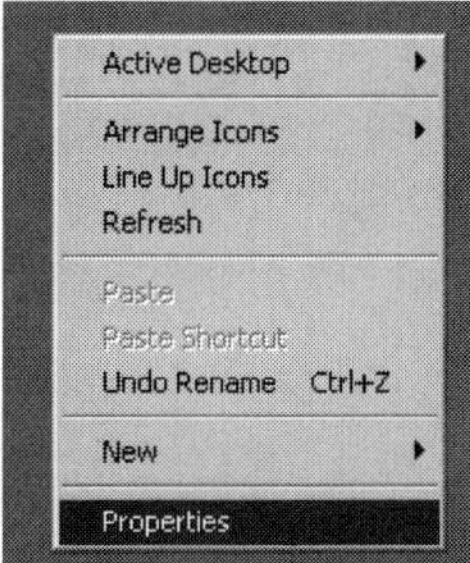

Figure B.10 Accessing the Display Properties dialog.

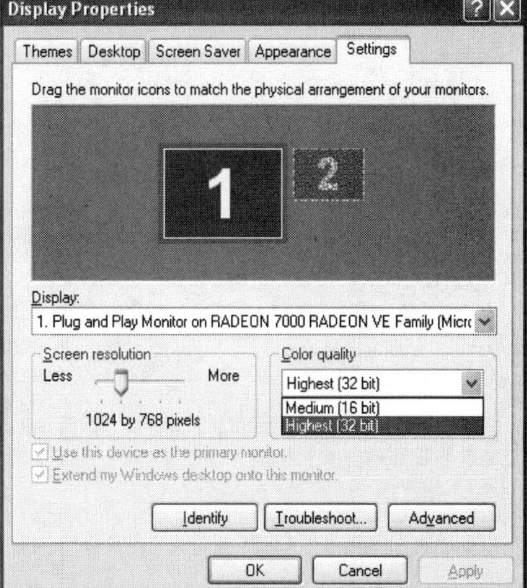

Figure B.11 Here's how you adjust display resolution and color depth.

No video or distorted video during DV capture

This section assumes Studio found the DV camera and did not produce the error message shown in Figure B.3. If you did receive the error message, see "To troubleshoot your DV card and camera," earlier.

If Studio "sees" your DV camera, but doesn't display video in the Player when the camera is running, try these solutions.

To troubleshoot no video or distorted video in the Player during DV capture:

1. Remove and reinsert the FireWire cable in both the camera and computer to ensure that it is properly seated.
2. Make sure you're running the latest graphics driver for the graphics card installed in your computer.
3. Make sure you're running the latest version of Direct X (www.microsoft.com/directx).
4. Make sure you're running the latest Studio update (Figure B.2).
5. Try different display resolutions and color depths. To do so, right-click on the Windows Desktop and choose Properties (**Figure B.10**).

   Windows opens the Display Properties dialog (**Figure B.11**).
6. Click the Settings tab.
7. Try all available resolutions above 800 x 600 and 16-bit, 24-bit, and/or 32-bit (if available) to find a combination that displays the videos.
8. Try a new FireWire cable.

✔ Tip

- If this doesn't work, check Pinnacle support at www.pinnaclesys.com/support for help with DirectX and advice specific to your graphics card.

No video or distorted video during analog capture

If you're having problems with your analog capture card, start by taking the steps described in "To troubleshoot your DV card and camera" to make sure the card is properly installed under Windows. If it is not properly installed, check your capture card documentation.

If the card is properly installed, try these steps to resolve your problem.

To troubleshoot no video or distorted video during analog capture:

1. Remove and reinsert the analog capture cable in both the camera and computer to ensure it is properly seated.
2. From the Studio menu, choose Setup > Capture Source (**Figure B.12**).

   Studio opens the Setup Options dialog open to the Capture source tab (**Figure B.13**).
3. Confirm that the proper video capture device is selected.
4. If the TV Standard box is active (not grayed out), ensure that it's set to the proper standard (NTSC in the US).
5. If the Capture preview checkbox is enabled, ensure that it's checked, and click OK.

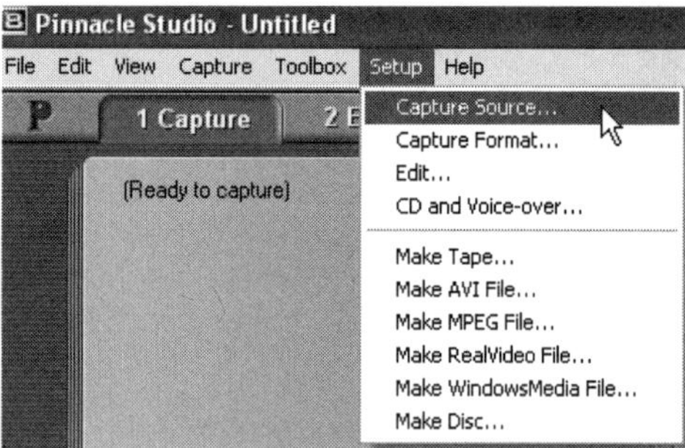

Figure B.12 Getting to the Capture source tab to check Studio setup options.

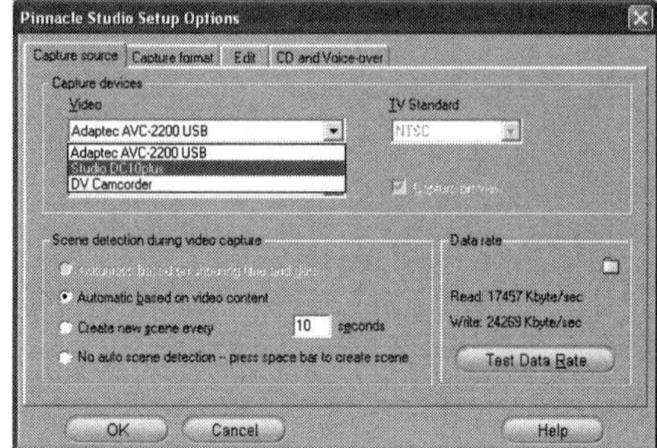

Figure B.13 Make sure you've got the right analog capture device selected.

Click here to open the Video input screen

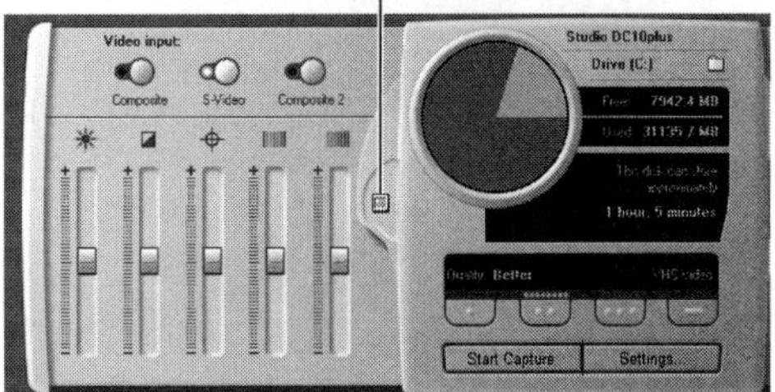

Figure B.14 And the right analog input.

6. In the Capture mode Video input screen, make sure the correct input is selected (**Figure B.14**).
7. Make sure you're running the latest graphics driver for the graphics card installed in your computer.
8. Make sure you're running the latest version of Direct X (www.microsoft.com/directx).
9. Make sure you're running the latest Studio update (Figure B.2).
10. Try different display resolutions and color depths. To do so, right-click on the Windows Desktop and choose Properties.

    Windows opens the Display Properties dialog.
11. Click the Settings tab.
12. Try all available resolutions above 800 x 600 and 16-bit, 24-bit, and/or 32-bit (if available) to find a combination that displays the videos.
13. Try a different analog capture cable.

Dropped frames

If you're having trouble with dropped frames, start with the steps described earlier under "To ensure a smooth installation," which should work with most computers. If all else fails, try these additional steps.

To troubleshoot frames dropped during capture or writing back to tape:

1. Save your project, reboot the system, and reload Studio before writing a project to tape.
2. During capture and writing back to tape, disable the network by pulling the cable from the network interface card.
3. Right-click on the Windows Desktop and choose Properties.
   Windows opens the Display Properties dialog (**Figure B.15**).
4. Click the Screen Saver tab.
5. Choose None from the Screen saver drop-down box.
6. On the bottom-right of the Screen Saver tab, click Power.
   Studio opens the Power Options Properties dialog open to the Power Schemes tab (**Figure B.16**).

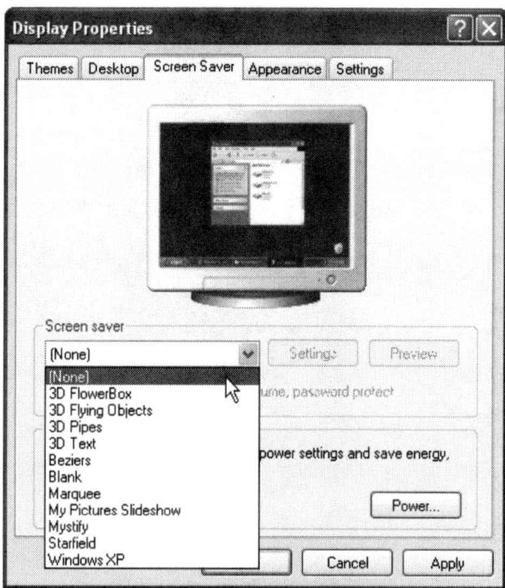

Figure B.15 Turn your screen saver off.

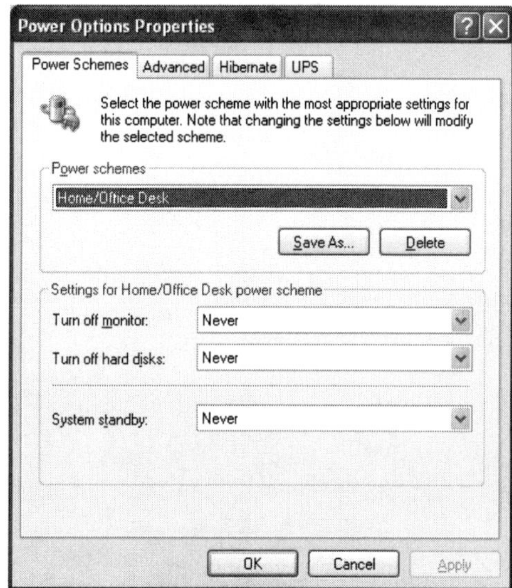

Figure B.16 Disabling your power-saving schemes.

Figure B.17 Closing all extraneous applications.

Figure B.18 Beware here, because you may end a crucial process.

7. Choose Never in the Turn off monitor, Turn off hard disks, and System standby drop-down boxes.

8. Close all extraneous programs by doing one of the following:
   - ▲ Close them one by one using normal program controls (if available).
   - ▲ Press Ctrl+Alt+Delete to load the Windows Task Manager, select the target program, and click End Task (**Figure B.17**).

✔ Tip

- If you click the Processes tab in the Windows Task Manager (**Figure B.18**), you'll see a lot more services and programs running. Resist the urge to freelance here and remove random programs, as you might unload a necessary service and crash the system (though Windows typically attempts to prevent this). You're better off working with a good start-up manager program (see Chapter 2).

No audio

Note that Studio doesn't play audio when capturing from DV. If you're not hearing audio during analog capture or during normal preview, read this section.

To troubleshoot no audio during capture or playback:

1. Load a file with known good audio in Windows Media Player or another application to see if the audio plays normally. If it doesn't, it's a system problem. Do the following:
   - ▲ Check that speakers are turned on.
   - ▲ Make sure speaker volume is turned up.
   - ▲ See if the speaker cable is connected to both the speaker system and computer.
   - ▲ See if the speaker cable is connected to the proper plug (usually the headphones icon).
   - ▲ Double-click the speaker in your Taskbar, or choose Start > Programs > Accessories > Entertainment > Volume Control to load Volume Control. Make sure that Wave Balance isn't muted and that both Wave and the Master Volume control are at reasonable levels (**Figure B.19**).
   - ▲ If available, plug in a set of headphones or alternate speakers and test whether these work. If they do, it's a speaker problem.
   - ▲ Following Steps 1 to 4 under "To troubleshoot your DV card and camera," open the Device Manager dialog, click the plus sign next to Sound, video and game controllers, and make sure your audio device is listed and working properly (Figure B.7.)

Figure B.19 Many times you can't hear audio because the volume is turned down (imagine that)!

Figure B.20 If your volume button doesn't flicker during capture, your captured files won't have any audio.

2. If Media Player plays the file normally, check to ensure that audio is captured with the file. In Windows Explorer, navigate to your capture directory and double-click a captured file, which should load into Media Player or other player program.

   If you can't hear audio during playback, somehow audio didn't get captured, normally only an issue with analog capture, since there's almost no way Studio can capture DV video without the audio.

   Verify your audio capture setup:

   ▲ Remove and reinsert the analog audio cables into both the computer and camcorder.

   ▲ Make certain the audio is plugged into the Line-in, not the Microphone port.

3. If audio isn't captured with the file, return to Studio in Capture mode.

4. In the Audio capture screen (**Figure B.20**), make sure Audio capture is turned on and that volume is not completely turned down. Start your camcorder and observe whether the audio meter is responding to the incoming audio. If there is no movement in the audio meter, audio is not getting to the system.

   If you've taken all the actions described in Steps 1 and 2, try swapping audio input cables.

5. If audio is captured with the file, and you still don't hear audio during preview, it's likely you muted the audio tracks or turned the sound down too low. Check "Using the Volume Tool" and "Adjusting Volume on the Timeline" in Chapter 11.

INDEX

B

C

INDEX

D

E

F

G

H

I

INDEX

T

W